Management for Professionals

More information about this series at http://www.springer.com/series/10101

R. Srinivasan

Platform Business Models

Frameworks, Concepts and Design

Springer

R. Srinivasan
Indian Institute of Management Bangalore
Bengaluru, India

ISSN 2192-8096 ISSN 2192-810X (electronic)
Management for Professionals
ISBN 978-981-16-2837-5 ISBN 978-981-16-2838-2 (eBook)
https://doi.org/10.1007/978-981-16-2838-2

This Springer imprint is published by the registered company Springer Nature Singapore Pte Ltd.
The registered company address is: 152 Beach Road, #21-01/04 Gateway East, Singapore 189721, Singapore

Preface

Firms that operate a platform business model have come to dominate the world today, in terms of both scale and performance (market capitalization). Some popular examples include Airbnb, Uber, Facebook, Amazon, and Google. Apart from these, there are quite a few firms operating as platform business models in their specific domestic markets, as well as reaching global consumers.

A unique feature of these platform business models (in contrast to pipeline business models) is that they operate as networks, quite often intermediating between different sides of users. Pretty much like an exchange, some of these firms facilitate interactions, reduce transaction costs, and help with matchmaking across specific user groups. Though such business models were not new, the proliferation of digital technologies and the easy access to the internet through mobile devices have provided the much-needed fillip to the growth and proliferation of these businesses.

This book is an exploration of the economics and strategies of these platform firms. As a student of strategy, I attempt to provide a template and framework for analyzing platform firms' economics and strategies, while acknowledging that each firm's strategy is unique (akin to its signature). I write this book as a guide to entrepreneurs and intrapreneurs in their journey of establishing and nurturing their platforms as well.

My journey into studying platforms started with a series of accidents. A friend of mine invited me to join his team meeting with a phrase, "we seem to be doing something right, but we are not able to explain why are succeeding." The team was actually building a platform, with a product framework. I spent a few hours with the team providing them with the basic concepts of network businesses and platforms, and things began to fall in place in their minds. Within a week of this meeting, a faculty colleague invited me to join a case-writing project which seemed unique. The executive in the firm was talking about leveraging network effects, and my faculty colleague (not from the strategy discipline) was not in sync with the theory and practice of platform business models. The case was being written at a time when the product firm was envisioning a transition to becoming a platform. The very next week after the case-writing conversation, I had to stand in for another colleague of mine for a start-up's meeting with its users. Over breakfast with the founders, we agreed that the best way for that start-up to scale was to reposition itself into a platform. These series of interactions of organizations large and small, mature and young, convinced me that there is a need for deeper understanding of platforms as business models. This exploration led me to seek more and more platform firms, and I got access to study a variety of platform firms, including those founded well before the turn of the millennium with rudimentary technology, which again convinced me of the need to highlight the role of technology as just an enabler in the design of platform business models. And like in most cases, practice was leading theory development.

I continued my exploration through three routes—case writing (using primary access to founders and leadership teams of these firms), consulting (I got involved with quite a few start-ups, and entrepreneurs wanted mentoring and advisory support in their journeys), and teaching (I designed and delivered courses on platform business models across business schools in India and Europe, primarily the Indian Institute of Management Bangalore and Friedrich–Alexander University of Erlangen–Nuremberg).

In the process, I have had the fortune of high-quality research support. Mayura walked in with a dilemma of whether to join a Ph.D. program and spent a good nine months; Sandeep and Pramoth also got bitten by the doctoral bug after completing their Advanced Management Programme at IIMB and joined the research team while pursuing their day jobs as well as their academic studies at other institutes; Padma had just completed her Ph.D. and was looking to join academics as a full-time researcher. I also had the good fortune of having passionate teaching assistants throughout my teaching journey—Sandeep, Padma, and Pramoth at IIMB; Hari, Aida, Aga, and Julius at FAU. Across various years, these teaching assistants made copious notes of my sessions and sometimes even audio recorded them and transcribed them into text for my use.

In addition, the team at the Friedrich–Alexander University of Erlangen–Nuremberg (especially Kathrin, Angela, and Albrecht) was constantly looking for opportunities to integrate my research on platforms with their focus on open innovation and servitization.

This book is a culmination of all these efforts—case writing, academic research, and consulting/mentoring firms that operate platform business models. Over the past three years, I have also invested in writing some of my thoughts on my personal blog page (r-srini.in). Though I would like to have been more regular in publishing the blog, it gave me the initial impetus to consolidate my learning into this volume. And during the COVID-19-induced lockdown and the resultant virtualization of teaching activities, I have also been able to record a MOOC on the same topic on EdX/ IIMBx (available at https://www.edx.org/course/platform-business-models), which would be a good supplement to this book.

Bengaluru, India R. Srinivasan

Acknowledgments

For providing me with space and freedom to explore my passion, IIMB.

For providing me with a boundary object to experiment and recalibrate my thoughts, FAU.

For putting up my numerous anecdotes and instances while I explained concepts, my students.

For providing me with these anecdotes, firms that gave me access to document cases.

For helping me test some of my ideas and strategies, my mentees from NSRCEL and the numerous start-ups/founders.

For being a good sounding board and converting a lot of my ideas into words, Sandeep and Pramoth.

For accommodating my idiosyncrasies in converting my thoughts into a MOOC, IIMBx team (Sanjana and Shwetha in particular).

For producing this idea into a coherent whole, Nupoor and Sharmila (Springer).

For being with me throughout this journey and beyond, my family.

Thank you!

Bengaluru, India R. Srinivasan

Contents

About the Author

R. Srinivasan is Professor of Strategy at the Indian Institute of Management Bangalore. He teaches courses on strategy and platform business models for MBA students at IIMB and the Friedrich Alexander University of Erlangen-Nuremberg, Germany. He has written a lot of cases and articles on platform businesses in India and Germany. He also engages with a variety of startups and businesses that operate platform business models as an advisor and consultant. He earned his doctoral degree from the Indian Institute of Management Ahmedabad.

Introduction

1

Have you ever wondered what differentiates an Airbnb from a traditional hotel? Or an Uber from a city taxi service? These are some of the many popular platforms that have come to dominate the world of business in the past decade. These platforms are typically asset light (Airbnb does not own a single hotel, nor does Uber a taxi) but have enough market power to lead their respective industries. Typically, such platform business firms intermediate between different sets of users, leverage network effects to grow the market, and in some markets dominate industries leveraging winner-takes-all economies. This chapter introduces the platforms as a unique business model and distinguishes them from traditional businesses.

What Are Business Models?

Models

A model is a replica of reality, a miniature, a life-like definition. It is common to use models to refer to an abstraction of something that exists in reality. Such models could take shape of prototypes that are used as a base for replication into life-size; an abstract representation of various scenarios and interdependencies like financial models; a description of a personality as in role models; or even fashion models that are used for demonstration purposes. Models abstract from the original. Some models help predict the future by connecting the dots. Models help in replications, visualizing connections and relationships, and for projections of the future. Models help in reducing the risk of failure and contribute to reduction in costs and/or elimination of rework.

R. Srinivasan, *Platform Business Models*, Management for Professionals,
https://doi.org/10.1007/978-981-16-2838-2_1

Business Models

Business model is a representation of the business. It diagrammatically represents who the primary customers are, what are their needs, what is the business' value proposition, how does the business interact with the customers, how does the business organize its operations, what are the specific resources required for these operations, and the costs and revenue structures of the business. Organized as a chart, the business model canvas, proposed by Alex Osterwalder, provides a template for representing the business model in a logical way (see Fig. 1.1).[1]

As one can see, the business model represents the various choices the firm has made, including its decision on specific customer segments, value offerings, and partnership arrangements; and the resultant resource requirements, value flows, and cash flows.

Platform Business Models

There are various things people refer to when they say platforms—a railway platform, a raised platform from where one could give an oration, or a technology or automotive platform that forms the basis for product design and manufacturing. The first thing that comes to everyone's mind when we say the word platform is a railway platform. Drawing from the analogy, a platform is a business model that brings together multiple sets of users—like trains and passengers. Imagine a railway station that has no signage or announcements on the arrivals and departures of specific trains! There would be chaos, right? A critical value offering of railway platforms is the provisioning of information to its users. The railway platform also provides a comfortable infrastructure for passengers to wait for the train, alight from or board the train. Another important value created by platforms is the specifications of the terms of usage or rules. In the absence of rules and norms, there could be serious chaos and inefficiencies. Put together, these three values—information, infrastructure, and rules—define how platforms operate.

In contrast to traditional businesses that Van Alstyne, Parker, and Chaudary (2016) refer to as pipelines, platforms add value in a different form.[2] In pipeline businesses like say, when a consumer buys bread, value flows from one direction to the other in the value chain—from the farmer who produced the wheat; to the small businessman that made the flour out of that wheat; to the baker that baked the bread; to the distributor and retailers that sold the bread; finally to the consumer. And the money flows the reverse direction—from the consumer to the retailer/distributor to the baker to the flour-maker to the farmer. These characterize pipeline businesses as money and value flow as fluids flow through a pipeline.

---

[1] Osterwalder, A. and Pigneur, Y. (2010). Business Model Generation: A handbook for visionaries, game changes and challengers, NJ: John Wiley & Sons.

[2] Van Alstyne, M.W., Parker, G.G., and Chaudary, S.P. (2016). Pipelines, Platforms, and the New Rules of Strategy, Harvard Business Review, April 2016.

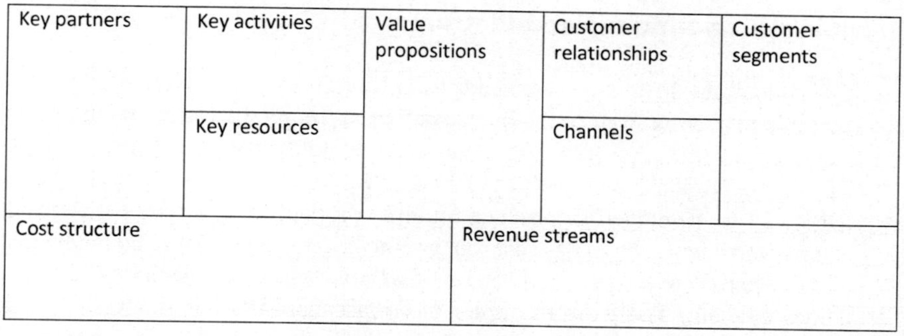

Fig. 1.1 Business model canvas. Adapted from: Osterwalder and Pigneur (2010)

In contrast platform businesses have different value flows. The transition from pipelines to platforms as business involves three key shifts: resource control to resource orchestration; internal organization to external interaction; and focus on customer value to ecosystem value (Van Alstyne et al. 2016). Take for instance a traditional newspaper. The newspaper caters to two user groups—the readers and the advertisers. The value flow is from the bureau (or the agencies) to the newspaper firm to the reader. If in consideration to this value, the readers paid the newspapers a commensurate fees, then the newspaper would still be a pipeline business. On the other hand, newspapers, in their interest to grow the readership, provide discounts to the readers, and make it up by charging advertisers. The value flow for advertisers come from the newspapers providing them space to communicate with the readers. In return for this value, the advertisers are willing to pay a significant amount to the newspaper. The operations of a traditional newspaper would work like this (i) source good quality news, produce a good newspaper (quality paper and printing), distribute efficiently (reach readers on time), and be open to feedback from readers; (ii) analyze the readership data—who're my readers and what do they like reading; and (iii) market space on the newspapers to those advertisers who are willing to pay for reaching their messages to the specific segments of readers that the newspaper caters to. In this two-way value creation process, newspapers can afford to subsidize the readers and make money from the advertisers; as the advertisers value more readers and are willing to pay to reach them. In such kind of platform business models, traditional frameworks that define customers may not be appropriate—as one cannot say who are the customers to a newspaper—the reader or the advertiser? It is also not correct to say that a newspaper caters to two separate sets of customers, as the value created and offered is interdependent—in the absence of readers, advertisers would not be willing to pay!

Single- and Multi-sided Platforms

An important distinction one needs to make in the discourse on platforms is that of simple platforms from multi-sided platforms. Simple platforms are those that cater to one set of users only, as in the case of automotive platforms or technology platforms. In these contexts, a platform refers to a base model or technological core that can be leveraged to produce multiple products and services. For instance, an automotive company may use an engine across multiple vehicle models. Or a technology core like a robotic engine that could be used to make multiple assembly lines efficient. These are examples of simple platforms, or single-sided platforms. Our focus in this book is going to be on multi-sided platforms, where the platform caters to multiple sets of users, like the newspaper adding value to readers and advertisers; or an airport providing services to passengers and airlines; or a marketplace that brings together buyers and sellers.

Network Effects

The core idea behind multi-sided platforms is the concept of network effects. By network effects, we refer to the value one set of users attach to the other set of users in the platform. The number and quality of users on one side attract users on the other side. For instance, the number and quality of the right segment of viewers of a television channel attracts specific advertisers to the channel. The more the number of children watching a particular channel, the more the advertiser targeting its communication to children is willing to pay to advertise on that channel. These network effects are referred to as cross-side or indirect network effects. Given that the willingness to pay is directly proportional to the number of specific users (on the other side), it is labeled as positive. Such network effects could also be indirectly proportional, as in the case of advertisements and readers in a newspaper. The more the readers, more the advertisers are willing to advertise and pay, but not vice versa. The more the space advertisements take in the newspaper, the less the readers are willing to read and pay for the newspaper. Such network effects are labeled negative cross-side network effects. There could also be contexts where more number of users on one side begets more users of the same side. For instance, social networking applications like Facebook attracts users to connect and commune with similar users—their friends, family, and colleagues. More people like oneself are active on Facebook, more likely that one will be active on Facebook. In such cases, the value of the social network is directly proportional to the number of users. Imagine a social networking site where none of your friends/acquaintances are active? It would be of no value at all. Such network effects where the value of the platform is directly proportional to the number and quality of users of the same side are called direct or same-side network effects. Such same-side network effects could also be negative. That is, when the value of the platform is indirectly proportional to the number of users of the same side, the network effects could be negative same

	Positive	Negative
Same-side or direct	Social networks like Facebook	Sellers on a B2B exchange
Cross-side or indirect	Marketplaces like Amazon	Advertisers on media

Fig. 1.2 Matrix of network effects

side. A good example of negative same-side network effects would be a B2B exchange. More the number of direct competitors one finds in a B2B exchange, the less value it is for individual businesses to affiliate with the platform. And therefore the willingness to pay to join such a platform is indirectly proportional to the number of direct competitors. In such cases where users value exclusivity or differentiation from other users, platforms may experience negative same-side network effects (Fig. 1.2).

Network effects are not the same as popularity or word-of-mouth attraction of users. In word-of-mouth attraction, users highlight the value they derived out of the business and therefore urge others to join and enjoy the same value. On the other hand, network effects highlight the increase in value added by the business to the users as more (or less) users join and use the same. In other words, the value created is proportional to the number of users (beyond simple economies of scale); the fact that there are more users (either on the same side or the other side), the platform is able to offer more value to everyone.

Platforms Make Markets Efficient

A lot of traditional industries are characterized by three classic information economics problems—information asymmetry, adverse selection, and moral hazard. ***Information asymmetry*** refers to the differences in the information available across different contracting (interacting) parties. Ideally, when one party has more or less information than the other, the contracts might be inefficient. Take the instance of a used-car market. The seller in the market has significantly more information about the vehicle than the buyer. In such a case, the seller has economic incentives to hide/suppress information about the vehicle, especially adverse information like accidents or product issues. When the seller exploits this asymmetric information to bargain higher prices at the cost of the buyer, this is known as ***adverse selection***. In the context of inefficient markets, adverse selection imposes significant costs of contracting, as the buyer (who has lesser information) has to invest time, energy, and additional costs in finding and verifying information provided by the seller. In spite of all this pre-contracting costs, there is a likelihood that such asymmetry may not be overcome. Post-contracting, a likelihood of a change in behaviour of one party that can have a material impact on the other party is known as ***moral hazard***. Moral hazards can manifest through reneging on contracts like change in pricing models, service commitments, or the like. In order to overcome moral hazards, it is important to write out detailed contracts involving governance and mediation.

Typically platforms when they intermediate between different sets of users, it allows for increasing the efficiency of these markets. Imagine a travel-support platform like TripAdvisor. In that platform, user reviews on the hotels and vacations bridge information asymmetry between service providers and clients; prior information about prices and packages published by the hotels help ameliorate the adverse selection issues; and intermediating all payments and reviews through the intermediary (TripAdvisor) insures against moral hazards. In most markets characterized by such inefficiencies, platforms have contributed significantly in improving economic value for both transacting parties.

Platform Roles

Typically platforms as businesses have multiple roles: ***providers, sponsors, and users***. First is that of platform provider—those providing the infrastructure and therefore interact with the users. On the other hand, sponsors do not deal directly with the users, but work in the background and design/ shape the information flows and rules.[3] It is the sponsors that define who can participate or not in the platform; what access would each set of users have; and the norms of interactions amongst users. Users are typically independent people/organizations that interact with the platform and other users. In some platforms, providers and sponsors are part of the same organization; and in some others, they could be independent. For instance, in the case of an electronic marketplace like eBay, the same firm controls both the roles—that of platform sponsor and provider. However, in platforms like music players using mp3, there could be multiple providers competing with each other in the market, using a common set of standards (in this case, mp3 is a sponsor, while hardware manufacturers like Apple or Samsung would be the providers). These roles form the basis for platform firms to architect their unique business models in their specific industries.

Platforms as Networks

Platforms typically operate in network markets. Network markets are characterized by four special features[4]: complementarity, compatibility, and standards; consumption externalities; switching costs and lock-in; and significant economies of

[3]For more details about platform sponsorship, please read Katz & Shapiro (1986). Technology adoption in the presence of network externalities, Journal of political economy, 94: 822–841.
[4]For more details, read Shy, O. (2004). The economics of network industries, Cambridge UK: Cambridge University Press. (Chapter 1).

scale in production. These market characteristics allow for specific economies and give rise to unique business models.

Complementarity, Compatibility, and Standards

In network markets, consumers consume products as systems together with complements: like hardware and software; music player hardware and the audio files; and cars and roads/pathways. Consumers shop for whole systems rather than just products or services. The video games one plays should be compatible with the hardware, and vice versa. For such complements to work with each other, it is imperative that the products are designed to be compatible with each other. In most cases, these compatibilities are defined by the setting and following of industry-level standards. For such standards to evolve, there is a need for conscious cooperation and coordination between producers of complementary products and services. Some markets could evolve to be served by a single/dominant standard, like Microsoft's operating system in PC markets or Android in mobile smart phones; or a small set of competing standards, like mp4, AAC, and WMV in digital consumer video formats. In markets with competing standards, there is a market for aggregators that are compatible with multiple standards or converters that help users convert content from one format to others.

Consumption Externalities

Consumption externalities refer to the increasing value of the product/service as more and more people adopt the same.

> How would like to be the only person in the world to own a telephone?

How valuable is an exclusive telephone? Pretty much useless, right? The value of the telephone increases proportionally to the number of people, especially those in your network, to own and use the telephone. The more the number of people using the telephone, the more valuable it is to you. These externalities are also referred to adoption externalities. In such markets with adoption externalities, there could be multiple equilibria. Either no one uses a telephone or everyone uses one.

In the case of normal goods that do not exhibit adoption externalities, the demand curve is downward sloping—as price decreases, demand should grow. But for products with adoption externalities, the slope may not be continuously uniform. There could be cases where beyond a point (after achieving a critical mass), the demand may disproportionately increase. This stems from the fact that the marginal utility for the nth customer is dependent not just on the inherent product quality but is also a function of the number of customers already in the network, n.

As more and more people start using a software utility like the ERP programme in an organization, more and more people get trained in using the programme, and the quality of experience improves. This results in higher marginal utilities resulting from the *externality* for subsequent users. An important concept to understand here is the concept of critical mass. Take, for example, fax machines.[5] Typical reduction in prices driven by fall in costs of electronic components did account for small growth in adoption of fax machines in the US market. However, once the market achieved a critical mass, the users in the corporations using fax machines used fax machines more and more to communicate with other users, and that led to a nonlinear growth in demand. Such adoption externalities are critical to the evolution of network markets. Below the critical mass, the adoption rates are linear and small, and above the critical mass, the demand expands significantly. Consequently, either no one uses these products and services, or everyone uses them!

Switching Costs and Lock-In

Network markets are also characterized by significant switching costs. As the network grows in size and penetration, the costs of switching increase exponentially.

Why is the world stuck with a QWERTY keyboard?

A common example of how network markets create switching costs is the prevalence of QWERTY keyboards as a dominant standard. The QWERTY keyboard was designed in the world of mechanical typewriters where it was important to have letters commonly used together arrive at the cylinder from different angles, lest a fast typist have the levers representing the letters jammed! In other words, a keyboard was designed with an intent (among other things) of slowing down typing. When mechanical typewriters gave way to electronic typewriters and subsequently computers and mobile phones, the world is still "stuck" with QWERTY keyboards! Due to the dominance of QWERTY as a standard, all those who used typewriters were trained on using the same. When electronic typewriters and early computers were introduced, it was easy for these users to transition to using those devices due to the acceptance of QWERTY keyboard as the standard. And eventually, everyone learnt using the QWERTY keyboard, and every device therefore had a QWERTY keyboard. It was not the case that there were no alternates, there

[5]For more detailed research on adoption externalities, read Economides & Himmelberg (1995). Critical mass and network evolution in telecommunications, in Brock G. (Ed). 1995. Toward a competitive telecommunications industry: Selected papers from the 1994 Telecommunications Policy Research Conference. Available on the internet at neconomides.stern.nyu.edu/networks/tprc.pdf (last accessed on 10.08.2020).

was a DVORAK keyboard, but the switching costs were so high, that the QWERTY keyboard continues to persist.

Firms can also deliberately build switching costs for their products and services. Some of the ways product manufacturers lock-in their customers are described below. These are some instances, and firms can choose a combination of a few of them as well.

a. Contracts: In the market for complements, firms can tie in their users with contracts for using their own/approved products as complements. For example, automotive and electronic product manufacturers mandate the use of approved spares during after-sales services, failing which the warranties may not be guaranteed. These mandates may be essential for continued efficiency, quality, and reliability of the product/service. So, when you buy a BMW car, you are pretty much locked-in to buying BMW spares only! If you want to break that, the risk is all yours!
b. Training and learning costs: In products and services with significant complexity of usage, the costs of training and learning may be critical upfront investments. Take the instance of an ERP product. Once all the employees, contractors and other stakeholders of the organization are trained into using that particular ERP product (which is a significant effort and cost in itself), it is pretty much difficult to switch to another product/service. The change management effort may be so significant that the firm continues with its existing product/service.
c. Backward compatibilities and data conversion costs: Another related switching cost in network markets is the maintenance of backward compatibilities with existing products and artefacts. For instance, while upgrading software, it is imperative that one maintains backward compatibility with existing IT artefacts (databases, email systems, and user files) as well as hardware products and services. This could be a significant switching costs for firms to upgrade their products from their own service providers rather than use something entirely new.
d. Bureaucratic costs of search: In some cases, the bureaucratic costs of searching and contracting with a new vendor might be so prohibitive that organizations might prefer to work with existing vendors and their products and services. Not just search costs, there may be significant costs involved in training the newly appointed vendors and their team members in quality standards and processes of the firm. In markets with tiered-global supply chains like in the fashion industry, it might be very difficult to train new vendors on quality expectations and delivery expectations.
e. Loyalty costs: In some markets with very little differentiation between competitors' products and services, service providers might lock-in participants with loyalty benefits. In such markets where the consumer might not be able to differentiate the quality of services (as in airlines) or might not be competent to evaluate the quality differences (as in doctors and hospitals), loyalty programmes may be very effective in increasing switching costs.

Significant Economies of Scale

As a consequence of these standards, externalities and switching costs, firms operating in these markets enjoy significant economies of scale.

What does it cost to produce the second copy of a software product?

These markets are characterized by high fixed (and sunk) costs upfront, with very little marginal costs of production. The average cost curve drops significantly to almost zero as the scale increases. As we had discussed before, once the critical mass is achieved in these markets, consumers' marginal utilities increase disproportionately, whereas the producers marginal costs drop exponentially as well, resulting in extraordinary contribution margins.

Platforms as Ecosystems

As it can be observed, platforms create, capture, and distribute value working as ecosystems, in collaboration and complementarily with multiple organizations. These groups of organizations have been defined using a biology metaphor—ecosystems. Moore, in a seminal article, introduced business ecosystems as an alternative to the traditional economic organizations: markets and hierarchies (Moore 2006).[6]

Business ecosystems have been studied in a variety of industries.[7] Ecosystems typically comprise numerous firms, individuals, and communities who may be independent and autonomous, but connected with each other through a technological core[8] (Baldwin 2012). This distributed nature of the ecosystems present four unique design parameters for organizing and value creation.

1. Modularity: The evolution of modularity in industries has led presented a lot of opportunities for growth. Modularity has helped achieve economies of scale in design, engineering, and manufacturing; facilitated reduced complexity in

[6]For a detailed description, Read, Moore, J.F. 2006. Business Ecosystems and the View from the Firm, The Antitrust Bulletin, 51, 1. Spring 2006.

[7]For more details, read: Adner R, Kapoor R. 2010. Value creation in investment ecosystems: how the structure of technological interdependence affects firm performance in new technology generations. Strategic Management Journal 31: 306–333; Baldwin C, Clark K. 2000. Design Rules, Volume 1, The Power of Modularity. MIT Press, Cambridge, MA.; Iansiti M, Levien R. 2004. The Keystone Advantage: What the New Dynamics of Business Ecosystems Mean for Strategy, Innovation, and Sustainability. Harvard Business School Press, Boston, MA.; and von Hippel E. 1988. The Sources of Innovation. Oxford University Press, Oxford, UK.

[8]See: Baldwin, C. Y. 2012. "Organization Design for Business Ecosystems." Special Issue on The Future of Organization Design, Journal of Organization Design 1, 1.

manufacturing by a variety of globally distributed and specialized manufacturers; and therefore helped customers with increased (backward and cross-brand) compatibility and resultant customer satisfaction. Baldwin and Clark (2000) had elaborated on the antecedents and consequences of modularity on industry evolution and profitability. Famously known as Joy's law,[9] many technology companies in the world believe in this: "No matter who you are, most of the smartest people work for someone else [other than you]". For such distributed value addition to happen, it is imperative that all constituents in the ecosystem work on specific aspects of the whole and have the ability to integrate.

2. Absorptive capacity: In an ecosystem, it is important that the firms overcome a set of biases, including "not-invented-here." Firms in the ecosystem should be open to receiving inputs and ideas from others and have the absorptive capacity to integrate the knowledge gathered from outside with that generated inside. This integrative capability is critical in the ecosystem co-creating value. Such capacity requires three sets of routines—ability to continuously scan the environment and engage with external innovators; ability to sift through the external body of knowledge out there and the internal innovation projects and their outcomes; and the ability to integrate these two streams of knowledge to create and capture value. These three capabilities are critical to work and create value in an ecosystem, else, there could be loss of control and centralization of value creation and capture. Of course, these capabilities are not evenly distributed across all the firms and actors in the ecosystem. There could be firms/actors that are central to the ecosystem, who set the standards, define the norms and rules of engagement, and stake higher claims on the value created (capture disproportionately more value). These "focal" firms are variedly referred to as orchestrators and facilitators in the ecosystem. Orchestrators define the norms and information flows; whereas facilitators provide the infrastructure for interaction among the members of the ecosystem.
3. Co-evolution: Co-evolution is about orchestrating and facilitating reciprocal interactions among technologies, business processes and routines, products and services, market mechanisms, firms, and regulators.[10] The process of co-evolution may involve a variety of activities including co-creating technological standards across competitors and complementors in an industry as well. Such co-evolutionary processes help entire ecosystems grow and flourish. Pretty much the biological metaphor of a biosphere, that support a variety of life forms, in symbiotic co-existence, co-evolution enables all the diverse actors in the business ecosystems co-create value for everyone involved.
4. Public goods: Given that an ecosystem is built around the principles of cooperation among complementary actors operating in their own niches while creating value for the whole, the outcomes of these ecosystems are most often treated as public goods. An innovation that is a product of the entire ecosystems'

[9] Anderson, C. 2012. Makers: The new industrial revolution, Crown Business.
[10] The process of co-evolution has been studied in complexity theory (Moore, 1996).

effort should be available for leverage by all participants in the ecosystems, with equity. Most often, this shared outcome is likely to be much larger than the sum of individual efforts, and that would be a significant incentive for participants to contribute to (and benefit out of) the business ecosystem.

These four ecosystem characteristics—modularity, absorptive capacity, co-evolution, and public goods—provide opportunities for platforms to architect ecosystems. Some platforms operate as focal firms, evangelizing and enabling other participants and actors to affiliate with others in the ecosystem. Presence of modularity is essential for seamless affiliation and value creation. In the absence of modularity, there may be requirements for participants to invest in specific assets, that are exclusive to that focal firm. It is also imperative that the focal firm manages its role carefully and allows for knowledge flows across the entire ecosystem. Some platforms do exhibit more control over the ecosystem than others, like the difference between the Apple's AppStore and Google's Play Store.

Key Platform Decisions

Given the unique nature of platform businesses, there are six key decisions to be undertaken by every platform business.

1. Platform firms need to decide and articulate the specific sets of users that they cater to, and define/discover/develop network effects. The strength, direction, and sustainability of these network effects for the basis for subsequent decisions —value architecture, pricing and network mobilization, growth strategies, and ecosystem development.
2. Platform firms need to clearly articulate their value architectures—what value do they provide and how. Each platform has to evolve a signature combination of utilities that constitute its value architecture.
3. Given the nature of interactions between users and the network effects, it is important to decide which side(s), it at all, to subsidize and monetize; and the impact it has on the network development and growth of users.
4. In platform businesses, given the network effects and interdependencies, no one joins unless everyone joins. Solving these chicken-egg problems or penguin problems is a critical platform decision and will shape the growth and sustainability of the platform.
5. How platforms compete with other firms and platforms, and vie for market dominance is another important decision, shaping industry evolution and market shares.
6. Platforms also have a significant impact on how they work with other complements and the evolution of the ecosystem. Conscious engagement with the ecosystem will shape the industry structures and standards as well.

These six critical decisions are to be undertaken by the firms' top management and leadership; and form the core of the subsequent chapters. Chapter 3 elaborates on how to analyze the strength and direction of network effects and the consequences of the same for growth. This chapter also provides a roadmap for product firms to transition to platforms. Chapter 5 focuses on the value architecture of platform firms, based on the four core utilities added by platforms. This chapter provides insights into how platformization will transform industries and enhance choice, reduce costs, and build communities.

Chapter 7 discusses the network mobilization issues and presents a long list of strategies for resolving the penguin problems and subsequent scaling of platforms. Chapter 11 elucidates the various pricing models and evolves the criteria for subsidization and monetization of specific user groups. Chapter 13 presents the various aspects of platform architecture and its implications for resource and capability development at the firm level.

Chapter 15 takes an industry perspective and defines the industry conditions for the existence of winner-takes-all markets. The chapter also discusses the nature of such industries and how governments and regulators deal with such firms. Chapter 17 elaborates the envelopment dynamics, where large multi-platform bundles envelop focused platforms. The implications for enveloping firms and those fighting the threat of envelopment are discussed in detail, apart from dilemmas faced by regulators managing such markets. Chapter 19 devolves into the issues of how firms operate multiple business models within the same firm to complement each other. For instance, business models like software-as-a-service (SaaS) and multi-sided platforms (MSP) complement each other in terms of capabilities, network mobilization and rapid scaling. The final chapter integrates all these issues and takes the ecosystem view to discuss contemporary issues around platforms. Some of the issues that have no easy solutions like global dominance by platforms in certain markets, existence of contestable markets, and the role of global and regional regulators are discussed in the concluding chapter.

GRAB.in™: Enabling Hyperlocal

2

Introduction

On a pleasant Friday morning in April, as the summer heat picked up intensity while Mumbai was slowly waking up, a group of delivery boys had started to gather near a popular eating joint. Orders for breakfast deliveries from nearby restaurants were pouring in from the residents as the delivery boys frantically checked their smartphones to make sure of what to order. Pratish, Nishant, and Jignesh (co-founders of Grab) were watching these from their office windows in Andheri (East), Mumbai. Once the orders were placed, a conversation about the gig economy ensued, and the former classmates began to ponder over several aspects of the changes they were contemplating in managing Grab.in and the sustainability of food delivery. Several questions lingered on in their minds:

- With so many of us attracted to take up jobs as delivery boys, what was the future of gig economy workers? Why would these restaurants not invest in their own delivery boys?
- What was the Grab.in business model—one of consolidation of orders, customer knowledge, or operational efficiency through outsourcing of logistics? Was it a

---

This case is an extension of Chapter 1 Introduction.

R Srinivasan (Professor of Strategy), IIM Bangalore, Sandeep Lakshmipathy (Research Scholar) and Pramoth Joseph (Research Scholar), prepared this case for class discussion. This case is not intended to serve as an endorsement, source of primary data, or to show effective or inefficient handling of decision or business processes.

R. Srinivasan, *Platform Business Models*, Management for Professionals,
https://doi.org/10.1007/978-981-16-2838-2_2

sustainable business model grounded in reality or a sight that would change once these firms run out of venture funding?

- Was this viable in tier-2 and tier-3 cities where the distances are not too much, and home delivery markets were not mature while restaurant eating was still a family experience?

Grab's Journey

The threesome of Pratish Sanghvi (Pratish), Nishant Vora (Nishant), and Jignesh Patel (Jignesh) started India's first hyperlocal service delivery aggregator Grab-A-Grub which operated the popular portal Grab.in. Although not from a logistics industry background, Pratish's experience came from closely following the money trail due to his earlier stint in investment banking at BlackRock for over 9 years. After a stint in Canada and after working with the Toyota group, Nishant returned to India with an urge to do something different and create an impact. Having known each other since schooldays, Pratish and Nishant got together with Jignesh in 2012 to register the Grab-A-Grub venture.

Amazed by the organized logistics market in the United States, the founders wondered if the Indian scenario could be an opportunity that was ripe for digital disruption. Similar to the US market, there seemed to be an evolving demand for intra-city delivery of food, grocery, and other items. After scouting for more information about the sector, the three Mumbai residents understood the early attempts made during the hey days of the dotcom boom wherein one of the internet darlings of the era, Kozmo.com, had raised significant funding to undertake under one-hour free delivery of small items as a business model. After a spectacular failure of Kozmo, this sector had not seen much investment worldwide, and lack of technology enablers had served as a dampener too. By 2012, the founders realized that Indian mobile smartphone penetration and internet backbone needed for hyperlocal delivery had come of age and were at a level of maturity that could support a sustainable business venture centered on hyperlocal delivery. Wanting to bring the convenience of fast local delivery to the urban population that was increasingly grappling with busy lifestyle choices and commute challenges, the founders realized that it may be an opportune time for a venture that focused on this space in the country.

As a way to test the space, in late 2009, the founders collected details of menus from restaurants in the Andheri West area in Mumbai to print a booklet that could be distributed in nearby localities. They also put up a portal that showcased details of what each restaurant offered. Tapping into the idle time of college going students, they were able to convince a few of the students to help out with food delivery during their free time. At a time when the rental concept did not exist, the founders had to invest capital to purchase four bikes that could be used by delivery boys to serve the nearby areas. On an experimental basis, they charged the restaurant about 25% of the order amount as delivery fee. In a few months, demand for the delivery service picked up with more enquiries flowing in and also with restaurants demanding for a fixed delivery price per order instead of a commission from the order value. The founders also faced their first tryst with elasticity issues when it came to seasonality of order placements and availability of delivery personnel to service the incoming orders. They understood the nuances of delivery logistics and the unit economics that would make the business a viable one. All this proved to be vital learnings for the young entrepreneurs who were, by 2012, ready to venture into a formal start-up by quitting their day jobs to dabble in hyperlocal delivery space.

Grab.In Business Model

The B2B Switch

Although Grab.in started out with a B2C model wherein it took food delivery orders over phone and through its portal to then interface with restaurants to finally deliver the content to the hungry patron, it soon began to dawn on the founders that the B2C approach was not a sustainable model in the longer. Restaurants saw the steep 25% commission as an overhead apart from the myriad other expenses they had to deal with including food preparation costs, rentals, administration, and salaries. Also, the more popular ones were worried that their brand value would be lost when the customer no longer interfaced with them and instead were speaking to an unknown entity who could one day take their business elsewhere. With a captive customer base, these popular restaurant chains in Mumbai had a business that could benefit if someone would handle the delivery logistics alone. Unlike in late 2018, where even private equity (PE) firms had started to invest in the food tech space, the situation in 2012 was different with smaller restaurant being capital starved. These smaller chains and neighborhood restaurants were looking for delivery partners so that they could concentrate on the core business of making and serving delicious food. Having their own delivery system was a revenue drag and inefficient use of the employed due to varying demand cycles. Working directly with the restaurants and transforming into their delivery partner, aka a B2B approach instead of directly interfacing with customers seemed to be a more lucrative proposition to the founders. Along with diversification into e-commerce delivery, partnering with the major e-commerce portals offered propositions of a scalable business model instead of being engaged in the cash hungry B2C model where the cost of customer acquisition was disproportionately growing by the year as more competition entered the arena. Pratish commented thus:

> There was this need to burn cash infinitely if we pursued down the B2C route – cost of customer acquisition is very high in this space. Pivoting to a B2B model in 2013 made so much sense since cost of adding new business partners to work with is way more manageable and does not have to be a mad rush to show numbers on the platform.

According to Nishant, almost 95% of the new restaurants were happy to work with food aggregators such as Swiggy and Zomato since these new eating outlets did not have an established customer base. However, for most of the restaurants that were served by Grab.in, they had a loyal following which needed home delivery option. The food aggregators were taking away 25–30% of the bill amount as commission, while Grab.in could address delivery needs of the restaurants for a fixed price per delivery. Established restaurants grappled without being able to understand how much of their existing customer base was being taken away by these new generation online food ordering apps which seemed to be ready to burn loads of cash to acquire customers while waiting forever to turn a profit for their investors. Restaurants worried about Swiggy and Zomato becoming bigger and more powerful brands than any major restaurant and that meant even more negotiating power rested with these platforms to squeeze out higher commissions. These fears of cannibalization and loss of brand value made restaurants look for a delivery aggregator who would not compete with them, but instead partner in their growth. Nishant commented on the advantages of switching to B2B model:

> We stopped worrying about demand generation which otherwise was burning a lot of cash. At the same time, we saw the unsustainability of the B2C model with increasing labor costs when it came to blue collar jobs.

Information transparency, or rather the lack of it, was another key concern that restaurants seemed to be concerned with. Platforms such as Swiggy and Zomato decided what information was shared with the restaurants and when. Also, the platform itself seemed to have absolute control of how it utilized the customer data and which restaurant it promoted. Local business outlets had witnessed nearly 95% fall in business when they were either blacklisted or dropped from these food aggregator platforms. Additionally, when faced with inadequate supply of riders, the customers wanting to order through the platforms would see all the restaurants in that area as offline, which resulted in a significant loss of business and credibility of the restaurants, especially on busy time periods. With lack of customer data, the ability of these businesses to plan and forecast business operations was taking a hit. Emergence of franchisee model and increasing corporatization of the food business was adding to the struggle for survival of these mom-and-pop stores that had built their business over decades. Nishant and Pratish strongly believed that brands such as Dominos would fight to ensure that the customer always got better value pricing on their portal than instead what was offered by Swiggy since they had a strong need to defend their brand value and customer recall that they cherished. Pratish's thoughts on the B2C to B2B switch summarized the benefits of the switch:

> The reason we moved away from the B2C approach was to bring in demand predictability & have a model which allowed us to do intra-day deliveries for other business categories in addition to the 30-minute food delivery business. Smoothening the delivery time demands was key for us. Even though food delivery had the best margins, it makes you bleed cash very fast – that's where most food only aggregators struggle and are looking to diversify.

Platform Architecture—Hot Spots and Bikers

Grab.in had a unique two-sided model wherein the delivery personnel comprised of one side of the platform whereas the other side was loaded with businesses that wanted to leverage Grab's last mile package delivery facilities. As the density of businesses onboard Grab.in increased, there was more demand for delivery, and hence, more delivery personnel who were willing to earn commission for dropping off parcels or food packets came onboard. As density of businesses on the Grab.in platform increased, it made even more sense for other businesses to also leverage the hyperlocal service since Grab.in would increase concentration of delivery personnel dedicated for serving the vicinity. As density of delivery personnel dedicated for a locality increased, it meant faster delivery timings per order and more deliveries per day with the delivery team being readily available all through the business hours.

With an intention to utilize the idle time between peak demands for food deliveries, the trucks from the distribution centers (DC) of subscribed e-commerce vendors would bring bags filled with bar-coded packages. These 30–40 packages that had to be delivered in the vicinity of the hot spot would be picked by the delivery personnel around 3 pm every day for the drop off to be completed before 7 pm. Parcels that could not be delivered for whatever reason would be taken back by the trucks from e-commerce vendors for another attempt for delivery the following day. The hot spot model helped multiple bikers avoid having to commute to the distribution centers of different e-commerce vendors at peak traffic hours. This hot spot worked well for Grab.in to make best use of idle delivery personnel as e-commerce sites were not as hard pressed for timely delivery and could wait for the 3 pm to 7 pm window for parcels to be dropped off daily. Some of the e-commerce vendors who utilized Grab's services had either Grab.in operate an exclusive DC for their needs or would deliver orders in an existing DC operated by Grab.in so that last mile delivery could happen. A couple of e-retailers had completely done away with their delivery teams and were dependent on Grab.in and its competitors for all their delivery needs.

Cash-on-delivery (CoD) items posed additional logistical challenges to Grab.in: wherein the area team leader (TL) had to gather the cash which was collected by the delivery personnel, and the TL had the responsibility to deposit the cash collected with the e-commerce DC the same night. With this setup, the TL became a micro-DC given all the transaction book-keeping that had to be performed in a single day. Naturally for Grab.in, this model was not scaling up well, and more logistical challenges began to creep in when returns post-delivery or multiple attempts to deliver goods were considered. Hot spot approach worked best for Grab.in when there was high concentration of orders from a single locality such as university campus areas or upscale residential blocks that were clustered together. Attempts to replicate the hot spot model outside Mumbai, Delhi, and Bengaluru were still at an experimental stage as scaling this model was turning out to be a challenge due to the dynamics involved. Nishant recalled another successful hot spot model thus:

> In areas which are remote, but have a high concentration of people who order online, a single biker carrying 200-300 parcels for delivery daily has been most effective model for us. Our delivery personnel have a few spots where they hand out these parcels from. People from these areas know these mini hot spots, and walk up to collect their parcels. This

happens a lot in the Tech Parks in Bengaluru and Hyderabad, or in University campuses where our personnel may not be allowed to do door-step delivery. But scaling the hot spot has definitely been challenging.

Pricing Model and Unit Economics

When Grab.in switched to the B2B model and was firmly in the logistics business, it was evident that they could not sustain with being married to a single sector such as the food business. This prompted the diversification into other delivery models such as groceries, pharmacies, and kirana stores (aka small retail outlets). Grab.in evolved into a truly hyperlocal logistics player which catered to multiple business within a single locality by handling delivery of goods for these business outlets. This diversification also made them a reliable business partner to the food and shopping outlets in the area without being perceived as a threat. The mix of technology and the human connect that the local business outlet could access seemed to make a stark difference in how these outlets accepted the model.

Fixed delivery price per order was charged provided the outlet promised a minimum quantum of deliveries per day. With this approach, businesses had the flexibility to adjust the delivery rates that they were charged based on the dynamism of business activities on any given day. As outlets made more transactions per day, they paid lower delivery rates to Grab.in due to the larger volumes that they brought in. Due to increasing daily labor wages across the country, it made more economical sense for these businesses to transfer their home delivery operations to a professional operator who had enough technology backup to scale and respond to elasticity of demand as needed (see Exhibit 1: blending demand peaks across sectors). This model brought in blended revenue of about ₹30[1] per order depending on various factors such as volume of operations, scale in the particular city, and other factors. The cost of operations for Grab.in in 2018 stood at around ₹25–26 per order on a blended basis, with a profit of about ₹4 per order delivered. Food and grocery delivery accounted for maximum margins with a profit of around ₹7 per order for Grab.in, while e-commerce gave lower margins, but helped achieve optimal utilization of labor force which helped to rake in additional revenues. For a single rider, he had the opportunity to deliver multiple e-commerce packages within the area on a single trip and thus have better returns even though the per parcel payback was lower. The e-commerce deliveries complemented through increased volumes. While Grab.in earned a revenue of around ₹20–21 per e-commerce delivery, the profit margins were lesser at around ₹3. Grab.in tried to maintain an operating margin of around 15%.

For the riders, Grab.in believed that the key to retaining the delivery personnel was how they structured the pay-outs and incentives. Schemes such as bonus of ₹1000 for working on all weekdays in the month, or a bonus of ₹1000 for logging in more than 250 h in a month, or even a ₹100 bonus for completing ten deliveries in the day were popular with the delivery teams as they strived to achieve these targets and rightfully collect the bonus that they earned. Cash for the day's delivery

[1]Currency exchange rate as of October 28, 2019: $1 (US) = ₹70.74.

was delivered to the delivery personnel on a daily basis, and that was a great enabler for the families of these personnel who had daily needs to attend to. While most bonus plans helped the rider to earn more, there was a penalty of ₹20 imposed whenever a rider declined a delivery instruction. These different bonus plans were put together in order to motivate the teams to deliver higher throughput and in turn benefit proportionately through monetary returns for their efforts (see Exhibits 2 and 3 for data on rider statistics and riders' earnings). With a team leader for every 40 delivery members, the TL had to ensure that the delivery teams performed well to satisfy the demanding local businesses who had something to deliver.

Full stack logistics companies such as Delhivery utilized services from hyperlocal operators such as Grab.in to handle their overflows. When demand from last mile delivery peaked, Delhivery would send the overflows that it could not handle to the Grab.in hot spots for package drop off. Since Grab.in had delivery personnel who were engaged in food or grocery delivery, they could deliver these parcels coming from Delhivery during the lean periods of the day which did not see much food or grocery orders. While Delhivery handled end-to-end logistics for its e-commerce and other clients, both inter-city and intra-city parcel drops, Grab.in differentiated itself with a focus of being hyperlocal. Taking advantage of its hyperlocal nature of operations and with fully decentralized operations backed by central technology backend, when the load from a vendor dropped during the day, the TL in the area could redirect the deliver personnel via Grab's proprietary routing application to drop packages for other e-commerce vendors or to a nearby restaurant to handle its delivery needs. A logistics player such as Delhivery did not have this flexibility. Having been perceived as a last mile service provider, Grab.in could deliver parcels in an area for Aramex, BlueDart and DHL, or for a few restaurants during the day, or for multiple e-commerce vendors by picking up parcels from their DCs. This flexibility gave enough opportunities to Grab.in to stay focused on the hyperlocal market with enough sectoral diversification to keep up revenues (refer Exhibit 4 for the market size of hyperlocal deliveries).

Better delivery quality, meaning deliveries completed on time with good customer interactions, through the riders helped ensure improved vendor brand perception that in turn translated into repeat orders and better customer ratings of their experiences with the brand. Although Grab.in could not help a brand such as Myntra increase direct sales, it could do the same through best-in-class delivery experiences for the customers. With the e-commerce vendors being fully aware of the details of each completed delivery, Grab.in ensured that each satisfied customer transformed into potentially new business opportunity in the near future which was inspired by the quality of service from Grab's riders. By monitoring the deliveries timelines across cities, Grab.in attempted to ensure appropriate timeliness for each delivery by addressing potential bottlenecks due to either sub-optimal allocation of riders or due to increased radius of operations of the vendors.

First Mover Advantage

By mid 2019, Grab.in had spread across 140 cities in India, with plans to expand into several other towns and cities over the course of next few quarters. With an intent to maintain the entrepreneurial streak, each of the city's Grab.in executives was allowed to manage the Grab.in operations as an individual P&L. For most of these cities, food delivery needs were the primary drivers followed by demand from e-commerce vendors. Being the first hyperlocal delivery agency in most of these cities in India, Grab.in had the opportunity to set a standard for online booking and delivery of food and other items which others had to follow through. With a central backend technology team in Mumbai, each of these cities were supported until they were fully up and running, after which each of the Grab.in centers in the city could function in a self-sustainable manner with continued backend support from the central teams.

With rising labor costs, most e-commerce firms were doing away with in-house last mile delivery teams and were instead looking at firms such as Grab.in to handle all last mile operations, from the distribution center to the customer's residence. Even dedicated logistics firms such as Delhivery were looking at leveraging Grab.in for handling delivery load spikes during festive seasons.

There were certain other daily delivery items that Grab.in had attempted and was even a first mover in some, but had decided to concede ground on them due to multiple reasons. One such aspect was delivering milk to households on a daily basis before 7 am every morning. After a few months of experimenting with the service, the team came to realize that the milk delivery service in the early mornings was only increasing their delivery windows and was not adding any complementary aspects. They were also up against unionized labor in this space. Since grocery deliveries were not mandatorily time-of-the-day specific, it aligned well for Grab.in to diversify into, but not so for milk delivery.

Delivery Challenges

When it came to the grocery delivery space, the founders were of the opinion that none of the players had yet figured out the best approach to address the demands or nuances of this sector. For the kind of customer acquisition investment that had been done by Amazon or BigBasket or BigBazaar, the corresponding densities in orders were yet to be realized. They expected this space to still evolve over the next few years to arrive at a model that would be the right way of handling the grocery delivery space without losing cash. Pilferages, damages due to hassles of dealing with perishable goods, handling returns, margin issues, transaction volumes for viability, and cost of customer acquisition were some of the challenges that Grab.in and other hyperlocal delivery platforms were dealing with in this space. Customer acceptability of delivered items was another variable when it came to grocery delivery as a pack of vegetables acceptable to one household may not be considered good enough for the other. For the delivery personnel, grocery delivery was the least lucrative—heavy items had to be carried around, was highly susceptible to customer dissatisfaction due to personal preferences, and had to be fast track ones similar to food parcels. Pratish visualized a potential successful longer-term model for grocery delivery thus:

> Indian grocery delivery story may likely get built around the traditional model by using the internet as a penetration tool. Digitizing the neighborhood kirana store, giving access to the hyperlocal consumers through an online platform for these stores and then providing a last mile delivery solution to bridge the dots seemed to be a viable approach. Real time inventory management is the challenge to realise this model, and is being worked on today.

According to the founders, for the average Indian consumer who went online to shop, the price comparison for the items that he/she was ordering online was still the primary challenge. This was only second to the quality of the product that would be delivered coupled with the fact that the customer had preferences on where the product would be delivered from. Online platforms were still gearing up to match these consumer demands.

Multi-homing

With the Grab.in business model, it seemed that multi-homing was an expected outcome. Restaurants and e-commerce portals were using services of Grab.in and others too at the same time to meet their business operation necessities. Restaurants would list on online food aggregators such as Swiggy and Zomato while also using Grab.in for local delivery of orders that came in directly to the outlets. On busy days of the week, when footfalls into the restaurants were expected to be anyway high, these restaurants preferred to go offline on the food aggregators and instead serve customers who were walking into the outlet since they could save on the 25–30% commission that they had to pay to these online portals. On days when there was less crowd, the online orders coming in through the aggregators were helpful to keep the capacity utilization at optimal levels for these food joints. Restaurants were confident that their strong brand pull would make the savvy foodie directly call the restaurant helpline for orders when she did not find the outlet listed on the aggregator's app. This helped save outflows due to commission pay-outs and also reinforced the brand value for the outlet. The business development and sales teams at Grab.in were constantly reaching out to restaurants to convince them to offload all delivery logistics to Grab.in, while they focused on serving in-house customers with quality food.

Even the online food aggregators utilized services of Grab.in to fulfill customer orders during peak hours. Elasticity was a key issue that any hyperlocal delivery channel had to deal with, and this meant that peak demand for 30 min delivery of food items was one of the toughest sectors. Swiggy and Zomato utilized services of Grab.in across cities in India wherein the strong technology backend integration with Grab's delivery services made it convenient for these food apps to divert delivery pickups to waiting Grab.in personnel. Area specialization approach of

Grab.in coupled with the hot spot model helped Grab.in respond easily to these demand spikes from the online portals. Similarly, the e-commerce vendors, who incidentally had less stringent delivery timelines as compared to food delivery, utilized Grab.in to address spikes in package delivery within the cities. During off-peak hours for food delivery, the time from 10 am to 12 noon or from 3 to 7 pm daily, e-commerce packages could be delivered to homes by picking them up from the Grab.in hot spots in different areas across the city. This helped Grab.in better utilize idle capacity when the demands from food delivery had slacked off for the off-peak hours of the day—between breakfast and lunch or between lunch and dinner.

Diverse Perspectives

An aspect that Grab.in prided itself was the way it worked hard to retain its delivery personnel in an era where every other hyperlocal or platform player was luring away blue-collar workers through incentive plans or better salary packages. According to Nishant, Grab.in gave the average delivery personnel the ideal job variation that one looked in this space:

> Grab.in provided the delivery boys with the option to switch what they were delivering – those who were keen to deliver higher volumes of parcels went in for the e-commerce deliveries, but then after a couple of months, they would switch to food delivery as e-commerce deliveries are very demanding due to large bags that had to be hauled around on bikes. Food deliveries were light and quick, but had to be point to point, and hence urgent micro managed trips.

Musings from the Delivery Team

Speaking to a team of delivery personnel in Grab.in helped understand the appeal of hyperlocal delivery from a job perspective wherein diversity of businesses catered to was perceived as key to continuous daily payments. Moving from a dedicated fast food delivery segment to a hyperlocal delivery unit such as Grab.in helped the delivery personnel stay focused on a smaller area of operations, thus increasing throughput and earnings. Challenged with untimely payments when employed directly by restaurants or fast food joints, these delivery riders were enamored by the professional approach of Grab.in which brought in technology-aided operations management, which was not possible for the small scale of operations of each business that operated their own delivery teams. With access to a rich trove of data accessible on the mobile application, the delivery personnel knew the progress he had made during the day in meeting his quota of deliveries so that he could be eligible for the firm's incentives for high performing delivery team members. Without being limited to a single merchant, the delivery rider had an opportunity to earn higher rewards by logging in extra hours during any given day to complete higher deliveries and plan out in such a way that he could optimize the time and route undertaken. Technology backbone provided by Grab.in to the delivery riders was seen as a key differentiator in working for a hyperdelivery focused firm such as Grab.in as against working for a single restaurant or super market in the locality. Most riders put in over 10 h a day to maximize their earnings. Most of them could target delivering a minimum of 3–4 orders an hour, while occasionally they could clock even six deliveries during peak hours. Having invested in a two-wheeler through a bank loan, one of the delivery riders was actively working toward earning daily wages to clear off these loans at the earliest.

Having streamlined the allocation of orders to the riders, the Grab.in operations team mixed technology with their ground level understanding of the localities to maximize speed of deliveries. With few customers even handing cash tips to the riders who deliver food, these riders seemed to enjoy working for hyperlocal deliveries. Many of the riders had varied levels of education with some of them had joined as delivery personnel after dropping out of school. With the needs of an aspirational population rising, hyperlocal deliveries created the much-needed blue-collar jobs for the urban population. With a formal referral system in place that handed over incentives for bringing in known accomplices to work as riders, Grab.in did not seem to have difficulty in getting prospective delivery boys. Various options for employment created by elements of the gig economy helped these riders to choose whom they wanted to work for based on multitude of conditions that differed for each individual. Local businesses allowed the delivery personnel to use their restrooms and refreshment facilities so that they could focus on the job. Training of delivery members on semantics of customer interactions helped prepare candidates from rural households to be equipped to handle demands of hyperlocal deliveries in the metros in India.

Operations Behold!

Lead generation through word of mouth was a primary means of acquiring new customers for Grab. With enquiries coming in through the company portal, Grab's investment toward acquiring new business through a dedicated sales team was minimal. With an average time of around 5 days to close a new customer, Grab.in operated a lean machine when it came to the sales process. With terms of engagement finalized, the operations team would then handle all customer interactions that encompassed initial trainings to the customer's staff on using the Grab.in platform, daily deliveries, surge capacity planning and settlements. Most merchants utilizing services of Grab.in punched in their orders on a daily basis. Although application programming interfaces (APIs) were available from Grab, most merchants were not savvy enough to get into API integrations to fully automate the order process and instead preferred to use the mobile application to punch in their orders every single time. Any escalations from the merchants regarding delivery services or the delivery personnel were handled through an established escalation mechanism at the city level with pre-defined service-level agreements

(SLAs) via Grab's technology platform. With a formalized feedback mechanism with 7-, 15-, and 30-day follow-ups, the Grab.in operations team ensured that newly onboarded merchants got the required level of services. Within this 30-day period, if a merchant wanted to quit the platform, the operations team analyzed the reasons for the same. The merchant could have been dissatisfied with the services offered by the platform, and that could be due to a variety of issues related to supply chain, grooming aspects of the delivery boys or even pricing.

The way the Grab.in teams were organized seemed to provide an edge over competition. Unlike the rest of the players in the market, Grab.in had an intentional design to the hierarchy that was put in place with the group leaders (GL) taking care of a single merchant in the area along with his team of delivery personnel. The team leader (TL) was accountable for a group of merchants but in the same area, and the area manager (AM) was connected to multiple areas with the responsibility of managing the areas with help from GLs and TLs in those places. GLs had delivery as their primary responsibility, apart from being a single point of service for a single merchant/ business. AMs also participated in periodic audits of riders and merchants to understand the quality of services delivered by Grab.in on the ground. These audits had proven to be a proactive measure to unearth issues related to rider discipline or other merchant business nuances that could stall quality of service. Without a dedicated sales and marketing team, AMs doubled up as business development managers to help Grab.in break new ground by clinching delivery opportunities from larger merchants or newer businesses in their areas given strong understanding of the geography under their management. With a clear understanding of the supply t available across their TLs and GLs and the demand that the teams were catering to, the AMs were suitably placed to redirect resources as needed. With increasing demand for well-trained delivery personnel, AMs also had the added responsibility of ensuring suitable retention policies to address attrition risks. With anti-poaching agreements between the e-commerce service providers and Grab, these firms ensured riders were not poached within the same DC.

Facing saturation in terms of cities to penetrate in the North, toward the end of 2018, Grab.in was looking toward increased presence in southern cities such as Mangalore, Mysuru, and Vizag. Grab.in would start operations in a new city with e-commerce deliveries, and once the delivery personnel pipeline and training aspects were well-established, Grab.in would then venture into serving delivery needs of local businesses. Hence, Grab's approach to penetrate a metro city vis-à-vis a tier-II city differed, wherein larger metros necessitated delivery personnel workforce to be already in place before starting operations at scale. City managers to sales teams and delivery boys along with a small recruitment team had to be in place before operations commenced in a major metro. In contrast, in non-metros, Grab.in typically started with one or two personnel who would then gradually build up the business based on the needs of strategic partners of Grab.in such as Aramax or other e-commerce vendors who needed coverage in the non-metro for hyperlocal delivery. With most of the hiring happening from the city in which operations were being set up, these personnel were well-equipped to handle the local geography, language demands, understanding of local business environment, restaurant preferences, bringing in other riders through referrals and other aspects critical for building successful operations. With no plans to go international in the near term, the Grab.in team was focused on penetrating more cities based on the potential these cities offered for growth in hyperlocal delivery opportunities.

Powering Technology

According to the founders, Grab.in followed a three-stack approach to technology—the App, APIs, and the dashboards. Grab.in offered different technology assets to each of its market sides—the riders had access to a mobile app that pulled new upcoming orders to be delivered, while the business outlets integrated into their point-of-sale (PoS) systems into the Grab.in backend to push demand. In the backend, there was an algorithm that assigned orders to the riders based on a variety of factors. For the business outlets, Grab.in provided multiple options to integrate—firstly through the APIs exposed by the Grab.in team that were integrated into the PoS system at the business outlet. This was the most popular means for business outlets to send delivery orders to the riders at Grab.in. Secondly, a different mobile app allowed business outlets to order for deliveries of goods to end customers. Thirdly, Grab.in also provided a Web-based dashboard on their portal wherein merchants could log in to send in delivery requests. Exposure to the dashboard also allowed the smaller retail outlets to visualize sales analytics to allow them to comprehend how their business was scaling up by providing an opportunity to understand repeat purchases, geo distribution of incoming orders, average ticket size, customer loyalties, and many other aspects to aid in customer relationship management.

Through the technology assets provided by Grab.in, merchants had the ability to accumulate orders for delivery so that they could order in the riders to arrive when they had gathered accumulated volume discounts.

Investments into Grab.in

Grab's first funding came in early 2014 through an Angel round, and in the same year, another investment came from Zomato which was looking at expanding its footprint across the country. Sixth Sense Ventures also invested in Grab.in along with Zomato during the same period. In 2015, Grab.in raised \$1 mn from Oliphans Capital and a private investor, and the very next year, Aramex committed to invest around \$3 mn. In early 2018, Grab.in raised another funding round of \$1.5 mn from Small Industries Development Bank of India's (SIDBI) wholly owned subsidiary SIDBI Venture Capital Limited. Being a government body, SIDBI foresaw the employment opportunities that Grab.in was generating for rural youth and wanted to be a part of the social impact that Grab.in was creating through its hyperlocal delivery business model. Even after these investments coming from different fund managers, the founders continued to hold significant portion of equity enabling them to guide the business to realize its vision of becoming the established hyperlocal business enabler.

In March 2019, Reliance Industries controlled Reliance Industrial Investment and Holdings Limited (RIIHL) acquired a majority stake in Grab.in for ₹1.06 billion.[2] With 83% holding, RIIHL committed to furthering Grab's investments in digital commerce initiatives and expanding its logistics services to cater to B2B and B2C segments.

Online food aggregators such as Swiggy and Zomato brought in different business risks for the average food retailer who had not been exposed to sophisticated aspects such as promotional offers, expedited on-demand delivery, commissions to third parties, and order refunds. Occasionally, when the online aggregator went offline due to technical difficulties on account of an unplanned outage, the various food joints that were critically dependent on these aggregators would have no means to easily cope up with the fall in demands. Due to dealing with perishable commodities, these restaurants were at risk of losing significant investments for each day of outage. In metros such as Mumbai and Bengaluru where traffic snarls were more common, online aggregators promised refunds to their customers if the order was not delivered within 30 min. This just meant that the restaurant had to take the brunt of a returned delivery which was unheard of in the traditional model in which they operated in the past. Much of the negotiating leverage existed with the aggregators who could dictate terms to the restaurants that had come to critically depend on such platforms for business continuity. Through a B2B relationship with Grab.in, restaurants could mitigate much of this as they had an opportunity to serve their customer base with home deliveries without having to depend on the all-encompassing food-tech aggregators. This created a niche for B2B players such as Grab.in, and investors saw an unserved need that could be profitably exploited.

Competitive Topography

Shadowfax

In late 2018, Shadowfax was one of India's highly funded B2B last mile delivery platform. As a technology-driven platform for hyperlocal and e-commerce logistics services in the country, it delivered food, pharmacy, grocery, and e-commerce. Its mission was to connect the fleet on the street and suppliers in logistics using a single platform/IoTs to bridge the information gap and eradicate inefficiencies across the value chain. Bangalore-based Shadowfax started operations in 2015 with 60-min food delivery orders and had grown the services from last mile deliveries in

[2]Gooptu, B. (2019) "*Reliance Industries' subsidiary inks pacts to acquire Grab A Grub and C-Square Info Solutions*," *ET Online*, March 4. Available at: https://tech.economictimes.indiatimes.com/news/startups/reliance-industries-subsidiary-inks-pacts-to-acquire-grab-a-grub-and-c-square-info-solutions/68245460 (Accessed: May 01, 2019).

intra-city to next-day inter-city deliveries. Shadofax had presence across 75 cities in India and provided services varying from bulky deliveries to express deliveries.

In November 2015, Shadowfax acquired Pickingo to start same-day pickup, and by the end of that year, it reached 15,000 orders per day. In March 2016, Shadowfax launched same-day delivery for fashion and grocery. By September 2016, Shadowfax was operationally positive for the first time serving 90% enterprise clients. By the end of 2016, it received Series B funding of $19 mn from Eight Road Ventures. Same-day delivery for bulk items such as furniture was launched in March 2017. In November 2017, it expanded its services to 70 cities by acquiring NuvoEx. In 2018, Shadowfax raised Series C funding of about USD 22 million.[3]

In 2017–2018, revenues stood at ₹763 mn from ₹317 mn from the previous year. Net losses shrank to ₹212 mn from ₹285 mn.[4] Shadowfax delivered everything ranging from food to medicines, packages to pallets, and luxury makeup to everyday grocery. E-commerce constituted 30% of its business, food, and groceries contributed 25%, and reverse logistics were at 20%.[5]

Dependo.com

Dependo Logistics Pvt. Ltd. was a subsidiary of Quess Corp, a leading business services provider, which assisted enterprises and emerging firms in managing their non-core activities and improving operational efficiencies. Quess Corp was a step-down subsidiary of Fairfax Financial Holdings Group, held through its Indian listed subsidiary, Thomas Cook India Limited. Dependo provided last mile logistics solutions and had offices in cities, and doorstep pickup was available in four cities —Mumbai, Delhi, Bangalore, and Chennai. Services on offer included First Mile solutions, last mile delivery, reverse logistics, distribution center management, and on-demand courier. With a daily average of handling 75,000 packages, they had offices spread across 36 cities in the country with more than 1500 professionals. Their first mile collection service helped to collect goods from sellers and deliver to the e-commerce hubs. The last mile delivery services features included cash and collection on deliver, managed drop-ship, smartphone equipped fleet, digital signatures, localized and product trained customer service, real-time status, next-day delivery, and GPS tracking. They also picked up return packages from the customers and sent them to the hub for aggregation. Their on-demand courier services were available across Bangalore, and delivery was within the city or across India.

[3]Athira Nair (2018) *On-demand delivery startup Shadowfax raises $22 million in Series C funding*, yourstory.com. Available at: https://yourstory.com/2018/08/demand-delivery-startup-Shadowfax-raises-22-million-series-c-funding (Accessed: May 4, 2019).

[4]Dearton Thomas Hector (2018) *Tech-enabled logistics startup Shadowfax trims FY18 loss as revenue soars*, techcircle.in. Available at: https://www.techcircle.in/2018/11/23/tech-enabled-logistics-startup-Shadowfax-trims-fy18-loss-as-revenue-soars (Accessed: May 4, 2019).

[5]Toms, M. P. and Hector, D. T. (2018) *Shadowfax: This 'Uber' for delivery personnel is getting logistics right*, vccircle.com. Available at: https://www.vccircle.com/Shadowfax-this-uber-for-delivery-personnel-is-getting-logistics-right/ (Accessed: May 27, 2019).

Ekart Logistics

Ekart logistics or Ekart courier was a courier delivery firm headquartered in Bangalore, India, with about 400 employees. Ekart was one of India's largest logistics and supply chain companies delivering 10 million shipments a month to more than 3800 locations. It was started as Flipkart's in-house supply chain arm in 2009 and controlled by way of a company named WS Retail Services, a major seller on Flipkart platform. Eventually Ekart was acquired in 2015 by Flipkart from WS Retail Services.[6] Ekart was handling all the deliveries for Flipkart. It helped in the growth of Flipkart with its innovations like cash on delivery, in-a-day guarantee, and same-day guarantee. Ekart logistics had diversified in 2018 and delivered parcels for other sectors such as pharma and local retailers. Flipkart had continued investments in Ekart logistics to develop the entity as an independent logistics business in the future. Ekart was the pioneer in introducing locker services in stores and supermarkets.

ElasticRun

ElasticRun is focused on last mile and middle mile operations for the e-commerce industry alongside primary and secondary distribution for pharma companies. ElasticRun was an aggregated variable-capacity transportation network built using idle transportation and logistics capacities from many dispersed entrepreneurs. ElasticRun raised about $8 mn funding in 2018.[7] ElasticRun, which used technology for transportation and supply chain operations, ran an asset-light, variable-capacity logistics network. The company's technology platform could build aggregated transportation capacity in tune with the requirements of its varied clientele. By aggregating resources across channels, the start-up eliminated fixed setup costs, thus helping its customers reduce logistics spending. The company catered to clients in e-commerce, pharmaceuticals, food, and automotive sectors with their primary distribution, secondary distribution, and last mile connectivity. In 2016–2017, its operational revenues rose to ₹91.3 mn from ₹65,688 in the previous year and posted a net loss of ₹73.9 mn up from ₹ 4 mn.

Hyperlocal Aspirations

According to the founders, Grab.in had cautiously expanded from one city to another. With an attempt to be prudent with the cash burn, Grab.in had approached expansion of operations in a phased manner by setting up strong local operations command

[6] Shrutika Verma and Mihir Dalal (2015) *Flipkart buys back logistics arm from WS Retail, Livemint.com*. Available at: https://www.livemint.com/Companies/DadIlWWt07oLLh3rdS8YUN/Flipkart-buys-back-logistics-arm-from-WS-Retail.html (Accessed: April 20, 2019).

[7] Vijayakumar Pitchiah (2018) *Norwest, Kalaari invest more into logistics tech startup ElasticRun, VCCircle.com*. Available at: https://www.vccircle.com/norwest-kalaari-invest-more-into-logistics-tech-startup-elasticrun/ (Accessed: May 27, 2019).

chain which would be capable of looking into adjacent territories for growth opportunities. For example, once the Delhi NCR operations were fully functional, the Delhi Grab.in team started to look at addressing delivery needs for nearby places such as Mathura as part of expanding reach. The team usually started operations at two ends of the city that they would get into and then slowly start increasing coverage to cover the entire geography. As a matter of policy, Grab.in aimed to make a new city's operations profitable in 4 months' time frame, and this approach helped keep costs to minimal. Once all the cities were profitable on their own operating terms, the central teams started to focus on turning the firm profitable overall. Once this goal was achieved in February 2018, the team started to focus on further expansions across the country. By hiring past entrepreneurs for key positions within a city, Grab.in kept the culture of thriving with frugality as a core tenet for each team. With this approach, by first quarter of 2019, barring the technology costs, Grab.in achieved net profitability. New cities to enter was seemingly dictated by demands from different e-commerce partners coupled with the likelihood of replicating the restaurant-based hyperlocal business in the city under consideration as this was central to Grab's operational efficiency. Each of the city heads had to focus on cash flows and turning their operations profitable in the shortest time possible.

Road Ahead

With new funding, the founders were looking at starting operations in newer cities with larger teams wherein the business operations could sustain a longer gestation period to turn profitable enabling double digit growth. Increased funding would also allow Grab.in to invest further in cities that were out-performing others with growing demand for food deliveries and ever-increasing e-commerce footprint.

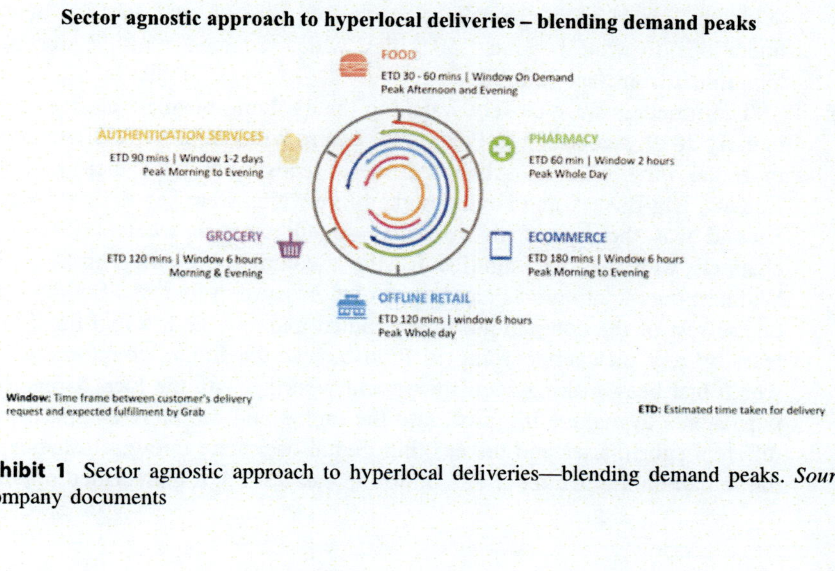

Exhibit 1 Sector agnostic approach to hyperlocal deliveries—blending demand peaks. *Source* Company documents

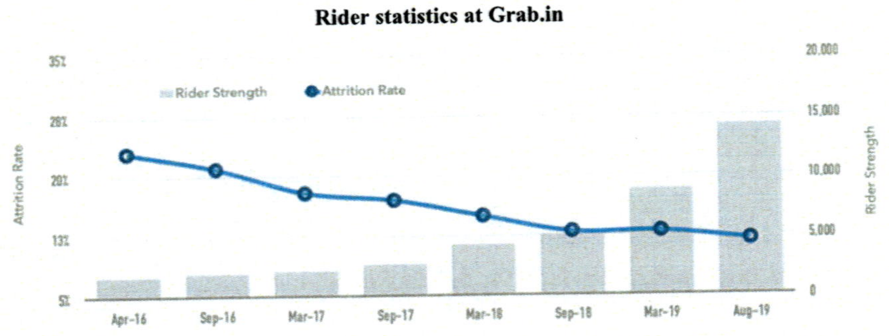

Exhibit 2 Rider statistics at Grab.in. *Source* Company documents

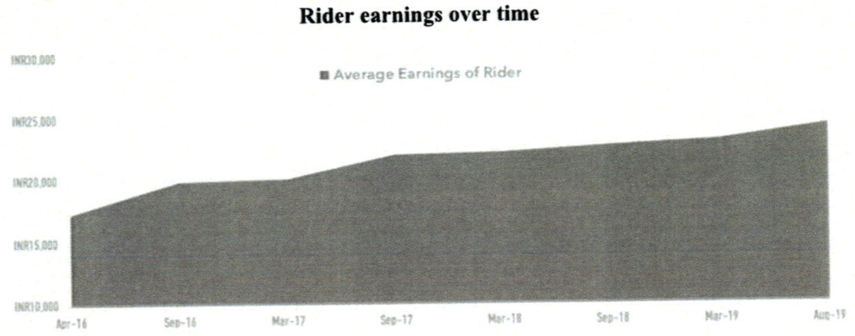

Exhibit 3 Rider earnings over time. *Source* Company documents

With an aim to grow the business five-fold, Pratish was looking at expanding operations to well beyond 250 cities which covered multiple sectors on the hyperlocal front (see Exhibit 4).

The founders were closely watching the evolving business ecosystems in India in early 2019. According to Pratish, they were witnessing four different ecosystems in India. First was the Alibaba centered ecosystem with their investments in Zomato, Big Basket, and Paytm marketplace which were key to drive consumption. Second was the ecosystem evolving around Amazon where online and offline channels were getting engulfed by the e-commerce giant. Third, the Flipkart–Walmart combination was another parallel ecosystem that was building up to take on the rest of the competition in the Indian markets. Fourth and final, but not the least by any means according to Pratish, was the Indian conglomerate Reliance which had been making acquisitions and working with the local kirana (mom and pop) stores to make a big push into the online and offline retail space through its different subsidiaries and the existing digital backbone through Reliance Jio. With the Indian online market at $22 billion in early 2019, it represented only about 5%

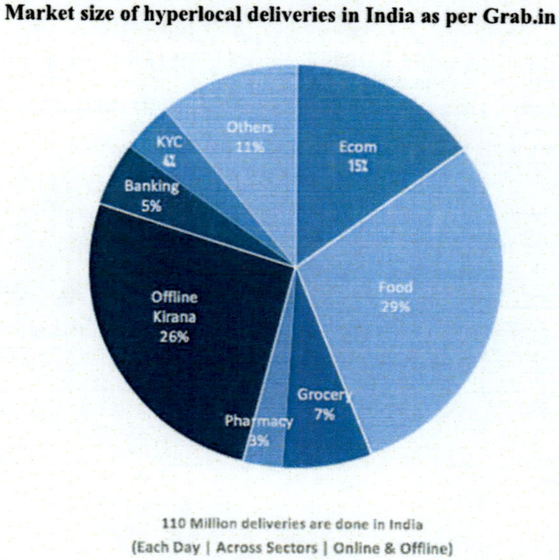

Exhibit 4 Market size of hyperlocal deliveries in India as per Grab.in. *Source* Company documents

of the Indian opportunity, while the remaining 95% was yet to be fully tapped into. Grab.in was keen to be part of one of these growing ecosystems so that it could grow its rider base by riding on the disruption that these different ecosystems would bring to the nascent Indian hyperlocal market scenario. With ramped up scale and operational capabilities, Grab.in wanted to be well placed to serve the growth of these ecosystems to in turn fuel its growth ambitions. According to Pratish, with just over 10 million uniquely identifiable addresses in India, the limitations of the online-only model is fairly straightforward and reminisced of how an online–offline model mix could propel the next push in retail volumes. Being part of one of the major ecosystems in India was the way forward for the founders to realize the exponential growth they were planning for as that would cement the needs on the supply front while the team could focus on driving the growth of rider volumes and delivery quality.

Network Effects

3

A typical platform business brings together multiple sets of users. This chapter elaborates the differences between pipeline and platform business models, provides a framework for analysis of network effects, and derives implications for growth and sustainability of platforms.

Externalities, Network Externalities, and Network Effects

Externalities refer to the costs or benefits accrued by a user due to the actions of other users. These externalities may be positive or negative and could be either enjoyed during production or consumption of the good (product/service). Network externalities have been defined by economists[1] as the change in benefit or surplus that an agent derives from a good when the other agents consuming the same kind of good changes (Leibowitz and Margolis 1995). The most common definition of network externalities is the value generated out of owning a network good like telephone: more the number of users owning a telephone, more the value of the telephone to the user. These network externalities are typically internalized by the users. That is, the additional utility of usage is being captured by the users, the telephone owners.

However, in the context of platforms, the owner of the platform or network may internalize some of these additional benefits, rather than the users themselves internalizing all the value added. In other words, when the users fail to internalize these externalities completely, the platform owner might as well internalize those

[1]For a detailed discussion, see Leibowitz, S.J. & Margolis, S.E. 1995. Are network externalities a new source of market failure? Research in Law and Economics, 17.

R. Srinivasan, *Platform Business Models*, Management for Professionals,
https://doi.org/10.1007/978-981-16-2838-2_3

benefits that the users did not. These benefits that are internalized by the platform owner are no longer externalities and are referred to as network effects.[2]

Defining Network Effects

The core concept in the context of platform markets is the presence of network effects. For simplicity sake, consider a two-sided platform, like Uber. A typical platform like Uber intermediates between supply-side users (drivers) and demand-side users (riders). Both sides of users interact with each other facilitated by the platform, as represented in Fig. 3.1.

In such a platform, the platform intermediary is represented in the middle with the users affiliating with the platform firm. The network effects are represented by arrows to indicate the direction. For instance, the arrows connecting from side 1 to side 2 and vice versa represent cross-side network effects, and the arrows within the sides represent same-side network effects.

In a platform like Uber, more riders in a city attract more drivers to affiliate with Uber and vice versa. These motivations indicate the presence of cross-side network effects. In a social networking platform like Facebook, users attract more users like them, representing same-side network effects. In a pay television, more viewers will attract advertisers, but not the other side. Viewers of a particular television show might write reviews about the same and attract others to watch the same. This act will surely increase the number of viewers, but do not represent network effects. Word-of-mouth marketing and user-driven promotions might increase scale on one side of the platform, but may not increase the utility for other users. Network effects occur when the increase in scale results in higher marginal utility for other users. In the case of television show reviews getting more users, the marginal utility for the new users is not any different than what was derived by the early users.

Network effects represent the utility (*Y*) derived by a given user from affiliating with a network being dependent on the number of other users (*n*) that the focal users can interact and/or transact. This utility is typically over and above the utility (*X*) derived from the standalone platform, unrelated to the scale. Therefore, the total utility (*U*) derived by a user from a network is the sum of these utilities. Hence,

$$U = X + Y(n)$$

where U is the total utility derived from the network; X is the utility derived from the standalone platform (independent of scale and scope), and $Y(n)$ is the utility derived rom the platform as a consequence of the platform having n users.

[2]For a more detailed analysis of these differences, read: Leibowitz, S.J., & Margolis, S.E. 1994. Network externality: An uncommon tragedy, Journal of Economic Perspectives, 8, 2. 133–50.

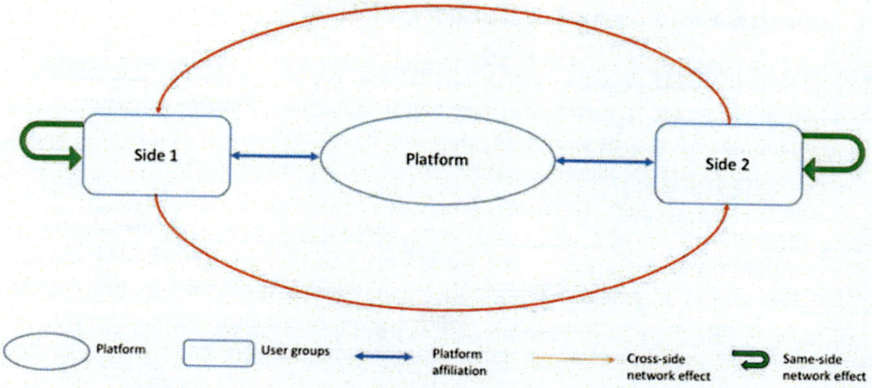

Fig. 3.1 Representation of platform network effects

Same-Side and Cross-Side Network Effects

Network effects drive businesses when users value the presence of other users in the platform. When a platform intermediates between multiple sets of users, there could be same-side and cross-side network effects.

Cross-side network effects or indirect network effects refer to the value attached to the number and quality of users on the other side of the platform. For example, in a ride-hailing platform, riders value the number and quality of drivers on the platform. More the number of drivers affiliated to the platform in that city, more valuable is the platform to the rider. Between competing ride-hailing platforms, other things being equal, riders are likely to choose that platform that has more drivers. And the same might hold good for the drivers too—more the riders on the platform, more business a driver on the platform is expected to get, and therefore more likely to join the platform.

Same-side network effects or direct network effects refer to the value attached by the users to the number and quality of users on the same side. For instance, in a social networking platform, users are likely to value the number of quality of their friends and family, as well as influencers on the platform as their peers (users on the same side of the platform). The value of the platform increases proportionately with the number of their peers the platform is able to attract and therefore facilitates interactions. It is also important to manage the quality of users and their specific preferences. It may not be the total number of users, but those users that the user would like to interact with regularly (in the social network) that matters in the definition of same-side network effects.

Positive and Negative Network Effects

These network effects may also be positive or negative. For instance, while advertisers on a newspaper or media platform highly value the number of readers/viewers, the converse may not be true. Readers might not value advertisements, and the network utility $Y(n)$ might be zero, i.e., they may just put up with the advertisements. However, when the advertisements become irrelevant or too many to disrupt the reading/viewing experience, there may be disutility. Which means, users negatively value the advertisements, and the readers may leave the platform. In summary, network effects may be positive (directly proportional), zero (no salient effect), or negative (indirectly proportional).

When there are positive network effects, users beget more users. As the number of users grow, the number of interactions amongst users may increase, and the utility might increase exponentially. These increased utilities might attract more and more users, sustaining rapid growth of the user base of the platform. On the other hand, negative network effects present limits to growth. When users negatively value scale in a platform, high-value users start leaving the platform, and the platform is at risk of shrinking or even collapse. It is important that platforms maintain appropriate controls on negative network effects and ensure value creation and capture for the users.

Properties of Network Effects

There are three properties of network effects that are relevant to analyze in the context of platform businesses.

- Strength of network effects
- Direction of network effects
- Nonlinearity.

Let us illustrate these with an instance each as we discuss these properties.

Strength of Network Effects

Think of a matrimony platform focused on recent graduates. Each user may have diverse expectations from the platform—some of their preferences may be very strong, while some others may not be. For instance, someone may significantly value socioeconomic matches, while some others may value psychological matches. Some users might really value the platform offering a long list of potential partners, while others might prefer a small curated list. Some users might prefer to initiate the conversation themselves and take things forwards, while some others might want some assistance to communicate and interact. Network effects are strong when users demand ***novelty, choice, and convenience*** from the platform. The relative strength of network effects across the sides of the platform is a key consideration in defining the architecture and economics of the platform. We could measure the strength of network effects using standard marketing research techniques, including conjoint analysis.

Network effects are strong when users value ***novelty*** in the platform. During repeated interactions, like in the decision to affiliate with a news aggregation platform, users would value their ability to access a variety of news from different sources. Users' willingness to join will largely depend on the breadth and depth of coverage of news from a variety of sources. As they continue to use the platform, users will value the quality of news, contributing to their willingness to stay. As the news aggregator continues to invest in breadth, depth of news coverage and improve the quality, the network effects will be stronger, resulting in a stronger association with the platform (willingness to join and willingness to stay).

In some other platforms, users value ***choice***. In platforms that aid users find and discover something as part of their decision-making, variety will increase the strength of network effects. Take the case of hyperlocal platforms like food delivery. User's willingness to join the platform will be dependent on the number of restaurants available for delivery in that geography. More the number of restaurants willing to deliver through that platform, more the users are willing to join. Willingness to pay would also be higher for platforms where there is more choice of restaurants/menu items, and the platform allows for restaurants to differentiate themselves on the platform.

In the context of platforms with complex interactions, users will value convenience. Take the case of travel aggregators. Users will value the platform's contribution in terms of enabling a variety of interactions in one single interface—deciding on the tour locations, search/select/book the hotel, search/select/book tour operators to local tours, and pay for all of these in the travelers' local currency (and that too without cultural hiccups like bargaining and tipping). If a platform would aggregate all these inter-related transactions on a single platform, ***convenience*** will increase the users' willingness to pay.

In sum, users value novelty, choice, and convenience. Depending on the nature and frequency of interactions on the platform, users will value a combination of novelty, choice, and convenience. In the case of high frequency transactions (like a social network), the network effects is largely determined by the novelty, whereas in the case of infrequent (but critical to customer experience) transactions (like property buying), the network effect will arise largely out of choice. In both cases, it is the variety of content that matters, but the source of network effects is different due to the frequency of interactions. In cases where there are high frictions in transactions (like hiring an intern), the network effects arise out of convenience. This frictions may arise due to common market inefficiencies (information asymmetry, moral hazard, and adverse selection) or due to the transaction costs of search, selection, and contracting.

Direction of Network Effects

The presence of negative network effects can become a serious hinderance to the growth of the platform. Like in the case of a traditional newspaper, too many, inappropriate (to the segment of readers) and irrelevant advertisements might discourage readers, and it requires a fine balance to keep the readership stable. This constant balancing of both sides' utilities is a pre-requisite for sustained growth of both sides of the platform.

Negative network effects amongst users of the same side can be more restraining for growth. Imagine a B2B marketplace like mjunction.in that caters to commodities like steel, coal, telecom spectrum, and tea. The more the number of direct competitors affiliated with mjunction, the less value it is for the users. The buyers and sellers value the number and quality of each other, but each buyer (and seller) would prefer less direct competition. It is important for the platform to allow for the participants/users to differentiate themselves from the competition, in terms of a variety of parameters, including brand, quality, perfect fit with the other side's requirements, and possibly even history (experience) of operating in that market. In the absence of this differentiation, it is possible that these negative same-side network effects would impose limits to growth of the user base, as beyond a certain scale, niche and differentiated users refrain from joining the commoditized platform. On the other hand, having a large number of undifferentiated users on one side will present with high costs of search, selection, and contracting by the other side users. These costs would result in a choice overload problem and create opportunities for niche platforms (that serve a narrow segment of users effectively) to evolve.

Nonlinearity of Network Effects

Network effects are not necessarily linear across all scale. For instance, up to a certain scale, network effects may be positive, and once the platform scale crosses a threshold, the network effects may be negative. Take for example, a telecommunication network. Given the fixed costs of the telecommunications infrastructure, the initial users will enjoy positive network effects. Once the infrastructure utilization approaches its capacity, users will perceive disutility as the network becomes congested.

Even with positive network effects, not all users perceive the same utility. As the number of users increases, the user utilities might follow a logistic function (a typical "S" curve). Beyond the first few transactions, the marginal utility increases at a decreasing rate. This may be due to (a) reduction in novelty of the platform for late adopters, (b) choice overload experienced by users as the network size increases, and (c) the bureaucratic costs of engaging with the growing network. And once the network reaches maturity, the marginal utility may even begin declining due to overcrowding of the network and the possibility of poor quality users proliferating the network (see Fig. 3.2). Given the concavity of the curve beyond a particular scale, traditional network value increase calculations based on Metcalfe's law may not hold true for platform businesses.[3]

Leveraging Networks for Growth

The three properties of network effects—strength, direction, and nonlinearity—determine platform growth. Stronger the positive network effects, more the marginal utility of platforms to the users. And when these utilities are a function of scale, users promote platform affiliation to other users and help the platform scale. Take for example a digital payment platform. As more and more users (payers) adopt that particular product/service, they bring in more and more shops and restaurants that they pay to. As more and more shops (receivers) adopt that product/service, other payers begin using the same. More users on one side begets more users on the other side, and once the platform achieves a critical mass, scaling up happens with little or no marketing effort by the platform. However, when the platform achieves network saturation (due to infrastructure constraints, increase in search and contracting costs, and/ or overall quality reduction), the platform growth may plateau and even begin tapering down. This point provides opportunities for firms to leverage their resources and enter into newer products/services and markets or start providing newer and additional value to the existing users. Gawer and Cusumano (2008) provide two strategies for firms to become "platform leaders"—coring and tipping.[4]

Coring

Coring refers to the set of activities firms use to create a new platform leveraging an element that is fundamental to the technological/market ecosystem. Typically coring strategies leverage a "core", something that resolves technical problems affecting a majority of users in that ecosystem. Short of establishing a dominant standard, coring encourages other participants in the business ecosystem to adopt that specific core. For a platform with leadership aspirations, it is important to take the lead in identifying, investing, and developing the core.

For instance, the Indian travel portal makemytrip.com began as providing travel services between USA and India and then expanded its services to Indian domestic travel. Apart from air travel bookings, Makemytrip extended its core to provide hotel bookings, holiday packages, train bookings, buses, cabs, and almost everything related to traveling and holidays. Not just leveraging the core offering of

[3]The core argument with network laws (Metcalfe's law and Reed's law) is based on the premise that the utility for all users is the same, which is not always true in the case of platform businesses. For a more detailed argument on this, read Briscoe, Odlyzko, and Tilly (2006). Metcalfe's Law is Wrong, IEEE Spectrum, July 2006. Available on the internet at spectrum.ieee.org/computing/networks/metcalfes-law-is-wrong (last accessed on 8th August 2020).

[4]For more details, read Gawer, A. & Cusumano, M. 2008. How companies become platform leaders, MIT Sloan Management Review, Winter 2008.

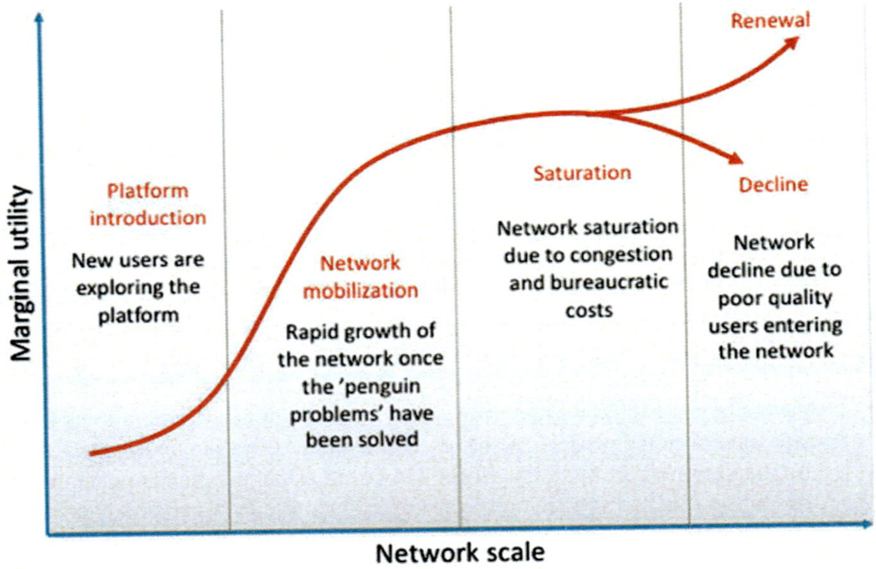

Fig. 3.2 Marginal utility as network scale increases

matching travelers with their needs, it began providing corporate services by setting up "implants"—mini travel desks within large organizations' travel desks. It had further extended the core to integrate travel insurance, foreign exchange dealerships, retail (offline) stores, as well as a franchise programme to expand its reach throughout the country.

In effect, for coring to be successful, platform leaders should identify and leverage its core; plus ensure that other partners in the ecosystem build on it. Without losing control over profit-making opportunities arising out of the core, it should enable complementary innovation around its core that would ensure profitability for its partners as well. Typically, coring solves an existential problem in the industry through building strong interdependencies between the platform and other complementors' business models that build on the core. In doing so, the relatively tight integration of the platform's core and its complementors act as strong switching costs for the complementors to engage with competing platforms.

Tipping

Tipping refers to how platform leaders sustain their market leadership in the context of platform wars between competing platforms by building momentum. Gawer and Cusumano (2008) list a variety of actions platforms may adopt for winning platform wars: competing to set standards, pricing, tipping across markets, and forming coalitions. Battles to set standards are common across a variety of ecosystems, including those where platforms are active. Across technology domains (design of railroads and automobiles), PC operating systems and application software ecosystems, as well as digital entertainment (audio and video compression standards), standards wars have been documented.[5] Between many competing platforms, the one that wins the standards war would surely be able to get more complementors to join its ecosystem and generate momentum for end-user adoption. Pricing is another tool available to swing the momentum towards one platform. By appropriately pricing and discounting one set of users, platform leaders may kick in network effects faster than their competitors and sustain the momentum. Pricing may also provide incentives for users to remain loyal with specific platforms by increasing switching costs. Another useful strategy used for gaining momentum of user adoption of a specific platform is to tip across markets. Use of standards and leveraging user groups from one market to another enables easy adoption and growth, to achieve the requisite critical mass. Co-evolution of standards along with the complementors is another strategy to ensure that the ecosystem achieves a critical mass.

Take for example the Apple iTunes. Apple introduced the iTunes for the iPod and subsequently tipped it to other markets, including iPhone. The evolution of common interfaces across devices and markets ensured easy adoption to other complementary products like the iCloud as well. Apple has also adopted a counter-intuitive pricing strategy for music, where they adopted the reverse razor-blade strategy (high hardware prices with low music prices). This ensured that voracious music listeners signed up to iPod first and ensured that the market achieved critical mass. Even though Apple introduced their own proprietary standards for audio and video compression, the critical mass was achieved in the face of superior design and branding amongst other things.

In effect, for tipping to be successful, platform leaders must engage with and leverage their complementors to evolve and evangelize standards that are adopted by a large section of the population. The development of these compelling features and making it an industry/ecosystem standard attracts and retains users. The ability to leverage these unique and valuable features across markets further strengthens the platform leaders' dominance over the ecosystem and helps them achieve scale and scope economies.

Products, Services, and Platforms

A key difference between products/services and platforms is the level of control the focal firm. In the case of a product/service, the focal firm owns the product/service standards, organizes resources and capabilities required to manufacture/deliver the product/service, as well as engages with the customers and end consumers. However, in the case of a platform, the focal firm may depend on a variety of ecosystem

[5]For a detailed study of standards wars, read Shapiro, C., & Varian, H.R. 1999. The art of standards wars, California Management Review, 41, 2. Winter 1999.

partners for any or all of these value creation functions. It is a critical strategic choice of the firm—on its source of advantage.

Would the firm rather control all activities of the value chain or not is a scope decision—and it studied as an outsourcing decision. Creating a platform business is much more than simply deciding what activities to outsource and what activities to in-source. In the case of outsourcing, firms still define the product quality standards and service levels. Even though outsourced, the firm owns the customers and is accountable for value creation, customer experience, and value capture. However, in the case of a platform, these firms may simply orchestrate the interactions between different sets of users without even controlling the resources for value creation, customer experience, or value capture. It is possible for some platforms to just focus on lubricating the transactions (or eliminating the frictions in the transactions) through process definitions and governance. That is the reason a lot of platforms may not own any physical assets or conventional resources. For instance, Uber owns no cars but may be the world's biggest taxi aggregator. Uber only owns the algorithm that helps drivers and riders find each other and transact with each other seamlessly. For this algorithm and governance before, during, and after the transaction (including background checks of drivers and incentives to ensure quality of cars; live tracking and safety features during the ride; and payment system integration, driver ratings, and customer service after the ride), Uber charges drivers and riders. This is a very distinct business model from owning a fleet of taxis, where the investments are in hard assets. Uber's investments are in technology and not hardware.

There have been instances where some products and services become industry standards and intend to transform into platforms. Products like mp3 that have become standards could also enjoy externalities. Traditionally externalities refer to the costs or benefits accrued by a user due to the actions of other users. The evolution of mp3 as an industry standard means that a music player manufacturer has a ready market for their hardware provided the products are able to play mp3 formats. The patent owner of such standards may charge a royalty from the hardware producers or may grant usage licenses for free. These royalties may not compensate for the costs they need to incur if there were to develop these standards independently. These are positive externalities for the hardware manufacturers. For these positive externalities to become network externalities and generate network effects, the role of the platform (or the network/technology) owner in internalizing and distributing these benefits becomes critical.

These firms that intend to leverage the product's externalities need to get multiple sets of users and complementors to innovate and develop add-ons and complementary products/services over and above the product. The firm's role then enlarges to include value creation and capture by other firms and users, apart from protecting the product's core value.

Faircent™: Powering P2P Lending Revolution

4

We are in the business of pricing loans right, not into lending
—*Vinay Mathews*

Introduction

"Note that we are in the business of loan pricing using data analytics, not into lending" was the closing statement from Vinay Mathews (Vinay), as he welcomed a group of potential lenders. He was explaining the business model of Faircent, the peer-to-peer (P2P) lending marketplace he had co-founded with Rajat Gandhi (Rajat) over 4 years ago. At the same time in another conference room next door, Sumit, an early adopter who had come onboard the Faircent marketplace to invest some of his surplus money was winding down his consultations with his Faircent portfolio manager. With meager attendance in office on a pleasant Saturday afternoon in late August at the Gurugram (near New Delhi, India) office, Rajat and Vinay, along with Sumit and the group of potential lenders who were considering onboarding the Faircent platform, headed out for lunch. As the group started

---

This case is an extension of Chapter 3 Network effects.

Srinivasan R, (Professor of Strategy), IIM Bangalore, Raghunathan R, (Associate Professor of Strategy), BITS Pilani, Sandeep Lakshmipathy Research Scholar, Pramoth Joseph, Research Scholar and Padmavathi Koride, Independent Researcher, prepared this case for class discussion. This case is not intended to serve as an endorsement, source of primary data, or to show effective or inefficient handling of decision or business processes.

R. Srinivasan, *Platform Business Models*, Management for Professionals,
https://doi.org/10.1007/978-981-16-2838-2_4

discussing the latest developments in the P2P markets worldwide, Rajat and Vinay began to ponder over a few issues.

- Had the P2P lending space matured enough to be considered by savvy investors as a main stay investment opportunity? If not, then how far away were we from P2P being widely accepted?
- Would it be in the best interest of the firm or the industry if Faircent decided to open source their technology stack with the intent of catalyzing P2P lending in the FinTech space?
- Was it prudent to expose Faircent's P2P lending marketplace APIs to third-party developers? Would it trigger rapid innovation and increased adoption?

Faircent's Journey

Rajat, Vinay, and Nitin Gupta (Nitin) joined hands and leveraged their significant experience with internet businesses and financial services to build an online peer-to-peer (P2P) lending marketplace called Faircent. Prior to coming together to bootstrap the new venture, Vinay and Rajat had worked for several Indian internet majors such as Rediff, Times Internet, and Sify, with over two decades of experience working on various early stage internet powered services centered around e-commerce, jobs, matrimony, and emails. With experience spanning technology and marketing, both Rajat and Vinay came together to start Faircent with Nitin acting as the advisor and non-executive co-founder. Diverse experiences of the founders acted as driving forces. Rajat was inspired by a personal experience as early as 2011 where a friend had crowdsourced funds to meet his dream need. This inspired him to further understand the peer lending ecosystem and a lack of formalized approach to bring this forth into the digital era that leveraged the expanding internet and smart phone penetration seemed as an incipient fortuity. Around the same time, startled to see the exorbitant rates charged by the credit card firm, Vinay explored alternative options for lower interest rate loans. Peer lending opportunity, as explained by Rajat, came forth as one credible approach that had not been explored in the Indian context. The fact that chit fund operations in India did not leverage the internet and hence could not bring together unrelated participants across the country came across to these budding co-founders as a timely window of opportunity. They nurtured the idea for few more months before incorporating Faircent in 2013. Both continued working on the business model that culminated with a formal launch in 2014 (refer to Exhibit 1).

The founders were keen to leverage technology to speed up the peer lending process and reduce costs. Faircent launched the online marketplace in October 2014 by when they had a sound understanding of the underpinnings of such an undertaking that involved credit to individual borrowers and small and medium businesses (SMBs). In the beginning, borrowers and lenders came together on the platform's website www.faircent.com to interact directly and to decide a mutually agreeable interest rate for their loans. The interest rates on the platform moved from

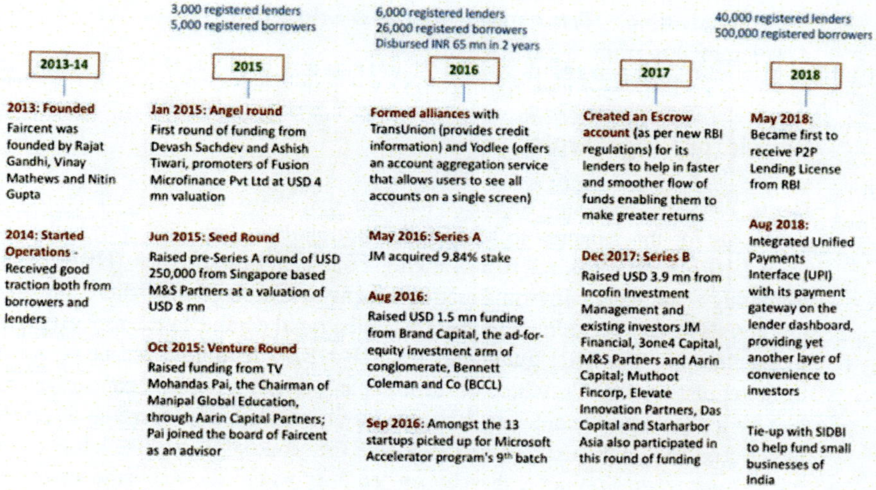

Exhibit 1 Company History—A Timeline View. *Source* Company documents

competitive bidding by borrowers to alignment to a minimum floor rate and then eventually to a maximum cap of few percentage points above the floor interest rate. Faircent never wavered in its decision to curate borrowers which they felt was an absolute need to mitigate risk for the lenders. In Q3 2018, Faircent operated its business in 450 + locations and had 120 employees. By late 2018, Faircent had onboarded about 550,000 borrowers and 86,000 lenders on the platform. It had facilitated over ₹550 mn ($7.1 mn) in disbursements to borrowers and had firm commitments for another ₹700 mn ($8.5 mn) from lenders registered on the portal.

Funding Support

Faircent started with some seed funding and then eventually moved onto Series A and B funding from marquee investors. It raised $250K from M&S Partners in June 2015. Faircent sold a 9.84% stake in the company for an undisclosed sum from JM Financial Limited, a unit of JM Financial Services in May 2016.[1] The company also raised an undisclosed amount of funding from Aarin Capital Partners in October 2016. Faircent raised $1.5 mn (₹90 mn) as part of the Series A funding. It raised $4 mn (₹250 mn) in a Series B funding led by key investors. Key existing investors such as JM Financial Services, Aarin Capital, and new partners such as Incofin Investment Management, Belgium, and Muthoot Fincorp contributed as part of

[1]Chopra, A. (2016) "*Faircent raises $1.5 million from BCCL's Brand Capital*," *Livemint,* August. 11, Available at: https://www.livemint.com/Home-Page/c977129GWuNj4MJoDzTfAN/Faircent-raises-15-million-from-BCCLs-Brand-Capital.html (Accessed: on October 1, 2018).

Series B funding.[2] The venture was also selected to be part of the Microsoft Accelerator Program Winter 2016 cohort.

Regulatory Rigmarole

Being early movers, the founders realized that there was lack of regulation and approvals for the business to be viable. The regulation on P2P was a clear take-off from RBI's regulations on Non-Banking Financial Corporations (NBFCs) in 2011, following a suffusion of Non-Banking Financial Corporation—Micro Finance Institution (NBFC-MFI) credit in the markets and a rapid decline in the recovery, causing a market failure. The RBI guidelines on P2P-NBFC lending were no different from those regulating NBFCs, where the central bank clearly stipulated caps on the amounts lent by lenders and the amounts borrowed by borrowers. It was meant to promote the larger objective of financial inclusion, where the scope of the loans included small and micro-borrowers. Similarly, the cap on lending, where the exposure of lenders was limited to ₹1 million across all P2P platforms, was designed to prevent inundation of funds in the market which had led to market collapse in 2011. Therefore, RBI brought forth explicit laws regulating the licensing, scope of activities, governance including choice of directors, and most importantly, caps on loan sizes and interest rates.

As part of regulating the P2P sector, RBI had floated a concept paper on this topic in April 2016[3] and had finally come out with new policy directions in October 2017 wherein it was made mandatory for the P2P marketplaces to register with RBI as NBFCs operating in the country. Although 30 firms were operating P2P lending businesses in early 2016, as of July 2018, there were only six firms which had moved forward to register with RBI as certified P2P marketplaces. With formal regulations in place, this space could also attract larger players as it provided an alternative investment opportunity with the conveniences of modern technology which eliminated geographical constraints related to demand and supply of credit. As of late 2018, FinTech players such as PayTM and IIFL-backed www.5paisa.com were expected to enter the fledgling P2P market.[4]

In late 2017, Faircent became the first legally ratified P2P lending platform in the country after being formally recognized by the banking regulator.[5] Securing the

[2]Dhanjal, S. S. (2016) "*JM Financial subsidiary invests in P2P lender Faircent,*" – *Livemint*, May.11, Available at: https://www.livemint.com/Companies/4daiUNfZQwd4YW19Tc5VwL/JM-Financial-subsidiary-invests-in-P2P-lender-Faircent.html (Accessed: on October 1, 2018).

[3]Reserve Bank of India (2016) "*Consultation Paper on Peer to Peer Lending,*" Mumbai. Available at: https://rbidocs.rbi.org.in/rdocs/content/pdfs/CPERR280416.pdf (Accessed on September 4, 2018).

[4]Nahata, P. (2018) "*Regulations Shrink India's Peer-To-Peer Lending Industry,*" *Bloomberg Quint,* August 3. Available at: https://www.bloombergquint.com/business/2018/08/03/regulations-shrink-indias-peer-to-peer-lending-industry#gs.kThU7Aw (Accessed: on September 4, 2018).

[5]Pani, P. (2018) "*Faircent.com receives NBFC-P2P certification from RBI,*" *The Hindu BusinessLine*, May.21, Available at: https://www.thehindubusinessline.com/money-and-banking/faircentcom-receives-nbfc-p2p-certification-from-rbi/article23948136.ece (Accessed on September 12, 2018).

NBFC-P2P license proved the legality of P2P lending operations and enabled borrowers to get easier access to credit while ensuring alternative investment category for lenders with surplus funds. RBI regulations mandated that P2P marketplaces would operate as NBFCs with liability to follow the requirements necessary for such firms to run operations legally in the country. As a regulatory body with the mandate to safeguard interests of investors, RBI had circulated guidelines related to operations of NBFCs that were operating as P2P lending exchanges. It was mandatory for these new age lending marketplaces to have net-owned funds of not less than ₹20 million as a pre-requisite for registering as a NBFC-P2P entity. This stipulation alone had ensured exit of several smaller players in the market as the RBI also intended to avoid fly-by-night operators in this sector. RBI also had to ensure that these marketplaces would make significant investments in technology, credit assessment-related investments, customer support through call centers to address borrower or lender issues so as to lend adequate credibility to the new model.

RBI guidelines required the marketplace to establish escrow accounts for borrowers and lenders with all fund transfers happening through these accounts alone[6] (refer to Exhibit 2). The marketplace was to play the role of a pure intermediary with no flow of funds through its channels or reflecting on its balance sheet. This helped increase transparency of operations and also was expected to safeguard the sector from money laundering. Vinay reminisced thus:

> Faircent was a front runner in launching escrow accounts in India under the trusteeship of ITSL (IDBI Trusteeship Services Ltd.). Launching of these escrow accounts in February 2017 smoothened financial transactions on the platform with both borrowers and lenders realizing a sense of security as funds started flowing directly between their accounts with the marketplace playing the intermediary. Faircent does not touch the fund flow.

RBI had even mandated the company structure for these P2P firms—if one desired to be operating in India as a P2P platform, then such a firm had to be registered as a company or a cooperative society as any other form of P2P business that is operated by individuals; proprietorships or Limited Liability Partnerships would not then fall under RBI purview and would be deemed illegal. These applicable rules were similar to the ones NBFCs faced and was natural for RBI to mandate the required legal structure so that these P2P firms came under the ambit of RBI jurisdiction. Other requirements mandated for the P2P marketplaces included having brick-and-mortar presence for its place of business, board members with adequate financial industry background, locally available executive staff, and business continuity plan (BCP) for all critical infrastructure as the marketplace was a custodian of agreements and cheques. With restrictions on cross-border transactions between residents and non-residents due to Foreign Exchange Management Act (FEMA) provisions, RBI restricted foreign investments through P2P

[6]ET Online (2018) "*RBI releases consultation paper on P2P lending, wants to classify it as NBFC*," *The Economic Times*, July.24, Available at: https://economictimes.indiatimes.com/news/economy/policy/rbi-releases-consultation-paper-on-p2p-lending-wants-to-classify-it-as-nbfc/articleshow/52024171.cms (Accessed on September 5, 2018).

Exhibit 2 Calculation of CPI. *Source* Lender dashboard on www.faircent.com)

marketplaces. As per RBI, the marketplace was prohibited from promising any kind of fixed returns either directly or indirectly and could only share the current statistics that were observed on the loans borrowed through the platform.

The marketplace was also expected to have a *living will* which was an alternative arrangement for continuation of operations if the firm that operated the marketplace was to go bankrupt. This would facilitate the borrowers and lenders to close out their ongoing transactions in a timely manner and exit. Adequate provisions for redressal of grievances from lenders and borrowers had to be put in place as per RBI regulations which were similar to what was applicable for other NBFC firms. These NBFC-P2Ps had to make sufficient provisions for ensuring confidentiality of customer data and prevent misuse from any side of the platform or by the platform operator itself. Detailed reporting stipulations at regular intervals that were applicable to NBFCs were also extended to these marketplaces.

Shrinkage of Competition

A viewpoint shared by several industry commentators was that regulation through RBI's intervention had resulted in driving several firms out of the P2P lending business. Stringent conditions put forth by the RBI would allow only few firms to formally remain in the business but had also helped eliminate firms that did not have the expertise or resources to sustain in the P2P lending space. RBI's own data had estimated that there were around 30 P2P lending marketplaces in the country in 2016, but only a handful of them had come forward to seek NBFC-P2P license from the regulator to legally operate P2P marketplaces in India. RBI had to balance the need for investor protection with that of nurturing the infant P2P lending industry to ensure the model could sustain in the mainstream financial market. RBI had the sole responsibility to shape the P2P marketplace into a lucrative asset class which could then provide investors alternative venues for parking surplus funds. Returns from P2P lending had the potential to match those from market-linked investments such as mutual funds and stocks, and it was prudent for regulators to oversee the rapid growth of a new asset class instead of letting it fall a victim to greed.

Faircent Business Model

From inception, Faircent had a clear objective of only being an information intermediary and not manifest into a business that pooled money from multiple willing lenders to issue credits to borrowers. Aware of stringent regulations that were in place for firms that operated as financial institutions, Faircent had to evolve a clear strategy of what value proposition they brought in for the average investors who were willing to invest some of their savings through the marketplace. The founders had recognized the need for serving sections of consumers and SMBs who were unserved by the banking system either due to credit unworthiness of the borrowers or due to high cost structure of traditional lending firms that made small unsecured lending transactions untenable. Increasing internet penetration in India, coupled with the fact that the average Indian was conversant with using the smartphone, presented the firm with a unique opportunity to address the gaps in financial inclusion. Since banks preferred lending to large creditworthy borrowers who could issue collaterals in the form of real estate, inventory, stocks, and others, the SMBs had to resort to very expensive means of borrowing money through local money lenders as they had very less to offer as collateral after raising initial rounds of funding from the banks. Faircent was one of the earliest marketplaces in India that brought credit seeking individuals and SMBs with varying degrees of repayment capability together with retail and institutional investors who were looking for better asset classes to invest in.

Platform Architecture—Lenders and Borrowers

Faircent was a two-sided platform (refer to Fig. 4.1) with borrowers and lenders occupying either sides, while the platform itself played the facilitator role to bring these two groups together to conduct a financial transaction. Since times immemorial, lending as a business had thrived within closed communities wherein people hailing from a certain caste or region or occupation borrowed money from within that community as trust was the basic tenet on which such lending was based. Although the founders were initially enamored by this approach and wanted to operationalize the same through a technological platform, they finally decided to keep it open for the masses where creditworthiness of an individual would then become the only basis on which the platform would encourage lending. For Faircent, the basics of lending was derived from how traditional banks operated. Vinay mentioned thus:

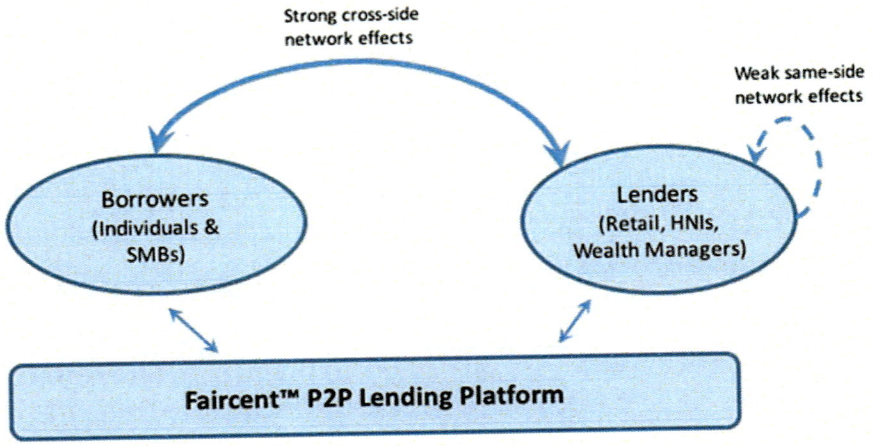

Fig. 4.1 Network effects at Faircent. *Source* Authors' representation

> We understood how the banks operated—distribute large amounts of capital sitting in current and savings account across large number of borrowers across multiple regions so as to spread the risk of lending. At the same time, similar to banks, there was need to offer large number of monetary products, such as personal loans, home loans, car loans and others, so as to serve the different needs of a spectrum of customers. If a financial services business was hyper concentrated, then it was a matter of time before it would go under due to being over leveraged in some way.

Early on, Faircent realized the need to curate borrowers before allowing them to borrow through the portal. Low-quality lending would have jeopardized the reputation of the platform as the default rate had to be kept to a minimum possible for lenders to gain confidence about lending through this new model. In the initial days, Faircent experimented with different models for deciding at what rate of interest would the lenders be allowed to lend. Earlier, lenders were allowed to decide the rate of interest at which they lent without the platform recommending a potential interest rate for the offered loan. However, very soon, Faircent moved away from this model as it realized that the average rate of lending through this new marketplace was not any lower than what was available through the informal markets out there. The average interest rate on the platform kept going up and became a barrier for new borrowers to evaluate the marketplace as a potential new source of availing affordable credit. In addition, this approach led to the lenders' greed to maximize interest rates that were charged which drastically increased default risk. Based on risk profiling of the borrowers, Faircent started to recommend the interest rates that the lenders should charge for the loan amount offered to a specific borrower, and also much before any regulatory restrictions, Faircent started to put in place additional restrictions such as not allowing a lender to lend more than 20% of the invested capital to a single borrower.

With origins from non-financial backgrounds, Rajat and Vinay had the unique opportunity to look at peer lending business as one that could identify and connect creditworthy people with needs to those who had surplus and not as a pure-play lending business. Early on, Faircent recognized the need for a see-saw balance required to maintain the ratio of borrowers and lenders on the platform. With the peer-to-peer lending platform such as Faircent, the founders understood the need to constantly pull in more of one side to satisfy the evolving needs of the other. If the supply side stood tall, then it was time for the firm to pull in more demand for capital by bringing in borrowers onto the platform. When there was excessive demand for capital, then the firm had to attract additional lenders and so on. Both the founders soon realized the nature of onboarding participants onto a peer lending platform, and in fact, the see-saw balance was seen as the desirable state of equilibrium for a steadily growing marketplace.

Faircent had maintained a low entry barrier for lenders and borrowers in terms of the quantum of loan that can be lent or availed through the marketplace. Although this ensured that the marketplace would attract maximum investors and borrowers, the platform had developed robust loan pricing mechanisms that ensured only quality loan lending was facilitated and those who were not creditworthy even at a higher risk of lending capital were eliminated. According to Rajat, only a fraction of the borrowers who register on the platform were in fact allowed to avail loans through the marketplace due to the stringent screening process in place (refer to Exhibit 3). Borrowers were measured on the basis of three critical factors:

- Ability to pay back loans based on incomes and cash flows from business or employment

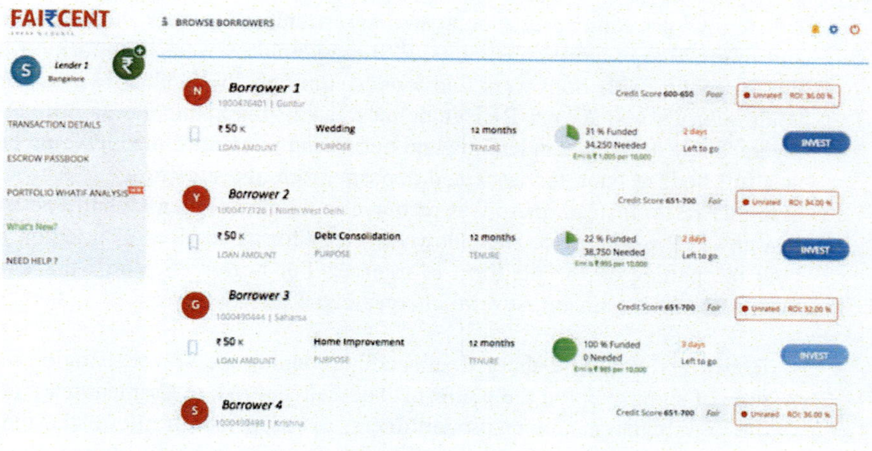

Exhibit 3 Lender dashboard on Faircent marketplace. *Source* Company portal

- Stability which covers aspects related to their professional capability for repayment including tenure of business operations, income variance, and stickiness to an area of operation
- Intent to which is covered through analysis of past loan records, late payments of monthly EMIs, credit scores, mobile data collected through the Faircent app and social media interactions which help derive inferences related to financial behavior of the borrower. Faircent believed that the behavioral traits drove the intent for repayment and this helped the platform determine how much to lend to a particular borrower.

Leveraging social media data and information access through the user's mobile phone had given Faircent an opportunity to put in a robust process when it came to assessing quality of the borrower who wished to borrow a certain sum of money from the P2P marketplace. When the platform started operations, CIBIL score constituted to nearly 50% weightage while determining if an individual or a small business was to be issued a collateral-free loan. However, CIBIL score weightage had come down by end of 2018 as other aspects related to social media interactions, phone logs, shopping patterns, and other online behaviors took precedence. Unconventional approach to doling out credit driven by data models also helped make each lender a bank unto herself and enjoy the rates of return that was privy of banks alone. While banks ended up not lending to many genuine cases, the approach taken by Faircent attempted to address some of these lending-related inconsistencies, and as a result, both individuals and SMBs in equal numbers were looking to raise money from the marketplace.

Pricing Model

Due to low operating costs as compared to institutional lenders, data-driven models, and minimal regulatory constraints, P2P marketplaces were in a position to share these benefits with borrowers and lenders through lower charges and simplified lending processes. As per RBI guidelines, a P2P marketplace was not allowed to leverage any difference in lending and borrowing rates since then it would be acting as a full-fledged bank that accepted deposits from investors to issue loans to others at higher rates. Instead, there was recourse in the form of lender and borrower fees that any P2P marketplace was allowed to levy for its services of bringing together both the parties on the platform to transact. For borrowers who were looking to borrow through Faircent, several charges came their way:

- Borrowers would be charged an account opening fee or a registration fee at the time of signing up on the platform. The Faircent risk assessment team evaluated the new registrant for creditworthiness, assessed risk profile of the individual, and completed the photo-id verification formalities before onboarding. Documents requested for registration purposes included salary slips, bank statements, income tax returns, balance sheets of firms owned, and among others. Termination of account or loan request due to any illegality or fraud meant no refund of the registration fees to the borrower.

- Every time the borrower requested for loans on the platform, there was a listing fee charged to cover the fully automated credit evaluation mechanism that assessed the latest creditworthiness status to ensure fair lending rates were extended to disciplined borrowers who had fulfilled all past loan obligations in a timely fashion. If the loan requested would get facilitated through Faircent, then the listing fee was adjusted against the loan processing fee so as to not burden the borrower through double levies.
- Few lending platforms also charged an additional borrower fee in the form of a small percentage of the loan amount or a fixed charge for each instance of loan disbursement.
- P2P platforms had a minimum period for which the borrower had to service a loan, and in the instance of the need to prepay, the borrower had to pay the full interest for the minimum set tenure which was usually around 3 months. Most P2P firms charged a fixed pre-payment fee to cover their expenses in closing out the transaction.
- If borrowers missed payment schedules, there was a penal interest that had to be borne by the borrower for every instance of delayed payment. Although these additional interests were transferred to the lenders, the marketplace also charged late payment fees to cover its loan recovery overheads.
- For delayed payments or other related issues which mandated the lending platform to issue legal notices, the borrower was charged nominal legal fees which could be remitted to the lenders or could be utilized by the marketplace. For an additional fee, many platforms allow lenders and borrowers to avail third-party legal services.

For lenders who were looking to invest through Faircent their surplus money, there were charges levied by the platform:

- Similar to borrowers, lenders too were charged an account opening fee at the time of signing up on the platform. The Faircent risk assessment team evaluated the new registrant for "Know-Your-Customer" (KYC) norms and completed the photo-id verification formalities before onboarding lenders.
- When a specific loan amount was disbursed based on the investment request from the lender, a small percentage or a fixed fee was charged to the lender.
- When borrowers defaulted on the payment schedule, Faircent's automated mechanisms sent in warning notices to the individuals or SMBs who had pending monthly payments. However, if these alerts were ignored and no payment came through, Faircent considered the loan instance as a default and initiated legal proceedings to recover the dues. There was a fixed percentage, around 5% of outstanding loan amount, levied as recovery charges by the platform to cover its legal expenses incurred.

- Few P2P platforms charged an exit fee to the lenders for withdrawing investment amount that was not disbursed as loans.

Faircent was also evaluating alternative revenues sources by offering analytical services to its lenders who could subscribe to different platform services that made P2P investing with more insights possible. Due to the rich data sets related to repayment behaviors that were gathered, Faircent was uniquely placed to deliver these additional data-driven solutions to its customers. Faircent offered various financial products to its borrowers in the form of different loans to suit unique personal and business needs. It had partnered up with a NBFC for offering gold loans where borrowers could pledge gold with finance firm's offices across India to avail themselves of additional loan amounts. Similarly, Faircent had partnered with home finance firms to fund home loans, while other partnerships helped toward automobile loans. On the topic of tenure of loans, Rajat mentioned thus:

> We have people borrowing money from our platform for all kinds of needs. Tenures can vary technically from one day to as long as 36 months. We have an online ticketing firm that leverages our APIs to borrow money for six day tenures to fund its customers who are looking for confirmed train reservations. Cash flow generated is tremendous and can fulfil the needs of a savvy investor who is looking to plough surplus cash into circulation at reasonable risk levels. Each lender has become a bank with the services offered by our marketplace.

Handling Investment Risks

Unlike the traditional banking system, wherein the prime lending rate (PLR) and other cost of funds determined the rate of interest of the collateralized loan that was offered, the P2P marketplaces had a differentiated approach. For these firms, profile of the borrower was the prime determinant of the interest rate.[7] Based on the proprietary scoring algorithms of each marketplace, the cost of borrowing was largely determined by the borrower's risk profile. Lending activity at Faircent was a multi-stage process. Once a borrower completed her loan application, Faircent's automated system was equipped to determine if the financial details furnished by the potential borrower qualified her business for a loan. Once determined, personal credit history of the borrower was gathered from the consumer credit bureau, along with the details of repayment of past loans and delayed payments, if any. Faircent then deployed a battery of data models to ascertain details about the suitability of lending to the business. Analysis of the local conditions, industry outlook, area of commercial operations, tax filings, existing liabilities, and other financial data were used as inputs to the credit model to sort the business into the appropriate risk grade

[7]Dhawan, S. (2018) "Are P2P platforms safe for lending and borrowing? Find out," *The Economic Times*, July 11. Available at: https://economictimes.indiatimes.com/wealth/borrow/are-p2p-lending-platforms-safe-for-lending-and-borrowing-find-out/articleshow/61654162.cms (Accessed on September 15, 2018).

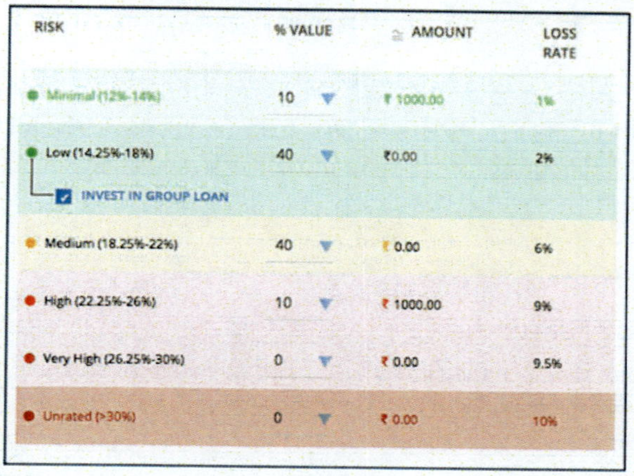

RISK	% VALUE	AMOUNT	LOSS RATE
Minimal (12%-14%)	10	₹ 1000.00	1%
Low (14.25%-18%) INVEST IN GROUP LOAN	40	₹0.00	2%
Medium (18.25%-22%)	40	₹ 0.00	6%
High (22.25%-26%)	10	₹ 1000.00	9%
Very High (26.25%-30%)	0	₹ 0.00	9.5%
Unrated (>30%)	0	₹ 0.00	10%

Exhibit 4 Faircent's auto invest allocation as per risk type. *Source* Company portal

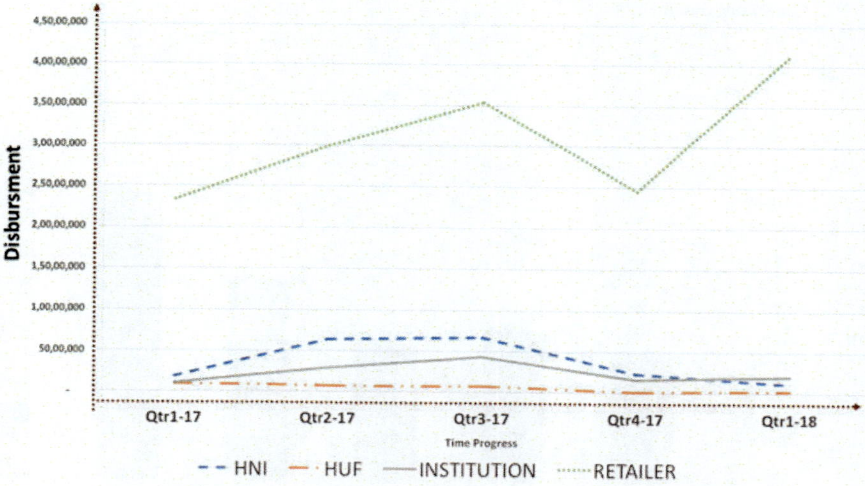

Exhibit 5 Disbursements with respect to lender categories. *Source* Company documents

(refer to Exhibit 4). With a good mix of automated and manual levers to help decide on the best possible interest rate at which unsecured loan could be offered to the borrower, Faircent leapfrogged the banks that applied legacy approach of relying on the banker's judgment even though they had access to similar data points (refer to Exhibits 5 and 6).

In a chit funds operation, supply of money preceded demand. When one individual needed working capital, she would withdraw the required money at a

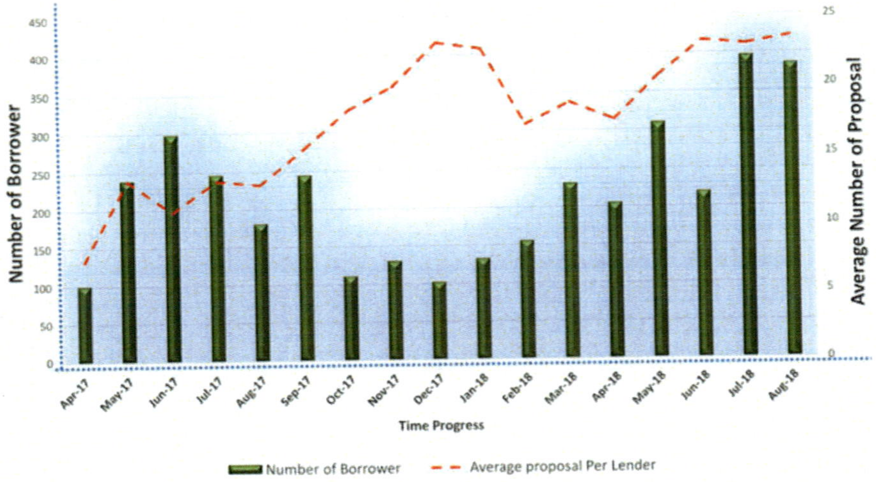

Exhibit 6 Average number of proposals from lender to each borrower over time. *Source* Company documents

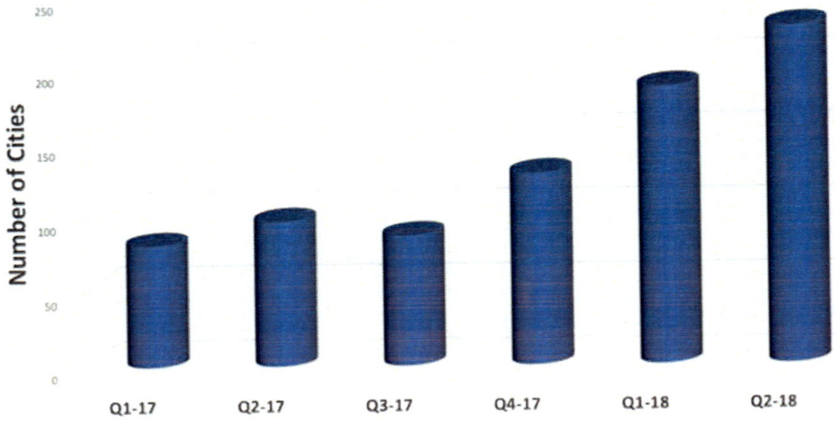

Exhibit 7 Geographical spread—Expansion across India. *Source* Company documents

discount, thus generating positive returns for others who stayed invested in the fund. Although in a holistic sense, the Faircent model was similar, and it was very different due to use of technology and the scope of operations which was represented by breadth of participation of lenders and borrowers that cut across regional boundaries and communities (refer to Exhibit 7). While the chit funds business was driven by relationship model where the intermediary brought together the participants, the Faircent model was agnostic of these traditional divisions that delimited the participation and lacked transparency. From the start, Faircent modeled itself around strict disclosures around interest rates charged and transparency of charges levied on lenders and borrowers as it helped increase confidence in the new online system. Eager to differentiate the platform from lenders in the informal network who charged high interest rates, transparency was viewed as a fundamental requirement around which the marketplace could thrive.

Any form of investment harbored varied degrees of risk, and P2P investing was no different. The lender had to understand the risk to capital invested as the borrowers could default on payments anytime, and the exchange could shut down leading to issues in collecting future EMIs or regulatory changes could make it difficult for the different sides to complete transactions. Lenders were advised to build diversified portfolio of P2P loans so that the exposure to one single big default is minimized. Since high interest rate loans also had propensity for higher defaults, lenders had to build a spread of low- and high-risk loans irrespective of how attractive the P2P lending business was. Defaulting borrowers would hurt their credit scores making it harder for them to secure future loans and faced stiff penalties and legal proceedings which could drag on for a while. For the lenders whose loans were facing recovery issues, there was an expectation that the platform would help enforce the contract agreed upon between the lender and the borrower. Most P2P exchanges handled the legal proceedings when there was a default either through offering third-party legal consulting or assisting in loan recovery. A portion of the recovered loan was taken away by the platform as recovery charges which helped cover the legal expenses for the marketplace. Rajat recounted thus:

> Businesses seem to go through a 7/8-year life cycle with respect to boom & bust cycles and this could have an impact on the P2P lending operations. There is a strong co-relation to the economy, and any job losses could trigger dip in appetite for both borrowing and lending through platforms such as ours.

First Mover Advantage

As an early starter in the P2P lending space, the Faircent.com team had the unstated necessity of ensuring legal correctness in the model they were putting in place such that it would stand the scrutiny of a regulator, who was yet to issue any form of regulation for the sector. This presented an opportunity for the fledgling firm to closely work with the banking regulator to apprise of the various models followed by the peer lending industry across the world. With the advantage of learning from the experiences of global P2P marketplaces such as Lending Club and Prosper, Faircent continued working with the RBI to facilitate formalization of P2P lending in the country. Faircent gained a distinct advantage by being one of the first NBFC-P2P companies and moved quickly to put in place the business model. They provided early feedback to RBI on the regulatory framework and relied on technology to launch an online platform for P2P. Launched in 2014, Faircent reported

5000 registered lenders, 20,000 registered borrowers, and a disbursement of ₹35 million in less than 16 months.[8] As of September 2018, Faircent processed loans of about ₹550 million a month.

Working closely with the RBI on the regulatory framework and compliance aspects enabled Faircent to take direct feedback from their functioning business to the regulator. This in turn helped Faircent solidify the business model as the technology platform and regulations took shape. The team worked closely with the RBI team to evolve the P2P lending model and thereby ensured the marketplace approach to lending was not adversarial to the thinking within the central bank. Faircent took upon itself the responsibility of raising awareness on P2P lending in the country along with other early movers. Investors and borrowers had to understand the opportunity this presented as compared to traditional investment avenues. Karun Thareja, who headed marketing at Faircent, commented:

> Being an early bird in P2P lending space, our biggest opportunity has been to educate the masses on peer lending and how it can work for them as an additional asset class for investments. People understand mutual funds which have had nearly two decades of history, while peer lending is very nascent in comparison, but awareness is growing at a faster rate with close to 9k lender registrations per month on our platform. Increasing smart phone and Internet penetration has enabled the common man to look for loan options beyond the traditional bank which would more often reject his request, and that is where they find platforms such as Faircent as alternative venues to borrow money.

Monetizing Faircent Stack, Open APIs, and Developer Ecosystem

In April 2018, Faircent announced the availability of its application programming interface (API) platform for developers. Faircent had integrated key features of online lending into its technology stack, namely automated borrower and lender verification, credit evaluation, underwriting tools, payments and disbursement of funds, integration with escrow bank accounts and rating agencies, analytics on defaults and loan pricing, EMI collections, and loan recovery. Faircent had envisaged that intermediaries would be willing to share data with partners, developers, and third-party service providers through its open API platform. Faircent thus hoped to enable new entrants into the FinTech industry and other offline businesses offering financial solutions to build new products atop its platform as well as integrate Faircent's existing solutions into partner's offerings.[9] Dr. Shakti Goel, Chief Product and Technology Officer at Faircent, elaborated on the plans:

[8]Kannan, U. (2016) "Lending money, the digital way," *The Deccan Herald,* May 1. Available at: https://www.deccanherald.com/content/543810/lending-money-digital-way.html (Accessed on September 15, 2018).

[9]Faircent (2018) "Faircent launches open API platform; invites developers to leverage tech infra," *Faircent.com,* April 11. Available at: https://www.faircent.com/Faircent-launches-open-API-platform-invites-developers-to-leverage-tech-infra.html (Accessed on September 19, 2018).

> From humble beginnings on the technology side, we have now evolved into having our own ERP system built from the ground up for P2P lending which allows our lenders to plan their investments based on desired risk profiles. Based on studies about good lending behaviors that we have observed on our platform, our financial tools allow investors to plan diversified investing that ensures credible returns. Although defaults may exist, our tools help enhance the probability of net positive returns from the investments and even help fix damaged portfolios.

Hosted as a software as a service (SaaS) on the AWS and Azure cloud ecosystems, Faircent was built as a completely modular P2P lending service wherein the APIs used by the firm's mobile apps on iOS/Android could be the same APIs which could be used by third parties for tighter integration with the marketplace. With a host of dashboards for every operation of the P2P marketplace, there was a growing sense in the team that the platform could evolve into a multi-tenant model that could host P2P systems for different markets across Asia. Faircent wished developers would eventually build apps on top of the public APIs exposed which would provide value-added services to lenders and borrowers. Leveraging anonymized data sets available on the marketplace to allow external partners and banks understand credit behavior was another untapped opportunity that the firm aimed to capitalize upon. Although Faircent appeared to be ahead of the curve on the technology front when compared with other competitors in India, it seemed to acknowledge the additional distance it had to travel when compared to international P2P lending firms such as Lending Club and Prosper. Open APIs enabled Faircent to offer line of credit (LoC) facilities for the first time through the peer lending platform to certified vendors of e-commerce portals and enabled it to earn high-quality returns over short tenures. Faircent even envisaged going down the open source route to allow closed communities to leverage portions of their tech stack to run peer lending operations such as a P2P network limited to an education campus. Similar to how Lending Club had exposed vast amounts of anonymized loan data for public consumption through data analytics, Faircent visualized itself make further forays in this path.

Competitive Topography

From 2015 onwards, venture capital (VC) funds had taken keen interest in the Indian FinTech space which was in line with the investments happening in similar firms in the United States and China. This cohort of start-ups in the financial services space was looking at disrupting established norms in an industry that moved money, but which itself had seen far lesser innovation. Saddled with opaque and complex processes, the operating costs at the traditional banking firms reeled of inefficiencies in the sector and the opportunities it offered for the nimble start-ups to bring disruption. Multiple firms across the United States, United Kingdom, China, and India entered the mature industry with intent to alter credit making decisions, while banks grappled with arcane infrastructure. Saddled with increasing banking regulations, the financial firms were more than keen to partner with firms that were propagating newer business models never witnessed before.

The P2P lending in India was in its nascent stages, with the best estimates pegging it at $15 million. Low awareness of platform business models and lower trust in the technology-driven initiatives, though dampening the business initially, were not large enough to dampen the rapid growth of the industry. Regulators taking a note of the growth and the potential of this sector made it mandatory for the lending platforms to obtain NBFC-RBI license. Following this, nearly five platforms obtained RBI's P2P-NBFC certification, Faircent being one of them. The certification provided the much-needed stamp of approval to the platform, filliping the business in no small way.

Most of the players in the fray reported a steady growth after the licensing. While the platforms followed the stringent norms from RBI, several of them offered risk adjusted interest rates to match the risk profiles of the borrowers. The lenders likewise were encouraged to invest based on their risk appetite, nevertheless adhering to the RBI limit of their exposure. Thus, all the platforms in the fray attempted to balance the lenders' interest, together with those of the borrowers. A few of them nevertheless pitched themselves as serving the hitherto unserved customers, by offering instant, small personal loans, for purposes unserved by banks. Each one of these players was backed by national or international investors wanting to cash in on their present growth and future projections. Given the even distribution of capability as well as ambition, it would be hard to predict who would lead the market, which, however, did not possess the winner-takes-it-all (WTA) dynamics.

Lending Club

Lending Club was launched as an application on Facebook where lenders and borrowers were matched based on their shared connections. Apart from risk matching, it leveraged shared connection between borrower and lender to build trust and credibility. At the same time, the Lending Club model was not limited to a pure social match where friends gave loans only to other friends as some of Lending Club's competitors were doing at the time. It created borrower grades from A to G and assigned each borrower a risk grade based on the risk evaluated from their credit score, transaction history, and other online behavior. Although the firm started to lend money secured through venture funding and other capital raised by Lending Club founders, it soon resorted to encouraging registered lenders to invest on loans for the borrowers. Lenders were then suggested portfolio recommendations based on their risk appetite and shared connections. Within a few months of its launch, it passed the $200k mark for the loan amount and set up an independent website outside of Facebook. The initial closed loop of shared connections allowed

Lending Club to test its algorithms to grade borrowers and build credibility on the investors' side. Lending Club allowed individual borrowers to borrow anywhere from $1000 to $40,000, whereas SMBs could borrow up to $300,000. It charged origination and service fee among other commissions it levied on the borrowers and lenders for the services provided by the platform. Compared to banks that had 5–7% operating costs, Lending Club could manage lean operations with a 2–3% overhead which greatly increased its ability to facilitate unsecured loans as compared to the traditional banking system.[10]

Soon after Lending Club was launched in May 2007, the United States suffered sub-prime mortgage crisis that shrunk credit available even for borrowers with good credit history. Unlike its competitors such as Prosper, Lending Club did not allow all borrowers to apply for loans on its platform, but only those with Fair Isaac Corporation (FICO) scores of more than 640 could apply. With the mortgage crisis deepening, it became difficult for even prime FICO borrowers to obtain loans at reasonable interest rates, and these borrowers were attracted to Lending Club. With downturn impacting the stock market, the P2P lending platforms appealed to risk savvy investors who wanted to build a diversified investment portfolio (refer to Exhibit 8). Secondary trading of loans on the Lending Club platform after regulatory approvals in 2008 ensured liquidity for investors. Although it started off with personal loans, it soon expanded reach to small businesses, mortgages, and automobile loans. Ever since its founding, Lending Club had roughly doubled the loan amount it had facilitated every year. In 2011, it attracted institutional investors to its platform, and in 2013, even a traditional bank signed up as an investor. Similar to Faircent, Lending Club had faced initial hiccups around too much lender money following too few quality borrowers. For banks that participated on Lending Club, lending large amounts to risky borrowers was unattractive, and by registering on Lending Club, banks were able to diversify by lending small amounts to many risky borrowers.

PayTM Micro-finance Platform

Following demonetization in November 2016, where old notes of larger denomination were banned by the Government of India, PayTM emerged as a leading payment option for millions of users across the country. As on May this year, the company crossed an annual gross transaction run rate of USD 29 billion. It attributed the growth to strong adoption of mobile payments and bank transfers on its platform. The rapid growth fueled investor investment, with players like Berkshire Hathaway planning to invest $356 million, adding muscle to the technology platform which sought to diversify into areas like investment management and e-commerce. Over the past couple of years, PayTM developed a moat to some

[10]Mandelbaum, R. (2015) "*What Lending Club's Success Means for the Future of Small-Business Lending*," Inc, May. Available at: https://www.inc.com/magazine/201505/robb-mandelbaum/lending-club-money-on-demand.html (Accessed on September 10, 2018).

Exhibit 8 Net Annualized Return (NAR) vs. Invested amount (July 2018). *Source* Company documents

extent through an e-wallet digital payment ecosystem. However, that seemed to be bridged by competitors with the emergence of UPI.

The platform, facilitating fund transfers between depositors and recipients, took advantage of its large customer base to morph itself from an e-Wallet platform to a payments bank. The morphing was made possible by the acceptance of savings by PayTM, whose transactions with the customers hitherto included compliance to KYC norms as well as documentation of PAN and Aadhar numbers. PayTM's distinct advantage was its knowledge of consumer payment behavior and transaction patterns. It could leverage the data by cross-selling insurance, financial products, and lending. The company's entry into P2P segment could provide the much-needed exposure to others in the segment. Its entry could trigger consolidation in the nascent P2P lending segment.[11] The PayTM bank, which received NBFC-P2P licensing, was already lending small sums to users. Sources close to the company point out how PayTM was trying to leverage the 7 million strong offline merchant base it had garnered and was giving out small-value short-term loans. The newly emerging PayTM bank would accept a deposit of up to ₹100,000 from the customers, whose continuous interactions helped the platform gain useful insights about them.

i2i Funding

i2i Funding went beyond the conventional P2P lending platforms who predominantly played a facilitation role between lenders and borrowers, by profiling the

[11] Devan, M. (2018) "PayTM bets on lending, seeks RBI license to become peer-to-peer lending platform", *The News Minute, March 23*. Available at: https://www.thenewsminute.com/article/paytm-bets-lending-seeks-rbi-license-become-peer-peer-lending-platform-78370 (Accessed on September 20, 2018).

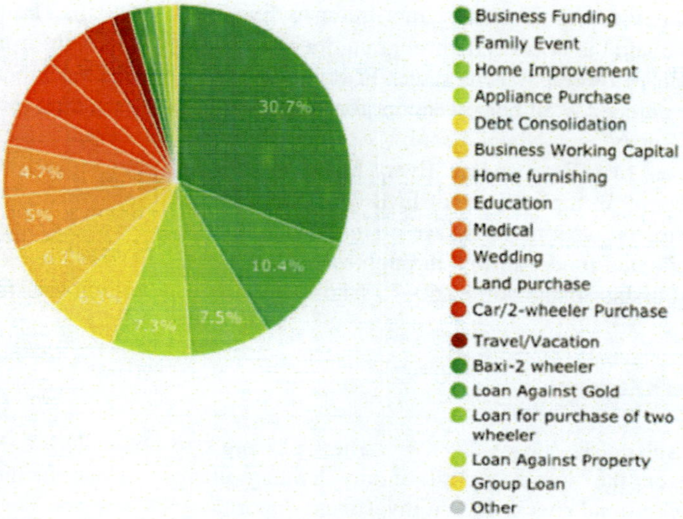

Exhibit 9 Loan Purpose (until November 2018). *Source* Company documents

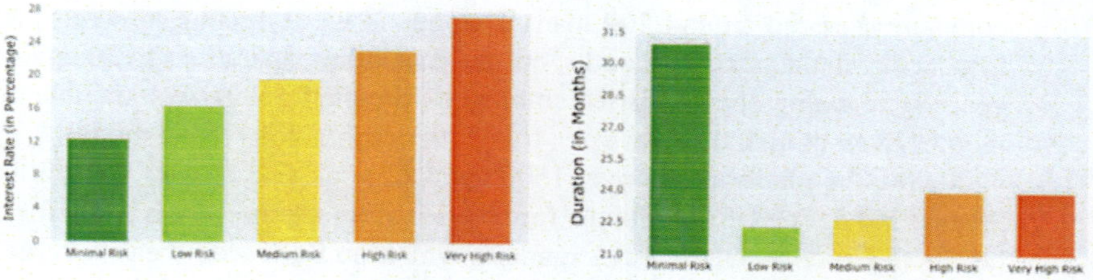

Exhibit 10 Loan Details by Risk Bucket: RoI Earned & Tenure (until November 2018). *Source* Company documents

loan riskiness through an examination of borrower's credit history.[12] The borrower risk profile was built by collecting personal, professional, and financial information —the in-house underwriting team of the platform accorded credit score and customized the interest rates. The platform allowed risk adjustment of interest rates to ensure lenders did not lose out by lending to high-risk borrowers and mitigated the risk by physically verifying the borrower documents. The risk adjustment further ensured all borrowers were not classified into the same category and therefore did

[12]Sangani, P. (2018) "i2iFunding plans to increase loans disbursal to Rs 200 crores over next two years," *ET Bureau,* May 16. Available at: https://economictimes.indiatimes.com/industry/banking/finance/i2ifunding-plans-to-increase-loans-disbursal-to-rs-200-cr-over-next-two-years/articleshow/58685873.cms (Accessed on September 20, 2018).

not pay the same interest rate (refer to Exhibits 9 and 10). The platform further handheld the borrowers throughout their borrowing cycle, right from loan approval stage to the repayment stage. In order to ensure timely repayment, the platform recommended all borrowers opt for auto EMI/Due amount from their bank account to Repayment Nodal Escrow Account through a *National Automated Clearing House (NACH)* mandate. Every EMI was deducted automatically from borrower's account. In the instance of EMI default or a delayed repayment, i2i offered to take corrective actions to ensure a smoother recovery process. Similar to Faircent, i2i facilitated fund transfers through escrow accounts.[13] As on 2018, the platform was disbursing loans worth ₹60–75 lakhs (10 lakhs = 1 million) per month.

CashKumar

CashKumar, one of the five earliest platforms to obtain NBFC-P2P license, followed the norms typical of any lending platform—loan facilitation, borrower background check, and an investment opportunity for lenders. The platform was in the lending space from 2016 onwards, long before the actual grant of RBI license. As per the company sources, the platform has been growing exponentially ever since, if measured by the number of onboarding borrowers. The platform operated in nine cities including Hyderabad, Coimbatore, and Ahmedabad. In 2018, the company serviced around 200 loans a month. It was targeting to service about 80 loans a day in the next six months, besides expanding operations to 20 cities by next year. By reaching out to salaried employees, the platform grew at the rate of 30% a month. Even though the loan sizes for debt consolidation were a modest ₹50,000 to ₹100,000, the platform had over 1500 loans of book size of over ₹60 million as of August 2018. The USP of the platform was in offering short-term credit for meeting necessities such as medical emergencies which no bank would easily serve. It also offered loans to pay pending EMIs and helped borrowers consolidate various loans, which constituted 15% of their portfolio. Such services helped enhance the popularity of the platform.[14,15]

[13]Sachdev, N. (2017) "P2P Lending Startup i2i Funding Helps Break Away from Traditional Banking," *The Tech Panda,* July 27. Available at: https://thetechpanda.com/2018/07/27/p2p-lending-startup-i2i-funding-helps-break-away-from-traditional-banking/ (Accessed on September 22, 2018).

[14]Dhar, D. (2018) "Cashkumar gets NBFC-P2P Certificate of Registration from RBI," *CashKumar,* July.13 Available at: https://cashkumar.com/cashkumar-nbfc-p2p-cor-rbi (Accessed on September 20, 2018).

[15]Revathy, L. (2018) "Cashkumar foresees huge potential in online lending for short-term credit," *Business Line,* August 3. Available at: https://www.thehindubusinessline.com/money-and-banking/cashkumar-foresees-huge-potential-in-online-lending-for-short-term-credit/article24595250.ece%0D (Accessed on September 25, 2018).

LenDenClub

LenDenClub, an online P2P lending platform, started with the explicit motive of financial inclusion, wherein borrowers from low-income groups, ineligible for bank loans, could borrow small sums against their salary.[16] Started in 2018, LenDenClub was the fifth P2P platform to obtain NBFC-P2P license from RBI. The platform's idea originated when its founder observed a friend with a salary of ₹28,000 per month, a couple of thousands short of ₹30,000, unable to access a personal loan. After spending ten years in the lending business, the founder realized that there were no products in banks or other financial institutions for the low-income clientele seeking small, personal loans to meet their urgent cash flow needs. The platform's idea was to cater to the small borrowers who apparently did not earn enough to qualify for a personal loan from banks. The platform growth followed the typical S-curve, with the first few clients signing up for the platform at one go, while the rest took time to adapt, primarily because of low trust in the platform's business model. This proved to be a hurdle in the early days before the platform obtained RBI NBFC-P2P license, where the borrowers onboarded primarily on word-of-mouth information. After obtaining license however, the platform attracted 50,000 borrowers from five cities every month, while lenders from smaller towns were also registering with the platform. The platform thrived on product innovation, including loans for home renovation and family functions, overlooked by traditional lending agencies, and planned to add more and more innovative products into its portfolio.

Monexo

Monexo, a P2P lending platform, pitched itself as an attractive investment option for lenders as well as an attractive borrowing option for borrowers. The platform promised return between 13 and 30% to lenders and a loan sanction within a minute of applying, to verified borrowers.[17] Monexo.co claimed to be India's first P2P marketplace where lenders were provided the ability to fully automate investment into loans listed. It allowed lenders on the platform to set rules of investment based on their risk appetite, and subsequent investments were taken care of in an automated manner when new lending opportunities arose.

Monexo distinguished itself by partnering with IDBI Trusteeship Services Limited (ITSL) where all the money of lenders and borrowers was received. This ensured Monexo had no access to lenders' and borrowers' funds for its own

[16]Rana (2018) "Lending platform LenDenClub gets NBFC-P2P certification from RBI," *Medianama,* July.20 Available at: https://www.medianama.com/2018/07/223-lending-platform-lendenclub-gets-nbfc-p2p-certification-from-rbi/ (Accessed on September 20, 2018).

[17]Palepu, A. R. (2018) *"P2P lending platform Monexo partners with Cube Wealth for new-clientele," Business Standard,* July.24 Available at: https://www.business-standard.com/article/companies/p2p-lending-platform-monexo-partners-with-cube-wealth-for-new-clientele-118072400553_1.html (Accessed: September 20, 2018).

expenses. The platform provided loans to borrowers in a single cheque and collected their repayments as well in a single cheque. The simplified processes enhanced borrower quality, whose background check was done by the platform through credit bureaus. The platform, a part of a plethora of P2P lending firms, aimed to choose the best quality borrowers and not the last resort borrowers, as evidenced in the literature where a suffusion of several, for-profit lenders led to a competition for the limited pool of honest and able borrowers.[18] By April 2018, the P2P lender had assets under management worth ₹20 million. Every investor on the platform could either opt for an automatic allocation of their investment across multiple borrowers or they could select the borrowers they wished to fund. The platform assured of transparency by allowing lenders to see borrowers' details through its online investment dashboard. The lenders could access borrowers' legal notices, repayment intimation, and collection calls the platform placed. The plan was to eventually scale up P2P lending to the self-employed class and small-medium enterprises by 2020, provided the regulatory environment allowed it.

Faircent's Aspirations

New FinTech phenomenon of P2P lending in India and across the globe held great potential in bringing a large chunk of unorganized money lending into its fold. Members of society with no credit history and those who needed quick loan disbursements for immediate personal or business needs could be catered to by these platforms. Mediocre credit assessment policies and mechanisms adopted by the traditional banking system ensured that only borrowers with pristine credit history, who could also offer collateral, were the only ones who get served with timely loans. This left a huge gap for new forms of financing to fill in so that financial inclusion of those in need of credit could be addressed. From an investment perspective, individuals with surplus money have had not many alternative channels to invest. Providing bank grade investment option coupled with data-driven credit-worthiness assessment and verification methods brought in by P2P marketplaces seemed to have ushered in new possibilities for the lenders. Recent regulations had provided the much-needed shot in the arm, lending legality to the P2P model. Toward the end of 2018, this sector seemed to be at the cusp of a take-off in terms of growing loan numbers and general acceptability from both lenders and borrowers.

Both the co-founders strongly believed that the complex financial company that they had founded was firmly at the forefront of a new wave of innovative firms that were taking on the old stewards in the financial services industry. In a short span of 5 years since idea conception, early P2P marketplaces such as Faircent had further accentuated the fact that investor financed loans can work and had laid the

[18]McIntosh, C. and Wydick, B., 2005. Competition and microfinance. *Journal of Development Economics*, *78*(2), 271–298.

foundation for further refinements. As the group was walking toward the restaurant for lunch, the co-founders pondered over a few queries.

- Would the growth in these metrics sustain over the coming years as new instances of additional regulations kick in as reaction to any fraudulent use of the new system? How soon would Faircent's business model adapt to any churn in the banking regulations that governed P2P lending in the country?
- What additional measures were required to increase investor confidence in the P2P lending system which would help reduce cost of capital so that borrowing from alternative systems was more attractive for individuals and SMBs?
- What degree of preparedness was needed for Faircent and other P2P marketplaces to weather the upheavals as none of these marketplaces were tested fully by an economic downturn? Would any form of diversification of services offered on the marketplace help mitigate the risks of a downturn?

What envelopment threats should Faircent be cognizant about in order to sustain in this market where it was playing the David with a new business model among the Goliaths in the form of established financial institutions all around?

Value Creation in Platforms

5

Platform firms have contributed to changes in a variety of industries, by making markets efficient. The manner in which each platform adds value to its users is a critical strategic choice for the entrepreneurs and managers of these firms. As is true for every strategic choice, the specific value creation and capture decisions can be compared to the firm's signature. Each platform is likely to be unique in its value architecture, and therefore, the trajectory of firm growth and impact on the industry, ecosystem, as well as the user groups.

Value Architecture

Osterwalder and Pigneur (2010) define a firm's value architecture as "the rationale of how and organization creates, delivers, and captures value." It consists of a firm's unique combination of value creation, delivery, and capture decisions. Value creation describes how firms design their offerings (value proposition) that meets their users' requirements. Value delivery, on other hand, focuses on how the firm interacts with the users to understand their requirements and facilitates the consumption experience (infrastructure and support). Value capture refers to how firms gain monetarily (or otherwise) through this value creation and delivery processes. In other words, value creation focuses on the product/service design; value delivery on the organizational routines and infrastructure (including relationships with the ecosystem); and value capture focuses on the outcomes.[1] Keen and Williams (2013) elaborate on value architecture as consisting of three inter-

[1]Martin, P.C.G., Schroeder, A. & Bigdeli, A.Z. 2019. The value architecture of servitization: Expanding the research scope, Journal of Business Research, 104, 438–449.

R. Srinivasan, *Platform Business Models*, Management for Professionals,
https://doi.org/10.1007/978-981-16-2838-2_5

connected decisions: value narrative (the plan to generate value); value engine (operational capabilities); and opportunity platform (business practices to capitalize on new opportunities).[2]

Platform business models have a differentiated business model that allows for a nuanced understanding of each firm's value architecture as unique to each firm. In understanding the value creation by platforms, there are four fundamental utilities that are to be considered: discovery, matching, transaction, and evaluation.

Discovery

The primary value added by most platforms is intermediating in markets that are plagued with inefficiencies. These intermediaries facilitate the process of how users on one side of the platform search, find, identify, and select specific partners to interact with. These platforms provide information as a service. There are users who demand information (demand-side users) to help them make decisions, and the platform facilitates their choice-making by providing them information about the other side (supply-side users). These are also referred to info-mediation platforms.[3]

Platforms like Craigslist in the USA and Just Dial in India help users look up for a specific local business that would potentially meet their needs. Platforms like Just Dial focused on enlisting hyperlocal businesses with no internet presence and therefore would not be searchable on Google. Just Dial had built a large and credible database of small businesses in every locality that provided the user with the specific products/service offerings of each of these firms along with their contact details. Craigslist, on the one hand, focused on hyperlocal availability of specific products—including those products and services that may be available for a short period of time only, like an antique piano on sale.

The value narrative in discovery platforms is the facilitation of discovery of credible users on the other side. Credibility arises from quality, relevance, and currency of the data. In order for discovery value to be created, platforms need to invest in and master three capabilities—extensive access to supply-side user data, clear understanding of the criteria used by demand-side users to make their choices, and leveraging the data on search behavior to provide insightful recommendations.

Deep engagement with the supply-side users is required to keep the data high quality and current (updated as required by the demand side), as errors of both omission and commission may be costly for the platform reputation. Imagine a hyperlocal restaurant discovery service. It is critical for the platform to have data on the real-time availability of menu items at those restaurants and present it to the demand-side users (hungry patrons) for ordering. In the absence of real-time or accurate data, there could be service failures like stockouts after the orders are

[2]Keen, P. & Williams, R. 2013. Value architectures for digital business: Beyond the business model, MIS Quarterly, 37, 2.

[3]Sawhney, M., Prandelli, E., and Verona, G. (2003). The power of innomediation, MIT Sloan Management Review, Winter 2003.

placed, or misplaced orders—wrong orders on incorrect restaurants. These could be expensive for the platform's growth prospects and revenue from both sides of the platform.

Insights into the consumer behavior of the demand-side users is critical to organize the information collected and presented to them for facilitating their choice-making. Given that the core value proposition is facilitating decision-making, it is absolutely imperative that the data is organized as per the users' decision criteria. Take for example, a dating platform that allows for young adults to meet with others. The platform needs to present the profiles with exactly that data points that the users look for, including say, photographs, interests, and links to their social media activity.

The platform will generate sufficient data arising out of user behaviors across the entire life of the interaction—during the search, finding, identifying, and selecting users on the other side. This rich data should be used appropriately (of course, subject to data privacy regulations) to segment and characterize the users' preferences and choices and therefore add to their repertoire of knowledge about those segments of users. This should help refine the algorithms that are used to prioritize search results that are presented to the demand-side users. Take for example, a search engine like Google. The search user remains loyal as over time, the search engine has perfected the understanding of the preferences, and the algorithm shows up the "most relevant" search results in the top of the results listing. "When was the last time you went looking for something on the sixth page of Google search results?" Most search engines are able to provide you the relevant results within the first fifty listings, even if you had misspelt your search terms or had not used the right framing of the question. Most times, these search engines are capable of even autocorrecting and pre-empting your actual search, based on your recent search history!

In summary, discovery as a utility is a critical value that platforms add to its user groups.

Utility	Value creation	Value delivery	Value capture
Discovery	Lubricating the friction in search (reducing the bureaucratic costs of search and selection)	Extensive access to the supply-side users to ensure quality, relevance, and currency of data	Deep understanding of the search criteria of the demand-side users; leveraging that data to (a) organize the supply-side users' data and (b) refine the algorithms for prioritizing and presenting search results

Matching

Matching utility goes beyond discovery—it enables choice-making by the users by sharpening the options presented to them, whereas discovery utility deals with search, find, identify, and select users of the other side; matching enables choice-making by ensuring the preferences of both sides of the users are aligned. In the context of discovery, there is a clear distinction between the demand side and the supply side of the intermediation. However, in the context of matching platforms, both sides are demand and supply sides—it is mutual. Take the example of an online grocery store, where shoppers are bargain-hunting. Search would result in the appropriate options for choice-making by the shoppers, and the shopper can choose from whatever she is presented to her. However, in an online dating platform, it is not sufficient for a user to like one on the other side, and it is important that the person(s) on the other side also have to like the user! In contrast to a shopping algorithm, where the tomato ketchup does not need to like the shopper, users from both sides need to prefer each other for a "match" to happen. In other words, matching is a two-say exercise where the preferences and behaviors of both sides need to be considered by the algorithms.

Not just dating and matrimony, matching platforms are commonly found in the context of sports coaches, fitness trainers, tutors, or two-player games like online chess. Take for example, an online chess-gaming platform like lichess.com. Depending on the proficiency levels and format preferences of both the players, the algorithm will match the users in pairs for playing against each other. A peer-to-peer (P2P) lending platform like Faircent matches lenders and borrowers depending on their credit scores and risk-return preferences.

The value narrative in matching platforms is the easing of choice-making by both sides of the users, through two-way search and filtering process. In order to do this efficiently and effectively, the platform should be able to understand/profile, categorize, and curate/customize the search results based on the expressed preferences and observed behaviors of both sides of users. In order to create matching value, platforms should possess three capabilities: ability to capture the preferences of users from both sides of the platform; segment the users based on these preferences; and therefore curate and customize the results to the specific users/user groups.

In order to understand the preferences of the users, matching platforms like eHarmony.com[4] require users to fill out a detailed form that captures their psychological predispositions and social preferences as well. Such detailed questionnaires not just capture the profiles of the users in depth, it also helps the platform to deter non-serious users from entering and exploiting the platform. This ensures quality of users on the platform, which the other side highly values.

Given the variety of expressed preferences in hyperlocal service delivery platforms like Urban Company,[5] it is important that the platform segments its users

[4]For a detailed description of the compatibility quiz at eHarmony, see https://www.eharmony.com/tour/what-is-the-compatibility-quiz/.

[5]See the Urban Company Website (https://www.urbancompany.com/bangalore) for the complexity of jobs.

based on categories of services, residence localities, and the complexity of the job required. A request for a plumber should be analyzed based on the location preferences of the plumber (the consumer's address should fall within the plumber's preference radius) and the complexity of the job (job for fixing a leaking tap should be matched with a different plumber than a job fixing a leaking roof requiring weather-proofing).

In order to provide curated and customized results to its users, recruitment platforms have begun using technologies like artificial intelligence (AI) to help match right candidates to job requirements.[6] Algorithms allow for matching based on the candidates' CV, and application behavior has been established to eliminate biases that humans invariably bring in into the recruitment and selection process. For the recruiter, use of such platforms provides three benefits: enlarges the pool of candidates to include passive candidates including former applicants and employees; helps write inclusive job descriptions; and eliminates biases in shortlisting and selection. For the candidates, these platforms provide fair opportunities to present their work experience and expertise, as well as eliminate frivolous and low-quality matches (that are not in line with their expressed career aspirations and goals.

In summary, matching is much more nuanced than discovery as it involves analysis of the preferences of both sides of users and ensures that the results are specifically curated to these individual users/segments.

Utility	Value creation	Value delivery	Value capture
Matching	Ease of choice-making by both sides of users (through a two-way search and filtering process)	Access to expressed preferences and observed behaviors of both sides of users	Ability to capture preferences from all user sides; segment the users based on these preferences; and curate/customize results to specific users/user groups

Transaction

Another critical utility provided by platforms is that of reducing transaction costs. While discovery utility is focused on reducing the bureaucratic costs of search, transaction platforms focus on lubricating the interaction between the user groups. There are various forms of transaction costs that arise when users interact: contracting or defining the terms of exchange, pricing or finding the fair value to be transacted, and arbitration or recourse when one party reneges on the contract. These costs may be pretty high in certain transactions. Take for instance, renting a self-driving car in a city that one infrequently travels into. Apart from the search

[6] See: https://forbes.com/sites/falonfatemi/2019/10/31/how-ai-is-uprooting-recruiting/.

(finding the appropriate car and the place where one can pick it up), the transaction costs include establishing authenticity of the person hiring the car (say a valid driving license and another identity document), setting up the terms of hiring (including what is included in the base fare and what is not), negotiating the price, and agreeing on the warranties and indemnities (recourse in the context of accidents, damage, criminal activity, or even material damage to the car and injuries to the driver and passengers). If one were to negotiate and agree on each of these issues one-to-one between the car owner and the car renter, it would possibly be too cumbersome and may result in inefficient contracts and transactions. It is exactly this friction that car rental platforms like Avis would seek to lubricate through internalizing traction utilities within the platform.

Transaction platforms are everywhere, right from online marketplaces like Amazon or casual worker hiring platforms like Upwork. In e-commerce platforms like Amazon, the users not only search products but could also place orders to buy the same. Amazon's transaction engine ensures that the sellers' and product data is presented accurately to the shopper, the shopper's order reaches the seller, shopper's payment is collected and transferred to the seller after appropriate verifications, ensures that the product is delivered to the shopper at the specified address/within stipulated time, enables returns and warranty claims if the products were found to be defective/not meeting the laid down terms, and intermediating between the seller and the buyers in any disputes. In essence, transaction platforms are not just about enabling financial transactions, they need to ensure sufficient, and accurate information is transacted as well.

The value narrative for transaction utility is, therefore, eliminating transaction costs for the users in the platform. For a transaction platform to lubricate the frictions in the interaction between user groups, it should possess three capabilities —ensure adequate and accurate information is collected from both parties and shared with each other; take responsibility for pricing and other monetary transactions; and be accountable for arbitration and recourse when disputes arise at any stage of the transaction process. Users will value such internalizing of transactions and would be willing to pay for the same, provided the utility is non-core to their transactions but critical to the engagement. For instance, negotiating on payment terms may not be a core process for an Airbnb host (she might want to focus more on customer experience), but is very critical to establish trust and credibility.

In order for transaction platforms to establish credibility between the user groups, it is imperative that the platform collects authentic and credible information regarding the users and their products/services that are being transacted on the platform. For instance, Airbnb has detailed tips for hosts to make their place stand out of the crowd.[7] These tips include the usage of quality photos of the interiors and exteriors of the property, detailed descriptions of the property including naming, and creating a good host profile. It is imperative that this information thus collected is credible and the platform does that by verifying the hosts' identities and the property details (apart from verifying guests' identities during booking/at site by the

[7]See: https://airbnb.co.in/d/tipstostandout/.

hosts). Therefore, a typical listing of a property on Airbnb contains not just details about the property and the host, but information on what to expect during the stay and specific norms of behavior expected of the guests as well. This additional information helps set mutual expectations and contributes significantly to reduction in transaction costs.

Price discovery and certainty are one of the most important components of transaction as a utility. Take for instance, the home healthcare services provider, Portea. Among other services, Portea provides comprehensive elder care services at home, and a core value proposition is a "care plan" that covers planned doctor visits, nutritionist consultations, and a customized program for the customers.[8] All for a fixed price. Such packages and plans eliminate anxieties around price discovery for users, especially when they are not fully covered by insurance or healthcare support. Not having to negotiate and pay for every visit is a core value proposition that Portea offers to its users.

Owning the end-to-end transaction process also requires that the platform provides for arbitration and recourse for the users when things go wrong or not as expected. Some platforms use an escrow process (holding on to the money till the service is delivered satisfactorily), whereas e-commerce firms have detailed recourse policies (returns, refunds, and replacements) that are explicitly called out during the ordering process. In the event of a product/service not meeting the expected and/or listed specifications, it is the platform's responsibility to arbitrate between the parties and ensure a fair recourse to the aggrieved party. These assurances and warranties for all users are critical for maintaining trust and credibility on the platform.

Transaction as a utility, therefore, is critical in intermediating between users and establishing credibility and trust in the entire ecosystem.

Utility	Value creation	Value delivery	Value capture
Transaction	Reducing the friction in the transaction (reducing transaction costs)	Extensive investments in capabilities to intermediate in the markets for information and financial transactions, thereby ensuring credible contracts around expectations, pricing, and arbitration	Ensuring reliability of the transactions by internalizing activities that are non-core to the transacting parties, but are critical for building/maintaining trust and resultant customer experience

[8]See: https://portea.com/elder-care/.

Evaluation

Evaluation is one of the most critical utilities provided by platforms to its users. Its criticality stems from its contribution in reducing the information asymmetry between the user groups. These evaluations help platforms close the loop between users' expressed preferences and actions. They bridge the stated and the actual. These evaluations may form the basis for decision-making by the users on the other side (as in restaurant ratings in Yelp used for choosing dining options) or for quality control by the platform (as in Uber using driver ratings to weed out poorly rated drivers off the platform).

Evaluation in multi-sided platforms may take four forms—ratings, reviews, recommendations, and feedback (3RF). Ratings are typically numeric and are used as an omnibus score for the product/service/experience. Ratings are used when the users value the whole more than the parts, and it is sufficient for the users to make their decision. Examples of ratings include seller ratings on an e-commerce platform. The products being branded, and the delivery and payments managed by the e-commerce platform (and is standardized), and the quality of experience is determined by the seller ratings only. In such cases, just a numeric rating is sufficient for the buyers to make the decision.

Reviews, on the other hand, are more nuanced and allow for evaluation of different components of the product/service/experience. Typically written out in text supported by a number, it provides a detailed evaluation of the specific functional, emotional, and self-expressive benefits. Reviews are very common in the context of experiences like music, movies, or theater. What value one expects to derive from a movie experience may be very different across users. While one user might value the story and screenplay more than music, the other user might value the quality of performance of the artists. It is to account for such variations in experiences, one would look for a nuanced evaluation of each of the components of the product/service/experience.

Recommendations go beyond simple reviews, where the quality of the evaluator is also valued. In ratings and reviews, more the number of evaluations, better it is. However, in the context of specialized products/services/experiences, users may value evaluations from experts like a critic's choice in music, or a celebrity endorsement for a fitness product. Higher the quality of evaluators, more the value of the recommendation, and users might just follow the recommendation while making their choices for engagement.

Feedback is qualitatively different from ratings, reviews, and recommendations in the sense that it is meant for the product designer/service provider/experience provider. Ratings, reviews, and recommendations on the other hand are meant for decision-making by other users. A movie review is used by users on the same side of the network, other movie goers to choose if they should watch that movie and what to expect. Feedback is typically provided for use by the other side of the network so that they make changes, if required for the future. Most often feedback is provided by users who may not be fully qualified or who may not have full information about the product/service/experience. Take for example, student evaluation of teaching in the context of higher education. These students' feedback is meant for the teacher to make changes, if she/he feels appropriate. Given that students may not have full information about the specific topic/program, their feedback may be useful for the teacher to tailor her/his delivery (style or pace) rather than making changes on the content of the course. Feedback is effective when it is constructive and helps the service provider to take appropriate action.

The value narrative for evaluation utility is therefore to improve reliability and quality of information provided on the platform. Bridging information asymmetry is a key utility in making platforms create and deliver value. Evaluation helps bridge information asymmetry by enabling users on the other side providing additional information and validating the information transacted on the platform. In the absence of such information flows, service providers might exploit the information asymmetry resulting in adverse selection. Imagine a travel facilitator like tripadvisor.com. The supply side (say hotels) on the platform has much more information about the service than the demand side (travelers). It is in the interest of the hotels to disclose only positive information and hide potentially negative information. In such markets, evaluation plays a key role in bridging information asymmetry and ensuring that adverse selection does not degenerate the market into a "market for lemons".[9]

In order for platforms to bridge information asymmetry through evaluations, platforms need to (a) enable credible ratings, reviews, and recommendations of the users; (b) internalize the risks of adverse selection; and (c) keep the information current and reliable. Credibility of ratings, reviews, or recommendations is typically established by ensuring that those who provide these evaluations are verified users of the service. For instance, when a user writes a review on airbnb.com, it is linked to a verified stay. One cannot just login to Airbnb and write a review about a host/guest without having used the service. The e-commerce marketplace, Amazon, qualifies product ratings and reviews with "verified purchase" tags to enhance credibility. In the absence of such credibility, it is possible that the users might game the system and enhance their standings in the market through, say paid reviews.

When these ratings and reviews are used by users on the other side to make their purchase/engagement decisions, they implicitly trust the platform for having ensured the credibility of the same. In spite of these credibility checks, when a service failure occurs, the users expect that the platform enables the aggrieved party by internalizing the cost of adverse selection. Take for example, the used vehicles marketplace is droom.in.[10] Droom has a detailed vehicle inspection process that certifies the quality of the vehicle apart from the seller ratings. In a market where the buyers and sellers may not be competent in evaluating the technical specifications and determining the fair price of the product, Droom's AI-enabled services like Orange Book Value, Eco, History, and Discovery provide the transacting parties with enough transparency in the process.

[9]See Ackerlof (1970). The market for "lemons": Quality uncertainty and the market mechanism, The quarterly journal of economics, 84, 3. 488–500.
[10]See https://droom.in/eco for Droom.in quality check document.

Apart from the quality and reliability of the information provided on the platform, it is imperative that the information presented is current and updated. For instance, travel portals like Travelocity provide information not just about the travelers' stays but the dates of stay and dates of reviews. They are sorted recent first and could be filtered for traveler types (like couples or with small children). Such time-stamping of reviews ensures that the users are provided with the most recent and current reviews, greatly helping in making right choices. Not just that, Travelocity also publishes responses from the hotel management staff to the reviews. Such close-looping of information provides further credibility to the reviews.

Utility	Value creation	Value delivery	Value capture
Evaluation	Bridging the information asymmetry between users (facilitating decision-making)	Enabling ratings, reviews, recommendations, and feedback on the services/experiences on one side/both sides	Ensuring that these (3RF) evaluations are credible, current, and high quality by internalizing the costs of adverse selection and close-looping of information flows

DMTE as a Cycle

As can be seen in the previous sections, one can conceptualize the platform utilities as a concentric cycle (see Fig. 5.1).

Starting from discovery that aids users find each other and reduces the search costs, platforms could add matching as a utility helping curate and customize value

Fig. 5.1 DMTE Cycle

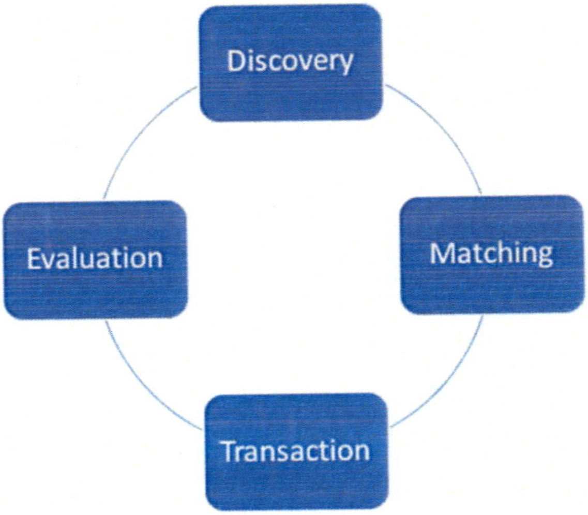

to each user group based on their expressed and revealed preferences, subsequently reduce transaction costs between different user groups through transaction as a utility, and finally aid decision-making through evaluation utilities. It is not necessary that all platforms must provide all these utilities, and every business has an opportunity to choose the right portfolio of utilities depending on the user groups they serve and the value creation intent. At the end of the day, the choice should enable strong network effects that power the business ecosystem like "flywheels." For instance, a platform like Airbnb that provides all the four utilities—it helps hosts and guests discover each other; ensures that the right options are provided to each user group and matched; enables seamless transaction of information and money flows; and helps hosts and guests rate each other. The Figs. 5.2, 5.3, and 5.4 depict the three flywheels—discovery and matching; transaction; and evaluation flywheels. These flywheels catalyze virtuous cycles of growth.

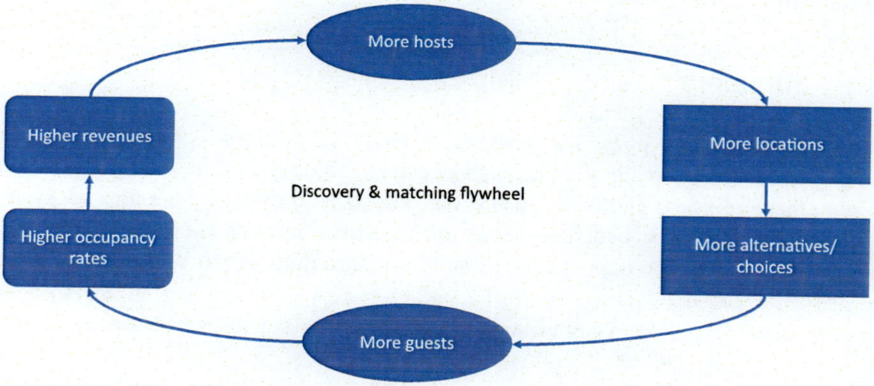

Fig. 5.2 Discovery and Matching flywheel

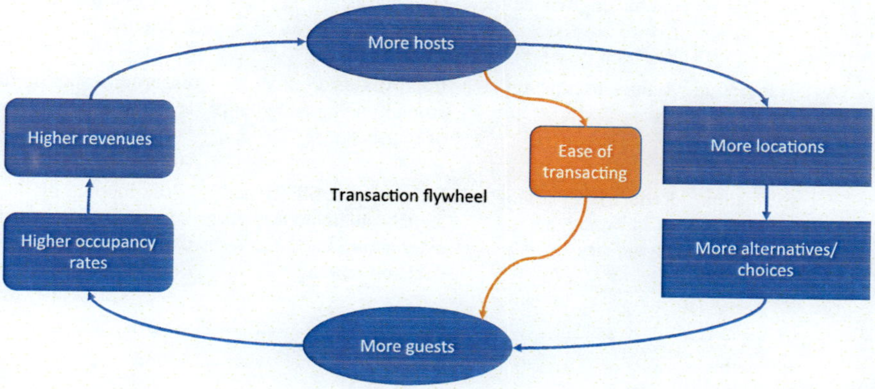

Fig. 5.3 Transaction flywheel

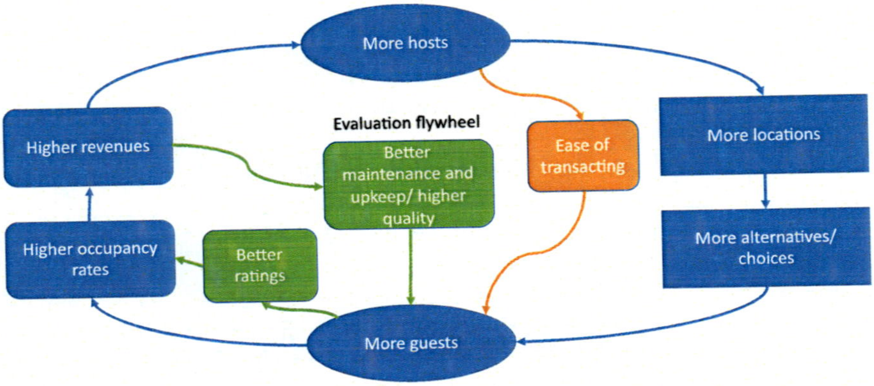

Fig. 5.4 Evaluation flywheel

Summary

In summary, platforms provide a range of utilities—discover, match, enable transactions, and govern through effective evaluation of the multiple sides. Through these utilities, platforms ensure that the stakeholders in the entire ecosystem reap three economic benefits—reduction in costs/improvement in efficiency; enhanced choice; and the opportunity to build a community/network of users.

Utility	Reduce cost/Improve efficiency	Enhance choice	Build community/Network
Discovery	Reduce search costs	Broaden scope of search	Effective segmentation of users into use cases
Matching	Reduce bureaucratic costs of contracting/reduce the risk of adverse selection	Effective filtering of search to match specific preferences	Smart recommender systems to curate, filter and aggregate user needs and preferences
Transaction	Reduce transaction costs	Improves credibility around pricing and quality of transactions	Ensuring responsibility and accountability, enabling fairness across all stakeholders in the platform
Evaluation	Reduce risks arising out of information asymmetry	Enhances credibility and signals quality to the other side, aiding in decision-making	Close-looping of information flows between user groups enabling decision-making

Swiggy™, Foodora™, and Yelp™: Hyperlocal Platforms

6

Introduction

On a late Saturday evening, a group of management students who were working on a research project realized that they may be working through the entire night and not have time to step out for dinner. One of the tech-savvy students grabbed her phone and instantly ordered food from the neighboring street's food joint and was utmost thrilled when she even received a cash back offer for using the app to order food from the app. Wondering about the immense potential, these local platforms could offer to traditionally offline businesses such as restaurants and food delivery catering vans, the student started to pen down few of her thoughts.

- What could be the business model of these hyperlocal delivery platforms and how easily could they scale operations as demand increased?
- Were there any same or cross-side network effects visible among participants who use these platforms?
- What kind of complementary services could these platforms venture into? Should they move beyond food delivery and into a full-fledged hyperlocal delivery service?

This case is an extension of Chapter 5 Value Creation in Platforms.
Srinivasan R, Professor of Strategy, Sandeep Lakshmipathy Research Scholar, and Pramoth Joseph, Research Scholar prepared this case for class discussion. This case is not intended to serve as an endorsement, source of primary data, or to show effective or inefficient handling of decision or business processes.

R. Srinivasan, *Platform Business Models*, Management for Professionals,
https://doi.org/10.1007/978-981-16-2838-2_6

- What could be some of the limiting constraints under which these hyperlocal platforms had to deliver business outcomes?

Food Delivery Business

Origin of the Journey

Not until long ago, most of the "phone and order" food deliveries were undertaken by pizza outlets in the metros (and similar restaurant-owned local delivery services) that catered to the hungry. However, with the emergence of smart phones and increasing internet penetration, patrons preferred to order food using mobile apps. Food delivery businesses were disrupted by digital forces wherein apps from Zomato, Swiggy, GrubHub, and others increased convenience and choices for all. Hungry patrons seemed to have a variety of restaurant choices which offered competitive pricing for their best offerings. Powered by reviews and recommendations coming from millions of patrons, the food delivery business and in general the hyperlocal delivery ecosystem were undergoing epic changes. Platforms such as Delivery Hero, Food Panda, Yelp, GrubHub, Swiggy, Zomato, and Just Eat had achieved global scale and some were considered unicorns,[1,2] or businesses which were valued at over a billion US dollars.

Hyperlocal is defined as "*relating to or focusing on matters concerning a small community or geographical area.*" Real-time information about happening places in the city or town, powered through reviews from real people who have undergone experiences at these outlets, held immense value for everyone else. Time sensitive information about local businesses helped patrons zero on the right one in a new locality. Neighborhood focused news, restaurant reviews and recommendations, food delivery from nearby restaurants along with grocery, and others constituted the scope of hyperlocal. Advertisers were interested in hyperlocal more than ever due to its ability to deliver relevant content as close to the patron as possible. Ability to deliver hyperlocal marketing at scale had puzzled many firms with considerable marketing budgets. However, emergence of hyperlocal platforms such as Yelp and Zomato changed the dynamics and has been successful in making impressions on the minds through personalized content that can be delivered in an automated manner. More recent incarnations of hyperlocal businesses enjoyed relatively better success as they were aided by satellite-based location services on smart phones. Along with improved mobile internet speeds, GPS-powered apps ensured more accurate real-time targeting of prospective patrons with individualized content.

[1]Anirban Sen (2018) *Swiggy enters unicorn club with $210 million funding from Naspers, Livemint*. Available at: https://www.livemint.com/Companies/AiJRVx5nIYGhuS5qSfZrHK/Swiggy-raises-210-million-in-fresh-funding-from-new-existi.html (Accessed: August 12, 2018).

[2]Lango, L. (2018) *Valuation Is Starting to Become a Concern for GrubHub Inc Stock, Yahoo Finance*. Available at: https://finance.yahoo.com/news/valuation-starting-become-concern-grubhub-220018888.html (Accessed: August 23, 2018).

Aggregation Versus Delivery

Aggregation platforms such as Yelp or Zomato started off with featuring restaurants and other local businesses on their portals and mobile apps which brought together reviews and recommendations from patrons who had experienced the concerned business' services prior to expressing their views on these portals. With this approach, advertising was the main avenue for revenue generation. The delivery part was mostly left to the restaurants to cater to and these aggregators focused on only getting additional customers into the store. Access to a variety of restaurants along with recommendations on what to eat at each outlet was key attractions that pulled patrons to these aggregator portals.

Recent delivery platforms that arrived on the international scene from 2010 onward had taken a different approach to food delivery. By building a fleet of delivery personnel from the ground up, these start-ups businesses not only managed to help the patrons with mobile apps that listed food to choose and order from but also partnered with the restaurants to handle the logistics of delivery of prepared food to the patrons. From the interface with the patrons to ensuring payments processing, these delivery platforms had reinvented the food business and the delivery ecosystem. This approach had brought in fresh investments and entirely new players into the market who spotted the potential. Flush with cash from venture funds, these delivery platforms had attracted huge investments and were looking to expand services to include patrons' other needs. These ventures advertised aggressively and had built brands with high recall and patron connect.

Swiggy

Bengaluru headquartered online food ordering hyperlocal start-up Swiggy started operations in 2014 to deliver food to hungry patrons who did not want to traverse the ever-increasing traffic snarls in the city. Founded by Rahul Jaimini, Sriharsha Majety, and Nandan Reddy and modeled to help patrons easily browse through the menu cards on the mobile app to order food from nearby restaurants, Swiggy allowed its patrons to pay through the app while it settled the food bills with the restaurants. Designed to be a full-blown food ordering and delivery solution that brought the dishes from neighboring restaurants, Swiggy had put in place a dedicated fleet of delivery personnel who picked food from the restaurants on behalf of patrons.

Food Delivery Process

Powered by its own delivery personnel who were equipped with smartphones, Swiggy used its home-grown routing algorithms on its app to ensure fastest possible delivery of freshly cooked food with each Swiggy delivery personnel dedicated to delivering a single order at a time (refer to Fig. 6.1). The delivery person would get notified when a new order was placed by a hungry patron who did not wish to drive down to the restaurant of choice. Keeping in mind the low-tech

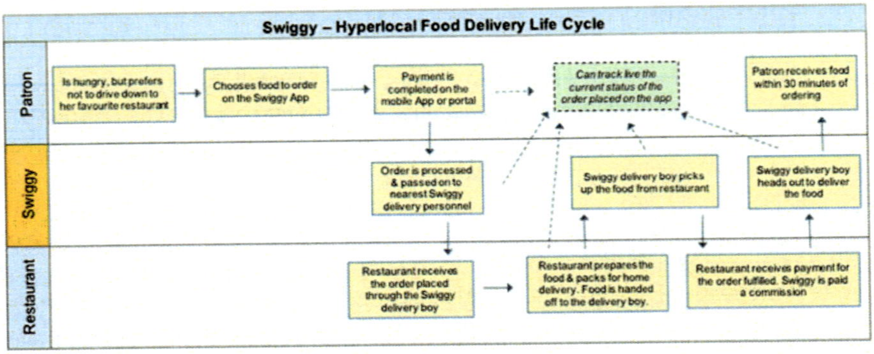

Fig. 6.1 Order flow through the Swiggy ecosystem. *Source* Authors' representation

approach of most Indian restaurants, Swiggy's integration with the restaurants was mostly manual wherein the delivery person would place the order for the patron's requested dishes and would ensure the restaurant was paid through Swiggy once the food was ready to be picked up. Swiggy allowed patrons to pay for the food they ordered through a variety of online and offline means and would transfer the payment to the restaurants after deducting its commission from the process. The delivery personnel would get paid for each delivery they made and also a fixed amount for every hour they spent engaged on the Swiggy platform. This model of work-based payments was attractive for a significant number of young Indians looking for job opportunities and they sought to be delivery personnel for Swiggy or similar platforms. With delivery times of around 30 min, Swiggy ranked next only to Dominos when it came to speed of food delivery in major Indian metros.

Business Model

Swiggy's business partners were the restaurants to which it brought traffic through its portal and mobile app. For every order that came through Swiggy, the restaurants were charged commissions of 10–30% making the restaurants the money side for the platform.[3] With discount offers to its patrons, Swiggy ensured the patrons were the subsidy side wherein they could even receive cash back offers for every order placed using the app which was above a minimum order price. There were nominal charges for food delivery due to distance of the delivery point from the restaurant or peak hour congestions. Swiggy also seemed to levy delivery charges in some cities based on a variety of considerations such as cost of delivery, traffic congestion, and others. It was apparent that the platform was still looking at ways to subsidize the

[3]Sayan Chakraborty (2017) Swiggy gets $80 million from Naspers and others, gains financial heft against Zomato—*Livemint*, *LiveMint E-Paper*. Available at: https://www.livemint.com/Companies/OvLqW673Z02PechgqA1fHP/Swiggy-raises-80-million-from-Naspers-others.html (Accessed: June 4, 2018).

patrons through variety of offers and discounts while making up for the revenue loss through commissions from restaurants. Compared to competitors such as Zomato, Swiggy seemed to command a higher commission rate from the restaurants.

With over $465 million raised through venture capital until August 2018[4] and enjoying a unicorn status as its valuation crossed $1 billion, Swiggy was looking at rapidly expanding its footprint across Indian cities to take on its rivals Zomato and Food Panda while trying to stay ahead of new entrants such as Uber Eats and Google's Areo.[5,6] Swiggy had started operations in Bengaluru, India, with six delivery executives and just 25 restaurants, but as of mid-2018, it had catapulted itself into India's largest food delivery service provider with 40,000 delivery executives and over 35,000 restaurant partners with presence in over 11 cities across the country including non-Metro such as Nagpur. Swiggy could be expected to set eyes on international expansion soon where competitors already enjoy a foothold.

Sustainability and Growth: Addressing Multi-homing and Envelopment

Swiggy had ensured need for low-tech integration from the restaurants by dealing with them through its delivery personnel who would walk into the restaurant to place orders on behalf of the patrons and pick up the food parcels for home and office delivery. This model ensured very low multi-homing costs for the restaurant who could also serve patrons coming through their own telephone systems, other online ordering platforms such as Zomato or Food Panda as well as their walk-in patrons. Once a few marquee restaurants were onboard Swiggy, it was sufficient to ensure other restaurants jumped onto the bandwagon or else risk being left out (fear of missing out, or FOMO) of a revenue stream through online orders. The FOMO for the restaurants ensured most neighborhood restaurants joined Swiggy and served their patrons through home delivery of fresh food. Presence of local favorite eating joints on Swiggy ensured even more patrons would come onboard to try out food ordering. In the fast-growing hyperlocal Indian food delivery market, there seemed to be no clear winners yet as the cost for multi-homing was not a sufficient barrier for the restaurants to choose one platform over the other to service online patrons.

For those restaurants which wanted to improve operations, Swiggy had built an owner app that provided visibility into flow of orders, patron feedbacks received,

---

[4]Salman S H (2018) Swiggy raises $100 million from Naspers, others—*Livemint*, *LiveMint E-Paper*. Available at: https://www.livemint.com/Companies/91Lju0nx1z32mAmUZh2y6O/Swiggy-raises-100-million-from-Naspers-others.html (Accessed: June 4, 2018).

[5]Anirban Sen (2018) Swiggy enters unicorn club with $210 million funding from Naspers, *Livemint*. Available at: https://www.livemint.com/Companies/AiJRVx5nIYGhuS5qSfZrHK/Swiggy-raises-210-million-in-fresh-funding-from-new-existi.html (Accessed: August 12, 2018).

[6]Sarah Perez (2017) Google Areo is a new app for ordering food or home services in India, TechCrunch. Available at: https://techcrunch.com/2017/04/13/google-areo-is-a-new-app-for-ordering-food-or-home-services-in-india/ (Accessed: August 12, 2018).

and menu analysis.[7] With real-time updates on the app, restaurant owners were presented with an opportunity to react based on patron feedback to improve order inflow. Through online presence on the Swiggy platform and improved brand equity, restaurants were presented with new business opportunities with a patron base not limited to the immediate neighborhood. As restaurants benefited from patron analytics provided by Swiggy, it helped the platform increase multi-homing costs for these restaurants. Another step in this direction was the introduction of Swiggy Access in late 2017, a kitchen backend facility in Bengaluru which provided free space for restaurant owners who wanted to expand patron base that they served but could not do so due to need for high capital investments. This was also a competitive reaction to Zomato which was stepping up its investment in cloud kitchens.[8] Operated as a warehousing facility or a central base, Swiggy Access hosts kitchens for multiple restaurants under the same roof. Designed to give instant access to the delivery fleet of Swiggy, these kitchen spaces, which were slated to come across multiple cities, provided restaurants additional benefits such as capacity planning, demand forecasting, and improved stock management. Restaurants had to bring in their appliances and hardware while space was provided free of cost along with access to other facilities on Swiggy's platform. Multiple restaurants were signing up for operating out of Swiggy Access bases due to increased prospect of access to newer patrons at reduced costs in neighborhoods where they did not have any presence.[9] Swiggy was planning to charge high commission rates to the restaurants that operated out of Swiggy Access as compared to rates on its marketplace model.

Swiggy's own private brands which had started operations in 2017 were also housed at these Access kitchens and competed with the rest of the restaurants on the platform.[10] How the restaurants would react to private labels from the platform provider was yet to unfold. Operating as a cloud kitchen, the white label restaurants launched by Swiggy was in direct competition with the restaurants that leveraged Swiggy as an order management and delivery platform. In contrasting approach, main competitor Zomato had decided to provide infrastructure services to its restaurant partners to help them scale while staying away from launching white labels. As strategic pivots and consolidations accelerated in the food-tech space, outcomes of these moves were yet untested.

[7]ANI (2018) Swiggy expands footprints, launches operations in Nagpur, *The Economic Times*. Available at: https://economictimes.indiatimes.com/small-biz/startups/newsbuzz/swiggy-expands-footprints-launches-operations-in-nagpur/articleshow/63938012.cms (Accessed: August 12, 2018).

[8]Srinivasan, S. (2018) "Food delivery battle brews in cloud kitchen, Zomato makes first move," *The Economic Times*, June 14 Available at: https://economictimes.indiatimes.com/small-biz/startups/newsbuzz/food-delivery-battle-brews-in-cloud-kitchen-zomato-leads/articleshow/64580974.cms.

[9]Salman S.H. (2017) Swiggy launches 'Access' kitchen for restaurant partners, *Livemint*. Available at: https://www.livemint.com/Companies/mgngNTra7jScvi0nzskqeK/Swiggy-launches-Access-kitchen-for-restaurant-partners.html (Accessed: August 12, 2018).

[10]Payal Ganguly (2017) Swiggy sets up cloud kitchen "The Bowl Company" in Bengaluru, *Times of India*. Available at: https://timesofindia.indiatimes.com/companies/swiggy-sets-up-cloud-kitchen-the-bowl-company-in-bengaluru/articleshow/56659238.cms (Accessed: August 12, 2018).

Swiggy had acquired few start-ups in its journey to become the leading hyperlocal food delivery platform in the country including its recent acquisition of Scootsy for around $8 million.[11] As of mid-2018, inorganic growth through acquisitions enabled Swiggy to acquire other start-ups such as 48East and was in talks to acquire "direct to home" milk delivery start-up SuprDaily. These acquisitions were undertaken to increase frequency of orders as items such as milk are bought by Indian households almost daily, whereas an average patron ordered food online through restaurants only 3–4 times a month. With substantial funding in place, Swiggy was looking into capacity creation that would help it expand services to other adjacent hyperlocal deliveries and push to enter newer markets. Although milk delivery yielded an average of ₹1000 per Indian household, the lower margins on these have made platforms consider attaching delivery of grocery and other items to these same households which are captive patrons.[12]

Swiggy had recently launched its capital assist program in partnership with a financial firm that provided collateral-free loans to Swiggy's restaurant partners to help small businesses tide over capital allocation issues that hindered most expansion plans. The Swiggy Capital Assist program was also aimed at increasing the switching cost for these restaurants and to dissuade them from multi-homing with other delivery platforms such as Zomato, Uber Eats, or others. These loans without an initial deposit, at attractive interest rates and often subsidized by Swiggy, were aimed at easing the hassle of obtaining loans through traditional channels to enable the restaurants to invest in additional capacity creation.[13]

By early 2017, it was evident that the ongoing consolidation in the food-tech industry in India would have room for only two major players—Swiggy and Zomato. How Swiggy takes on the more experienced rival in Zomato was something to be witnessed as the duopoly unfolded. Swiggy's ability to sustain its expanding fleet of delivery personnel was critical to its long-term success as a key hyperlocal platform. How well Swiggy leveraged lean time of delivery personnel in the food business to cater to delivery of other services to its install base would determine profitability. With milk deliveries mostly skewed toward deliveries in the morning hours, and with food orders from restaurants limited to lunch and dinner

[11]Supraja Srinivasan (2018) Swiggy acquires on-demand delivery firm Scootsy for Rs 50 crore, *The Economic Times*. Available at: https://tech.economictimes.indiatimes.com/news/startups/swiggy-acquires-on-demand-delivery-firm-scootsy-for-rs-50-crore/65238251 (Accessed: August 12, 2018).

[12]Varsha Bansal (2018) Swiggy, BigBasket discover next cash cow: Milk supply, *The Economic Times*. Available at: https://economictimes.indiatimes.com/small-biz/startups/newsbuzz/swiggy-bigbasket-discover-next-cash-cow-milk-supply/articleshow/64377983.cms (Accessed: August 12, 2018).

[13]Supraja Srinivasan (2017) Swiggy partners with Indifi Tech to launch financing program for restaurant partners, *The Economic Times*. Available at: https://tech.economictimes.indiatimes.com/news/internet/swiggy-partners-with-indifi-tech-to-launch-financing-program-for-restaurant-partners/61049835 (Accessed: August 12, 2018).

times, there was scope for delivery of grocery and medicines during the remaining lean hours of the day which could put to use the idle delivery personnel. As commanding a higher commission would be a herculean task in non-food delivery areas, Swiggy may have to contend with lower commission rates in milk, grocery, and alcohol deliveries.

In early 2018, Swiggy's main rival Zomato launched Zomato Gold—a monthly paid subscription service that promised zero delivery charges for patrons who ordered through Zomato. With over 150,000 patrons embracing the Gold program in the first 90 days of its launch, the subscription program from Zomato was a run-away success by the food-tech business standards. With this unprecedented response to a paid subscription model, Swiggy had to evolve its own competitive subscription offer that assured patrons of zero surcharge delivery even during peak hours. With intent to lock-in patrons onto the Swiggy platform, and increase stickiness, Swiggy launched the Swiggy SUPER paid subscription program which assured patrons of free food deliveries without any convenience charges irrespective of time of day or distance of the restaurant.[14] Also promised as part of the subscription program were amenities such as, dedicated patron care and faster resolution of disputes. Available as one-month and three-month subscription packs, Swiggy was charging anywhere from ₹99–149 per month and was looking to add paid subscriptions as a key revenue source apart from commissions from restaurants.

Foodora

Founded in October 2014 in Munich by Konstatin Mehl, Foodora secured backing from Rocket Internet in April 2015. It offered a platform that connected hungry patrons with restaurants in German cities to start with. Foodora eventually merged with Delivery Hero in September 2015[15] as part of the consolidation of food-tech businesses in Rocket Internet's portfolio.[16] Headquartered in Berlin, Delivery Hero had a market capitalization of €8.66 ($10.01) billion after mergers with Foodora and others. Delivery Hero operated through different brands in various regions—Foodora in Germany, Foodpanda in India, pizza.de, and lieferheld among others. It offered products and services to the catering business in the form of assistance for

[14]Supraja Srinivasan (2018) Swiggy follows Zomato's steps, rolls out first paid subscription plan for users, *The Economic Times*. Available at: https://economictimes.indiatimes.com/small-biz/startups/newsbuzz/swiggy-follows-zomatos-steps-rolls-out-first-paid-subscription-plan-for-users/articleshow/65201912.cms (Accessed: August 12, 2018).

[15]Steve O'Hear (2016) Delivery Hero acquires Foodpanda as Rocket Internet shuffles online takeout pack once again, *TechCrunch*. Available at: https://techcrunch.com/2016/12/10/delivery-hero-captures-foodbanda/ (Accessed: August 23, 2018).

[16]Delivery Hero Inc (2015) Delivery Hero acquires 100% of Foodora from Rocket Internet—The Easiest Way to Your Favorite Food. Available at: https://www.deliveryhero.com/delivery-hero-acquires-100-of-foodora-from-rocket-internet/ (Accessed: August 23, 2018).

packing, advertising, and printing services. Delivery Hero had business presence across Europe, Asia, North America, Middle East, and North Africa.[17]

Food Delivery Process

During the early days, hungry patrons accessed Foodora primarily through their portal, but later shifted to the mobile app as the preferred choice for food ordering. Users could enter their postal code and view a curated list of restaurants in their neighborhood or the mobile app leveraged GPS info to show the options available to order from. Once they had found their restaurant and meal of choice, patrons could place the order from the comfort of their home or office, paying online through Foodora's secure platform. Once payment was complete, restaurant received the confirmed order along with the delivery personnel's details with the estimated time of order pickup so that the restaurant could then prepare the requested meal.

With an endeavor for faster delivery of freshly cooked food and accompanied by a conscious attempt to be environment friendly, Foodora preferred bike-borne delivery personnel. To enable speed of delivery, Foodora had earmarked smaller delivery zones for its riders which was typically around 1 mile which in turn enabled a higher utilization of its riders. The entire delivery process (refer to Fig. 6.2) was transparent to both the patron who had placed the order and the restaurant which was serving food. Patrons were intimated about the estimated delivery time before placing the order. Once the order was submitted, they could monitor the progress of the order through the mobile app or the website. Once the Foodora rider (aka Independent rider or Unabhängige reiter) picked up the order for delivery, the rider could be tracked to the exact location. Patrons had an option to choose Foodora logistics team or the restaurant's own drivers for food delivery. Food delivery was typically done by riders within 35 min from the moment the completed order was placed.

Business Model

The business model followed by Foodora ensured that all the parties involved benefited out of this transaction. The patrons were charged for the order that was booked on the app or the website. The delivery fee varied according to the city the patron belonged to. The restaurant paid a flat 30% commission on the total amount of the food order to Foodora. The rider who picked up the order and delivered it was paid a flat rate per hour plus tips, if any. In typically most instances, restaurants had kept prices for delivery menu similar to in restaurant prices and thereby raked in higher revenues owing to lower taxes on take-out orders. The food delivery model was a good match for restaurants to utilize idle capacity and not incur additional costs for delivery orders. Very popular restaurants perceived the food delivery model as an additional revenue stream which would have otherwise been

[17]Stefan Nicola (2016) Delivery Hero's Foodora Expands as Rivalry Intensifies, *Bloomberg*. Available at: https://www.bloomberg.com/news/articles/2016-02-19/delivery-hero-s-foodora-expands-in-europe-as-rivalry-intensifies (Accessed: August 23, 2018).

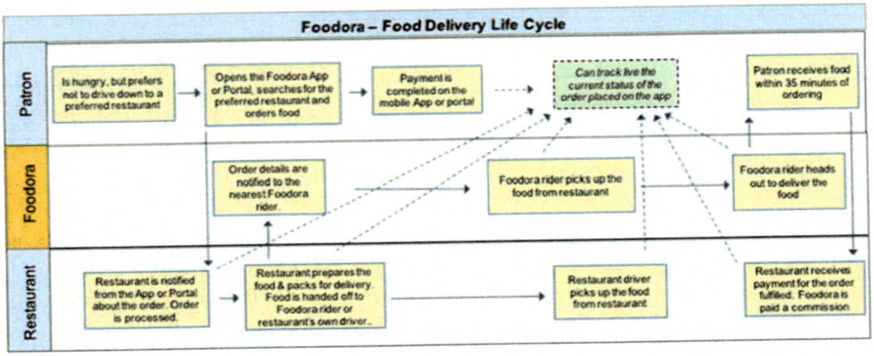

Fig. 6.2 Order flow through Delivery Hero/Foodora. *Source* Authors' representation

lost due to high levels of demand and near impossibility of obtaining reservations for a dine-in.

Unlike other subsidiaries of Delivery Hero, Foodora's delivery own fleet was complemented by freelancers to helped deliver parcels within a 2–3 km radius. A vast majority of Foodora's riders were students who garnered additional income based on their assigned shifts and deliveries made. It also followed an asset-light model whereby it owned no bikes. Foodora provided the pink delivery boxes, a helmet, and a jacket for the Unabhängige reiter. They were only required to own a smartphone and a bike to make the food delivery.[18]

Foodora also provided discount coupons which helped patrons save money when they paid for their food orders online. Early on, Foodora charged the restaurants a one-time setup fee and a monthly subscription in addition to a 14% commission on the order value.[19] In 2018, Foodora did not charge a setup fee anymore and moved to a flat percentage commission on the order value.

Sustainability and Growth Opportunities

Though Delivery Hero focused on the food delivery business, it had two service offerings: (i) asset-light model where it only provided software access for both food orders and delivery management and (ii) the integrated model where it owned delivery logistics in addition to software access. Foodora's approach followed the integrated model wherein it handled the delivery logistics along with demand generation and order management. Profitability was higher in developed markets

[18]Miltok (2016) Foodora—A digital revolution of the food delivery industry—Technology and Operations Management, HBS Digital Initiative Forum. Available at: https://rctom.hbs.org/submission/foodora-a-digital-revolution-of-the-food-delivery-industry/ (Accessed: 12 November 2018).

[19]Vasagar, J. (2014) "Delivery Hero plans to use $88 m in internet takeaway push," *Financial Times*, January 19. Available at: https://www.ft.com/content/801931ba-7f8e-11e3-b6a7-00144feabdc0.

for the integrated approach of Foodora. In developing markets, marketing and other operational costs were higher which in turn subdued profit margins.

Prior to acquisition by Delivery Hero, Foodora had expanded to 50 cities across 10 countries. By late 2018, Foodora's parent Delivery Hero provided services in 42 countries working with more than 150,000 restaurants and more than 12,000 riders.[20] Stickiness with returning patrons was high and that accounted for about 70% of the business volume (see Footnote 19). With commissions constituting up to 73% of revenues, 2017 revenues for Delivery Hero stood at €544 m ($602 m) and Q1 2018 were at €171 m (see Footnote 19). Overall, the food-tech business opportunity in Europe and the existing low penetration levels of food delivery apps presented Delivery Hero with major growth potential (refer to Exhibit 6.1).

Rising valuations was an indication of the prospective growth opportunity in food-tech industry. In August 2016, Delivery Hero, the parent of Foodora, was valued at €2.7 billion and in September 2017, Naspers acquired 12.15% stake in Delivery Hero from Rocket Internet by valuing the company at €5.5 billion valuation.[21] Operating margins were still negative, and for 2017, Delivery Hero generated €3.8 billion in Gross Merchandise Value (GMV), a key metric for food delivery aggregators (see Footnote 19). McKinsey reported that on average, close to 70% of patrons had never switched aggregator platforms such as Foodora across various countries (refer to Exhibit 6.2).

Food delivery market was driven by three significant trends: (i) Engaging patrons via internet and mobile apps, (ii) providing food on demand accompanied with logistics for last mile delivery, and (iii) business growth driven by the continued upward mobility of patrons in their spending habits and the comfort of ordering food without having to drive down to the restaurant. Yet another driving factor for sustainability and profitability was the food order value. Delivery Hero claimed the leadership position in 39 countries, whereas Just Eat was supposedly market leader in 13 countries when it came to order size.[22] While Delivery Hero reported increasing order frequency across key food delivery markets in a 20–95% range, these firms understood that sustainable growth would have to come from winning the markets they were already entrenched in and not from newer ones.[23] This could help the platforms focus on the returning patrons and the consistent revenue generated through these loyal patrons.

---

[20]Delivery Hero Inc. (2018) Delivery Hero—Company presentation. Available at: https://ir.deliveryhero.com/download/companies/delivery/Presentations/20180802_Company_Presentation_vf.pdf (Accessed: August 23, 2018).

[21]Timetric (2018) Delivery Hero AG—Company Capsule. Available at: https://www.marketresearch.com/Timetric-v3917/Consumer-Goods-Retailing-c80/1.html (Accessed: August 23, 2018).

[22]Wijngaarde, Y. et al. (2017) Food Delivery Tech: Battle for the European Consumer. Available at: https://blog.dealroom.co/wp-content/uploads/2017/10/Food-Tech-Prez-FINAL.pdf (Accessed: August 23, 2018).

[23]Ahmed, M. (2016) "Just Eat, Delivery Hero and Takeaway.com fight for dominance," *Financial Times*, January 1, Available at: https://www.ft.com/content/cfa6d3d8-a285-11e5-8d70-42b68cfae6e4 (Accessed: August 10, 2018).

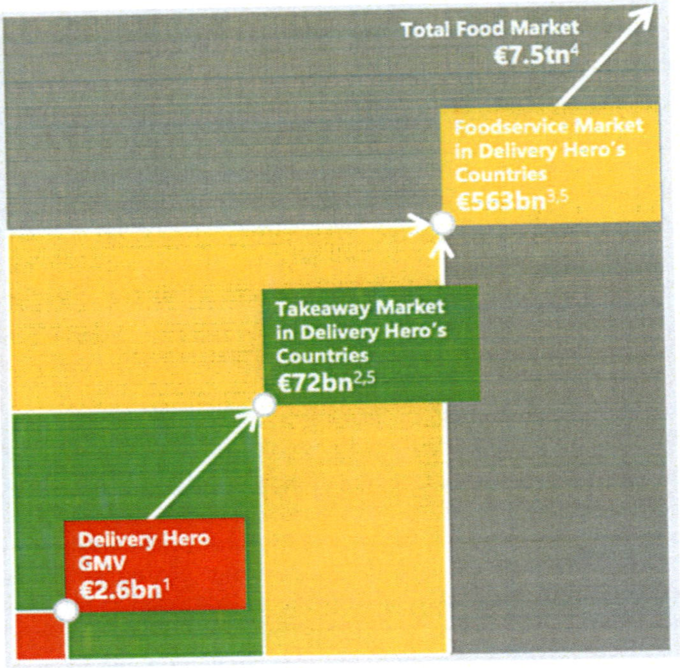

Exhibit 6.1 Delivery Hero—market opportunity—as assessed at end of 2016. *Source* Delivery Hero—company portal. Available at: https://www.deliveryhero.com/wp-content/uploads/2017/05/Public-Company-Presentation-20170509.pdf

Delivery Hero had focused on growth via acquisitions since 2012. The firm had also prudently exited the UK and China markets that were challenging and thereby laying a growth path. Delivery Hero relied on technology and integration to bring full visibility of the supply chain process to the businesses. This helped in rolling out key initiatives to smoothen the process for the patrons, the restaurant, and the delivery personnel. By bolstering its own technology capabilities, Delivery Hero ensured leadership but the path was unclear when Delivery Hero would rake in a profit.

Yelp

Started in 2004, Yelp helped connect people to local businesses such as restaurants, shopping outlets, travel, fitness, nightlife, and others. Headquartered in San Francisco, California, this hyperlocal platform was one of the earliest to link local city dwellers to happening places around them. Yelp started out by publishing crowd-sourced reviews about local businesses and had begun allowing online

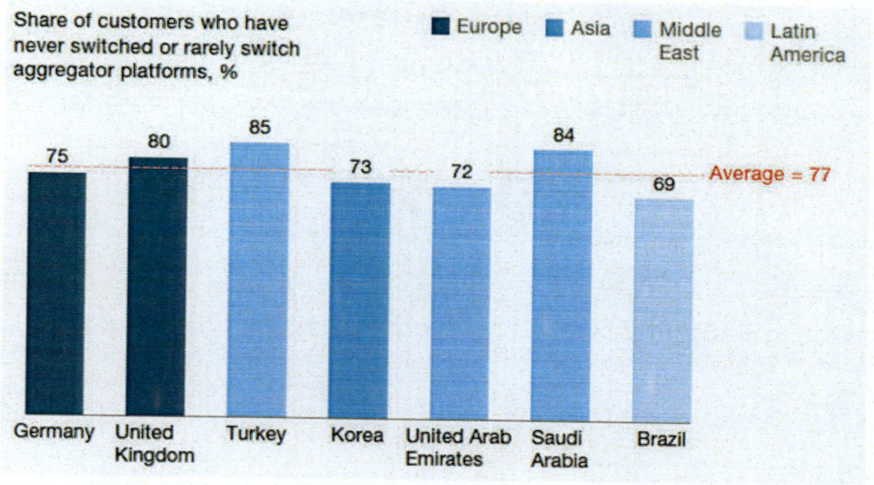

Exhibit 6.2 Ability to retain patrons. *Source* McKinsey & Company. Available at: https://www.mckinsey.com/industries/high-tech/our-insights/the-changing-market-for-food-delivery

reservations. With a major presence in North American metros, Yelp had become a review portal that allowed its visitors to network on the site regarding their evaluations of local business outlets which in turn could publish information about their products and services offered.

On the one side of Yelp were the patrons looking for happening places in their neighborhood while the other side had local businesses vying for mindshare of these patrons. Yelp platform had a unique third side in the form of advertisers (refer to Fig. 6.3) who were keen on placing ads on Yelp. Local businesses and popular brands were the key money sides for Yelp platform as they advertised on the portal. Yelp's patrons enjoyed zero transaction costs for their access to reviews, recommendations, bookings, and interactions with local businesses. However, patrons usually paid a small delivery fee if they wished to have food delivered from local restaurants that were featured on Yelp.

Business Model

From a modest revenue of $83 million when Yelp went public in March 2012, the business had come a long way to report a net projected revenue of around $950 million for 2018 which was a tenfold increase.[24] From a platform that was mainly focused on patrons who navigated the Yelp website in 2011 to a predominantly mobile traffic in 2018, Yelp's patron base had evolved in its preferences and expectations from the platform (refer to Exhibit 6.3). With a mission to connect patrons with local businesses in each city, Yelp's pricing model had evolved from a

[24]Yelp (2018) Yelp Shareholder Letter. Available at: http://www.yelp-ir.com/static-files/4c4c615f-5cbb-494c-8a84-9859a42766e5 (Accessed: August 10, 2018).

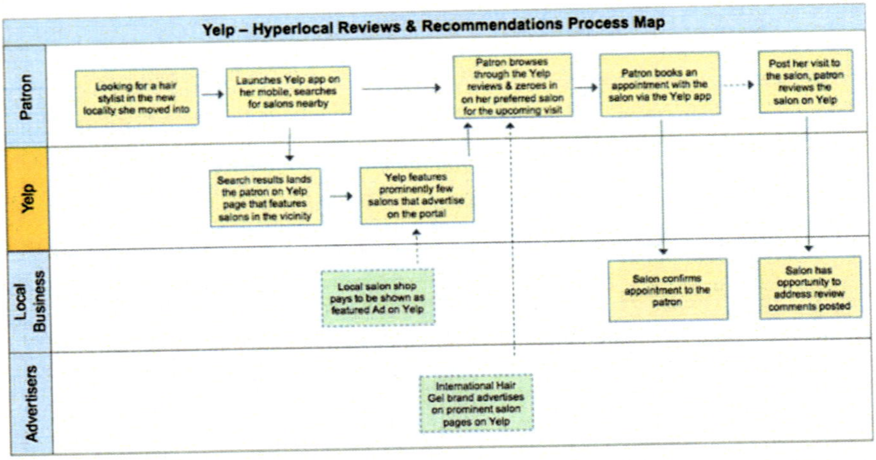

Fig. 6.3 Yelp process map—ensuring participation of all sides. *Source* Authors' representation

single advertising solution that catered to small and medium businesses to one that was now customizable so that it could cater to multiple markets across the world. Yelp had started to offer marketing solutions that addressed unique needs of advertisers at the local and national levels. With presence on more than one-thirds of the smart phones in the USA, the Yelp mobile app claimed deep penetration and witnessed increasing usage for restaurant-related transactions. With more than half the revenues in 2018 expected to come from restaurant reviews and food delivery activities, Yelp's partnership with GrubHub was expected to further drive up revenues from this category. Along with restaurants, home and local services were an emerging category for Yelp for which it was customizing its advertising and go-to-market strategies. Yelp Custom Ads were offered to local businesses that advertise with Yelp to enable them to moderate the photos and reviews that were visible in the ad campaigns.

With an advertising revenue of $214 million in Q1 2018, Yelp local Salesforce was focused on increasing Yelp's portion of the overall spend on advertising. It witnessed a 27% year-on-year jump in paying advertising accounts due to its movement away from fixed term contracts with local businesses for advertising with Yelp. It also derived commissions from GrubHub for every restaurant fulfillment order that originated from Yelp. Yelp had put in more focus to bring local businesses that were transactional in nature and not limit itself to only being an aggregator in all categories. Huge patron base gave leverage to Yelp as it negotiated advertising rates with major brands that vied for presence on the platform.

Growth Opportunity

With over 150 million monthly unique visitors, Yelp was a highly trafficked site on the internet built atop a robust review and evaluation platform. With year-on-year growth of over 20% in cumulative reviews, by end of 2017, reviews done on Yelp

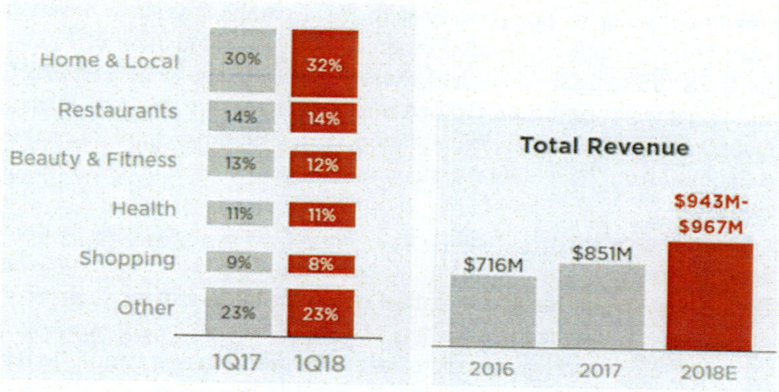

Exhibit 6.3 Yelp—advertising revenue by category. *Source* Yelp Inc.—Q1 2018 Shareholder Letter. Available at: http://www.yelp-ir.com/static-files/4c4c615f-5cbb-494c-8a84-9859a42766e5

stood at 148 million.[25] With a large advertiser base of over 160,000, the business was witnessing over 20% growth year-on-year. Many of the local businesses that were reviewed on Yelp also advertised on the platform to attract and engage more patrons. Independent advertisers also leveraged the platform to promote branded products sold through local outlets that had presence on Yelp.

Personal digital assistants such as Amazon's Alexa and Apple's Siri were integrated with Yelp's content to respond to local search queries from users.[26,27] When users of these devices sought reviews and recommendations for nearby restaurants or salons or hotels, they were served with search results from Yelp's content. This was helping drive up the mobile traffic for Yelp and was expected to be a major source of revenue as more internet users consumed content through their mobile devices. More users using Yelp services meant more reviews and recommendations for the nearby businesses which in turn would find it even more attractive to advertise on Yelp. These mobile devices and personal assistant gadgets were expected to drive up user engagement levels for services such as Yelp as these recommendations got better only when more people used it daily to keep them relevant and up to date.

Online food ordering constituted the largest category of transactions by revenue and volume on the Yelp platform and was currently available through partners such as GrubHub. Consolidation in the food delivery business was aimed at reducing

---

[25] Yelp Inc. (2017) Yelp Reports Fourth Quarter and Full Year 2017 Financial Results, *Yelp*. Available at: http://www.yelp-ir.com/news-releases/news-release-details/yelp-reports-fourth-quarter-and-full-year-2017-financial-results (Accessed: August 15, 2018).

[26] Richard Lawler (2015) Amazon Echo links with Yelp to find info on local restaurants, *Engadget*. Available at: https://www.engadget.com/2015/10/24/amazon-echo-links-with-yelp-to-find-info-on-local-restaurants/ (Accessed: August 14, 2018).

[27] Trefis Team (2012) *Apple Shows Yelp Some Siri-ous Love, Forbes*. Available at: https://www.forbes.com/sites/greatspeculations/2012/03/23/apple-shows-yelp-some-siri-ous-love-sends-it-more-traffic/-d4652194ea86 (Accessed: August 14, 2018).

delivery charges or doing away with them completely since these charges sometimes were as high as the food ordered. With the acquisition of Eat24 from Yelp[28] for $288 million, GrubHub had exclusive partnership with Yelp for food delivery and this integration meant GrubHub had an edge over rivals such as Uber Eats and DoorDash. With the recent integration, Yelp and GrubHub had enabled patrons to order food from over 80,000 restaurants spread across 1200 cities that were featured on Yelp.

Yelp's geo-targeting facility had enabled local businesses to define the target area around their business for the ads that they posted on the Yelp platform. Businesses could specify a radius of 5–25 miles around their primary area of operations as the target area for serving these ads. Any web or mobile users browsing Yelp content for related services in this range would be served targeted ads about the business. Yelp tried to allocate a wide range for service-based businesses as compared to local brick-and-mortar ones. With robust Search Engine Optimization (SEO), Yelp pages appeared prominently on Google search results and hence helped businesses that advertised on Yelp receive more traffic from other portals than just Yelp's own internal traffic. With increasing competition from Google's own home services offerings that were attempting to garner more ad revenues from these very same local businesses, Yelp had to differentiate its offering to fight off the envelopment threat.

Sustainability of the Business Model

Reviewers were motivated by badges and honors they received for being the first to review a new location, or the attention they gathered from other users who benefited from the reviews posted on Yelp. In order to maintain the authenticity of the reviews posted, reviewers were encouraged to use real names and photos on the portal while registering. While strong network effects existed among the local businesses as no one wanted to be left behind (FOMO) when a platform was making it convenient to bring foot fall to the stores, the presence of diverse businesses was a great attraction for even more patrons to use Yelp for discovering local experiences. Similarly, the presence of large patrons looking for outlets in the neighborhood was a great pull for more and more businesses to want to be on the Yelp platform so that they had an opportunity to engage with the patrons on the other side. According to the portal, Yelp uses automated software that can recommend useful and reliable reviews wherein the software looks at dozens of different signals, including various measures of quality, reliability, and activity on the portal, and this process, according to Yelp, has nothing to do with whether a business advertises on Yelp or not.

Businesses could set up a free account on Yelp to post photos and message their patrons. The ability to get back in touch with patrons who had visited the local business provided the business owners a unique opportunity to address service

[28]Joshua Brustein (2017) GrubHub Buys Yelp's Eat24 for $288 Million, *Bloomberg*. Available at: https://www.bloomberg.com/news/articles/2017-08-03/grubhub-buys-yelp-s-eat24-for-288-million (Accessed: August 15, 2018).

delivery gaps. It also provided an opportunity to communicate with patrons and inform them of the new services that have been introduced by the business since their last visit. In order to give its patrons a seamless experience in choosing what to order from the restaurants which were reviewed, Yelp introduced the popular dishes feature. It helped hungry patrons to quickly know what the best dishes on offer at the restaurant were, without having to wade through thousands of reviews. With these automated recommendations on what to order, Yelp was increasing stickiness to its local search services and adding entry barriers as newcomers would not have the rich data sets that were helping such recommendations to be made. Powered by modern machine learning algorithms that could go through tons of reviews and photos posted to emerge with dish recommendations, Yelp was leveraging data collected from the reviews posted on the platform to further its competitive advantage against newcomers such as Uber Eats. In addition to reviews, Yelp helped patrons find events happening in the city and to also talk with other Yelpers.

Although thronged by millions, Yelp faced its own challenges when it came to queries related to how it used the reviews and recommendations to direct advertisement traffic. Yelp was considered more expensive than Google or Facebook Ads which were other alternatives for local businesses to advertise on. With a higher cost-per-click rate, Yelp faced criticism for lack of transparency on what keywords or topics were local businesses spending ad dollars upon. Yelp has been accused of not displaying all reviews and giving preferential treatment to those businesses that advertised on Yelp. Many local businesses found it difficult to justify the economic value of the traffic coming in through Yelp pages and the higher rates they paid for their Yelp Ads. With Google making it easy for businesses to launch customized websites featuring photos and reviews, understand customer behaviors with timely insights and leverage advantage of tight integration with Google Maps, it was ramping up its focus on the hyperlocal market as an adjacency to its dominant search business. On the other hand, Facebook, as the front runner in social media interactions, was also expected to compete strongly with Yelp and Google to grab a share of the advertising revenues from these local businesses. Facebook was a portal frequented by patrons on a daily basis and any reviews posted by friends on the local businesses' pages were bound to gather traction.

The Road Ahead

With robust forecast for the coming years (refer to Exhibit 6.4), the hyperlocal platforms were poised for a period of great growth. Food delivery platforms such as Swiggy were already looking at transforming into full-fledged hyperlocal delivery platform by leveraging and expanding their existing patron base. Delivery of milk, alcohol, medicines, and grocery were high on the list of expanded services that these platforms were targeting. Through acquisitions or partnerships, these hyperlocal platforms were looking to expand service offerings to take on competition more effectively. Availability of funding and consolidation proceedings in the

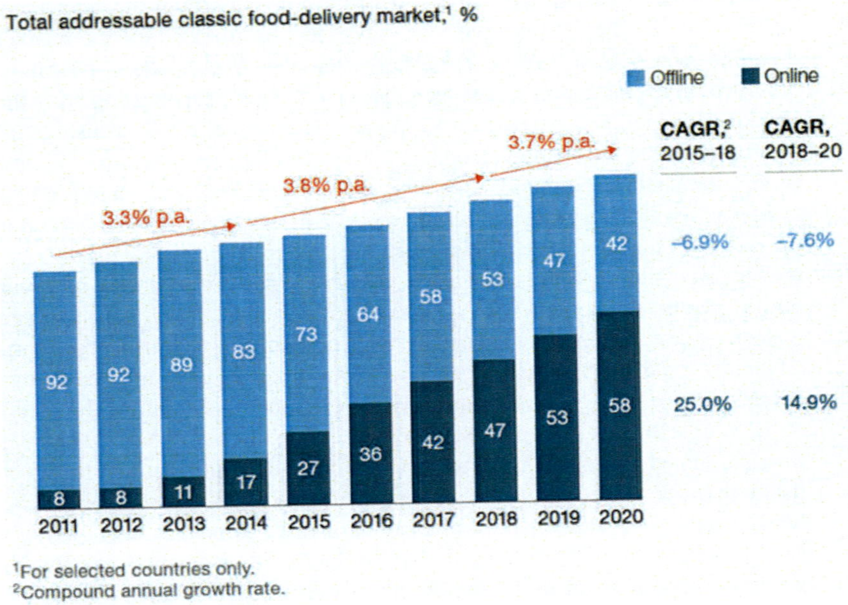

Exhibit 6.4 Projected growth rate for food delivery market. *Source* McKinsey & Company. Available at: https://www.mckinsey.com/industries/high-tech/our-insights/the-changing-market-for-food-delivery

sector were also driving the platforms to offer additional services to keep up growth rates. Sustaining large delivery workforce and staying profitable were still ongoing endeavors at these firms which were figuring out the right balance in an industry that was still in its infancy. With increasing patron loyalty and low switching rates, these platforms were building additional lock-ins that ensured engagement of the burgeoning patron base. However, as of late 2018, stiff competition between Swiggy and Zomato in India had seen an unusual beneficiary—the local delivery personnel who saw their incentives steadily climb up as competition intensified. Rising food delivery costs was another challenge that these platforms across the markets needed to mitigate.[29]

It is imperative that we observe how each of these platforms were able to capitalize on their core competencies as they entered new adjacencies. Some questions though lingered in the professor's mind as he keenly followed the hyperlocal space:

[29] Ahuja, A. and Sen, A. (2018) "Swiggy, Zomato hike delivery boy salaries as competition grows," *LiveMint E-Paper*, 26 July. Available at: https://www.livemint.com/Companies/cYbdfsYk93HFhMuC0XgaNN/Swiggy-Zomato-hike-delivery-boy-salaries-as-competition-gro.html.

- To what extent should these hyperlocal platforms compete with their own partners through initiatives such as white labels, cloud kitchens, or dark stores? When would the resident restaurants and local businesses on the platform bail off by sensing the threat from these actions wherein the platform itself was emerging as a provider of services?
- How would the strategies of these platforms evolve as they take on the bigger rivals in their turf? Swiggy would run into BigBasket on the hyperlocal delivery front in India, while Yelp would run into Google and Facebook on the advertising space.

Network Mobilization

7

Cross-side network effects or indirect network externalities present an interesting scenario[1]: To attract buyers, a platform should have a base of registered sellers, but the sellers will be willing to sell on the platform only if they expect many buyers to show up. Be it newspapers which have been around for centuries or the cab hailing apps, a platform needs to make explicit attempts to get onboard each side so that it is appealing for the other sides to also participate. This challenge of getting critical numbers on each side is commonly referred to as solving the Penguin problem.[2] The penguins which want to dive into the waters to find food delay the same since they fear the lurking predators. Each would prefer the other to test the waters first before they go in. Similarly, there is no incentive for any one participant on the platform to get the bandwagon rolling unless the others are already onboard.

Solving the challenge of onboarding initial set of users is crucial to have a viable business model, especially when the switching and multi-homing costs for partic-

[1]Bernard Caillaud and Bruno Jullien, "Chicken & Egg: Competition among Intermediation Service Providers," The RAND Journal of Economics 34, no. 2 (2003): 309–28.
[2]Joseph Farrell and Garth Saloner, "Installed Base and Compatibility: Innovation, Product Preannouncements, and Predation," The American Economic Review, 1986, https://doi.org/10.2307/1816461.

This chapter is primarily written by Sandeep Lakshmipathy, under the guidance of R. Srinivasan.

R. Srinivasan, *Platform Business Models*, Management for Professionals,
https://doi.org/10.1007/978-981-16-2838-2_7

ipants are low during the early stages of association.[3] This chapter explores ways different platform firms have approached this challenge. Network mobilization strategies depend on two dimensions of growth: the extent to which the firm leverages its existing resources and the path it takes to acquire its first set of users. These two decisions are crucial in the context of platform growth.

Strategic Dimensions: Resources and Users

Strategically, firms would approach the challenge based on the kind of resources at their disposal and the set of initial users they want to target. Hence, analyzing the firm's approach to building critical mass requires strategizing along two dimensions: users and resources. There are three primary sources for the initial set of users: port users from existing pipeline (or platform) business, target marquee users first, and attract altogether new users. Platforms leverage resources in three major ways: use existing firm resources (coring), leverage resources from the ecosystem to augment existing resources (tipping), and invest in new resources that can power the platform growth.

User Dimension

Users could be individuals or institutions such as government agencies or other large corporations which are looking for means to reach out to the other side(s) of the platform. Users choose to affiliate with one platform over another based on multiple considerations including past reputation of the sponsors of the platform, quality of products/services, business models offered, and privacy provisions. In platforms that exhibit significant cross-side network effects, the number and quality of users on the other side is one of the primary considerations for platform affiliation.

Porting Users: Porting is defined as migration of existing users of a firm to a new product or service to be launched by the same firm. Established firms that have an existing user base can offer new services by porting all users onto a new platform offering. All sides of the new platform may emerge from users or entities that are ported from the existing base of the firm. For instance, Amazon.com ported its publishers and book buyers from its e-commerce bookstore during the launch of its

[3]Joseph Farrell and Garth Solaner, "Competition, Compatability and Standards: The Economics of Horses, Penguins and Lemmings," in L.G. Gabel (Ed), Production Standardization and Competitive Strategies (Amsterdam: North-Holland, 1987); David S. Evans, "The Antitrust Economics of Two-Sided Markets," Yale Journal on Regulation 20, no. 2 (2003): 325–81, https://doi.org/10.2139/ssrn.332022.

Kindle e-book reader.[4] Porting from a captive installed base of available users is one of the least expensive ways to build critical mass for a fledgling platform business.

Attract New Users (at least on one side): Some platforms are ground breaking in that they tend to create entirely new markets where none existed before. Users may not have experienced similar services in its traditional form either due to transaction frictions inherent in the old ways or due to access issues. The platform could provide new means of expression to its members and in turn make it desirable for the other sides to also come onboard to interact. When the video-sharing platform YouTube was launched, it was a disruptive new service for users who produced and consumed videos.[5] New users could come in the form of consumer groups, audiences who are targets for advertisers or even new suppliers who are coming onboard an e-commerce portal. When this new user group joins the portal or the product, a multi-sided platform is then born.

Target Marquee Users: Multiple platform firms that have emerged since the internet took wings have used marquee users or events as their rallying point to invoke network effects and attract new users onto the platform. Marquees come in different forms and sizes[6] as they could be important personalities such as rock stars or politicians, reputed entities such as the government or marquee brands that can pull users. A platform could target marquee events such as the Olympics or a presidential election. The online micro-blogging platform Twitter effectively used the 2008 US Presidential candidate Barack Obama's supporters to attract a large base of users to sign-up for its services.[7] It could also be a disruptive event such as sudden changes in politico-economic situation in the country such as the role of Facebook in the Tunisian revolution.[8] Endorsement by marquees is seen as testament to the fact that the platform affiliation is valuable to the audience. If a platform can provide exclusive access to the marquee, then users who seek to interact may even attach a premium to be on the same platform.

---

[4]Sarah Perez, "Amazon Invites Children's Book Authors To Kindle Direct Publishing, Rolls Out Kids' Book Creator Software | TechCrunch," 2014, https://techcrunch.com/2014/09/03/amazon-invites-childrens-book-authors-to-kindle-direct-publishing-rolls-out-kids-book-creator-software/.

[5]Karel Cool et al., YouTube, Google, and the Rise of Internet Video, 1 Kellogg School of Management Cases 1–25 (2017).

[6]Dave Centeno and Jeff Jianfeng Wang, "Celebrities as Human Brands: An Inquiry on Stakeholder-Actor Co-Creation of Brand Identities," Journal of Business Research 74 (May 1, 2017): 133–38, https://doi.org/10.1016/J.JBUSRES.2016.10.024.

[7]Aaron Smith, "The Internet's role in campaign 2008," Pew Research Center (Internet & Technology), https://pewreserch.org/internet/2009/04/15/the-internets-role-in-campaign-2008.

[8]Anita Breuer, Todd Landman, and Dorothea Farquhar, "Social Media and Protest Mobilization: Evidence from the Tunisian Revolution," Democratization 22, no. 4 (2015): 764–92, https://doi.org/10.1080/02614367.2016.1188137; Soumaya Ben Letaifa, Bo Edvardsson, and Bård Tronvoll, "The Role of Social Platforms in Transforming Service Ecosystems," Journal of Business Research 69, no. 5 (2016): 1933–38, https://doi.org/10.1016/j.jbusres.2015.10.083.

Resource Dimension

Firms traditionally leverage resources at their disposal to build sustainable businesses where possible, or develop new resources using their other capabilities. In business models with cross-side network effects, the source of firm resources is a critical dimension in staging its growth.[9] Which resources are leveraged (costs, control, and fungibility of resources) influences pricing models, direction of growth, and pace of network mobilization.

Leverage Existing Resources: Firms can leverage their current/existing resources in their offerings on the new platform so that users who value those resources will onboard. Resources held by a firm could include tangible resources such as capital-intensive machinery that gives it a manufacturing advantage, or intangible resources such as an established brand, a network of users, or routines/processes, that can be leveraged for the new platform. For instance, Uber could leverage its matching algorithm (matching drivers with riders) to expand its scope to Uber Freight.[10]

Develop New Resources: When a firm develops an entirely new resource in-house, it is aiming at solving a core technical issue or a market imperfection/ market failure. When a platform offers to solve issues in a better manner than ever before, it attracts customer groups away from other established offerings as they see the benefits of the new approach. For instance, Airbnb solved the market failure in the matching of demand and supply of hotel rooms.[11] Leveraging technology, Airbnb made available surplus rooms in homes to price-sensitive budget travelers.

Leverage Resources from the Ecosystem: A firm may not by itself own the necessary resources to directly build a critical mass of followers for its new platform but could leverage resources the firm has access to through partnerships with other firms or through complements. While complementary products are built by external firms using public interfaces exposed by the platform, firms have also launched new platforms by entering into joint ventures with partners. Instead of the firm having to do all the innovations, complements and partnerships help the platform address a broader problem domain. These have the potential to attract entirely new user groups who otherwise would not have considered the platform. When a gaming application is included as part of a social network, then the complementary product

[9]Michael A Cusumano and Annabelle Gawer, "The Elements of Platform Leadership," MIT Sloan Management Review 43, no. 3 (2002): 51–58.

[10]Darrell Etherington, "Uber Freight Launches to Connect Truck Drivers with Available Shipments | TechCrunch," TechCrunch, 2017, https://techcrunch.com/2017/05/18/uber-freight-launches-to-connect-truck-drivers-with-available-shipments/.

[11]Benoit et al., "A Triadic Framework for Collaborative Consumption (CC): Motives, Activities and Resources & Capabilities of Actors"; Barbara Hartl, Eva Hofmann, and Erich Kirchler, "Do We Need Rules for 'What's Mine Is Yours'? Governance in Collaborative Consumption Communities," Journal of Business Research 69, no. 8 (2016): 2756–63, https://doi.org/10.1016/j.jbusres.2015.11.011.

keeps existing users engaged. For instance, Zynga leveraged Facebook Application Programming Interfaces (APIs)[12] to launch a popular gaming platform, which in turn increased the appeal of Facebook.

Solving the Penguin Problem

Geoffrey Parker, Sangeet Paul Choudary, and Marshall W. Van Alstyne[13] have enumerated a list of strategies platform firms adopt to solve the penguin problem. The list includes (a) follow-the-rabbit strategy, (b) piggyback strategy, (c) seeding strategy, (d) marquee strategy, (e) single-side strategy, (f) producer evangelism strategy, (g) big bang adoption strategy and (h) the micro-market strategy. This chapter brings together the two dimensions (users and resources) to evolve a two-dimensional framework for solving the penguin problem (see Table 7.1).

Leverage existing resources to port users

Amazon leveraged its existing assets such as tablets, streaming devices and AWS compute infrastructure to bootstrap two platforms. Amazon Video Direct was launched in May 2016[14] as a video publishing platform competing with commercial YouTube videos in the user-generated video market wherein independent film makers could upload videos and leverage existing Amazon Prime viewership base. Here, Amazon customers were ported to the new video publishing platform as viewers and creators of videos. With advertisers already onboard the Amazon Prime ecosystem, Amazon Video Direct evolved into a three-sided platform with strong network effects. Kindle Direct Publishing platform followed a similar strategy to allow Amazon customers publish e-books and paperbacks free of cost to gain access to users on Kindle devices, Kindle apps and Amazon portal worldwide.[15]

To successfully port users to a new platform using existing resources, it is evident that the platform strategy needs to include consistency in portability of users with a strong focus on quality. Firms must ensure they maintain high switching costs to prevent user groups from migrating to rival platforms. Quality of existing services plays a vital role as users who are not happy with the existing product or service would not flock to a new offering by the same firm. It is critical for the firm to maintain consistency with respect to what it is offering as part of the new platform to which it is porting its users. For example, any attempt to port users

[12]Leena Rao, "Facebook And Zynga Enter Into Five Year Partnership, Expand Use Of Facebook Credits | TechCrunch," TechCrunch, 2010, https://techcrunch.com/2010/05/18/facebook-and-zynga-enter-into-five-year-partnership-expand-use-of-facebook-credits/.

[13]Geoffrey Parker, Sangeet Paul Choudary, and Marshall W. Van Alstyne, Platform Revolution, First Edit (New York: W. W. Norton & Company, 2016).

[14]Jason Guerrasio, "How Amazon Is Trying to Lure in Indie Filmmakers with a $100,000 Bonus | Business Insider India," Business Insider, 2017, http://www.businessinsider.in/How-Amazon-is-trying-to-lure-in-indie-filmmakers-with-a-100000-bonus/articleshow/56901436.cms.

[15]Perez, "Amazon Invites Children's Book Authors To Kindle Direct Publishing, Rolls Out Kids' Book Creator Software | TechCrunch".

Table 7.1 Network mobilization examples

		Where do users come from?		
		Port users (or all sides)	Attract users via marquees (marquee users/events/brands)	Attract new users (at least on one side)
Where do resources come from?	Leverage existing resources (from same firm)	Kindle Direct Publishing; Amazon Video Direct	Microsoft XBox	Uber EATS
	Leverage ecosystem resources (via partnerships/complements)	Alipay	Twitter	Salesforce AppExchange
	Develop new resources (in-house development)	Vodafone M-Pesa	Airbnb	YouTube

onboard a matrimonial site to a new dating platform launched by the same firm could have disastrous consequences. Users on the matrimonial site have different expectations from the platform as compared to what a casual dating user would expect.

If existing users value the brand they are associated with and trust the firm to provide similar or improved services with the new offering, then porting would have higher chances of success. This expectation helps firms leverage existing user base on one side and easily attract users onto the platform. Other user groups could then be enticed to participate on the same platform as they value transacting with the former user groups.

Leverage ecosystem resources to port users

Payment platforms such as Apple Pay, Android Pay and Alipay partnered with credit card firms such as Visa and MasterCard to leverage their banking expertise. Alipay, a third-party online payment platform launched in 2004 by the Alibaba group controlled a major share of online payments in China.[16] By 2004, Alibaba.com was already a growing B2B and B2C marketplace through its different entities and needed a robust payment platform that could handle financial transactions in-house. Alipay provided an escrow service for buyers on Alibaba.com, allowing them to verify the products received before releasing payments and helped Alibaba overcome buyer apprehensions arising out of relatively weak consumer protection laws in China. Alibaba ported its large install base of business entities, both buyers and sellers, from Alibaba.com to Alipay.

[16]Asim Shah, "Alipay Surpasses PayPal as Leading Mobile Payments Platform—Bobsguide. Com," bobsguide, 2014, http://www.bobsguide.com/guide/news/2014/Feb/12/alipay-surpasses-paypal-as-leading-mobile-payments-platform/; Ayoub Aouad, "Alipay Is Setting up for Global Dominance—Business Insider," Business Insider, 2017, http://www.businessinsider.com/alipay-is-setting-up-for-global-dominance-2017-5?IR=T.

Value co-creation and sharing is a critical aspect visible in an ecosystem approach. Multiple firms come together to pool resources to create a new offering that offers compelling value proposition to the user.[17] Firms with an open mindset to collaborate will be most successful in this setting. Platform firms must ensure that partners can leverage the complements across the entire ecosystem without the need to rebuild the complements all over again. Given that the platform firm wants to expand reach, it should focus its forward and backward integration approaches so that partner firm's assets can be leveraged to gather resources for the new platform. Firm should look for different ways in which it can develop complementary resources—acquisitions, joint ventures, and partnerships. Firms should also look for unique ways in which it can incentivize complementors better than their competitors. Ability of platforms to sustain price erosion and intense competition improves when rich partnerships and complements are available to enhance the value proposition of the base platform.

Develop new resources to port users

Consider the M-Pesa platform launched by Safaricom, a subsidiary of Vodafone, in Kenya and Tanzania in 2007 that enabled mobile phone-based branchless banking. It allowed users to deposit and withdraw money using secure SMS messages and using retail outlets (who charged a commission for every transaction) as banking nodes. M-Pesa had become the most successful mobile phone-based financial service providing access to financial system for millions in Africa by providing remittances, bill payments and micro-credit services.[18] Safaricom leveraged its mobile customer base to port both sides, the end users who want to transfer their money and retail merchants who work as banking nodes, on to the banking platform.

Most platform firms focus on solving core problems, either technological or process related, that helps reduce transaction frictions. Not sacrificing on quality is critical as users will expect the firm to provide a high-quality experience when it addresses existing pain points. Identifying adjacencies where the firm can extend its offerings is an important strategic decision. Firms must ensure that the new resources being developed are closely related to the user base that it is looking to port. Straying too far away in terms of the type of new resources developed would lead to lesser effectiveness in porting the existing users onto the new platform.

Leverage existing resources to attract users via marquees

Microsoft leveraged its dominant position and expertise in building computer operating systems to enter the gaming consoles market with Xbox. It acquired the reputed game developer Bungie and released the much anticipated marquee game

[17]Adner and Kapoor, "Value Creation in Innovation Ecosystems: How the Structure of Technological Interdependence Affects Firm Performance in New Technology Generations".
[18]Daniel Runde, "M-Pesa And The Rise Of The Global Mobile Money Market," Forbes, August 2015, https://www.forbes.com/sites/danielrunde/2015/08/12/m-pesa-and-the-rise-of-the-global-mobile-money-market/#350dc98c5aec.

titled "Halo" just in time for the 2001 launch of Xbox.[19] Halo became a first-person shooter game developed exclusively for Xbox that sold millions of copies and helped bootstrap Xbox's games portfolio. As gaming enthusiasts on boarded the Xbox platform, it attracted even more game developers to build new games or port existing ones onto Xbox.

Firms targeting a marquee user or event need to ensure that there is a possibility to maintain sustained engagement with the users through the marquee personality. If it is a onetime act, then the firm will struggle to retain the users who came in due to the marquee customer. In the case of a rock star, users should be able to expect frequent interactions which will keep the teenagers engaged on the platform. Similarly, if the government can use a trading platform for all its ongoing procurements, then it will attract more vendors to participate and engage. If it is a marquee brand, then users would expect to see new releases from the brand to stay engaged on the platform with the brand. Firms must look for crowd pullers who can attract new users onto the platform. Through sustained marketing efforts, the firm must onboard key personalities or opinion leaders whose usage of the platform will send the right message to the other side of users.

Leverage ecosystem resources to attract users via marquees

Launched in 2006, Twitter received first big public exposure during the marquee digital media conference SXSW in March 2007. However, the stage was set for rapid growth of Twitter when it opened up its APIs right at its public launch in August 2006. The ability for complements to build useful near real-time apps using APIs helped the small team at Twitter achieve broader acceptance and address newer outcomes as compared to what the firm itself had envisioned. Marquee users greatly assisted Twitter in keeping up the growth momentum when President Obama[20] used Twitter during the 2008 election campaign. Twitter's decision to embrace open architecture enabled its growth as a robust communication platform with a thriving ecosystem where popular apps such as Twhirl, TweekDeck and Twitterific[21] have helped bring more users.

Along with an early decision to open access, the platform firm needs to time the launch so that it has the desired impact of attracting the users when they are most primed for the service. If targeting a timed event (such as the Olympic games) for the launch of a platform service, the firm must right size the feature set, its degree of openness and the timing of the availability of the preview to its partners so that they too receive an opportunity to develop the right extensions. Complements or partners in the ecosystem can help onboard users even during subsequent growth phases for the platform as they bring in the possibility of new value to the different sides due to

[19]Rick Marshall, "The History of the Xbox | Digital Trends," Digital Trends, 2013, https://www.digitaltrends.com/gaming/the-history-of-the-xbox/.

[20]Chris Hughes et al., "Obama and the Power of Social Media and Technology," The European Business Review, no. June (2010): 16–21.

[21]Sarah Milstein et al., "Twitter and the Micro-Messaging Revolution: Communication, Connections, and Immediacy-140 Characters at a Time," O'Reilly Radar, 2008.

the extensions they develop to the core perceived value of the platform when it started out.

A marquee user ascertains the quality dimensions of the platform by its ability to help target the exact intended audience,[22] number of returning users, and degree of engagement that the users would get into. Marquee users themselves would not choose a platform that does not help them connect with the right kind of users they wish to be associated with.

Develop new resources to attract users via marquees

Airbnb founders capitalized on a popular design conference in San Francisco to launch their venture. When the founders rented their own apartment and found that they could sell beds, they realized a great business idea fuelled by shortage and high prices of hotel rooms during peak demand. Airbnb built a new platform which inspired home owners to list and travelers to book easily.[23] Airbnb hired professional photographers to post high-quality pictures to help customers make stay decisions easily and set the quality standard for future postings across the globe.

Timing it right is critical for firms that look to leverage marquees while developing new assets. Firms need to be opportunistic to recognize the unserved need of the target customer base and move quickly to address core issues. When the timing is right, the impact of the solution offered by the platform is more profound and could help the platform go viral given the strong network effects. After the marquee event, it is crucial for the firm to ensure strategies to maintain sustained engagement of all parties on the platform.

Leverage existing resources to attract new users

Uber used taxi drivers on the platform to launch new platforms looking for sectors ripe for disruption. Uber Eats emerged as an online meal ordering and delivery platform that partnered with restaurants in over 90 cities around the world to deliver an integrated experience to the user. Uber Eats evolved into a three-sided platform with restaurants, customers, and drivers as its different sides. While Uber started out building the network of drivers and commuters as part of its taxi hailing service, Uber Eats leveraged these same drivers on the new platform to diversify into food delivering business, leveraging its existing matching infrastructure while attracting a new user group: restaurants.[24] Similarly, Uber Freight allowed truck drivers to collaborate with businesses looking for logistics help without need for prolonged negotiations.[25]

---

[22]Hughes et al., "Obama and the Power of Social Media and Technology".

[23]Leigh Gallagher, The Airbnb Story, First Edit (Boston: Houghton Mifflin Harcourt, 2017).

[24]Davey Alba, "Uber Just Launched Its Food Delivery Uber Eats App in First US Cities | WIRED," Wired, March 2016, https://www.wired.com/2016/03/ubereats-standalone-app-launches-us/.

[25]Etherington, "Uber Freight Launches to Connect Truck Drivers with Available Shipments | TechCrunch".

Once a firm has substantial user base through other services or holds other critical assets such as an established supply chain, distribution network, patents or regulatory approvals, it could approach the challenge of attracting new users onto a new platform offering by just subsidizing users to onboard. When the platform subsidizes one side to onboard the platform, it can expect other interested sides would in fact pay to participate on the platform to transact. When taxi hailing platform Uber was launched in new cities, it subsidized the taxi drivers to onboard the platform first so that ride seekers can find a taxi easily at any point of time.[26] Firms should leverage brand image and the core product offerings to attract new users who would want access to existing firm resources. Innovation to solve core issues is critical in this segment where firms of any size can flourish.

Leverage ecosystem resources to attract new users

Salesforce AppExchange was a cloud computing marketplace where partners leveraged the open architecture of Salesforce to build plugins. On the one side, the partners developed plugins and extensions using APIs that extended the Salesforce CRM for the enterprises (the other side of the AppExchange platform). Salesforce attracted new enterprises on to its platform due to the rich variety of extensions available.[27] It also attracted developers to customize Salesforce and leverage the new extensions to reduce the implementation effort.

With the success of the core offerings in the case of firms like Salesforce and Apple, these firms have explored newer ways of increasing demand for their core products and services. Firms have leveraged their existing products and extended their capabilities either through open interfaces or through partnerships. With the deep investments that these firms are capable of, there is significant value co-creation that they can do in order to attract partners who wish to get a small pie of the large market that the platform firm is attempting to build. Having open architecture as the strategy cornerstone along with willingness to build on partnerships is important when firms are trying to build new platforms on the strength of complements. When partners are enabled to extend platform functionalities, they get empowered to create new value propositions for the entire ecosystem.

Develop new resources to attract new users

YouTube was a three-sided platform serving content creators, viewers, and advertisers. Viewers gained access to quality content in different genres for free; producers gained easy access to a wider audience; and advertisers acquired the targeted audience.[28] YouTube solved the penguin problem in its early days by attracting content creators on to its platform through a sustained marketing

[26] Adam Lashinsky, Wild Ride: Inside Uber's Quest for World Domination, First Edit (New York: Portfolio, 2017).

[27] Natalie Gagliordi, "Salesforce Launches AppExchange Partner Program, New $100 Million Platform Fund," ZDNet, 2017, http://www.zdnet.com/article/salesforce-launches-appexchange-partner-program-new-100-million-platform-fund/.

[28] Paul A Soukup, "Looking at, with, and through YouTubeTM," Communication Research Trends 33, no. 3 (2014): 3–35.

campaign and by providing better video tools. The recommendation engine also ensured new videos were recommended every time a viewer came back to the portal. Ability to view videos using a Flash plugin which was widely deployed across PC systems coupled with the ability to embed videos on other sites encouraged viewers to prefer YouTube as it solved key technical issues that were stopping mass adoption of video sharing. YouTube also invested heavily in hosting and streaming infrastructure to ensure seamless viewing experience.

To attract new users through the new assets that the firm has developed, the firm should make sure that it is indeed solving an existential problem such that an entirely new user base is attracted by the innovative solution the firm offers. Firms could start with a focus on specific segment before diversifying the solution into others. The firm must try to develop unique and compelling features as part of the new offering on the platform such that it is hard to imitate and attracts users. This will help give confidence to the new users who are onboarding the platform that the firm is serious about addressing the issue at hand and has the deep expertise to address the same.

A summary of the strategy recommendations for the different user attraction and resource leverage strategies conditions is shown in Table 7.2.

User Attraction Strategies

It can be seen that firms that tend to port users have deep pockets and are capable of investing heavily in the new platform due to sustained cash flows from their existing businesses. They typically have a sizeable loyal user base that allowed the firm to provide additional services to the same customers. These users would have high switching costs as they were deeply invested in the services offered. Net cost of acquiring new customers was near zero and they would be set up to transact on the platform instantly due to their prior engagement with the firm.

Platform firms that leverage marquees were aiming to solve customer issues that were yet unaddressed. Easing customer experiences through frictionless transaction on the platform seemed to be the aim. These end-user issues could be sudden needs that arise from changes in the marketplace or long-standing ones that have remained unaddressed. In the case of marquee events, the events could be either well-planned or could occur with no prior notice. In the case of GST tax reforms in India, it was a well-planned tax reform event wherein platform firms had the opportunity to onboard retail businesses on to the new tax regime.[29] In the case of demonetization of high currency notes in India in November 2016,[30] the financial platform firms had no prior notice of the marquee event and had to quickly repurpose assets to

[29]Karan Choudhury, "The Rs 35,000-Cr Business of Making India GST-Ready," Business Standard, June 12, 2017, http://www.business-standard.com/article/economy-policy/the-rs-35-000-cr-business-of-making-india-gst-ready-117061100607_1.html.

[30]Ravi Prakash Kumar, "Rs 500 and Rs 1000: What Is Demonetisation and Why Was It Done," The Economic Times, November 9, 2016, http://economictimes.indiatimes.com/news/economy/policy/what-is-demonetisation-and-why-was-it-done/articleshow/55326862.cms.

Table 7.2 Network mobilization strategies

Where do resources come from?	Where do users come from?				
		Port users (on all sides)	Attract users via marquees (marquee users/events/brands)	Attract new users (at least on one side)	
	Leverage existing resources (from same firm)	Consistency in portability Quality focus Resource relevance	Time it right Find crowd pullers	Just subsidize Leverage brand Innovate	**Strong presence** **Market leaders** **Translate quality to brand**
	Leverage ecosystem resources (via partnerships/complements)	Ecosystem play Vertical integration Incentivize complementors	Open architecture Leverage partnerships	Open architecture Leverage partnerships Ecosystem play	**Extending/re-application of resources** **Value co-creation** **Vertical integration**
	Develop new resources (in-house development)	Solve core problems Identify adjacencies	Build communities and sustain engagement	Solve core problems Start with specific segment	**Opportunistic entry/diversification** **Easing of discovery, matching and transaction costs**
		Have large, loyal user base **Deep pockets** **High switching costs**	**Users with unserved needs** **Easing user experiences**	**Big marketing spends** **Big brands**	**Observations from sample firms ↑** **←**

leverage the spike in digital transactions. In case of natural calamities that throw up business opportunities, there is again hardly any time to prepare as witnessed in the surge in usage of ride sharing apps such as BlaBlaCar due to the volcanic eruptions in Iceland in 2010 that disrupted air traffic in continental Europe.

Successful firms that have built new platforms by attracting new users had big marketing spends or were well-funded. These were big brands that users easily recognized and would want to be part of a new platform launched by these firms. With the success of their core products, these firms explored other ways of further increasing demand for their core products and services. For instance, in the Amazon Web Services (AWS) marketplace, the core offering from AWS prompted a variety of ISVs to participate in the migration to cloud computing.

Resource Leverage Strategies

Firms that have leveraged existing in-house resources to launch new platforms had strong market presence. Be it Amazon, Microsoft, or Uber, these firms were market leaders in their categories. These firms had access to critical resources such as key patents or technology that made it easy for them to launch new platforms centered on these resources. These firms were also able to transfer quality of their core assets onto the new platform which helped onboard users. Without proven quality of the core assets, no user group would be willing to onboard the new platforms that are launched by these established entities.

Firms that launched new platforms by leveraging partnerships or complementary assets were extending the utility of their own products through open interfaces or have leveraged partnerships well. Firms such as Facebook and Twitter invested in value co-creation that allowed the platform to be extended in a variety of ways. These firms also focused on fulfilling user needs through forward or backward integration by leveraging related assets from their own portfolio or by leveraging assets of partner firms. Complements and partnerships helped these platforms in extending the platform value in unintended ways leading to new competitive advantages. Platforms that offered a rich set of complements were also perceived to be superior in quality[31] to ones which either did not have open interfaces or where the sponsor wishes to build all the functionalities in-house. Even competition among complement providers enriched the platform as it expanded the appeal to diverse user groups. The number of complements available on the platform was perceived as a sign of quality of the platform that attracted even more complements and users. As the platform sponsor of iOS App Store, Apple has always reserved the right to verify and exclude any third-party applications that do not meet the

[31]Carmelo Cennamo and Juan Santaló, "Value Creation and Free-Riding in Platform Markets: The Asymmetric Impact of Competition on Quality across the Platform Life Cycle," 2015, https://ssrn.com/abstract=2662407.

strict quality standards. This has helped Apple maintain an edge over other app stores with better quality control over what is available for download.[32]

Firms that developed new assets before launching their platforms leveraged the opportunity for early entry into a new segment. Some firms diversified into new businesses by developing new assets that would allow them an opportunity to generate additional revenue streams. In the case of M-Pesa, it was an opportunistic entry into a new market of mobile payments. M-Pesa captured significant additional value for the parent firm due to its significant reach across countries.

Summary

As can be seen, there are numerous strategies that platforms adopt for network mobilization. Choosing the right strategy has implications for sustenance and growth of platforms, in terms of both user acquisition and revenue growth. Pricing and subsidies play a significant part of network mobilization, but as discussed in this chapter, there is more to network mobilization than just subsidies.

[32]Kevin J Boudreau and Andrei Hagiu, "Platform Rules: Multi-Sided Platforms as Regulators.," Platforms, Markets and Innoation, 2009, 163–91, https://doi.org/10.2139/ssrn.1269966.

BharatMatrimony.com

8

A hot and humid day in Chennai, India was not new in the month of March. However, Friday, March 29, 2013 was a very pleasant day with early evening showers and a gentle sea breeze. Inside his office facing the Bay of Bengal, Murugavel Janakiraman (Muruga) had little time to enjoy the small pleasantries that the Chennai weather had to offer. The financial year was ending through the weekend, and he had to answer a few questions to himself before he met the company's top management team and investors. First on his mind was the extent of diversification of the group—had they diversified enough, or were their opportunities in the form of markets waiting for the BharatMatrimony.com type of platforms to transform them? What learning can BharatMatrimony.com consolidate and leverage across these markets? As he pondered, he was sure that his investors would support him in his efforts to develop the enterprise, chase new opportunities, and leverage the learning. However, he had to be absolutely sure of it himself.

Matrimony in India

Matrimony among Indians has been a huge market. Given the extent of diversity in the cultures, religion, languages, and even food habits, matchmaking has been serious business. It was believed that, unlike in most other cultures, matrimony is a marriage between two families, rather than two individuals. Most sons continued to live with

This case is an extension of Chapter 7 Network Mobilization.
R Srinivasan, Professor of Strategy and Menaka Rao, prepared this case for class discussion. This case is not intended to serve as an endorsement, source of primary data, or to show effective or inefficient handling of decision or business processes.

R. Srinivasan, *Platform Business Models*, Management for Professionals,
https://doi.org/10.1007/978-981-16-2838-2_8

their parents under a single roof even after their marriage and they raised their own children in traditional joint families. Even when job and professional commitments forced them to leave the city, parents who were retired or did not have serious commitments back home, moved in with their sons. Such joint families often acted as economic and social support systems. Apart from parents, siblings also shared the "family home." Matchmaking in this social context had its special challenges. Yes, people do fall in love with each other, and it is imperative that they take the consent and support of both their families before getting married. This is especially critical when they belong to different religions, castes, or even different states.

The traditional form of matchmaking was popularly known as "arranged" marriages. The responsibility of finding a bride/groom rested with the parents. Parents, with the help of their social networks, would tap into information about available brides and grooms, circulate the profile of their own sons/daughters in the "market" (among family friends/astrologers/priests), and seek out matches. Once a potential match was found, one of the parents would establish contact with the family, then arrange for the groom and bride to meet, and make a decision. Akin to the professional employment market, the criteria for choice making could be sometimes extremely complex, sometimes including criteria such as professional compatibility (a doctor would like to marry another doctor—"only he/she would understand my professional commitments"), caste (food and social habits are largely caste-driven), and even physical characteristics such as fairness, height, and obesity.

With social change inducing the evolution of nuclear families, the close relationship parents shared with their grown-up children underwent a transformation. With urban migration, the social and religious networks had shrunk considerably too. These shifts paved the way for professional matchmakers or "marriage brokers" who would sometimes organize themselves as a "matrimonial bureau." These professionals and organizations acted as agents, bringing families together through face-to-face meetings. Also popular were the matrimonial classified advertisements in newspapers and magazines. However, such searches were severely constrained by the geographies or niches they covered. For instance, a Tamilian family living in Delhi or Mumbai would not be able to access profiles as easily as those in Tamil Nadu nor would they be sure of finding a match among the limited profiles with these brokers or bureaus. Online matrimony provided a great opportunity to overcome these constraints. Online matrimonial sites in India were the 13th most popular mainstream online activity and in 2013, with over 12 million people using online matrimony searches in the online matchmaking market, were estimated to be over Rs. 3 billion.

Evolution of BharatMatrimony.com

Matrimony.com (formerly Consim Info, an acronym for consumer services through internet and mobile) owned a string of matrimony-related consumer internet properties, including BharatMatrimony.com. Consim Info was founded by Murugavel Janakiraman in 1997 and was an early mover in the internet matrimony space. Muruga, a graduate in Statistics, completed his Masters in Computer Applications

(MCA) from the University of Madras and worked for a year in India. Attracted by overseas opportunities, he moved to Singapore in 1994 and then to New Jersey, USA, in 1996. Working as a consultant for leading companies on software projects, he was fascinated by the power of the internet and began exploring what Netscape and related software had to offer. He realized that internet, which was at that time dominated by B2B applications, would be a great enabler in the B2C markets as well. Even though he was not sure of how to monetize the "eyeballs" that landed on a site, he was convinced that if ever there was a focused community site, it would surely attract many visitors. Hailing from Tamil Nadu, with his affinity to the Tamil language, he began a portal targeted at the Tamil-speaking community. He differentiated his offerings from other content-based portals, by establishing a service-based portal. One of the services that this portal offered was matrimony. Started on an auspicious day, April 14, 1997 (being the Tamil New Year), the matrimony section on his portal became very popular among the expatriate Tamil community. By 1999, when he saw that the matrimony section was attracting the most traffic, he decided to focus on matrimony as the flagship service of his portal, and gradually weaned away from other services. He established an exclusive matrimony website, and the first seeds of BharatMatrimony.com were sown.

Initially, it was a one-man show. Muruga was the designer, developer, and service support, operating part-time from home along with his day job. He initially created two channels in the website for Tamil and Telugu matrimony services. As the site continued to grow in popularity, he added other communities but had no clue of how to promote them. His initial venture was focused on the Tamil-speaking community, and that user base became the seed for his matrimony services. However, with other communities, he did not know how to market the site. He would leave flyers at grocery stores, send emails to friends and relatives, and promote his site at festival celebrations.

By the time the dotcom bubble burst, many things had changed. Muruga had lost his day job; the matrimony services had grown considerably to 15 micro-sites under the umbrella brand of BharatMatrimony.com; and much traffic to the site was flowing in from India (not just expats in the USA and Europe). He decided to relocate to India and began operating from a small office in Chennai. In the Indian market, there were a few competitors: SYS India offered internet matrimony listings; online portals such as sify.com, rediff.com, and MSN India launched their own matrimony channels. BharatMatrimony.com tied up with sify.com and merged the matrimony database listings. MSN India used BharatMatrimony.com to build its micro-site. The market continued to grow and remained profitable, in spite of the dotcom bust. For a customer, it would cost Rs. 300[1] to register on the BharatMatrimony.com site for a three-month period. The number of customers rose exponentially, with increased internet penetration and greater mobility of brides/grooms across India.

The period 2002–03 was a watershed year for Muruga and BharatMatrimony.com. BharatMatrimony.com had become a very strong brand, as it was perceived as a service that was effective in preserving the traditional essence and sanctity of the

[1]Rs. represents Indian Rupees; As on June 30, 2013, I US$ = Rs. 59.53.

Indian marriage ecosystem, albeit using modern technology. Leveraging on the success and popularity, Muruga decided to expand geographically into other Indian cities from Chennai, where it was first located. They moved to a bigger office as well as began setting up offices in other cities to establish local, on-the-street presence. Some of these offices were very small. Muruga reminisced:

> I remember our office in Hyderabad. It was a garage with 200 sq. feet of space. You open the shutter, there was a curtain and that was our office. The small office at that time served our purpose as it was just to mark our presence in the city, act as a collection center, and provide a local contact (phone) number for people to get in touch.

From Hyderabad, they moved to Mumbai and Delhi, and other major metros, outside their stronghold of South India. These small offices were used to collect money from its customers but did not provide any other service. By 2004–05, Muruga reversed his customer acquisition strategy: instead of customers approaching the firm for services through the internet and these offices, BharatMatrimony.com would reach out to potential customers through these offices. These local offices organized events and fairs, tele-marketed their services, and became the face of the company to the internet-wary older generation, namely the parents. They expanded their service offerings as well, to include services such as verification and references. BharatMatrimony.com became the first mover in ensuring that profiles were validated. Registered users had to provide their mobile numbers on the website. Muruga remarked:

> When you marry someone, you come to our site and give so much of your personal information, it is not only the most important decision of your life but for us to get that kind of information, we need to be the most trusted site. And that's why we talk of validation and pushed all our efforts on the "trust" factor. And though we had to give up a couple of lakhs[2] of profiles on a small issue like not having their mobile number on the profile, our focus and guarantee was on safety and security on our site.

Riding on the visibility gained from the online matrimonial services, events such as Swayamvara[3] and specific community meets were held with several people attending them. Services such as voice matrimony and video matrimony were soon introduced to increase the popularity of the site and make it more robust. First among many other firsts, through voice/video matrimony, one could call and leave an audio/video message for the opposite person. To avail of the voice/video service, users had to pay Rs. 6 initially, but later a message could be recorded free of cost. They also started an SMS service (short code 5050) by tying up with a few service providers; however, they soon abandoned it as it proved to be very cumbersome to customize.

---

[2] 1 lakh = 100,000 or hundred thousands.

[3] Swayamvara was a traditional Indian practice of choosing a husband, from among a lineup of suitors, by a girl of marriageable age. *Swayam* in Sanskrit means self and *vara* means choice or desire (it is also synonymous with bridegroom).

Diversification

Muruga believed that BharatMatrimony.com had helped them perfect the core of the platform architecture to connect customers at two ends of the platform. In 2005, he decided to extend the business model to other verticals such as employment (clickjobs.com), automobiles (indiaautomobiles.com), yellow pages (indiapages.-com), loans and advances (indialoanwala.com), property and real estate (indiaproperty.com). The performance of these portals was varied and they suffered significant losses, pushing the company to recapitalize through venture capital funds. Reflecting on those days, Muruga said:

> I didn't have a lot of expertise those days and though we were making Rs. 14 to 15 crores[4] per annum, the valuation of the organization did not work out and all the VCs we approached were not convinced of our business model and felt we were not worth funding. We literally had nowhere to turn at that time but thankfully it happened.

In 2006, BharatMatrimony.com raised its first round of funding, followed by a second round of funding in 2008. As the global economic meltdown loomed large, Muruga took a hard look at his businesses. Matrimony was their core business and remained their cash generator. Although platforms such as clickjobs.com were built on unique business models (under clickjobs.com, passive job seekers would get paid every time a potential employer accessed their profile), they had to be sold for want of adequate leadership attention and funding. He remarked:

> This was the most challenging period in my entire entrepreneurial journey. I had to let go of 300–400 people and had to forego on a lot of things and for the first time I looked at each and every aspect of the business and thought deeply on how to make it profitable – we were bleeding about Rs. 4–5 crores a year.

The loss was huge and crippling. Muruga then decided to close or sell some verticals and concentrate on two core verticals—matrimony and indiaproperty.com. The impact of the focus was a remarkable turnaround within a short period of 4–5 months. By then, the company had increased to a total of 15 matrimonial websites under BharatMatrimony.com and over 300 websites under Community Matrimony. The organization had transformed from a one-man venture 15 years ago to a professionally run company with over 4000 employees and 20 million registered members (on the matrimony site). BharatMatrimony had also gained an entry into the *Limca Book of Records* for facilitating a record number of marriages. By 2013, BharatMatrimony.com was considering an IPO to raise more money and fuel its growth plans.[5]

---

[4]1 crore = 100 lakhs = 10 million = 10,000,000.

[5]Sharma Samidha & Kurian Boby, Bharat Matrimony plans $125 m IPO this year, *The Times of India*, January 23, 2013.

Platform Architecture

BharatMatrimony.com was an umbrella brand, under which there were multiple micro-sites on specific verticals (such as tamilmatrimony.com and sindhimatrimony.com). There were over 15 such language-based portals. Later, he launched CommunityMatrimony.com, a conglomerate of 300 such community-oriented portals under the Matrimony.com banner. Apart from these community portals, the customers were also segmented on the bases of their service needs. For instance, Elite Matrimony focused on the higher income customers and celebrities; Assisted Matrimony provided customers with a dedicated relationship manager who acted as a concierge; Popular Matrimony focused on the lowest rung of the economic spectrum; and Defense Matrimony served the exclusive needs of armed forces personnel.

To create a profile on BharatMatrimony.com (with automatic classification into any of the micro-sites), a customer had to register on the website and provide all her/his details. Going by the Indian tradition of the family assisting in the matrimony process, the site allowed parents or siblings to register on behalf of the bride/groom. In order to verify the authenticity of details posted on the profile, BharatMatrimony.com conducted verification checks of the mobile numbers attached to the registered profiles. There were two categories of listing—free listing and paid listing. Registered users could search for profiles on the website, but to be able to view the contact details of the other side, one had to be a paid member. Membership fees for basic registration was Rs. 3290 for a three-month subscription (it had grown 10% every year from the earlier Rs. 300); Rs. 19,000 for Assisted Matrimony, and Rs. 50,000 for Elite Matrimony.

Apart from registering/searching on the website, customers could also interact at the retail outlets. BharatMatrimony.com had established over 180 company-owned retail outlets across the country. These brick-and-mortar centers attracted parents from the older generation, who did not have good access or were not comfortable using technology to engage with the site. At these centers, customers could update their profiles (such as having their picture taken and uploaded on the site), browse through profiles, shortlist/select and print a few profiles for offline sharing with others, and even seek counseling services. Muruga remarked:

> Although the Internet is growing fast, there are limitations in the number of users. A combination of both online and offline centers helps us go beyond the 35 million Internet users in India, making offline a profitable business opportunity.

In order to use the offline services at the retail centers, customers were charged Rs. 1250 for a three-month subscription, and Rs. 5800 for a nine-month subscription. Muruga said:

> The local promotions help us not just in increasing brand visibility, but also in building a strong brand identity.

Marriage-Related Services

With a strong foothold in the matrimony market space, BharatMatrimony.com diversified into the wedding gifts and return gifts market too. The online gifting market in India was estimated at over Rs. 1000 crores and was growing rapidly. MatrimonyGifts.com aggregated and retailed gifts to be provided to the bride and the groom, whereas Tambulya provided the bride/groom with options for choosing the return gifts to those who attend the wedding. Other wedding-related services such as venues, decorations, catering, photography services, event management services, and even honeymoon planning were aggregated under the portal MatrimonyDirectory.com.

IndiaProperty.com

One of the two verticals that survived the rationalization of diversification was the property and real estate business, under the brand name of IndiaProperty.com. The Indian real estate market was valued at over US$12 billion and was witnessing an annual growth rate of about 30% in 2013. Property buying in India was traditionally controlled by a network of entrenched real estate agents, who with their opportunistic behavior had created a market akin to the "market for lemons." Property developers and builders had limited marketing expertise to reach the masses and they had to depend on these agents for reaching out to customers. Given that a typical customer bought one or at most two properties in the same geography in her/his lifetime, these property brokers had distorted the market with artificial prices by creating opacity in demand and supply.

IndiaProperty.com provided builders, developers, and property owners (sellers) a platform to connect directly with agents, corporates and individuals (buyers), and IndiaProperty.com was positioned to attract end customers (individual and corporate property buyers). Leveraging on the backend technology that drove BharatMatrimony.com, IndiaProperty.com also provided end-to-end solutions from "search" to "completion of transaction" on the platform. As of 2013, the site listed over 20,000 unique properties classified into 20 different types under five broad categories. The site had unique features such as the ability to list multiple properties by the same seller, uploading of floor plans and approvals, and the ability to complete the entire transaction on the platform. Similar to AssistedMatrimony.com (with an engagement manager) and *Swayamvara* (marriage fairs), IndiaProperty.com introduced AssistedProperty.com and *Gruhapravesha* (property fairs).

Way Forward

As the financial year 2013 came to an end, Muruga was wondering about his next steps to fuel the growth of this enterprise. From a reluctant start in 1997 as part of a larger services portal, BharatMatrimony.com had come a full circle to become the flagship brand in a larger portfolio of services. With global aspirations, the company had sought out and acquired the domain name Matrimony.com. The platform business model connecting two groups of customers had succeeded in matrimony and property, but had failed (or had met with limited success) in other services such as loan aggregation, employment, and even automobiles. As he prepared for the year-end presentation to his investors and top management team, he reflected on the lessons that the organization had learnt and its future growth opportunities.

Just Dial Limited

9

Just Dial Limited (Just Dial) was the leading local search engine in India, offering search services to users across multiple platforms such as the internet, mobile interne, over the telephone (voice), and text (SMS).[1] Just Dial's search service connected users (consumers) and local businesses (mostly small and medium-sized businesses), helping the users find relevant providers of products and services quickly and helping businesses market their offerings to the right consumers.[2] Just Dial had also introduced in 2013–14,[3] a new service labeled "JD Search Plus" that extended search/listing services to enable transactions in over 17 categories.[4] In May 2015, Just Dial expanded its offerings by entering the product e-commerce

[1]Source: Company website, available on the internet at http://cms.justdial.com/overview, last accessed on June 12, 2015.
[2]Source: Company website, available on the internet at http://cms.justdial.com/overview, last accessed on June 12, 2015.
[3]Source: Company annual report, 2012–13, available on the internet at http://images.jdmagicbox.com/investors/Justdial-Annual-Report-130905075453.pdf, last accessed on June 12, 2015.
[4]Source: Company website, available on the internet at http://www.justdial.com/JD-On-Mobile, last accessed on June 12, 2015.

This case is an extension of Chapter 7 Network Mobilization.
R Srinivasan, Professor of Strategy and Menaka Rao, prepared this case for class discussion. This case is not intended to serve as an endorsement, source of primary data, or to show effective or inefficient handling of decision or business processes.

R. Srinivasan, *Platform Business Models*, Management for Professionals,
https://doi.org/10.1007/978-981-16-2838-2_9

marketplace.[5] Given the "local" advantage that Just Dial enjoyed, it would be interesting to see how Just Dial would perform in comparison with other national e-commerce firms such as Flipkart (www.flipkart.com), Amazon (www.amazon.in), and Snapdeal (www.snapdeal.com), as well as a variety of regional marketplaces such as deals in Chennai (www.dealsinchennai.com).

Evolution of Just Dial

Just Dial Limited (Just Dial) was founded in 1996 as A&M Communications Pvt. Ltd. in a frugal office in Mumbai. The small office space, including furniture and computers were rented to keep their costs low.[6] The company began offering local search solutions through voice-based solutions in Mumbai with the telephone number 022-8888888.[7] In the early days of business, the company did not advertise, but focused on the phone number and the brand name—the "7 times 8" number and the Just Dial brand name.[8] The "Just Dial" brand name was registered in 1997, and in 2006, the company name was changed to Just Dial Pvt. Limited. The initial operations were focused on putting together a sizeable database of businesses in Mumbai (where they began) by literally going door-to-door and asking their clients and their employees to use their services. The company launched their internet-based services through their website www.justdial.com as late as 2007, even though they owned the domain name since the brand registration.[9] The founder VSS Mani was so skeptical about the growth of the internet that he refused to join the dotcom boom during 1999–2000. He did sell some part of his personal equity to an American company that wanted to start the internet version of Just

[5]Source: Paul, Binu, Just Dial integrates ecommerce marketplace with its local business listings platform, *VCCircle Newsletter* (May 18, 2015), available on the internet at http://www.vccircle.com/news/technology/2015/05/18/just-dial-integrates-e-commerce-marketplace-its-local-business-listings, last accessed on June 12, 2015.

[6]Source: Anon. Just Dial Story in Founder Mani's words, YourStory (June 13, 2011), available on the Internet at http://yourstory.com/2011/06/justdial-story-in-founder-manis-words/, last accessed on June 12, 2015; and Chidambaram Varsha, Speed Dial for Growth—CEO Interview, CIO.IN (June 5, 2012). http://www.cio.in/ceo-interviews/it-has-helped-just-dial-turnaround-dynamic-business-needs-considerably-short-spans-ti last accessed on June 12, 2015.

[7]Source: Just Dial Annual Report, 2012–13 page 8. Available on the Internet at http://images.jdmagicbox.com/investors/Justdial-Annual-Report-130905075453.pdf last accessed on June 12, 2015.

[8]Source: Dharamsi Khyati, How Just Dial founder VSS Mani founded the 'Indian Google', MoneyControl SME StepUp, (November 22, 2012), available on the Internet at http://www.moneycontrol.com/sme-stepup/news/how_justdial_founder_vss_mani_built_the_indian_google-786199.html, last accessed on June 12, 2015.

[9]Source: Gokahley, Madhavi, VSS Mani: Dial a dream, *The Smart Manager*, September–October 2010, available on the internet at http://www.thesmartmanager.com/file/071010260601_TheSmartManager,smart_talk-VSS_Mani,_Sep-Oct-10.pdf, last accessed on June 12, 2015.

Dial, only to make a few million dollars for himself and see the venture fail.[10] Throughout the first 10 years of the company's founding, Just Dial focused on building its telephone-based services and therefore built a strong brand name that leveraged the power of "local" in search. Leveraging on the growth of mobile penetration in India, Just Dial launched its text (SMS-based) services in 2004 and an app for smartphones in 2011.[11]

Through 2006–12, the company attracted venture capital investments from a list of reputed global investors and went public with an initial public offering (IPO) in 2013.

As on March 31, 2014, Just Dial had attracted 1125 million searches and 31 million ratings from its consumers, leveraging a database of 11.8 million business listings and 262,150 paid campaigns.[12]

The (Traditional) Just Dial Business Model

Just Dial operated a discovery platform that connected consumers with local businesses. Inherently, this was different from the traditional broad search offered by search engines such as Google in two ways. First, Google with its search algorithm would focus on providing a broader range of results around the search criteria. Further, this difference arose out of Just Dial's local presence, with its foot soldiers who combed the market and updated the details of businesses; a majority of them not even present online, with accurate and updated phone numbers and contact details. The second difference between Just Dial and a search engine, such as Google, was the ability of Just Dial to match the precise location of the search consumer and "local" businesses. Although Google and other search engines were working toward more and more localization, Just Dial continued its dominance in niche searches.

Consumers could connect to the businesses on the other side of the platform through any of the four means—voice calls to a local number (088888888), text (SMS), the Just Dial mobile app, and the internet (www.justdial.com). The search services (leading to discovery of local businesses) were free to consumers. The businesses could reach customers on the other side either through a free listing or a paid listing. There were two kinds of paid listings—premium listing (comprising platinum and diamond categories) or a non-premium listing. Just Dial offered the SMEs (business customers) various packages that suited their financial requirements—from weekly or monthly payment plans to annual

[10]Source: Gokahley, Madhavi, VSS Mani: Dial a dream, *The Smart Manager*, September–October, 2010, available on the internet at http://www.thesmartmanager.com/file/071010260601_TheSmartManager,smart_talk-VSS_Mani,_Sep-Oct-10.pdf, last accessed on June 12, 2015.

[11]Source: Bhat, Shravan, Just Dial: New world, new game for VSS Mani, *Forbes India*, September 15, 2014, available on the Internet at http://forbesindia.com/article/big-bet/just-dial-new-world-new-game-for-vss-mani/38615/1, last accessed June 12, 2015.

[12]Source: Company annual report, 2013–14, page 4, available on the internet at http://images.jdmagicbox.com/investors/Justdial-Annual-Report-2013-14-140903125933.pdf, last accessed on June 12, 2015.

plans.[13] Apart from fixed price contracts (premium products), SMEs could also choose to run a specific campaign for a pre-defined time. During 2012–13, Just Dial's customers conducted 206,500 campaigns (non-premium services) contributing to 2.28% of the total listing,[14] which grew to 262,150 campaigns in 2013–14.[15]

For consumers searching a local business, the results were provided instantaneously backed by a robust technology backbone and a large base of 2068 information retrieval officers that extracted data from a database that was constantly updated by over 1076 field sales team (feet on the street) members.[16] Just Dial's geo-location services (JD maps) additionally helped customers reach the right businesses with accurate information.

For the small or medium-sized business enterprises, Just Dial's listing provided an opportunity to access a large pool of consumers, who they would have otherwise not been able to access. Since over 98% of the retail stores in India were offline (with no online presence), their only option to attract consumers was through traditional means of promotion—print, radio, or TV. Just Dial, with its strong database on consumers and their search history, provided them with a cost-efficient option to focus their marketing efforts to the right consumer segments. Just Dial's services helped firms that were inherently local (such as a laundry service) to access the right consumers.

Initially, there was much resistance on the part of consumers to provide their names, phone numbers, and emails to Just Dial, when they called in for some information. However, over time consumers realized that Just Dial would not provide this data to the tele-marketers but provided such data to essentially keep their search services free. As Mani said, "Our revenues come from sponsored customers. And sponsored customers need to see tangible results. Our sole purpose of being is to help people out with information. The end result of which leads to sales for paying clients.[17]"

The JD Search Plus Business Model

Leveraging on the traditional search business model, Just Dial ventured into JD Search Plus services in 2013–14, transforming the company from one of "local search" to "search and transact" destination. Just Dial offered JD Search Plus services

[13]Source: Mathai, Adit, Wait, don't JustDial, *Outlook Business* (August 17, 2013), available on the Internet at http://www.outlookbusiness.com/markets/feature/wait-dont-justdial-379, last accessed on June 12, 2015.

[14]Source: Company annual report, 2012–13, available on the internet at http://images.jdmagicbox.com/investors/Justdial-Annual-Report-130905075453.pdf, last accessed on June 12, 2015.

[15]Source: Company annual report, 2013–14, page 10, available on the internet at http://images.jdmagicbox.com/investors/Justdial-Annual-Report-2013-14-140903125933.pdf, last accessed on June 12, 2015.

[16]Source: Company annual report, 2013–14, page 19, available on the internet at http://images.jdmagicbox.com/investors/Justdial-Annual-Report-2013-14-140903125933.pdf, last accessed on June 12, 2015.

[17]Source: VSS Mani: Chasing a dream with Rs. 50K in your pocket, CiteHR, http://www.citehr.com/106169-just-dial-story-check-out-times-india.html, last accessed on June 12, 2015.

in four broad categories of services—ordering services, scheduling services, ticketing/travel services, and buying online/shopfront/reverse auctions.[18] One unique feature of the JD Search Plus service was the integration of "social" networks into the search and transact process. Consumers could tag their friends on the Just Dial platform and could therefore receive appropriate reviews, ratings, and recommendations on particular products/services/firms from those tagged friends. This integration provided consumers with rich and valuable bases for decision-making. These ratings and reviews also provide much needed feedback for the businesses.

An important component of JD Search Plus service was the reverse auction feature. Just Dial helped consumers in their best price discovery process by providing them with search results of local vendors, along with trust factors as well as their best price quotes for the selected products. These quotes enabled consumers to evaluate the various options/firms and make informed purchasing decisions.

The "JD Shop Online"

In May 2015, Just Dial introduced its e-commerce marketplace offering through its "Shop Online" service. It listed products across various categories including those that were already popularly sold online in India (such as mobile phones, appliances, and electronics), as well as categories such as floor tiles, sanitary-ware, bicycles, and paints that were not being actively sold/bought through the popular e-commerce platforms in India.[19]

In addition, Just Dial offered a "7-h express delivery" service for orders placed before 2 p.m., and the offer was supported by a Just Dial written guarantee in addition to the manufacturer's warranty and original invoice.[20]

Given the high mobile penetration and the rapid growth of e-commerce in India, the competition among various marketplaces was already on the rise. However, it remained to be seen if Just Dial might bring in an additional twist to the story with, what it called the "Online to Offline" business—customers who are online shopping from businesses that remain offline. Such a capability could enable Just Dial expand the entire e-commerce pie to include newer (inherently local, small, and offline) firms and therefore bring on board entirely new product and service categories.

[18]Source: Company annual report, 2013–14, page 10, available on the internet at http://images.jdmagicbox.com/investors/Justdial-Annual-Report-2013-14-140903125933.pdf, last accessed on June 12, 2015.

[19]Source: Paul, Binu, Just Dial integrates ecommerce marketplace with its local business listings platform, *VCCircle Newsletter* (May 18, 2015), available on the internet at http://www.vccircle.com/news/technology/2015/05/18/just-dial-integrates-e-commerce-marketplace-its-local-business-listings, last accessed on June 12, 2015.

[20]Source: Paul, Binu, Just Dial integrates ecommerce marketplace with its local business listings platform, *VCCircle Newsletter* (May 18, 2015), available on the internet at http://www.vccircle.com/news/technology/2015/05/18/just-dial-integrates-e-commerce-marketplace-its-local-business-listings, last accessed on June 12, 2015.

Practo

10

Practo was a matching platform that brought patients and doctors together. Founded in 2008 by Shashank ND and Abhinav Lal,[1] Practo Technologies (hereinafter referred to as Practo) sought to offer solutions for the following.

(a) Practice management and digitization of medical records
(b) Search and book appointments with the right doctor for free
(c) Easy access and sharing of digital records.[2]

In order to ensure this, Practo had to create a platform with enough doctors on one side, and a large number of patients on the other side seeking to consult these doctors. Given the industry structure characterized by doctors running their own clinics/practice with little or no marketing efforts, it was important to bring them onboard first. In May 2009, Practo Ray version 1 was launched, and the first sale was made to a doctor.[3] Practo expanded to include doctors from Chennai, Mumbai, Hyderabad, and Pune over the next 3 years. The adoption of Practo Ray grew

[1]Source: Company Website: https://www.practo.com/company/story (last accessed January 14, 2015).
[2]Source: The Practo Story: https://www.youtube.com/watch?v=6SHF5ndhGME (last accessed January 14, 2015).
[3]Source: Company Website: https://www.practo.com/company/story (last accessed January 14, 2015).

This case is an extension of Chapter 7 Network Mobilization.
R Srinivasan, Professor of Strategy, prepared this case for class discussion. This case is not intended to serve as an endorsement, source of primary data, or to show effective or inefficient handling of decision or business processes.

R. Srinivasan, *Platform Business Models*, Management for Professionals,
https://doi.org/10.1007/978-981-16-2838-2_10

continuously and by July–August 2012 achieved over five million appointments through Practo Ray. Through the adoption of Practo Ray by doctors and their clinics, Practo launched Android and iPhone Apps for use by the doctors.

Having built a sufficient base of doctors on the one side, Practo launched Practo.com through which patients could book appointments with doctors directly. The rapid adoption of Practo Ray continued as Practo expanded to Singapore and achieved 10 million appointments through Practo Ray in November 2013. In the meantime, Practo Search (through Practo.com) continued to grow and included 95,702 doctors and 42,914 clinics listed across 263 Indian cities and 116 locations in Singapore by May 30, 2014, grossing 164,188 appointments until that date.[4]

Making Practice Management Easy: About Practo Ray

Practo's value proposition for the doctors/clinics was three-fold.

- Free listing (on Practo.com) that brought them patients
- Practice management, provided through a software as a service (SaaS) platform over the cloud that integrated patient management (managing appointments, communication, and follow-up), clinical and medical record management, and prescriptions
- Practice management services that included billing, managing inventories, generating reports, training of staff, clinic automation, as well as support in accounting and taxation.

The software solution Practo Ray integrated the practice management solutions. The features provided by Practo Ray included the following.

(i) Calendar services[5]: Facilitated scheduling of patients, doctors, and consultation/surgical/treatment facilities in a clinic. Seamless integration of the software across devices and users ensured that doctors received visibility of the entire day's schedule through SMS on their phones, as well as patient queues through the day/week/month and provide efficient allocation of doctors' time as well as clinic infrastructure using the availability view.

(ii) Contacts[6]: Documented and helped doctors to personalize their patients' profiles, medical history, lifestyle habits, and personal information. Along with a unique patient id for the clinic, this feature also facilitated linking of various patients from the same family.

[4]Source: Company Website: https://www.practo.com/practo-search/practo-ranking-algorithm (last accessed January 14, 2015).

[5]Source: Company Website: https://www.practo.com/ray/features/calendar (last accessed January 14, 2015).

[6]Source: Company Website: https://www.practo.com/ray/features/contacts (last accessed January 14, 2015).

(iii) Electronic medical records (EMR)[7]: Helped consolidate each patient's medical information and medical history, including clinical treatment plans. With the ability to store all patient-related files such as MRI images, X-rays, and pathological test reports, this feature allowed generation/management of prescriptions, thereby ensuring comprehensive clinical documentation.

(iv) Billing[8]: This feature was integrated with diagnosis and enabled accurate billing of patients, communication of bills to them through printouts/email, sending reminders for overdue payments, and even enabled taking advance payments and providing refunds.

(v) Communications[9]: Practo Ray enabled seamless communication with patients through SMS and email for confirmation and reminders of appointments, SMS/emails of their prescriptions, or even wishing them on their birthdays, ensuring continuous engagement with patients.

(vi) Financial reports[10]: Provided the practice with detailed income and expense statements, itemized bill analysis, and amount due from patients.

(vii) Printouts[11]: of everything in the practice—bills, prescriptions, invoices, inventory lists, case histories, and treatment plans—on any type of printer was also enabled.

(viii) IVR system[12]: Enabled personalized routing of calls, maintenance of call logs, along with SMS integration.

(ix) Mobile[13]: Practo Ray mobile app (for Android and iOS devices) provided access to all appointments and patient records and included an option to add pictures to patient records from the phone.

(x) Integration[14]: Practo Ray enabled doctors manage their Practo.com profile from within the Practo Ray application, syncs the calendars across Practo Ray and Practo.com, and enabled integration with the clinic's website/blog/Facebook page as well.

(xi) Inventory: Practo Ray enabled clinics manage inventory of their drugs/consumables by providing them real-time stock data based on consumption/sale, including reminders for re-ordering stock.

---

[7]Source: Company Website: https://www.practo.com/ray/features/emr (last accessed January 14, 2015).

[8]Source: Company Website: https://www.practo.com/ray/features/billing (last accessed January 14, 2015).

[9]Source: Company Website: https://www.practo.com/ray/features/communications (last accessed January 14, 2015).

[10]Source: Company Website: https://www.practo.com/ray/features/reports (last accessed January 14, 2015).

[11]Source: Company Website: https://www.practo.com/ray/features/printouts (last accessed January 14, 2015).

[12]Source: Company Website: https://www.practo.com/ray/features/hello (last accessed January 14, 2015).

[13]Source: Company Website: https://www.practo.com/ray/features/mobile (last accessed January 14, 2015).

[14]Source: Company Website: https://www.practo.com/ray/features/integration (last accessed January 14, 2015).

Pricing of Practo Ray was based on two plans—the basic plan ('999 per month) and the advanced plan ('1999 per month). The advanced plan provided all the services offered by the basic plan, plus a round-the-clock IVR service (along with a single telephone number for the practice).[15] As of December 2014, Practo Ray had over 40,000 customers[16] (doctors).

Helping Patients Find Doctors: Practo Search Through Practo.com

The Practo.com website allowed patients to search for listed doctors. As of December 2014, the Practo Search service listed over 100,000 doctor profiles across India and Singapore.[17] The Practo Search service was free to both patients and doctors. Through this website, patients could search for, browse, and book appointments with the doctors.[18]

The value proposition for the patients was that they could find the "best" doctors by searching online/through their mobile phones. The site (Practo.com and the Android app) provided details about the doctor, the clinic, the timings, consultation fees, pictures of the clinic, as well as ratings based on other patients' search results/choices.

racto Search used a proprietary Practo Ranking Algorithm to determine the position of doctors and practices in the Practo Search results. The three factors that contributed to the ranking algorithm were relevance, appointment experience, and preference. Relevance matched the specific query with the specialties and super-specialties of the practice listings and the location of the search, providing results within a radius of 2 km. Appointment experience incorporated the feedback of other patients about the doctor/practice. Preference contributed to ranking through user interest (number of appointments booked through Practo.com in the last 30 days and number of page views of the doctor's profile on Google Search results) and the strength of the doctor's profile (such as achievements, certifications, and awards).

Doctors were required to update their profiles at least once in every 10 weeks, even if there was no change to the profile. Such an automated profile expiry mechanism ensured that the doctors' profiles were up to date.

[15]For more details on the services offered under the two pricing plans, visit https://www.practo.com/ray/plans (last accessed January 14, 2015).

[16]Source: Company Website: https://www.practo.com/ray (last accessed January 14, 2015).

[17]Source: Company Website: https://help.practo.com/practo-search/what-is-practo-search/ (last accessed January 14, 2015).

[18]Source: http://yourstory.com/2014/08/practo-growth-story/ (last accessed January 14, 2015).

Practo Ads

Practo also displayed advertisements of registered clinics/practices for a given specialty and given set of localities (zone), much similar to the sponsored links that appear alongside Google search results.[19] The number of sponsored listings for a specialty-zone combination was decided by Practo and was dependent on the site traffic. Ads did not appear on those doctor profile pages who had themselves signed up for sponsored listings.

[19]Source: Company Website: https://www.practo.com/health/advertise (last accessed January 14, 2015).

11 Pricing and Subsidies

Pricing in the context of platforms is a crucial decision and has to be thought through differently than in the case of pipeline firms. Given the network effects and the need to scale both sides of the platform, it is important to reimagine pricing in the context of platform firms. Let us, for instance, consider a two-sided platform with strong cross-side network effects between sides A and B. Let us assume that the strengths of network effects are not the same between sides A and B, i.e., users from side A value users from side B more than the other way. In such a situation, the platform's growth strategy will be focused on attracting users from side B more than A. The platform would spend disproportionately more on getting side B users, who, in turn, will attract side A users. Therefore, platforms are more likely to subsidize side A users, so that they affiliate with the platform in large numbers, attracting side B users to the platform. The platform can therefore monetize its services offered to side B users, as they value the number and right quality of side A users.

Take the example of conventional print newspapers. The newspapers cater to two sets of users—readers and advertisers. They provide news (including opinion, editorial, and analytical information) to the readers through their network of employed and outsourced reporters/agencies. The readers value the quality and breadth of the news provided and are willing to subscribe to the newspaper. On the other side of the newspapers, there are advertisers who value the large number and quality of readers that the newspapers reach and are willing to affiliate with the newspaper if their segments match. For successful matches, the advertisers are willing to pay premium prices, so that their advertisements reach the intended number of users in a specific segment. Given that the advertisers are willing to pay, the newspapers can actually afford to subsidize the prices charged from the readers. In fact, for a successful newspaper with a substantial circulation, it is possible that the newspaper could actually give away the newspapers to the readers for free. However, they may charge a small price from the readers, so that they "value" the content in the newspapers and do not recycle/scrap the newsprint without reading it. Remember, it is the act of reading/seeing the advertisements that the advertisers

R. Srinivasan, *Platform Business Models*, Management for Professionals,
https://doi.org/10.1007/978-981-16-2838-2_11

want, and if they realize that the readers are actually not doing that, they may not be willing to pay the premium! Therefore, the newspapers would subsidize the readers to a price that is marginally higher than the value a buyer would make from selling it as scrap in the recycling market, so that they actually buy the newspaper to read it.

Such subsidies would attract a large number of readers, as they get a significant value out of the newspaper for a lower price, a price that is lower than their willingness to pay. These large numbers of readers (circulation and readership numbers) are used by the newspapers to market their advertising services and attract more advertisers with higher willingness to pay. Every new reader added to the platform increases the value for the advertisers and increases the pricing power of the newspaper.

In other words, as the newspaper focuses on increasing its number, quality and loyalty of readers, the value it can create for the advertisers increases proportionately due to the existence of cross-side network effects. As long as the newspaper is able to create and sustain these cross-side network effects, it would be possible to charge premium prices from the advertisers.

In the context of platforms, we refer to these sides as "subsidy side" and "money side," respectively. A critical decision for platforms is to balance the demand across the two sides by the right kind of pricing. Pricing decisions include three primary choices—which side to subsidize and which side to monetize; what pricing model to use and how much to charge; and how to use pricing as a competitive tool against other competing platforms. In this chapter, we will discuss these issues including the impact of pricing on platform scale and scope.

Subsidy and Money Sides

Choosing which side to subsidize and which side to monetize is a critical platform decision. This decision has significant influence on platform evolution and scale. We identify six criteria for making this decision:

(a) Relative strength of cross-side network effects
(b) Relative price sensitivity
(c) Relative value attached to quality of products and services
(d) Marginal costs of user addition
(e) Relative differentiation among users
(f) Relative bargaining power of complementors

These six criteria, independently and collectively, should provide us with a guide to making the decision on which side to subsidize and which side to monetize, if at all. Before we proceed further exploring each of these criteria, let us define the phrases.

Subsidy side: A group of users, who when affiliated with a platform in large numbers are highly valued by the users on the other side of the platform.

Money side: A group of users who demonstrate high willingness to affiliate, willingness to pay, and/or willingness to remain loyal to a platform due to the continued affiliation and usage/engagement of users on the other side.

Notice that the definition of money side includes all three—willingness to affiliate, pay, and stay loyal to the platform. Even though the platform may not charge a price from the platform from the money side at all times, there is a possibility of monetizing the affiliation and engagement at appropriate time and scale of the platform.

Relative Strength of Cross-Side Network Effects

The first premise in platform value creation and capture is to encourage the development of cross-side network effects. It is the basis on which the platform intermediates between two sets of users and therefore is able to monetize one set of users. It is in this context, we study the relative strengths of cross-side network effects across the two sides.

Take the example of a conventional FM radio broadcasting station. Similar to the newspaper example discussed above, the advertisers value the large number of relevant listeners to the radio station and therefore are willing to advertise on the platform, pay a price for the same, and are willing to continue to advertise on the said radio station as long as the numbers justify the price. On the other hand, radio listeners are fully subsidized—they do not pay for listening to a specific station (apart from the fixed cost of the radio/device). The advertisers value the number of listeners to that radio station and the specific programming and are willing to pay to reach them. In this case, the listeners are the subsidy side and the advertisers are the money side.

A crucial role that is played by the platform here is the intermediation between the money and subsidy sides. It would be very difficult/expensive for the money side (advertisers) to reach the subsidy side (listeners) without the intermediation of the platform (radio station). Imagine if there were many alternate ways for the advertisers to reach their intended audience other than through the radio, the willingness to pay for the radio advertising would surely come down. Especially, if the advertisers were able to reach their audience directly, without the need for any intermediation, then their willingness to pay would drop further lower.

Take the instance of online flight booking intermediaries like makemytrip.com. Such websites aggregate flight details across multiple airlines and provide other services apart from just ticket booking (including holiday packages, hotel booking, local car booking, and conducted tours) to attract travelers. In such platforms, the travelers have many options to book their tickets, including booking it directly from the airlines' websites. When the prices of air tickets are comparable between the airlines directly and the platform intermediary, it is more likely the traveler would book directly from the airline. When they do so, they avoid paying the platform any transaction fees as well. More importantly, the intermediary operates as a simple discovery platform (where one searches and finalizes the itinerary) and not a transaction platform. In order for the platform intermediary to enable the transaction, it is important to heavily subsidize the travelers, and offer significantly higher value (discounts, cash backs, loyalty bonuses, and the like). Such subsidies have to be financed through the prices charged from the money side, i.e., the airlines (or other hospitality/tourism businesses). For the airlines to pay a fees to these platform intermediaries, they should be able to see a significant increase in volumes coming from through these platforms than organically through their own ticketing websites. It is important for the platform to ensure adequate volumes of tickets to the airlines to justify the fees. Quite often, the airlines' willingness to join such platforms (set aside some inventory of seats for sale through these platforms) would be dependent on the volumes they bring in; their willingness to pay is very low (the relative price differences between airlines' own websites and the listed prices on the platforms); and their willingness to stay loyal would depend on the competitiveness of the intermediation business, i.e., the relative market share of the platform vis-à-vis its competitors. Therefore, in most cases, the platform intermediaries would seek to compensate their user subsidies through engaging with a third side on the platform, like advertisers (for related products and services). This third side of the platform is not just interested in the number of travelers or airlines on the platform, but highly values the interaction between travelers and airlines. For instance, more the number of tickets booked to a holiday destination, more the tour operators in those destinations are willing to advertise on the platform.

Therefore, we can conclude

(a) Subsidize the side that is more valued by the other side.
(b) If the money side can directly interact with the subsidy side, the willingness to pay is significantly low; increase the value of intermediation.
(c) If the subsidy side can multi-home and engage with the money side through a variety of means, focus on bringing in another side to the platform that values the interaction between the other two sides.

Relative Price Sensitivity

Between the different sets of users, it is important to assess the relative price sensitivity and the ease with which users can switch or multi-home. For instance, in a hyperlocal platform (like Yelp.com in the USA or Just Dial in India) that connects users with local businesses, the search users are price sensitive and are not willing to pay to discover the local businesses—they could just walk across to the business and discover it themselves, or use a variety of other social media networks to discover and access information about local businesses. Whereas on the other side, the local businesses are willing to pay to reach the right users. These platforms, with their rich database that includes search preferences and demographic data, are extremely valuable to the local businesses to target the right users for their brand communication and sales offers. In such cases, it is quite clear that these platforms subsidize the users and monetize the local businesses.

However, when the users (on one side are price sensitive) but experience high multi-homing or high switching costs, there is a possibility to reduce the subsidies and charge them appropriately. However, in doing so, it is likely that competing platforms will work toward reducing the multi-homing and/switching costs by monetizing the price-insensitive user groups. Take the example of Acrobat Reader from Adobe. Adobe subsidized readers by giving the Acrobat Reader for free; and charged the Acrobat writers. The fact that the Acrobat Reader was free attracted millions of users and encouraged the other side (writers) to pay premium prices for the Acrobat software to create PDF documents. And Acrobat has leveraged these network effects to become the industry standard. In spite of the low switching costs for readers (most browsers can be used to read PDF documents today), readers continue to download Acrobat Reader as it was free to use. By the same count, in spite of many ways of creating PDF documents (most desktop applications allow for saving/printing as PDF), writers continue to pay for and use Acrobat writers, as they value its specific features.

Therefore, we can conclude

(a) Subsidize the price-sensitive users and monetize the price-insensitive users.
(b) Switching and multi-homing costs provide guidance to the levels of subsidies (given the competitive context) but do not help determine the subsidy/money side.

Relative Value Attached to Quality of Products and Services

Like most pricing decisions, users' quality perception is a critical input in platform pricing. Let us elaborate this criterion beginning with an example. Take the case of console-based video games. The sides of the platform include game developers on one side and game players on the other side. The game developers make decisions to affiliate with a given platform and make commitments in terms of developing the game on the platform-specific software standards, thereby incurring huge fixed costs of affiliation. Even the game development process is highly labor and capital intensive resulting in substantial upfront investments. On the other side of the platform are the game players, who also have to make commitments in terms of buying consoles (that are specific to the platform) that are fixed costs and incur variable costs in buying specific games. Given these investments, the game players are typically young adults, who play a specific game intensively over a period of five–six months and socially benchmark their progress with their peers. And they value really high-quality games. Lower-quality games on the platform will dissuade these users, not just from buying/playing that specific game but may tilt their preferences away from the entire platform to other competing platforms. Therefore, it is imperative that the platform ensures that the quality of games in the platform is very high.

In such contexts, the platform typically monetizes the game developers and subsidizes the game players. By charging the game developers, the platforms allow the market to only select the best quality developers and drive out poor quality game developers out. These game developers, having incurred high fixed costs of affiliation to a specific platform including the royalties charged by the platform, plus the costs of game development, would seek to recover these investments from a large base of game players. They would therefore charge a price that the (quality and price sensitive) game players can afford, while investing heavily in marketing their games. In doing this, the game developers attract a large number of game players to the platform as well, resulting in high console sales (which the platform typically subsidize from the high royalties earned from game developers). In the process, the platform has only high-quality game developers.

This example adequately highlights how platforms should decide on the subsidy side based on quality requirements—monetize the side that produces quality, while subsidizing the side that seeks quality. It might seem counter-intuitive in the first place. Imagine for a moment if the decision were reversed—subsidies for the quality providers and monetizing the quality seekers. Once the platform begins subsidizing the quality providers, there would be millions of game developers seeking to develop games on the platform, and the platform's bureaucratic and transaction costs of selecting and contracting with only high-quality developers will be very high. In the absence of such investment by the platform, the game players will be faced with these costs. And when the platform is monetizing these game players with a premium pricing, it is unlikely that they are willing to stay affiliated with the platform that offers them with varied quality games. Therefore, it is a good strategy to use pricing as a filtering mechanism to select only good quality game developers affiliate with the platform.

Not just in video gaming platforms, such decisions are visible in a variety of platforms like job search, hyperlocal business listing, food delivery, and the like. The principle is to monetize the quality provider and subsidize the quality-seeking side. The more the number of quality seekers on the platform (that are attracted due to subsidies), the more the value perceived by the quality providers in affiliating with the platform, and therefore their willingness to affiliate and willingness to pay increases. This pricing scheme reduces the costs of evaluating quality by the demand side of users (quality seekers). On the other hand, for the supply-side users (quality providers) it reduces the costs of searching for the right users: those who value the quality provided in the product/service.

Therefore, we can conclude

(a) Subsidize the side that seeks quality, while monetizing the side that provides quality.
(b) Platforms could use pricing as a strategy to reduce the quality-evaluation costs for the quality-seeking side and therefore rake up large number of users, that are valuable to the quality-providing side, reducing their search costs.

Marginal Costs of User Addition

A very important consideration in deciding which side to monetize and which side to subsidize is the marginal cost of adding every user. It is imperative that the marginal cost of adding a user should be less than the prices charged from these users. If the platform spends about $30 in adding a new user, the price charged to that user should be equal to or greater than $30. Take for example, a matrimony platform that bridges people looking for partners. If the marginal cost of onboarding a user on to the platform, including data collection and validation, was $30, it is imperative that every user is charged at least that amount. Else, the platform would be making a unit-loss for every new user added, and would need to find some other side of users to finance the same.

It is also imperative to study the variable costs of engaging with these users on the platform. If the platform has to spend some variable costs for every engagement with the subsidy-side users, then that costs also need to be recovered from the users (of either of the sides), for every transaction.

An excellent illustration of this criterion can be found in the 1999 experiment by a firm, aptly titled, Free-PC.com.[1] The firm intended to give away 10,000 personal computers with internet access to consumers, in return for accessing their browsing habits and exposure to a set of advertisements. The firm expected to spend about $600 per user and hoped to recoup the money through targeted advertisements. Apart from the costs of the PC installation, the firm had to incur variable costs of providing internet access to these users (remember, we are talking 1999, where internet was not as ubiquitous as today). However, no advertisers were willing to advertise to these users! Users who had signed up to such an arrangement and had segmented themselves as those who were extremely price sensitive! By providing a product that cost them $600 per user free, the Free-PC platform should have found sufficient number of users on the other side who would value these consumers—

[1]See http://edition.cnn.com/TECH/computing/9902/10/freepc.idg/ for a newspaper report on the business model.

those users who were willing to share their personal browsing history. However, the advertisers that they reached out to were looking for customers who would be willing to buy their products and services after exposure to their advertisements. Obviously, the firm did not survive long enough!

Therefore, we can conclude

(a) Ensure that the marginal costs (to the platform) of adding a new user should be less than the prices charged. That is, the subsidy side should ideally consist of users who could be added to the platform with very low marginal costs.
(b) Beware of variable costs of engagement with the users—if there are costs incurred by the platform per transaction, then those costs have to be recovered from either/both of the users for every transaction.

Relative Differentiation Among Users

Platform firms should be aware of the relative differentiation among users on the same side. More the differentiation between the users, the more likely that platforms can use exclusion as a strategy to monetize that side of users. Imagine a shopping mall that is reaching out to shops as tenants on the mall. More differentiated the tenants from each other, the mall can then resort to monetizing the tenant side based on providing exclusive contracts (like ensuring that there is only one multi-brand footwear retailer in the mall). If these tenants were not differentiated, that is, if everyone were similarly positioned and competing with each other, then their willingness to pay may be significantly lower. As the number of direct competitors remains small, the willingness to pay may be driven by the "fear of missing out" (or FOMO) in reaching out to the other side—the opportunity loss of not being present in the mall and losing access to the footfalls. However, as the number of undifferentiated direct competitors increases, the willingness to pay may start declining, and beyond a threshold, negative same-side network effects may even start kicking in. In other words, if there were to be too many direct competitors in the same platform, the value that I hope to derive from the platform might significantly reduce due to crowding experienced by the users on the other side. They may experience information and choice overload and may switch away from the platform.

Therefore, exclusion as a strategy might provide platform owners with the ability to charge premium prices, provided they can ensure that they attract sufficient users on the other side (ensure strong positive cross-side network effects).

On the other side, if there is no differentiation among users, and they are equally valued by users of the other side, then this side would contribute to significant cross-side network effects in the platform, and therefore should be subsidized. When subsidized, these users will join in large numbers, and might enable the platform to monetize the other side.

Therefore, we can conclude

(a) Monetize the side that has differentiated users. Platforms can use exclusion to charge premium prices from users who want to sustain their differentiation.
(b) Subsidize the side where the users are not differentiated and are equally valued by users on the other side.

Relative Bargaining Power of Complementors

In some intermediation platforms, there is a likelihood that the users from one side value association with specific users (also referred to as marquee users) on the side, more than the value of the platform affiliation. These marquee users might disproportionately attract more users on the other side of the platform, than others. The relative bargaining power of those marquee users with respect to the platform brand value might be higher, and therefore, these users should be treated more like complementors to the platform, rather than just any other users. Take the example of video games, where users buy the console to play specific games and where the brand value of the games and game developers like EA might be more stronger than that of the platforms (like X-Box or PS-2). In such situations, it becomes imperative that the platform works to increase the willingness to affiliate and willingness to remain loyal to the platform, rather than willingness to pay from these marquee users. The platform might have to significantly subsidize certain marquee users, in order to generate the network effects, and attract users on the other side and/or the same side. While the platform may continue to monetize the side that includes such marquee users but provide these specific users with other concessions, like exclusive or early access to certain data/services by the platform. In such cases, it is also important to evaluate the types of concessions one provides these marquee users and how other non-marquee users may react to such concessions.

Therefore, we can conclude

(a) Monetize the side the contains marquee users (who disproportionately attract more users on the other side).
(b) Treat these marquee users as complementors and focus on increasing their willingness to affiliate and willingness to remain loyal to the platform.

The decision on monetizing and subsidizing should be based on all these six criteria, taken together and is summarized in the Table 11.1 below.

Table 11.1 Criteria for monetizing and subsidizing

Monetize the side …	Subsidize the side …
… that values the other side users … where users are price insensitive … that provides quality in the products and services … where the marginal costs of adding a new user is high … that has differentiated users … that contains marquee users	… that is more valued by other side … where users are price sensitive … that seeks quality in the products and services … where the marginal costs of adding a new user is low … where users are not differentiated and are equally valued by the other side … where users are attracted by the marquee users

Having decided which side to subsidize and which side to monetize, we now turn our attention to the various pricing models that are available to platforms.

Pricing Models

There are various ways to define pricing in the context of platforms. Given that platforms present myriad value creation opportunities, there could be a variety of pricing models. Primary among them are the following.

(a) Subscription pricing models
(b) On-demand pricing models
(c) Razor-blade and reverse razor-blade pricing models
(d) Freemium pricing models
(e) Auction pricing models
(f) Free pricing models

Subscription Pricing Models

Subscription pricing models are typically used when the platform wants to encourage demand-side users to continue using with the product/service offered more and/or frequently. The value created by the platform could arise out of either aggregating millions of users to enjoy economies of scale and scope (in the supply side) or when a product is provided as a service, where the consumer rather than buying a product signs up for a period subscription (like a lease).

Another example of subscription pricing is video streaming platforms like Netflix and Amazon Prime (aggregation economies in supply side). In the case of video streaming, the platform enjoys economies of scale and scope by amassing a vast library of content and streaming it to the demand-side users. Users value the variety of content and the flexibility of streaming whenever they want to watch a movie without having to either buy a licensed version or watch it at the time chosen by the television broadcaster.

Another example of subscription pricing is cloud storage services or software as a service (servitization). In the case of servitizing products, (demand-side) users convert fixed costs of ownership into variable costs. When the platform wants to encourage the users to engage more and more with the platform through more number of transactions and frequent usage, and not engage with any other competing platform, a period subscription model would serve the purpose.

Given that the marginal costs of transactions (for the platform) is close to zero (both in the streaming and servitization example, the bandwidth costs are paid for by the user), the platform can afford to price them as a period subscription model. Such pricing also encourages the users to utilize the products/services more and more and sometimes even indulge in "binge usage." Such usage contributes to higher multi-homing costs and results in increased loyalty.

In summary, subscription pricing models are used when

(a) Platforms utilize economies of scale and scope in providing access to products and services (aggregation economies in the supply side)
(b) Demand-side users value variety and/or flexibility in their consumption of products and services
(c) Platforms encourage higher usage and frequent/continued engagement with the platform
(d) Platforms increase multi-homing costs for the demand-side users
(e) Platforms experience zero or minimal marginal costs of transactions

On-Demand Pricing Models

In contrast with the subscription pricing models, on-demand pricing works best when the transactions on the platform are fewer, less frequent, but are critical. The platform invests in having the supply side ready for the demand and incurs non-trivial variable costs per transaction. The demand-side users value rapid scaling up and scaling down of supply as per their demand fluctuations and are willing to pay per transaction. Such pricing could be either based on the number of transactions (volumes) or the denomination of each transaction (value) or a combination of both. The platform may require the supply side to make commitments to transacting on the platform with some specific investments. This asset specificity will ensure high switching costs for the users and therefore enhance the platform's ability to respond to demand fluctuations.

A good example for on-demand pricing is the app-based cab hiring platforms. In such platforms, the supply side (drivers and cars) are on-boarded first and are trained/expected to provide consistent quality of service. The demand-side users (riders) hail cabs whenever they want and expect that cabs be available wherever they are within reasonable times. These may result in surges in peak demand within days as well as weeks. The platform is expected to manage these fluctuations in demand and ensure that the supply is matched with demand. And for this dynamic matching of supply and demand, the riders are willing to pay even premium prices in the form of surge pricing.

Another good example of on-demand pricing model is that of hyper-local food delivery. Similar to the previous example, hungry patrons expect the platform to be able to scale up and down supply to match demand volatility and are willing to pay a premium price per transaction, depending on the criticality of the demand (peak hours vs. lean hours).

In summary, on-demand pricing models are used when

(a) Platforms invest in having the supply side ready and scalable to match the volatility in demand.
(b) Demand-side users value supply being available when and where they need.
(c) Platforms use pricing as a leverage to scale up and scale down demand to match demand fluctuations.
(d) Platforms force supply-side users to make specific investments, locking them to the platform and increasing their switching costs.
(e) Platforms incur non-trivial variable costs for every transaction.

Razor-Blade and Reverse Razor-Blade Pricing Models

There are instances where platforms incur both fixed and variable costs in value creation. When these costs are significant, some platforms adopt a razor-blade pricing model. That is the platform subsidizes the fixed investments by the users (typically made upfront during the platform affiliation) and makes substantial profits through higher prices for the consumables (post-platform affiliation). Such strategies are commonly referred to as razor-blade pricing strategies (since most shaving products firms give away the razors at very cheap prices and make money through selling the cartridges/blades at very high prices). This kind of razor-blade pricing is adopted by platforms where the users have to make fixed investments for affiliation as well as incur variable costs of engagement with the platform. When these are specifically tied to each other, the commitment to a specific platform is made when the users make the affiliation decision.

One good example of razor-blade pricing model can be seen in video gaming platforms. The gaming firms give away the consoles for a very small price and make money through sales of the consumables—the various games bought by the gamers throughout the life of the console. The decision to buy a particular console locks-in the gamer to play only those games that are available on that platform.

Another example of such razor-blade strategy adopted by platforms is that of e-book readers. The hardware that is used to read the e-books is heavily subsidized with the platform hoping to make money by selling books. Given that the user has committed to a particular e-book reader, she is locked in to buying books that are compatible with that.

There have been some platforms that have inverted this argument on razor-blade pricing, by adopting a reverse razor-blade pricing. By reversing the pricing model, i.e., pricing the upfront investment for a premium and subsidizing the consumables, Apple disrupted the industry.[2] Apple gave away music at prices that made no margins for the iTunes platform, while charging premium prices for the iPod music player. The premium prices paid by the users for the iPod serves as the lock-in for the platform, and the users continue to remain loyal to iTunes and consume large volumes of music (as they are subsidized).

In sum, razor-blade pricing strategies are used when

(a) Platforms incur both fixed and variable costs in creating and delivering value.
(b) Platforms lock-in demand-side users by subsidizing either the upfront investment or the consumables, and ensuring a tight integration and complementarity between the two value offers (say, hardware, and software).
(c) Demand-side users are willing to make commitments to a specific platform through incurring either high fixed costs or high variable costs in return for convenience and compatibility.

Freemium Pricing Models

These pricing models have become very popular in the recent years. Such models are typically used in the context of platforms where there are multiple segments of users and the network effects are not the same across segments. For instance, in the case of professional networking platforms like LinkedIn, there could be a large segment of users who are passively building their profile on the platform and a relatively smaller segment of users who are actively seeking jobs. Such platforms have to actively discriminate their pricing strategies across these segments for essentially the same products or services.[3] However, these segments may not be water tight, and users may move from one segment to another and choose premium services. Such mobility can be encouraged by free trials and providing limited basket of services to the free users. Once the free users as a segment enjoy the services and realizes the value of premium services, they may move up to the other segment and be willing to pay. Given that the pricing model includes both free and premium users, these models are commonly referred to as freemium models. Of course, in order to efficiently implement a freemium pricing model, platforms

[2]Johnson, MW, Christensen, CM., and Kagermann, H. 2008. Reinventing your business model, Harvard Business Review, December 2008. 59–67.

[3]Price discrimination can be studied using three types. First degree price discrimination refers to a case when a platform can charge unique prices to specific users depending on the willingness to pay of that particular user. Second degree price discrimination happens when the pricing is dependent on the volume of usage (say, bulk discounts). And third degree price discrimination refers to a pricing model where the price is dependent on the segment users belong to. For more details: Narahari, Y., Raju, CVL., Ravikumar, K., and Shah, S. 2005. Dynamic pricing models for electronic business, Sadhana, 30, 2/3, 231–256.

should be able to segment the market and ensure that the premium services are highly valued by the premium users, who are willing to pay premium prices.

Another good example of freemium pricing is consumer cloud storage services. While free users get limited storage space and restricted features, premium users get access to variety of services (not just higher storage), including archiving services and analytics.

Freemium models are typically used when

(a) There are different segments of demand-side users with staggered value expectations.
(b) The platform can efficiently segment the market and engage in price discrimination.
(c) There is a high chance that the free users will experience the platforms' products and services (as a trial) and a few of them will move to the premium segment seeking differentiated services.

Auction Pricing Models

As the name suggests, platforms can also offer auction pricing to its customers. The primary assumption in using auctions is that each user values the product/service differently and is willing to pay that price. Auctions are best ways to "discover" the right price each individual customer is willing to pay. In markets with high information asymmetry, like the used goods market, auction pricing is common. Good examples of auction pricing include eBay[4] and other consumer-to-consumer marketplaces like olx.in or quikr.com. In these, the platform typically charges a commission as a proportion of the value of the transaction.

For instance, Indian used car marketplace platforms like Cars24 bring together sellers and buyers, and once they have assessed the various parameters of the car being sold, puts it up for an auction to the buyers.[5] By putting up the car for auction, the true market price of the car is discovered for the seller, who may feel short-changed if the intermediary would offer a price itself.

Auction pricing models are useful when

(a) There is high information asymmetry among the users and between the user and the platform.
(b) Different users value the product/service offered uniquely, and the primary role of the platform is to help discover the right price.

[4]See https://sellglobal.ebay.in/seller-central/seller-benefits/ for how eBay adds value to sellers.

[5]See https://www.cars24.com/become-our-partner/ for details about the auction process in Cars24.com.

Free Pricing Models

Apart from all these models, some platforms just provide their products and services for free to one set of users, while making money from other users, like the ubiquitous internet search engines that provide search services for free to search users, while making money from website owners and advertisers. Typically, website owners are priced on a freemium pricing model, and the advertisers are priced using an on-demand pricing model.

As can be seen above, these pricing models are stylized examples of pure types. Platforms, depending on their context and the users' needs, will choose the appropriate pricing model. The pricing model chosen might also be a function of the maturity of the market, or the competitive strategy of the platform. For instance, a start-up platform competing against an established platform with very high market shares might adopt a penetrative pricing strategy to gain market share.

Pricing and Platform Scale

It is important to understand decisions around pricing as part of the overall platform strategy around scaling. Choosing the right pricing model will have significant impact on how users engage with the platform and affect their willingness to affiliate, willingness to pay, and willingness to remain loyal to the platform.

Users willingness to pay (WTP) for a platform is typically a function of three platform attributes—strength of cross-side network effects (value of having users on the other side of the platform), value created by the platform, and strength of same-side network effects (value of having other users on the same side of the platform). Typically value creation by the platform can happen through reduction in transaction costs including the costs incurred in overcoming information asymmetries and adverse selection problems. Such costs can be observed through reduction in search and selection costs, costs of contracting for efficient transactions, and the costs of governing such contracts. As long as the prices charged by the platform are lower than these, users would be willing to pay.

The willingness to affiliate (or willingness to join—WTJ) and willingness to remain loyal (or willingness to stay—WTS) to the platform are different from the willingness to pay. WTJ and WTS depend on the switching and multi-homing costs in the platform. These switching and multi-homing costs are a function of how much the users have to invest specifically to join the platform (costs of onboarding—including costs of adapting their processes to fit with the platforms'), asset-specific investments required to engage on the platform, and the costs of exiting the platform. This is apart from the competitive context of the industry, i.e., the number of direct competing platforms available in the industry.

Platform firms, therefore, have to expend equal energy in understanding and increasing all these—WTP, WTJ, and WTS of the users/user groups. And pricing plays an important role in these.

Apart from pricing, the ease with which users may be able to engage with the platform and other users is also critical to enable platform scaling, which is what we will turn our attention to in the next chapter.

Zomato™ Gold: Platform Overreach

12

Introduction

Rashmi had just returned to her restaurant after meeting a corporate client in the city of Bangalore. Rashmi and her friends had started a niche fine dining restaurant serving exclusive Franconian food, targeted at the growing expat German population a few years ago. Her manager alerted her to a series of calls from the local Zomato account manager offering the Zomato Gold program for delivery services. Rashmi had been following up on the National Restaurants Association of India (NRAI) campaign against the Zomato Gold program (that she had signed up last year) for dine-in services and wondering if she should also log out of the program. She had a decision to make on the dine-in Zomato Gold program, and now there was this offer to join the delivery program. She was left wondering if she could afford the sign-up costs as well as finance the discounts. She asked herself:

- Had Zomato bitten off more than they can chew by being over ambitious to monetize the vast user base with a premium subscription service? Did they misjudge user acceptability by changing the terms of operations quite frequently? What are the implications of the media and social media coverage on restaurants signing out of Zomato Gold on her customers?

This case is an extension of Chapter 11 Pricing and Subsidies.

R Srinivasan (Professor of Strategy), Sandeep Lakshmipathy (Research Scholar, BITS Pilani, Hyderabad), and Pramoth Joseph (Researcher Scholar, IIIT Bangalore) prepared this case for class discussion. This case is not intended to serve as an endorsement, source of primary data, or to show effective or inefficient handling of decision or business processes.

R. Srinivasan, *Platform Business Models*, Management for Professionals,
https://doi.org/10.1007/978-981-16-2838-2_12

- When she signed up for the Zomato Gold program, it was about attracting premium (frequent/non-price sensitive) customers to the restaurant. However, with the widespread adoption of the program, is there a risk of increasing price sensitive consumers? More still, will this expansion affect the loyalty and willingness-to-pay of the premium consumers?

Hyperlocal Food Delivery Business

Hyperlocal is defined as "relating to or focusing on matters concerning a small community or geographical area." Neighborhood-focused restaurant reviews, news items and event recommendations, and food delivery from nearby restaurants and grocery delivery constituted the scope of hyperlocal business. Advertisers were interested in hyperlocal more than ever due to its ability to deliver relevant content as close to the patron as possible. Ability to deliver hyperlocal marketing at scale had puzzled many firms with considerable marketing budgets. However, emergence of hyperlocal platforms such as Zomato and Swiggy changed the dynamics, and they were successful in making impression on the minds of customers through personalized content that can be delivered in an automated manner. Compared to the past iterations of home delivery start-ups, more recent incarnations of hyperlocal businesses enjoyed relatively better success as they were aided by GPS services on smart phones.

Firm's Origin

The idea for Zomato occurred to Deepinder Goyal (Goyal) and Pankaj Chaddah (Chaddah) when they attempted to make available offline the menu of their then employer's (Bain & Company) cafeteria on the intranet to ease the employees' pain of ordering food. The immense welcome of the idea received helped them with the version 1.0 (called Foodiebay) of their offering—making available the menus (as images) of different restaurants along with the relevant contact number for placing orders. The concept solved a genuine logistical challenge and revenue started trickling in as restaurants flocked to Foodiebay with advertisements. It was a win–win situation where the average restaurant goer could have access to menu details on his smartphone or on a portal while the local restaurant gained a web presence and more footfalls owing to the efforts of Foodiebay.

Goyal and Chaddah bootstrapped the venture for the first 2 years and eventually expanded Foodiebay to include other cities. With continued success, Foodiebay received its first funding in 2010 from InfoEdge which funded other companies such as Naukri.com and 99acres.com. Foodiebay, then rebranded as Zomato, rapidly expanded to other cities in India and launched a companion mobile app that made it convenient for end customers to interact with their favorite restaurants to place orders and track them (refer to Fig. 12.1). As the app led from the front in onboarding users, InfoEdge led the subsequent funding of $3 million in 2011 and

$2.3 million in 2012. The lure of larger ticket sizes in the United Arab Emirates prompted Goyal to expand overseas rather than expanding vertically to other businesses. The founder's conviction was upheld when the UAE operations broke even in just 4 months. While Zomato continued to expand to other countries such as the UK, New Zealand, Portugal, Turkey, and Brazil among others, funding continued to swell led by InfoEdge and Sequoia Capital. It acquired a string of companies (competitors) in various countries leading an expansion led by acquisitions as well. However, as funding tightened in 2015, Zomato quickly moved to cut its losses, exited or scaled back operations in a few countries focusing on shoring up revenues. Zomato became profitable in 2016–2017 and continued with key and critical acquisitions on a need basis.[1]

Its revenue for 2015–2016 was pegged at $28.2 million, FY17 at $51 million, and FY18 at $74 million while EBITDA 2015–2016 losses were at $75 million.[2] Losses from FY18 were at $11 million and FY17 were at $15 million.[3] By March 2019, the losses had catapulted to $ 295 million while revenues were significantly up at $ 206 million.[4] Advertising contributed to around 60% of its revenues, food delivery about 30%, and Zomato Gold about 12%.

Zomato's Gold Program

Looking at adjacencies and a possible new revenue stream, Zomato launched its premium subscription service *Zomato Gold* in March 2017 in Lisbon (Portugal), Dubai, and Abu Dhabi.[5] Zomato Gold quickly moved up to 700 K subscribers by 2017–2018 and in August 2019 stood at $1–1.3 million.[6,7] Zomato Gold had about

[1]Thomas, A. S. (2017, October 8). "*Batting It Out Of The Park: Zomato Founder And CEO Deepinder Goyal*", Entrepreneur.com. Available at: https://www.entrepreneur.com/article/302209 (Accessed: August 30, 2019).

[2]KJ, Shashidhar (2016, May 25) "*Zomato reports EBITDA losses of Rs 492 Cr; revenues of Rs 185 Cr in FY16*", Medianama.com. Available at: https://www.medianama.com/2016/05/223-zomato-earnings-march-2016 (Accessed: August 31, 2019).

[3]OfficeChai Team. (2018, April 2) "*This Is Where Zomato Now Earns Its Revenue From*", OfficeChai.com. Available at: https://officechai.com/startups/zomato-revenue-split/ (Accessed: September 1, 2019).

[4]PTI (2019, April 5) "Zomato posts USD 294 mn loss for FY19; revenue up threefold to USD 206 mn", Economic Times. Available at: https://economictimes.indiatimes.com/small-biz/startups/newsbuzz/zomato-posts-usd-294-mn-loss-for-fy19-revenue-up-3-fold-to-usd-206-mn/articleshow/68743020.cms?from=mdr (Accessed: September 1, 2019).

[5]KJ, Shashidhar (2017, March 16) "*Zomato launches a subscription service in Dubai and Abu Dhabi*," Medianama.com. Available at: https://www.medianama.com/2017/03/223-zomato-gold/ (Accessed: August 31, 2019).

[6]Payal Ganguly. (2019, February 21) "*Zomato eyes $25 million in revenues from subscription programme*," TechCircle.in. Available at: https://www.techcircle.in/2019/02/21/zomato-eyes-25-million-in-revenues-from-subscription-programme (Accessed: September 1, 2019).

[7]Financial Express Online. (2019, August 30) "*As Zomato Gold numbers swelled, restaurants had to foot the bill for higher valuation*," Online, Financial Express. Available at: https://www.financialexpress.com/industry/as-zomato-gold-numbers-swelled-restaurants-had-to-foot-the-bill-for-higher-valuation/1691000/ (Accessed: September 1, 2019).

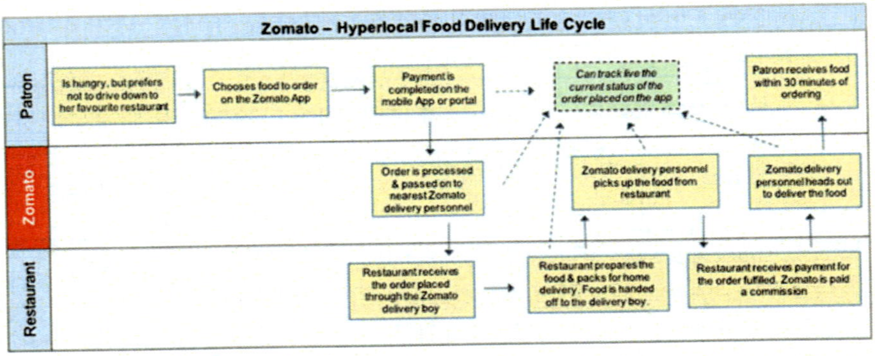

Fig. 12.1 Order flow through the Zomato's ecosystem. *Source* Authors' representation

150,000 subscribers and a 500,000 long waiting list as of April 2018. Zomato launched its Gold subscription service in India in November 2017.[8,9] Immediately after this popular debut, it was purported to be an "*Invite Only*" service. In late 2018, Zomato altered the terms and conditions of its offerings bringing in user limit: reducing the number of unlocks that users could choose at a table with additional restrictions on the count of diners. Zomato offered variants of its Gold pack called as "Starter" and "Medium" with lesser benefits in early 2019.[10,11]

Zomato Gold Design: A Unique "*Loyalty*" Program

When Zomato sensed demand for the *Zomato Gold* service in India, the firm began with a smaller service offering called *Zomato Treat*: a free dessert with every meal ordered for an annual subscription of ₹249.[12] Operational in April 2017, *Zomato Treat* attracted over 21,500 subscribers (and over 100,000 desserts served) in

[8]Franchise India Bureau. (2017, November 16) "*Online Food ordering Zomato Launches Zomato Gold In India*", RestaurantIndia.in. Available at: https://www.restaurantindia.in/news/Online-Food-ordering-Zomato-Launches-Zomato-Gold-In-India.n15029 (Accessed: September 1, 2019).

[9]Sindhu Kashyaap. (2017, November 15) "*Zomato brings 'Gold' its premium subscription offering to India*", YourStory.in. Available at: https://yourstory.com/2017/11/zomato-brings-gold-premium-subscription-offering-india (Accessed: September 1, 2019).

[10]Anwesha Madhukalya. (2018, September 17) "*Zomato Gold users say they've been 'cheated' as user-limit restricted*," Business Today. Available at: https://www.businesstoday.in/current/corporate/zomato-gold-users-say-they-ve-been-cheated-user-limit-restricted/story/282497.html (Accessed: August 31, 2019).

[11]News18 (2019, February 22) "*First Bite: Zomato Now Has New Gold Membership Powerpacks With No Validity Limits And Lower Prices*," News18.com, February. Available at: https://www.news18.com/news/tech/first-bite-zomato-now-has-new-gold-membership-powerpacks-with-no-validity-limits-and-lower-prices-2045023.html (Accessed: August 31, 2019).

[12]Mukund Kulashekaran (2017, April 11). "*Introducing Zomato Treats*", Zomato.com. Available at: https://www.zomato.com/blog/introducing-zomato-treats (Accessed: August 31, 2019).

4 months and was expected to further grow faster.[13] However, after running it as a stand-alone offer for about 18 months, Zomato decided to shut it down in November 2018.[14]

Zomato Gold was launched as a loyalty program by Zomato in November 2017 to increase diners' multi-homing costs (across competing apps). *Zomato Gold* gave diners a buy-one-get-one offer on food and buy-two-get-two offer on drinks. *Zomato Gold* came in with two offers for diners—at ₹300 for a starter pack that offered three uses per year, or ₹1050 for an unlimited pack that offered unlimited usage for up to one year.[15] The starter pack was subsequently discontinued, and the subscription rate was revised to ₹1800 per year.[16] As on March 2018, *Zomato Gold* and *Zomato Treats* had over 280,000 subscribers[17]; grew to 700,000 by end of 2018, and to 800,000 by February 2019. These programs facilitated $20–25 million in revenue by the end of 2019.[18] *Zomato Gold* had been one of Zomato's crown jewels and that was when Zomato sold its delivery business in the United Arab Emirates to the German firm Delivery Hero in March 2019, but decided to retain the Gold business. Although the number of subscribers for Zomato Gold was rising fivefold, the revenues only increased twofold (April 2018–March 2019).[19] The average revenue realizations were falling, but Zomato responded by launching *Zomato Infinity* in July 2019. Infinity allowed Gold members unlimited food and drinks for a fixed price! Though only available for high-rated restaurants, it reduced the value available for restaurants.

Positive Network Effects for Restaurants

Zomato Gold was a program that premium restaurants could not ignore. Since it was launched as an exclusive premium service for diners who were willing to pay, the expectation was that it would attract the fine diners. That segment of diners who

[13]Taslima Khan (2017, August 22). "*Zomato Treats crosses 21,500 subscriptions in 4 months*", ET Bureau. Available At: https://economictimes.indiatimes.com/small-biz/startups/zomato-treats-crosses-21500-subscriptions-in-four-months/articleshow/60168369.cms (Accessed: August 30, 2019).

[14]Jai Vardhan (2018, November 12). "*Exclusive: Zomato suspends its first paid subscription service Zomato Treats*", Entrackr.com. Available at: https://entrackr.com/2018/11/exclusive-zomato-treats-suspend/ (Accessed: August 30, 2019).

[15]Pradip Kumar Saha (2019, March 5). "*Zomato's Gold Millions*". Available at: https://the-ken.com/story/zomato-gold-loyalty/ (Accessed: August 30, 2019).

[16]Zomato's Terms & Conditions. Available at: https://www.zomato.com/conditions?country_id=1&page_type=SUBSCRIPTION&gold_plan_page=1 (Accessed: August 30, 2019).

[17]Deepinder Goyal (2018, April 2). "*Zomato – 'Short Form' Annual Report FY18*". Available at: https://www.zomato.com/blog/annual-report-fy18 (Accessed: August 30, 2019).

[18]Biswarup Gooptu (2019, February 21). "*Zomato Gold to bring in $20-25 M in revenue by the end of 2019*". Available at: https://tech.economictimes.indiatimes.com/news/startups/zomato-gold-to-bring-in-20-25-million-in-revenue-by-the-end-of-2019/68085537 (Accessed: August 31, 2019).

[19]Abhinaya Vijayaraghavan (2019, August 21). "*Restaurants take control as Zomato Gold loses Midas touch*". Available at: https://the-ken.com/story/restaurants-take-control-as-zomato-gold-loses-midas-touch/ (Accessed: August 30, 2019).

were less price sensitive and those who valued a fine dining experience were those it was supposed to attract. It would not make sense for a restaurant to let go of this opportunity to affiliate with Zomato Gold and risk losing these fine diners to competitors. The best restaurants signed up soon.

Negative Network Effects

The terms and conditions of Zomato Gold subscription service kept evolving. What started as an open-to-all service (anyone can buy the subscription) in November 2017, became invitation-only in April 2018. By September 2018, it restricted the unlocking to one per group of three persons at a restaurant table instead of one unlock per person. This meant, when you dine as a group of three people, only one of the three could use their *Zomato Gold* subscription. In February 2019, it introduced Zomato Gold Powerpacks for people who ate out less frequently—at ₹300 for three unlocks and ₹700 for ten unlocks. These changes enraged a lot of users as well (refer to Fig. 12.2)—as more and more subscribers signed up for the Zomato Gold subscription, the less valuable it became for the existing subscribers! The really high volumes forced Zomato to squeeze subscription benefits, and the growth of subscribers also stalled.

Fig. 12.2 Enraged Zomato Gold user venting frustration on Twitter. *Source* https://twitter.com/deep__sanghvi/status/1038764352835383296, accessed from the Internet on 13 December 2019

The restaurants who had signed up with the platforms were already pressurized on three counts—the commissions charged by the platforms were increasing; the ranking algorithms used by the platforms in a user search were increasingly becoming opaque; and the platforms had stopped sharing customer data with the restaurants citing customer safety and privacy issues. Additionally, the platforms were expanding their capacity by setting up cloud kitchens in popular geographies.[20]

The indiscriminate growth in number of diners actually turned the tables for the restaurants. The Zomato Gold program began attracting bargain hunters, quite a different segment than the fine diners as originally intended by the Zomato Gold program. The restaurants began losing money servicing the Zomato Gold customers. Sahil Sambhi, a partner at three restaurants in Delhi, including the microbrewery—The Drunken Botanist, said that while Gold would bring in more diners, it did not necessarily translate into higher sales.

> Last month, I made certain parts of my menu inaccessible to Gold and my sales went down by ₹10-12 lakh ($13,924-16,709) a month. That shows the customer is very Gold loyal. So, more diners are coming in, but my sales are going down.[21]

Given that the loyalty program only increased loyalty to the Zomato app, but not the specific restaurants, restaurant partners were unwilling to indiscriminately service these bargain hunters. Thomas Fenn, a partner at Mahabelly, a restaurant in Delhi said:

> We saw that they were not premium customers because the entry barrier was lowered. There is no stickiness, the day I am not on Gold, they might not come.[22]

The fear of missing out (FOMO) effect kept the restaurants going with the Gold program for some time, but when the costs were higher than what they could bear, they began protesting.

Restaurants' Reactions

At 1.3 million subscribers and 4570 restaurants on the *Zomato Gold* program, the number of bargain hunters landing up at restaurant tables was growing substantially. Given that the revenues from the *Zomato Gold* subscription went directly into

[20]Kuwar Singh (2019, August 27). "*How India's restaurateurs united on WhatsApp in five hours to fight food delivery apps*". Interview with Anurag Katriar, NRAI Mumbai Chapter. Available at https://qz.com/india/1695796/why-some-indian-restaurants-are-fighting-zomato-swiggy-ubereats/ (Accessed: August 30, 2019).

[21]Abhinaya Vijayaraghavan (2019, August 21). "*Restaurants take control as Zomato Gold loses Midas touch*". Available at: https://the-ken.com/story/restaurants-take-control-as-zomato-gold-loses-midas-touch/ (Accessed: August 30, 2019).

[22]Abhinaya Vijayaraghavan (2019, August 21). "*Restaurants take control as Zomato Gold loses Midas touch*". Available at: https://the-ken.com/story/restaurants-take-control-as-zomato-gold-loses-midas-touch/ (Accessed: August 30, 2019).

Personal message to you regarding Zomato Gold

Today at 5:51 PM

Dear Partner,

Hope you are well!

This is a personal message to you, given the recent logout campaign. It pains us to see that we failed to create a sustainable Gold program which works as well for restaurants as it does for consumers. We have already reached out to the NRAI to introduce a few changes to Gold going forward.

In the meanwhile, we want to hear your concerns and pain points as a restaurant owner. Specifically, when it comes to Zomato Gold, what is the top pain point for you? And how do you think we can help solve it?

We will look forward to your reply, and collaboratively make something more sustainable for you, and our customers.

Thanks
Deepinder
Founder & CEO, Zomato

Fig. 12.3 Zomato CEO Deepinder Goyal's email to restaurants. *Source* Abhinaya Vijayaraghavan (2019, August 21). "*Restaurants take control as Zomato Gold loses Midas touch*". Available at: https://the-ken.com/story/restaurants-take-control-as-zomato-gold-loses-midas-touch/ (Accessed: August 30, 2019)

Zomato's bottom line, and all the discounts were funded by the restaurants,[23] the burden became too much for the restaurant partners to bear. In August 2019, the hitherto unorganized restaurants under the aegis of NRAI (https://nrai.org) collectively began protesting against deep discounting by Zomato (and other platforms) using the ***#logout*** campaign. Zomato responded by restricting the number of *Zomato Gold* unlocks per table to two, one unlock per day for every user, and providing ad credits to restaurants that managed more than 1000 unlocks a quarter (restaurants with over 600 unlocks would get video content). The NRAI labeled these changes as cosmetic and not addressing the core problem—one of deep discounting.[24] As Zomato continued expanding the number of subscribers, both the subscribers (fine diners) and the restaurants lost value. The FOMO kept the restaurants going for some time until NRAI started the Twitter campaign. Then one by one, the frustrated restaurants owners began leaving the Gold program. The one-time fee the restaurants paid (₹40,000) was not much to lose, but the 45-day notice period to leave the service was what kept the restaurants logged in.

The Way Forward

When Rashmi received another call on her mobile phone from the local Zomato manager, she knew she had to answer her either way about joining the Zomato Gold delivery program. She had also received an email from Zomato's CEO Deepinder Goyal asking restaurateurs to share their pain points (see Fig. 12.3). She was wondering what she should do now: Should she join this organized rebellion (#logout campaign) that involved leaving not just the Zomato Gold program, but the platform itself?

[23]Kuwar Singh (2019, August 27). "*How India's restaurateurs united on WhatsApp in five hours to fight food delivery apps*". Interview with Anurag Katriar, NRAI Mumbai Chapter. Available at https://qz.com/india/1695796/why-some-indian-restaurants-are-fighting-zomato-swiggy-ubereats/ (Accessed: August 30, 2019).

[24]Abhinaya Vijayaraghavan (2019, August 21). "*Restaurants take control as Zomato Gold loses Midas touch*". Available at: https://the-ken.com/story/restaurants-take-control-as-zomato-gold-loses-midas-touch/ (Accessed: August 30, 2019).

13 Platform Architecture

Platform business models create substantial value through engaging with a wide network of partners and complementors. The more the number and variety of such complementors, the platform has an opportunity to contribute to developing and partaking value in an ecosystem. Such ecosystems could be designed around a specific technology (like artificial intelligence), a business domain (like aviation and aerospace), or a geographic cluster (like the Silicon Valley). For these ecosystems to thrive and create value for its partners and users, there needs to be significant compatibilities and complementarities among its value creating partners. There are three key trade-offs that platform firms need to address in shaping the evolution and value creation opportunity of not just the platform, but for the entire ecosystem including its partners and complementors. These include how much the platform is open or closed; to make the platform core proprietary or shared; and the setting of standards for wide adoption across the ecosystem partners and users. This chapter elaborates on each of these trade-offs for platform firms and elaborates on the implications for platform strategy and growth.

Ecosystem Value

Before we study the architecture of platforms, let us appreciate value creation in ecosystems. There are three layers of value creation in the context of ecosystems—core, configuration, and customization (see Fig. 13.1).

The core layer is the primary value created by the product/service for which the customer is willing to pay. In technology products like desktop computers, the core product includes the micro-processor, power units/batteries, BIOS, storage devices, and other hardware. Quite a lot of times, the computer assemblers include the operating system as well as some basic applications as part of the core products. Configurations might include those that are assembled at the retail store, like the size of the monitors, types of keyboards and trackpads, and other peripherals.

R. Srinivasan, *Platform Business Models*, Management for Professionals,
https://doi.org/10.1007/978-981-16-2838-2_13

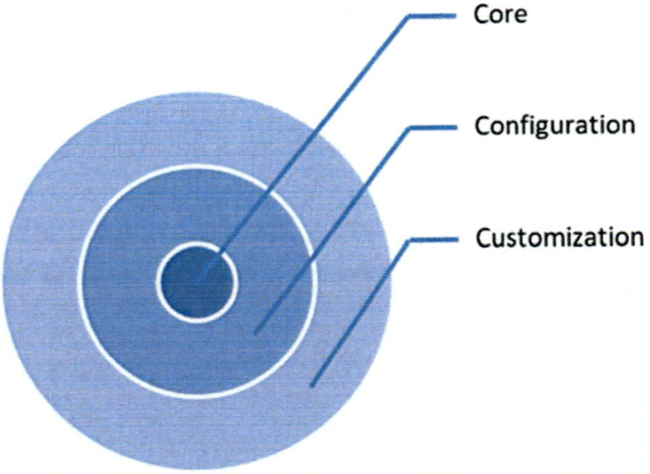

Fig. 13.1 Value creation layers in ecosystems

Customizations might include specific designs/stickers on the desktop, images/logos on the screensavers, firm-specific enterprise software, and services like email setup. In the same market, some brands allow for only basic configuration and most other products/services are internalized inside the core, allowing for the firms to sell different variants, depending on the configurations/customizations. On the other hand, some firms allow for extensive configuration and customization, and derive higher value out of the services provided, than the core product.

In summary, the core layer is available mandatorily for all users, whereas configuration is done for specific consumer segments (based on their specific needs and preferences), and customization is done for every consumer. In pure products like television screens, configurations manifest in terms of models offered by the manufacturers themselves, with consumers being able to make minimal customizations of their televisions. However, in services like fine dining restaurants, end consumers have significant options to customize their meal, over and top of the menu offered (the menu is the configuration layer). In ecosystems like the Android mobile OS, the core is owned by Google, phone hardware manufacturers do the configurations, and the consumers can customize their phones sufficiently. As modularity and compatibilities increase, the opportunities for configuration shifts toward end users, as they have more options.

As we can see, it is possible for a single firm to take ownership of all the three layers—core, configuration, and customization, and move toward more and more productization of the market. And on the other hand, it is also possible for the markets to move toward more and more configuration and customization, leading to servitization. Typically, servitization involves participation of multiple complementors providing customization and configuration value to end consumers, over and above the core value added by the platform. Therefore, it is imperative to understand ecosystem value creation answering two questions—what is the mix of core–configuration–customization offering in the ecosystem; and how many (and which) complementors provide these value creations?

Open and Closed Platforms

The most significant trade-off platform architects and designers are faced with is on their decisions to open their platforms. The more open a platform is, the more likely it would be easier for third-party complementors to affiliate with the platform and develop products/services on the platform. At the other end, a closed platform allows for the platform to charge premium prices from its users for access.

Openness is defined as the extent to which the platform firms share their technologies with independent or third-party partners. The intent of opening the technology is to enable these partners to extend the utility of the platform by building a variety of applications and extensions on top of the core platform technology. Such applications would bring in a wider variety of users and use cases for both the platform firm, as well as those that developed the applications on top of the platform. The platform firm gets more and diverse sets of users; and the application developers get a standard set of core technologies that they do not need to invest in, for their application development. Both the platform firm and the application developers benefit from each other's brand names and adoption externalities and would be able to scale really fast. Such growth of the platform along with the complements also provides opportunities for setting standards for the entire ecosystem.

In open platforms, there are no restrictions on who can affiliate with the platform in its development (of the core), extensions (complementary additions in terms of applications), commercialization (marketing both the platform and its complementary applications), and use (for both personal and commercial ends).[1] This allows for a variety of technology and business complementors to engage with the platform and partake in the growth of the platform/ecosystem. In contrast, closed platforms place restrictions on who can affiliate with the platform in any of its roles. An example of a fully closed platform would be a bunch of legacy applications custom-built for a specific enterprise client.

Platforms engage with multiple stakeholder groups, who perform a variety of roles. We discussed three roles in the first chapter—platform providers, sponsors, and users. Platform users are independent agents that affiliate with the platform for creating or capturing value. Platform providers build and enable the infrastructure for users' interactions with the platform and among themselves. On the other hand, platform sponsors define the rules of engagement and shape information flows. The way these roles are delineated and orchestrated shapes a platform's architecture and

[1]Eisenmann, TE, Parker, G., and Van Alstyne, M. 2008. Opening platforms: How, when, and why? In Gawer, A. (Ed.) Platforms, Markets, and Innovation, Edward Elgar: Cheltenham, UK.

subsequent business model. For instance, there could be platforms like eBay, where the same firm performs both the sponsor and provider roles. On the other hand, we could have technologies like mp3 (sponsor being mp3), where there could be multiple providers (consumer hardware for listening to music).

When we talk of open and closed platforms, we should discuss this in the context of multiple platform roles. Platforms may be open or closed in any or more of these roles. It is pretty common to observe around us that most platforms are in between truly open (open for all the roles) and fully closed (closed for all roles). For example, in the operating systems market, we can see that the Linux ecosystem is truly open for both demand-side users and supply-side users (application developers), as well as supporting wide adoption by a variety of hardware users (providers), and contribution by an open community in developing the core Linux platform. On the other hand, the Apple ecosystem is open only to the end users, whereas the firm controls the operating software and the related IP, produces its own hardware, and controls the participation of independent developers on the AppStore. In between these two extremes, there could be Android platform, where Google owns the operating system and the IP rights to the core technology, allowing independent hardware producers like Samsung and Lenovo to produce hardware; and third-party application developers to create and sell apps on the Play Store. On the other hand, Tesla's proprietary car operating system is embedded in their own car (hardware), while keeping it compatible for application development and commercialization by independent App developers (e.g., infotainment systems).[2] The Table 13.1 below summarizes the range of openness using the examples cited above.

Table 13.1 Levels of openness in multi-sided platforms

	Demand-side user (end user)	Supply-side user (application developers)	Platform providers (hardware)	Platform sponsors (operating system)
Linux	Open	Open	Open	Open
Android	Open	Open	Open	Closed
Tesla Car OS	Open	Open	Closed	Closed
iOS/Apple	Open	Closed	Closed	Closed

Adapted from Eisenmann, TE, Parker, G., and Van Alstyne, M. 2008. Opening platforms: How, when, and why? In Gawer, A. (Ed.) Platforms, Markets, and Innovation, Edward Elgar: Cheltenham, UK

[2]Source: https://www.zdnet.com/article/tesla-starts-to-release-its-cars-open-source-linux-software-code/, last accessed on 23 January 2021.

Trade-Offs in Opening Platforms

Open platforms encourage compatibilities between the platform core technologies and the complements. Such compatibilities increase versatility of the platform and attract a wide variety of application developers, as they incur lesser costs of development and faster development cycles (compared to developing the core technology plus the application). Such variety greatly enhances the value of the platform and in turn attracts more users to adopt the platform. This user base attracts more and more application developers to the platform, triggering cross-side network effects and ensuring rapid adoption of the platform.

Internalizing complementarities: The primary trade-off is between diseconomies of scope arising out of the same firm wanting to produce the core platform as well as secondary complements (may require different competencies and might have different shapes of cost curves) and the costs of ensuring compatibility between the core platform and complements, including transaction costs of engaging with independent developers, governance mechanisms (IP protection and other trade practices), and enabling complementors' profitability. While the first strategy favors opening up the platform, the costs need be surmounted for openness to provide economic value to the platform firm.

Economics of openness: The second trade-off is around pricing and profiting economically from the platform. There are three pricing models available for platforms.

1. It could price the core platform very low and charge a fee from the supply side for the compatibility, who could pass on these costs to the demand side users, by pricing their complements higher.
2. It could sell the platform core technology at a high price and encourage development of a variety of cheaper complements, after a large number of consumers had adopted the platform.
3. It could keep the platform closed for some time, selling its own proprietary complements before opening it out to independent partners.

Each of these pricing models has its own implications on speed, scale, profit potential, and sustainability of the platform.

Innovation and adaptation to technology change: The third trade-off in opening platforms is around the innovation. What is the platform firm's responsibility in ensuring innovation in the ecosystem? While keeping it completely closed, the platform takes full responsibility for ensuring innovation and sustained value creation. In industries that experience rapid technology change and/or evolution of consumer preferences, it could be pretty daunting to secure and sustain its competitive advantage over other platforms. On the other hand, opening up of the platforms to either have independent providers or supply-side complements enables the ecosystem to rapidly adopt technology and consumer changes. However, the platform core needs to be sufficiently flexible for this adaptation to be successful. In such cases, it might be better off to even allow independent complementors to contribute to the platform core technologies. These decisions have implications for speed of adoption and sustainability of the platform/ecosystem.

In summary, there are three trade-offs in the decision to open platform core—relative costs of internalizing or externalizing complementary products; the relative economics of profiting from the core or complements and volume or variety of complements; and the capabilities to innovate and adapt to technology change. While there can be no prescriptions, these choices around complementarity, pricing, and innovation determine platform strategies toward scale, scope, and ecosystem power.

Shared and Proprietary Platforms

Building on openness of the platforms, another critical architectural element in platform firms is the platform design in terms of shared or proprietary platforms. A proprietary platform has a single sponsor who is also the sole provider. A good example of proprietary platforms is the Apple iOS ecosystem. On the other extreme, is a fully shared platform, where there exist multiple sponsors and multiple providers. An example of shared platform is the Universal Product Code (UPC), or more popularly, the barcode. In these shared platforms, many firms may collaborate in defining the product standards, and subsequently compete in providing differentiated but compatible solutions. The presence of compatibility ensures that users have access to the entire range of complements, irrespective of which firm produced it.

In between these two ends of proprietary and shared platforms, there are joint venture platforms and licensing platforms.[3] Joint venture platforms refer to those where multiple firms cooperate in platform design, but a single firm is the platform provider. Example of joint venture platforms is cooperative airline alliances like Star Alliance or the One World alliance. These code sharing alliances are built through the cooperation of multiple airlines who are otherwise competing. However, when it comes to providing services like loyalty benefits or airport lounge services, there is just a single provider. Licensing platforms are those where a single firm serves as the platform sponsor, but many firms competing as platform providers. An example of licensing platforms is the Android operating system, where the sponsor (Google) licenses its use by many phone manufacturers. It is critical to note that the licensing is provided to the phone manufacturer (provider), rather than to the end user.

[3]Eisenmann, TE. 2008. Managing proprietary and shared platforms, California Management Review, 50,4.

Proprietary Platform

A proprietary platform exists when there are incompatibilities across competing platforms. Complements are exclusive to specific competitors, and users who affiliate with a specific platform would typically have access to only those complements that were designed for that platform, and not for other competing platforms. This has two implications for users—the switching costs are very high, as they would lose access to not just the platform as well as its specific complements as they switch; and for the fear of being locked-in, users may not commit to making any investments specific to that platform or the complements.

Therefore, one would typically find proprietary platforms in markets where the users are loyal to the platform, do not value too much variety of complements—that is, they use the platform for a specific set of predictable and repeatable activities, and engage in frequent interactions with the platform. Examples of proprietary platforms are enterprise software, where the businesses do not mind locking-in to a platform and its complements, in return for the efficiency and tight integration of the enterprise software with the business' activities and data. In such cases, given that the switching costs are very high, users spend considerable amounts of time and energy in making the decision to affiliate with a proprietary platform.

In order to be successful as a proprietary platform, a firm has to have significant technological advantage over its rivals to attract users (demand side). This technological advantage should also be good enough to attract a wide variety of complements (supply side) to affiliate with the platform, and therefore be attractive enough for the users to commit their resources to the platform.

Another source of advantage for proprietary platforms is their control over resources that are critical to success in that market. For instance, a tight control over hardware and operating system software allows for Apple to sustain its advantage over its supply-side complements (App Developers and telecom service providers) as well as build loyalty among the demand-side users (consumers) in the iPhone ecosystem. Such control allows for the platform to (a) perform its gatekeeping roles —deciding who can participate and who cannot participate; (b) price access to the platform and its complements/users appropriately to the other side; and (c) enable sufficient transaction control—define what kinds of transactions can take place within the platform and what not. These three critical roles in proprietary platforms are performed by the same firm—which is both platform providers and sponsors.

Figure 13.2 below depicts a proprietary platform ecosystem.

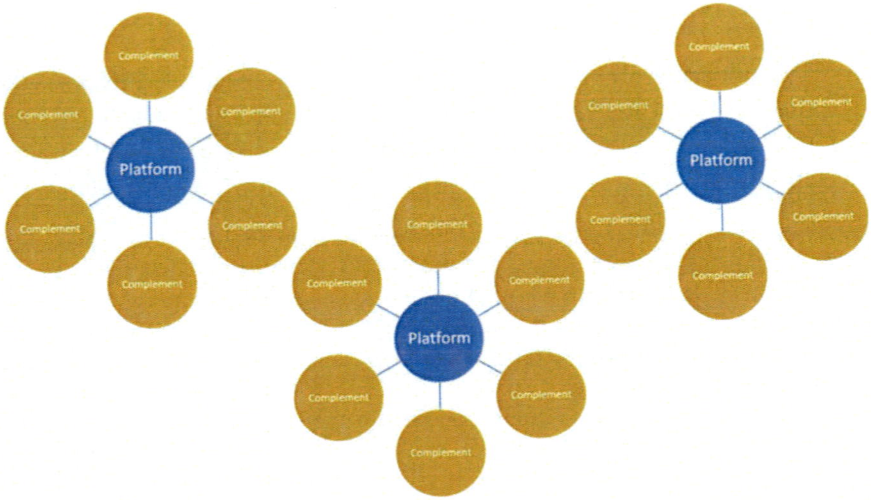

Fig. 13.2 Proprietary platform ecosystem

Shared Platform

A shared platform exists in an ecosystem where there are compatibilities across competing platforms. Therefore, such platforms attract many and wide variety of complements as they can leverage their investments across multiple platforms. In these cases, the platforms and complements differentiate themselves on other features, rather than just compatibility with the platform. More users would be attracted to the platforms, as they could access the utilities of multiple complements. Given the variety, any investments that the users make may not be specific to any platform, and their switching and multi-homing costs may be low. Platform and/or complementor choice and loyalty would, therefore, be based on other factors of differentiation.

One would typically find shared platforms in markets where the technology standards are mature, and users value variety of complements. Users may use platforms for a wide range of utilities, including some infrequent and unpredictable transactions. Examples of shared platforms would include online news aggregation platforms like InShorts, or video sharing platforms like YouTube, where users seek variety of content, and users do not wish to be locked in to one platform. The switching and multi-homing costs are low, and users would typically consume content from multiple sources.

In order to be successful as a shared platform, a firm has to ensure compatibility across a wide variety of complements and use that to attract a large number and diverse sets of complements (supply side). The large volume and variety of content, along with the strong brand of the platform, should attract large number of users (demand side) to the platform. These large numbers should kick-in cross-side network effects and therefore attract more and more supply- and demand-side users.

For developing shared platforms, there may be huge investments required—in both technological core and marketing and branding to attract the initial sets of users. Even after the critical mass of users are attracted, it is imperative that the platform continues its branding efforts to sustain the engagement and retain the user base, as the users' switching costs and multi-homing costs are very low.

In such shared platform ecosystems, there is also a likelihood that there may be fast followers, who appropriate disproportionately more value than their investments. The initial market may be developed through high capital and branding investments by the first mover (to set standards), and fast followers may begin exploiting these investments, by adopting shared standards. Given that the opportunities for technological differentiation are limited, shared platforms use a variety of differentiation mechanisms including attracting marquee brands as complements (like signing up of exclusive contracts with top-grossing artists in a music streaming platform).

Figure 13.3 below depicts a shared platform ecosystem.

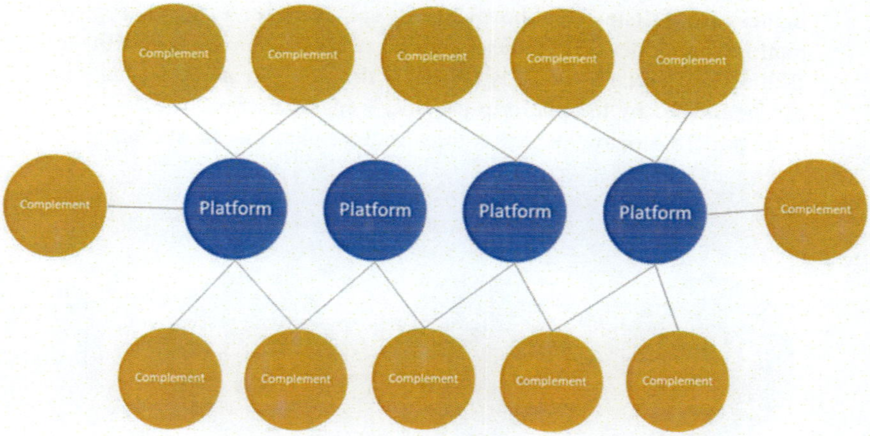

Fig. 13.3 Shared platform ecosystem

Joint Venture Platforms

Joint venture platforms exist in markets where the initial investments in platform design are very high, and no single firm wants to commit to making those commitments, say in setting standards. When the value appropriation opportunities are higher in the platform sponsor role, where the standards are set and the technological core is defined, one might see firms competing to set standards. The platform provider might require economies of scale and scope and might be non-core but critical to value creation. And therefore, one would find these competitors collaborating for these activities.

A critical condition for the existence of joint venture platforms is the strong intellectual protection available to platform sponsors. In an evolving market like the electric vehicle ecosystem, multiple firms may compete in developing efficient batteries and related vehicle design technologies but may collaborate in setting up charging infrastructure across the country. The proportion of value created in design and manufacturing of batteries is surely higher and could be protected through patents and other means. Setting up the consumer charging infrastructure for electric vehicles is time consuming, scale-economic, and could be done through a complement/partner. This is critical to the development of the ecosystem and user adoption but is non-core to the technological evolution and efficiency improvement.

In order to succeed as a joint venture platform, firms need to ensure that their technological core is protected through patents, copyrights, and/or strong brands. While the firms invest heavily in platform design and protecting their intellectual property, firms need to distinguish between those parameters that drive user adoption and loyalty.

In joint venture platforms, platform sponsor quality typically drives user willingness to affiliate with the platform, and the user experience provided by the platform provider drives user willingness to remain loyal to the platform. Willingness to pay is typically driven by the platform sponsor quality and brand but can be limited by the platform provider's inefficiencies.

Figure 13.4 below depicts a joint venture platform ecosystem.

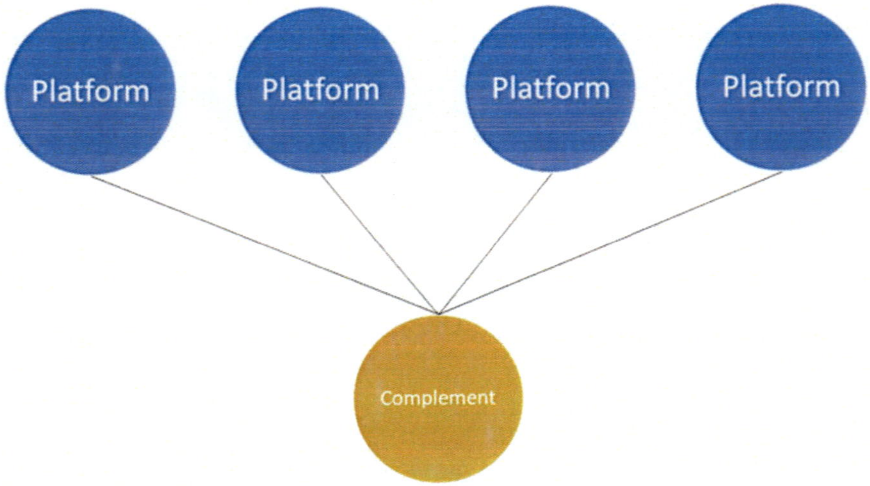

Fig. 13.4 Joint venture platform ecosystem

Licensing Platforms

Licensing platforms exist in markets where the initial investments in platforms are very high, but the returns from these investments are appropriable through the existence of wide complements. In such markets, users attach significant value both the platform core technology and those provided by the complementors.

A typical condition of the existence of licensing platforms is the presence of few platform sponsors that own the intellectual property of the technological core, and such core technology is licensed to a variety of complements. These complementors build on top of the core and provide users with a variety of utilities, including configuration (providing specific suite of products to specific customers) and customization (providing specific value addition to specific users). An example of licensing platforms is India's Unified Payment Interface (UPI), sponsored by the National Payment Corporation of India (NPCI). The NPCI built the payment processes (including backend infrastructure) and has licensed it to be interoperable across multiple partners, who are brands in themselves.

In order to succeed as a licensing platform, the licensees (complementors) should possess unique capabilities that are valued by the platform users and could not be provided by the platform sponsor. The licensees are typically strong brands that the platform leverages to acquire scale and scope.

These markets typically are characterized by a variety of complementors, including some who are exclusive to specific platforms, and some others who may be affiliated with multiple platforms. In typical licensing platform ecosystems, there are different segments of users that value different value propositions, and therefore, the platform licenses the core technology to multiple complementors to serve each of these segments. It is also likely that the users value variety of complements, allowing these complementors to differentiate their products and services. And therefore, it may happen that the complementors' brands may be significantly stronger than the core platform brand in these markets.

Figure 13.5 below depicts a licensing platform ecosystem.

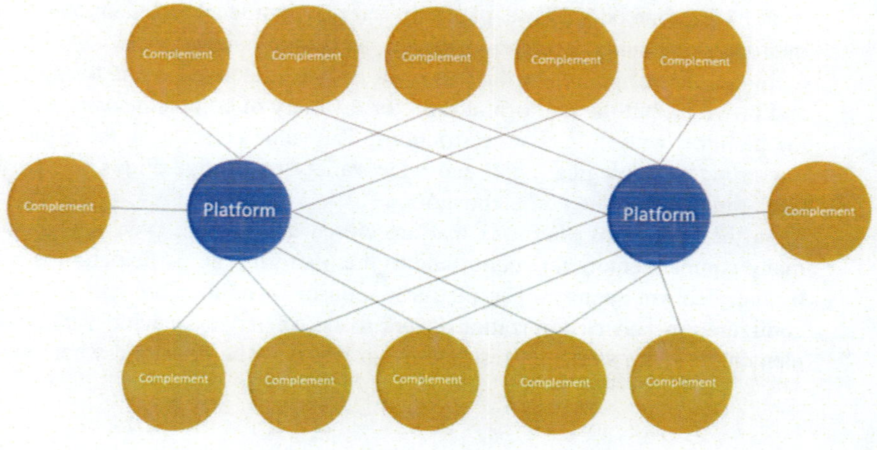

Fig. 13.5 Licensing platform ecosystem

Platform Design in WTA Markets

In markets that are characterized by winner-takes-all dynamics, there is a race to set standards and move the closer ecosystem to proprietary platforms. Given that the multi-homing costs are low in shared platforms, platforms invest heavily in attracting and retaining users through a variety of means, including subsidies, personalization of experiences (say, using recommendation algorithms), and exclusive access to highly preferred complements. In doing so, the attempt is to increase the users' engagement and subsequent investment in the platform, so that there is a lock-in. Take for example, even when cloud-based email services are available free, most users do not multi-home beyond a couple of such emails. The transaction costs of broadcasting a new email address to all their contacts (which may not be easily accessible to the user as a database) and sustaining the differentiation across different emails might dissuade them from signing up for more email addresses. A service like Gmail actively also allows users to classify their emails into multiple folders and categories, thereby enveloping the need for special preferences into their service bundles.

Therefore, we can conclude that, as markets tend towards becoming shared, platform competitors invest heavily in increasing user multi-homing costs, generate significant cross-side network effects, and envelop user special preferences. In effect, the attempt is to move the market to winner-takes-all dynamics, where only one or a few platforms dominate and capture value.

Matrix of Platform Architecture

Putting these two dimensions of open–closed and shared–proprietary platforms together, we would get a landscape like depicted in the Fig. 13.6 below.

In platforms that are open and shared, there exist multiple sponsors and providers, and there are no restrictions on its usage. A typical example of these platforms is the UPC barcode. These platforms create significant value through enabling interoperable standards across platforms and complements.

In the case of platforms that are open and proprietary, there is a single sponsor and provider, but the platform allows for a variety of complements to engage with the platform with little or no restrictions. The value creation by these platforms is the strong technological core, and wide variety of configurations and customizations provided by the complementors.

In the context of platforms that are closed and shared, even though there are many complementors that contribute to the platform, the participation is restricted by the platform sponsor. The platform sponsor owns the core and allows for the configuration and customization layers to be offered by a wide variety of complementors (with sufficient restrictions on what can be done and what cannot be).

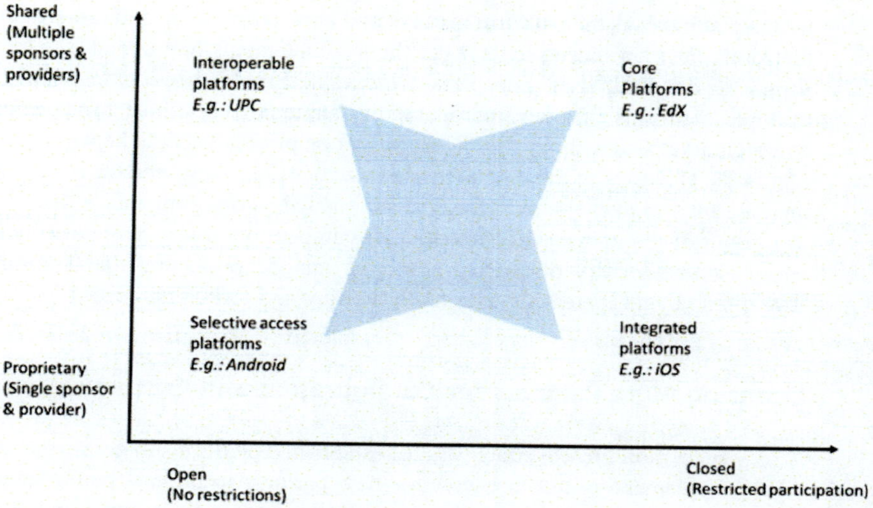

Fig. 13.6 Platform architecture landscape

A good example of a core platform is the EdX platform that owns the core and sets tight quality restrictions on both the supply-side complementors (content providing schools and faculty) and demand-side (learners).

In platforms that are proprietary and closed, all the three layers—core, configuration, and customization—are owned by the same firm. That is, there is no role for independent complementors in adding value to the platform, as all the three value creation options are internalized by the platform firm. The Apple ecosystem includes the iOS operating system, hardware, most critical applications, and service provided by a single firm.

Platform Architecture and Growth

We have so far discussed three main decisions around platform architecture: (a) core, configuration, customization decisions; (b) open–closed continuum; and (c) shared–proprietary continuum. We will now dwell upon the implications of these decisions on platform scale/sustainability and value appropriation.

Interoperability

As we had discussed before, the more open the platform, more likely it would attract complementors, and the wide variety and quality of complements would attract more users. The trade-off here is between rapid scaling of the platform and value capture by the platform. As the platform matures and attracts and more and more users, rival platforms have an incentive to make their complements interoperable across platforms, so that their users can partake the value provided by complements across multiple platforms. If such interoperability strategies contribute to increasing the overall market size without significant impact on prices, it should be welcome by the platforms. However, if the overall market size does not grow, and the rival platforms increase their market shares at the cost of established platform and/or the prices fall as a result of the increased competition, incumbent platforms may erect barriers to entry. Common entry deterrence strategies include protecting the IP, building a strong brand, and increasing user multi-homing and switching costs.

Licensing More Partners for Configuration and Customization

A very successful growth strategy is for established platforms to not restrict entry of other complementors but to encourage new partners to provide configuration and customization value. Such platforms typically protect their core, and the large number of configuration and customization partners helps the market grow. In markets where standards are yet to be set, and when rival platforms are competing against each other for market dominance, onboarding a large number of complementors will help build scale and scope advantages over competition, helping in successful *coring* and *tipping* of the markets (read Chap. 2 for coring and tipping strategies). However, platforms need to ensure that the brand value of the complements does not become stronger than that of the platform, and the users value configuration and customization more than the core.

Opening the Core

Coring and tipping strategies work in relatively stable markets. However, in markets with rapid technological and/or consumer preference evolution, rivalry among platforms might turn counterproductive. No one single firm would be willing to make commitments on a specific technological core, lest technology change makes that redundant/obsolete. Rapid technological obsolescence pushes firms to postpone investments, and the market continues to remain a state of flux. No competitor captures value in such markets. In such markets, it might be beneficial to open the core technology for multiple competing platforms to co-create and evolve standards. When standards evolve, all competitors that contributed to the core get access to value creation opportunities and benefit from widespread adoption of a single standard across the entire ecosystem.

When such standards evolve, and the entire ecosystem adopts these standards, there is likelihood of exclusion of other platforms that do not adhere to these standards. And these markets could demonstrate winner-takes-all (WTA) dynamics, which is the subject of our next chapter.

14 Delhivery: Leveraging the Platform

It was a hot summer day in the North Indian city of Gurugram. In the offices of Delhivery, the top management team had gotten together for an impromptu discussion on their growth aspirations. The group was led by Sahil Barua (CEO) with Mohit Tandon (CSO), Ajith Pai (CFO), Suraj Saharan (COO), Bhavesh Manglani (COO), Kapil Bharati (CTO), Sandeep Barasia (MD of Business Development), and Suraju Dutta (MD of Operations and Engineering) in attendance. The group was discussing how technology had transformed their industry. From the traditional transportation and warehousing business that was laden with unpredictability and inefficiencies, internet technology had helped improve efficiencies that would form the basis of success for the entire internet retail industry. Delhivery had played a significant role in shaping this. While the e-commerce retail firms competed with each other on discounts and low prices, it was imperative that their back-end partners provide them with significant advantage in terms of costs and efficiencies.

In the short period of time (about 5 years) since its founding, Delhivery was considering how it could leverage its technology that had the capability to power the back end of a distributed operation and the last mile distribution knowledge that could provide predictable services to the end consumers of e-commerce and logistics businesses to other domains and geographies. The team reminisced on how it all began and where they had reached. They needed clarity on if and how they

---

R Srinivasan, Professor of Strategy, Sreecharan Rachakonda, and Raj Kovid KR, prepared this case for class discussion. This case is not intended to serve as an endorsement, source of primary data, or to show effective or inefficient handling of decision or business processes.

R. Srinivasan, *Platform Business Models*, Management for Professionals,
https://doi.org/10.1007/978-981-16-2838-2_14

would prioritize between leveraging their technology capabilities to introduce new products, reduce costs for their customers, and enter new markets.

About Delhivery

Initial Thoughts of the Idea[1]

In early 2008, while studying at IIM Bangalore, Sahil and Ajith conceived an idea for a start-up—to help other start-ups by augmenting their operations and finance teams and provide resources to scale their business. However, with the economy going south at that time, the idea could not take flight. Sahil went on to join Bain in their Delhi office, and Ajith joined the Lodha Group in Mumbai. It was at Bain that Suraj, Mohit, and Sahil first met. After working together for 3 years at Bain across private equity and telecommunications, it was clear to all three of them that the internet revolution had just begun in India and that it was the right time for them to set out on the path that would eventually lead to Delhivery.

The three of them already had an interest in the internet space and were impressed with the growth potential of the sector. They were good friends with the co-founders of Zomato, with whom they conducted several brainstorming sessions as they were starting the business. They observed that Zomato was doing fantastic business online but wondered why no one had built a delivery network for restaurants to fulfill the orders. The idea for Delhivery was born out of this discussion. They would tie up with local restaurants and store and fulfill orders placed by customers with these restaurants and stores in 30 min. Shutl, a UK-based start-up, which subsequently became e-Bay was the pioneer in this space. Postmates and Instacart would bring this model to the US markets in May 2011 and 2012, respectively.

The next challenge was getting the company operational. Shortly after coming up with the idea, one night, Sahil and Suraj ordered food from a restaurant in Gurugram. As they were talking to the delivery agent, they understood that the restaurant was shutting down. They rushed to meet the restaurant owner who was surprisingly still there and was keen on his staff being absorbed elsewhere. All of the restaurant's delivery staff was hired on the spot, and this led to the birth of Delhivery.

The first branch of the firm was set up in a 250 ft^2 room in Gurugram, which was their corporate office, dispatch center, call center, and development center all rolled into one. When they started, there were ten people in all, including four delivery agents. Soon, they started clocking in over 100 orders a day in Gurugram and at this point in time, an investor friend of theirs nudged them toward the burgeoning e-commerce space.

The logic was that the peak demand for Delhivery at the time was during lunch and dinner hours, but the agents had little or nothing to do in between. The Delhivery team decided to use those slack hours to deliver consignments for

[1]Source: http://www.nextbigwhat.com/delhivery-startup-journey-297/.

e-commerce companies to customers in Gurugram. Parcels would be delivered on the same day, cash collected could be returned in 24 h, and Delhivery's slack capacity would be fully utilized. This was a win-win for the e-commerce companies, their customers, and Delhivery as well. Delhivery kicked off operations with Urban Touch, Indiatimes, and HealthKart in Gurugram in the summer of 2011. By winter, their order volumes had grown to nearly 600 a day and their clients were demanding expansion to new cities.

To further understand the space, the co-founders began analyzing companies such as Blue Dart and DTDC, which would become their future competitors. They started transferring packages to each other through different delivery services. They ordered a number of products online to understand the strengths and weaknesses of the existing players. Soon they realized that traditional logistics players had limited understanding of the scope of e-commerce fulfillment, which was fundamentally different from traditional freight or mail logistics. Given that the e-commerce market was expected to grow to nearly $100 billion by 2020, the Delhivery team decided to pivot to focus purely on the e-commerce fulfillment opportunity, sacrificing their hyperlocal business for the time being.

Enterprise Story 2011–2015

Delhivery began as a simple intra-city transportation service provider. When they started out in 2011, they had a simple value proposition—they would deliver faster, provide real-time tracking of shipments, and manage cash more effectively than the incumbent players. They could deliver faster because they did not use a classic hub-and-spoke model, thereby eliminating a number of unnecessary steps in the process. They could provide real-time tracking to customers by implementing predictive tracking rather than a reactive or scan-based tracking. Also, no other logistics company had built processes to automate cash handling at that time. They believed that once they were able to solve these three problems, two things should start happening—customer confidence would grow which would lead to larger repeat purchasing, and return rates would drop.

At that time, the return rates of some of the e-commerce companies were as high as 37–38% and they would receive payments from logistics companies once a month. Consumers were wary of repeat purchases owing to delays in product delivery and poor delivery. So, Delhivery sought to measure its success based on how well they were able to improve these metrics. Within the first 6 months, the return rates went down from 38 to 16% through their faster delivery and clearer tracking. After the initial burst, however, they had hit a wall and could not bring it below 16%. On further examination, they realized that the problem was not with consumer behavior, but with the pre-shipping leg of the supply chain. Merchants and warehouses were shipping products 7 days after the order had been placed in some instances. So, even with Delhivery delivering orders on the same day or within 2 days, by the time the customer received the product, it would be 10 days since he had placed the order. The next step for Delhivery was clear. Suraj was tasked with creating Delhivery's warehousing vertical, with the goal of fulfilling an order, end to end, within 48 h of order placement on the website.

To support the new business, Delhivery raised $7.5 M in capital from Times Internet Limited and Nexus Venture Partners in 2012 and 2013. They had studied e-commerce models around the world and concluded that building their own systems in-house for transportation and warehouse management would become a huge competitive advantage. They started with transportation and then expanded into fulfillment and order management systems. In their early days, the original and only purpose of technology was to adapt the paper-based model of delivery into a Web console. At this level, the system acted more similar to an assistant. As their volumes and network started to grow, they came across new challenges and started writing rules back into the system. The next level they added to the system was basic user permissions. Then came in the requirements of cash on delivery (COD) collections and reporting mechanisms. Slowly, the system emerged from being a mere assistant to a guide for the finance team, the operations team, and the management team as well. Similarly, that is how they intended to build technology for the fulfillment side as well—by moving in as an assistant first and then functioning as a guide.

In order to enhance the express and fulfillment businesses, Delhivery put together a small team of people to work on Data Science. The intent of Data Science was to look at 55 million packages over a billion scans and produce results which would push them from a guided to directed system. Having collected such volumes of data, they could define the expected path for any shipment, optimally balancing time, cost, and distance. They attempted to get to a point where the system could tell what the next step of a shipment should be, even if it was mis-routed, thereby eliminating human error in decision-making. The team also worked on services such as address disambiguation, network planning and simulation, and universal catalog among other innovative services.

Around 2013–2014, the market grew nearly 3.5 times and Delhivery grew 4 times as well and gained share, but the fact is that they could have grown over 6 or 7 times by capitalizing on the rising tide. Despite having the capital and growing as fast they could, they could not build enough capacity to keep pace with the market because they did not have the people or the time. Then, they realized that this was going to be a continuous feature. Also, regulatory constraints in India were beginning to ease at that time. Goods and Services Tax (GST) was on its way, state taxation was improving, and it became easier to move in and out of cities. They realized that soon the competitive advantages of the national players were going to diminish over time, and the local players were going to hit back at the aggregators and undercut them on price, as it had already been happening around the world to FedEx, UPS, and DHL by then. So, Delhivery decided to power the local players instead and weave them into their system. Around end of 2014, they started opening up their technology. They had been re-architecting their systems to make them open; they started releasing parts of their code base and exposing application program interfaces (APIs) to third parties.

When they came back to the hyperlocal business in 2015, Delhivery's intention was to get the local mom and pop shops and kirana stores online. They observed that if they could get all levels of inventory—at the local store, at a platform level, at an individual seller, and at a fulfillment center—in one view, they could cut down on cost drastically. This kind of inventory aggregation is extremely valuable for e-commerce platforms as well. For instance, Delhivery could essentially leverage this and source a product from somewhere else if a client's platform did not have the stock. They had not enabled it yet, but they possessed the functionality to do this. Since October 2015, Delhivery engaged a separate team for on-demand delivery (ODX), which carried out primarily food and C2C delivery. Each had its own issues and opportunities. They piloted ideas such as sharing their existing fleet between express and hyperlocal delivery since they usually had different peak hours, or undertook 2–4 h food deliveries instead of 30–40 min, which could be much more valuable to some customers, etc. Scheduling and fleet allocation become extremely critical in these businesses and were problems being tackled by the Data Sciences team.

Delhivery has also been looking at co-developing warehouses with entrepreneurs. Given that there is much spare warehousing capacity lying vacant in India, instead of building everything on their own from scratch, they approached existing warehousing owners who had already sunk in the capital. Also, many of them had profitability issues. Delhivery's discovery team worked with warehouse owners to actively manage warehouses instead of only managing real estate by leasing technology, helping with design, setting up and training the operations teams, and assisting with local business development as well. In exchange, Delhivery took a small revenue share per order moving out of the warehouse. On how they would find warehouses, Sahil commented:

> Given the size of the opportunity, we usually find good warehousing space relatively easily. There is active supply of high-quality mid-size warehouses so it is fairly easy to avoid the poor ones. For instance, we could go to any industrial area and find warehouses compliant with our design requirements. So we would go to 30 miles outside Jaipur or 20 miles outside Surat and set up high quality infrastructure. Though we suspect that once we start hitting second and third tier cities, the problem will be more thorny.

Growth Over the Years

Table 14.1 summarizes the growth of the firm since 2011. During 2018–2019, Delhivery witnessed a 42% revenue growth to Rs. 1070 crores, over the previous year, and its net losses were Rs. 684 crores.[2] It had been one of the well-funded start-ups in the Indian logistics industry, counting on marquee investors.

[2] 1 USD = Rs. (INR) 70, on December 1, 2018; 1 crore = 10 millions.

Table 14.1 Growth of Delhivery

	2011–12	2012–13	2013–14	2014–15	2015–16	2016–17	2017–18	2018–19
Cities	2	31	130	175	400	500	1200	1700
Clients	6	75	600	800	1950	3000	3000	3500
Sellers	20	53	10,000	25,000	100,000	100,000	150,000	150,000
Products/day	500	9000	40,000	90,000	200,000	320,000	350,000	400,000
Team size	150+	1000+	2500+	5000+	14,500	NA	15,000+	21,000+
Fulfillment space (ft^2)	5000	10,000+	40,000+	0.5 + million	1 million	1 million	1 million	6 million
Revenue (US$ million/Rs.)	$0.5 million	$2.8 million	$10.4 million	$37.2 million	$107.7 million	Rs. 743.70 Cr[a]	Rs. 1023.05 Cr[a]	Rs. 1070 Cr[b]
Net losses (Rs.)						Rs. 629.21 Cr[a]	Rs. 637.83 Cr[a]	Rs. 684 Cr[b]

Sources http://www.delhivery.com/about.html; company corporate profile (available with authors)
[a]https://www.vccircle.com/softbank-vision-fund-to-pick-38-stake-in-delhivery-in-latest-india-bet/
[b]https://tech.economictimes.indiatimes.com/news/startups/delhivery-sees-strong-growth-in-revenue-in-fy18/67256285

Table 14.2 Pin code coverage of Delhivery compared to other logistics companies (as of June 2016)

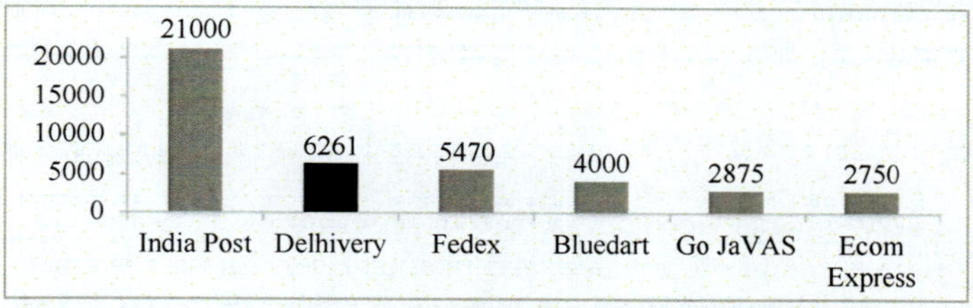

Sources http://www.delhivery.com/about.html; company corporate profile (available with authors)

Current Status[3]

As of December 2018, Delhivery operated four service lines—express delivery, fulfillment services, Omni-channel services, and cross-border services. They had 30 fulfillment centers, across 12 cities. The company had fulfilled over 250 million shipments in 2018 and was well set to cross 350 million by the end of the financial year. Table 14.2 shows the pin code coverage of Delhivery compared to other logistics companies.

Delhivery Businesses

Delhivery's businesses could be broadly classified into four sets of customer-facing activities:

1. Express services, focused on last mile delivery for e-commerce retail firms
2. Fulfillment services, storage, pick-and-pack, and shipping services
3. C2C delivery
4. Focused on individual customers sending packets to other individuals, and hyperlocal, focused on food delivery in hyperlocal markets.

Express Services

Delhivery began as a pure-play transportation company focused on e-commerce fulfillment. This was a B2B sales process targeted at e-commerce retailers and online marketplaces. By being last mile delivery partners, Delhivery was also directly in touch with the end consumers of these retailers. As the e-commerce

[3]Company corporate profile (available with authors); https://www.delhivery.com/about/.

industry matured and more sellers and retailers entered the online space, the need for end-to-end supply chain services and a broader access to infrastructure was heightened.

Customer Segments

Delhivery's has serviced primarily four segments of customers. The largest segment has been e-commerce retailers and marketplaces. These customers have generated demand and passed orders and fulfillment schedules to Delhivery. For these customers, Delhivery also had capabilities to directly pick up products from sellers' warehouses/depots/factories or to store and ship products on behalf of these sellers and the marketplaces from Delhivery's own fulfillment centers. A nationwide last mile feet-on-the-street distribution network tightly integrated with a world-class fulfillment center operation was the key success factor in managing the expectations of this customer segment.

The second segment of customers included small and medium businesses who wanted to extend their offline services to online or entrepreneurs building first time online businesses from scratch. These customers were typically producers or traders of products who wanted to reach a larger end consumer base through e-commerce. These small and medium businesses would either have invested in their own niche e-commerce websites or would list on one or more of the marketplaces. These customers typically demanded nationwide transportation services and last mile delivery of products from a single or a few source locations along with fulfillment center support for storage and pick–pack–ship services.

The third segment of customers consisted of offline brands going online—what Delhivery called their enterprise segment. Customers such as Arvind Mills or Madura Garments or Welspun would supplement their brick-and-mortar retail network with an online presence and would look for partners such as Delhivery for various flexible fulfillment and delivery solutions. Each of these retailers planned to invest heavily in acquiring and deploying sophisticated e-commerce platforms themselves that would augment their vast offline retail and distribution infrastructure. Their key expectation from partners such as Delhivery was providing seamless omni-channel fulfillment capabilities. Another service these enterprise customers looked for is pure logistics between their manufacturing/warehousing locations to their distributors/retailers located across the country.

The fourth segment of customers was individual consumers. Consumer demand could manifest as either traditional retail parcel shipping or one-off procurement by a small business owner. This segment required cheap, effective pickup, and last mile delivery capabilities.

Delhivery was serving all of these segments of customers nationwide by 2016.

Operations

Delivery's express services were designed to operate in three layers—the first layer was the order-capture layer or the discovery layer; the second layer was the inventory layer; the third was the transportation layer. The discovery layer helped Delhivery receive consumer location, product information as well as the source location (where the items were available at the time of order) from their customers, say, an e-commerce retailer. Delhivery did not play a significant role in defining and optimizing this layer, especially for the larger customers. In the instance of a small and medium business, Delhivery might advise on the same, but it would ultimately be the customer's choice of how to operate and optimize this layer.

Delhivery's significant value addition was in the inventory layer. This is the activity that follows the discovery layer where the coordinates of the end consumer and the product have been identified. A typical e-commerce order may contain multiple items, and these could be located in different warehouses across the country. Delhivery had to optimize the transportation based on three criteria—need for kitting them together, time taken for transportation, and cost of transportation. For instance, there could be fashion or book orders, where there is no value of kitting all the items of the order together and they could be delivered independently as suborders. In that instance, each item/location combination was considered a suborder and the last mile delivery was planned accordingly. However, when there is need to integrate all the items of the order together into a kit (such as a keyboard, mouse, monitor, and a CPU in a desktop order), the optimization of where to ship these independent items for kitting is decided on basis of the time taken for transportation and the cost of transportation. For instance, it is likely that a very bulky item is located in a warehouse closer to the final delivery location, all other items may be shipped to that warehouse and kitted there for last mile delivery. Sometimes, because of taxation and regulatory restrictions, it might not be possible for moving certain items into a particular state. In that instance, the items are all transported to a central warehouse and kitted there for transportation to the delivery location.

Ideally, this consolidation would be performed at a pre-last mile location to leverage on the economies of scale and scope available at the fulfillment centers, rather than at the last mile. The inventory layer is a combination of two sub-layers when there is a need for consolidation. Delhivery clearly separates its warehousing activities from the transportation activities—the transportation layer does not touch the package before it is ready to ship but focuses only on pick and pack. Any consolidation or kitting would be done at a warehouse (fulfillment center) and not in transit or in the last mile.

The transportation layer was the third layer of services. There were two legs to the transportation layer—an inbound transportation of goods to the fulfillment center (FC) and an outbound transportation from the fulfillment center to the dispatch center (DC). There were two possible scenarios here—when the products were stored at the Delhivery-operated FC from the start, that is, even before the orders, and when the product would be picked up from the customer warehouse

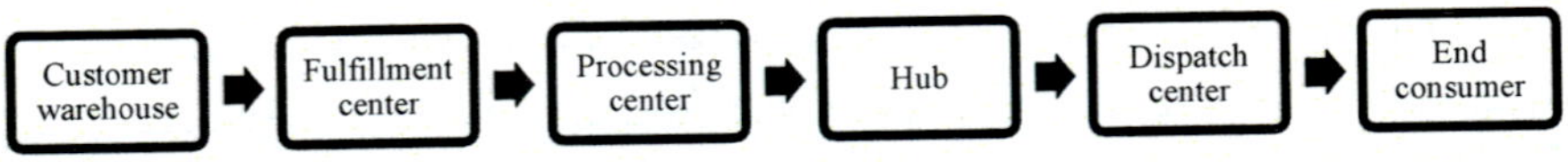

Fig. 14.1 Typical transportation layer

only after receipt of the order. In the first scenario, the outbound transportation would be fulfilled from the FC stock. In the second instance where the inbound transportation happens after the order receipt, there would be just-in-time (JIT) fulfillment, where the products would be cross-docked directly from the inbound to outbound transportation. Delhivery operated 19 fulfillment centers, 40 hubs, 730 dispatch stations, and 13 automated sortation centers across the country (as on June 2016) and was rapidly growing in penetration. Dispatch stations would deliver last mile to the end consumer.

Figure 14.1 depicts a typical transportation layer. After receiving orders, items were picked up from the customer warehouse to the fulfillment center (inbound). At the fulfillment center, they were picked, packed, and transported to the processing centers. These processing centers sorted and bagged the items for specific locations (serviceable areas). These bags were then transported to hubs where they were either shipped to the dispatch centers (if they are to be delivered within the same city) or transferred to delivery partners (line haul) for shipping to outstation dispatch centers. It was possible that Delhivery's customers used delivery partners other than Delhivery and used Delhivery's fulfillment centers only. Once the bags were received at the dispatch centers, they were opened and sorted into specific runs (routes taken by local delivery persons) for delivery.

In instances, where the volumes for a specific delivery city were very low or sporadic to justify establishment of a dedicated dispatch center, Delhivery operated Distributed Processing Centers (DPCs), which received bags containing shipments to a collection of such small volume cities. These bags were then opened at the DPCs, and then the orders were delivered either through the nearest DCs or directly to the end consumers from the DPCs.

One of the major requirements for express services by e-commerce retailers and marketplaces in India has been for the last mile delivery partner to collect cash/payment for the goods sold through the COD. This model has been driving the phenomenal growth rates of the Indian e-commerce volumes. This placed a huge demand on the last mile logistics partner to collect cash/payment from the end consumer on behalf of the customer. Delhivery managed this cash in two ways—in larger DCs where large amount of cash was collected daily, the banks' representatives would pick up the cash from the DCs by the end of the day. In smaller DCs with lesser cash, the DCs stored the cash in lockers and deposited them the next day in the local bank branches. These cash transactions were reconciled by the end of the day daily with the deliveries at the DC level as well as the national level.

Another defining feature of Indian e-commerce market has been the volume of returns. Given the intense competition in the e-commerce retailers/marketplaces, consumers were presented with significant choice. This often resulted in significant volumes of returns as well. Combined with the option of paying COD, Indian consumers had begun exercising their power of choice by delaying decision-making until the time the product arrived at their doorstep. Therefore, managing returns was another significant expectation from the logistics partners. There were two kinds of returns: doorstep returns where the customer did not even take delivery of the product, and post-sale returns where the customer took delivery of the product and then chose to return the product later. Managing doorstep returns was intuitive and easy; it was the post-sale return that differentiated Delhivery. The same staff on that route would pick up the returns from the end consumers toward the DCs. Returns were handled with almost the same process as the forward logistics, with the DCs sending the returned items back to the Return Processing Centers (in most large cities) or to the processing centers for re-bagging returns to the seller.

Fulfillment Services

Delhivery's vision for their fulfillment business was inspired by Amazon Web Services (AWS). Just as AWS provided computing capacity to businesses of all sizes across the world, allowing them to transform fixed computing costs into pay-as-you-use variable costs, Delhivery intended to provide third-party warehousing/fulfillment services to businesses backed by their formidable warehouse management and supply chain technology while saving their customers the capital expenditure of setting up warehouses on their own. The basic premise was to convert fixed warehousing costs which are very high during lean periods and convert them to variable costs depending on volume of business done by the customer, while maintaining exceptionally high service standards and precision.

Delhivery followed two models of fulfillment. One was to support marketplace models where sellers would stock in the Delhivery FCs and use Delhivery's channel management services to sell across multiple demand channels. The other was the inventory model where sellers/retailers/manufacturers would stock in Delhivery's FCs for their own channel/demand.

Delhivery's FCs offered services such as inbound logistics into the FC, packaging and labeling, pick–pack–ship, and express services. In the inventory model, Delhivery maintained the inventory on behalf of the seller in the FCs. When an order was placed for the item through either the seller's website or one of the e-commerce marketplaces, then Delhivery would pick, pack, and provide express services/transfer to another delivery partner. For instance, a seller of mobile phones might utilize Delhivery's inventory services, receive an order through a marketplace, and use the express services of the logistics subsidiary of the e-commerce company. One of the critical competencies in the marketplace fulfillment model was the ability to provide cross-docking services. In cross-docking, the FC only receives the items, labels/relabels the items, and ships them outward. Exhibit 14.1 depicts the marketplace model, and Exhibit 14.2 depicts the inventory model.

Exhibit 14.1 Marketplace model of fulfillment. *Source* Authors' representation

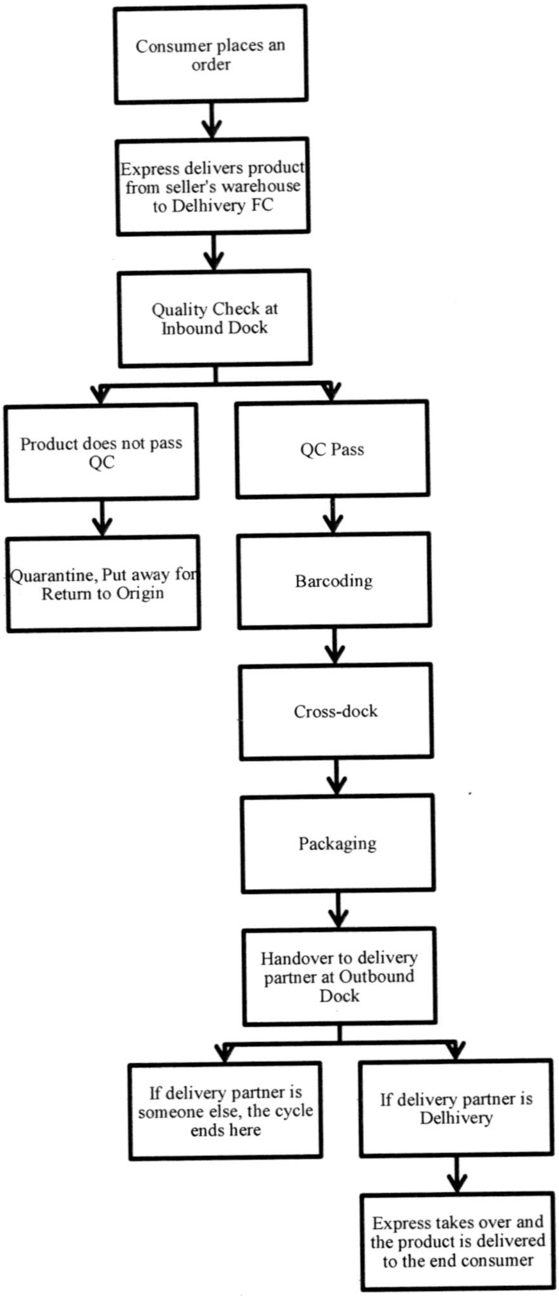

Exhibit 14.2 Inventory model of fulfillment. *Source* Authors' representation

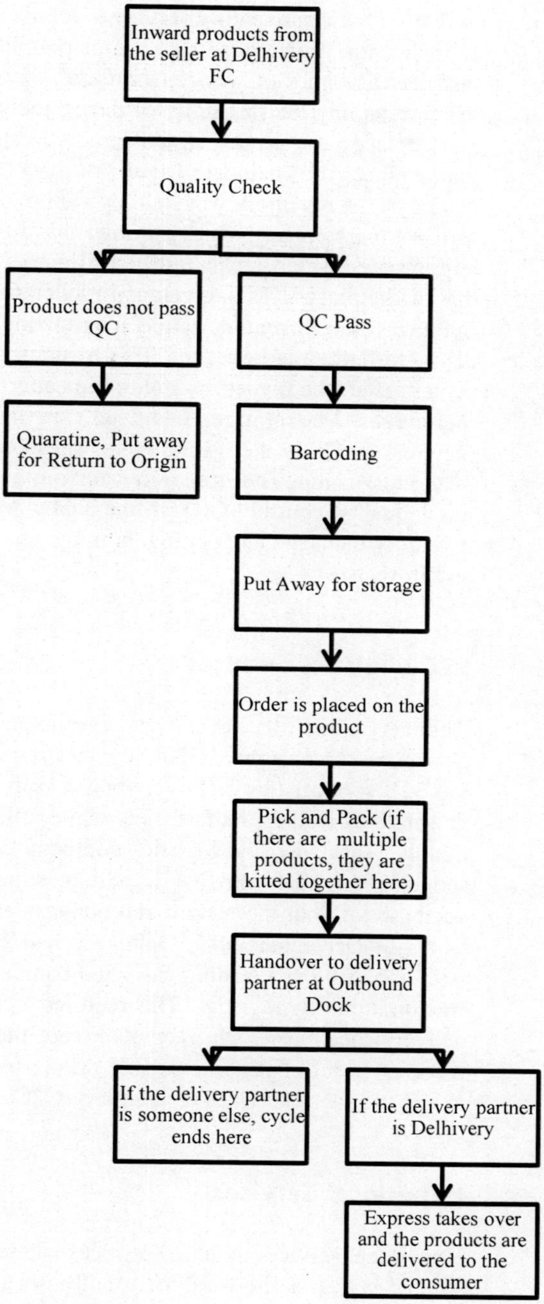

Through their inventory services, Delhivery allowed sellers to provide visibility of their entire inventory to all the marketplaces that the seller was listed on. For instance, a vendor of wooden furniture may have a total inventory of 100 chairs. While retaining the flexibility of listing the inventory across multiple e-commerce marketplaces, the vendor would be able to showcase the entire inventory in all the marketplaces the chairs are listed. All marketplaces showed the availability as 100 chairs, as the inventory was held by Delhivery, who could fulfill demand from any of these marketplaces. Once an order was fulfilled for any of the marketplaces, the appropriate inventory was reduced from the total, and the same was updated in all the marketplaces. This inventory model fulfillment service allowed vendors to optimize their inventory while maximizing their visibility and chances of sale across different marketplaces. This inventory held by Delhivery in their fulfillment centers could be owned by either the seller or, sometimes, even the marketplaces themselves. Marketplaces could procure fast moving items in bulk from manufacturers and hold the inventory for subsequent sale, when the orders arrived.

Critical competencies required for running an efficient fulfillment service were good quality control (QC) as the items were received at the FC, and efficient inventory management (coding, binning, and tracking) of individual items in the FC and in transit.

C2C Logistics Services

Delhivery had its eyes set on expanding its C2C logistics as well. Consumer-to-consumer (C2C) logistics required a different set of capabilities from the B2B services that Delhivery began with. It required a consumer interface at the first mile as well as the last mile, while utilizing the same line haul services in the middle. That way, the logistics company could leverage economies of scale and scope in the back end, while adding significantly to its consumer geo-location database (at both the pickup and delivery ends).

As of December 2015, Delhivery had seeded its C2C business in partnership with one of India's leading classified companies. Initially, the focus of the business was on intra-city logistics. This required tight coordination between the source and delivery locations, such as making sure that the seller (or shipper) and buyer (or receiver) would both be available during pick-up or drop-off. Delhivery had plans to expand these services to inter-city C2C services as well.

Hyperlocal Services

Hyperlocal services included services where the source and delivery locations were located within a short radius, usually not more than 6 km. In the hyperlocal services, the delivery partner received an order from the end consumer that was placed at a vendor/seller. For the order to be fulfilled, the delivery partner should have real-time visibility of the vendor's inventory, as well as have capabilities to deliver the items within extremely short timelines, typically 30–60 min. Speed of pickup and delivery has been a critical success factor in the instance of hyperlocal delivery services.

Delhivery forayed into hyperlocal food delivery services in 12 cities. In order to ensure visibility of vendor inventory in a locality, Delhivery invested in encouraging the vendors to use their point-of-sale (PoS) devices. As soon as an item was ready and available, Delhivery had visibility of the same through the PoS system and the ability to aggregate the same over a specific geography. So, when a customer ordered for a particular item, Delhivery had full real-time information of what items were available, where and at what price.

The PoS installed at the vendors provided Delhivery with an equivalent of a virtual disaggregated "dark store."[4] This visibility into the vendor inventory was a significant source of data for Delhivery, where it could help the vendors with predictive analytics and consult on decisions such as pricing, flash sale, and inventory buildup for a season. This data was available on the cloud and, when it attained a specific scale, could be significantly useful to the customer for making sense based on the local realities and end consumer needs. For instance, an apparel store owner located near a school might be able to build inventory of a particular color and size of trousers to cater to the demand for uniforms from the school students. Delhivery sold the PoS, an integrated hardware and software solution for use by the hyperlocal merchants, with the ability to store the inventory data on the cloud. Delhivery, thence, had the abilities to provide visibility to this data on the cloud to specialized marketplaces such as zomato.com, who responded to this real-time data with orders sourced from end consumers.

Delhivery had developed an on-demand delivery platform, called ODX. Through this platform, Delhivery used the lean periods of the day for the delivery persons (lunch and dinner time) to enter food delivery from hyperlocal locations. These delivery persons were provided handhelds, and their locations were easily traceable. Given that the infrastructure existed, it was imperative to connect all the dots—vendor inventory availability, visibility of that inventory on a food ordering platform, receiving customer orders, passing of that order to the restaurant's virtual dark store, locating the delivery person in the near vicinity of the restaurant, and the end consumer, and therefore fulfilling the same. All these exchanges were real-time data exchanges driven by technology, resulting in the delivery person's handheld receiving information about the restaurant address, order details, and the consumer address. Once this was done, hyperlocal delivery could be done in a matter of minutes of the item being available. Delhivery pilot tested the ODX platform in December 2015 and released it in early 2016 to enable all its point-to-point transportation operations.

[4]Dark Store: Large retail facility that resembles a conventional supermarket or other store but is not open to the public, housing goods used to fulfil orders placed online. http://www.oxforddictionaries.com/definition/english/dark-store.

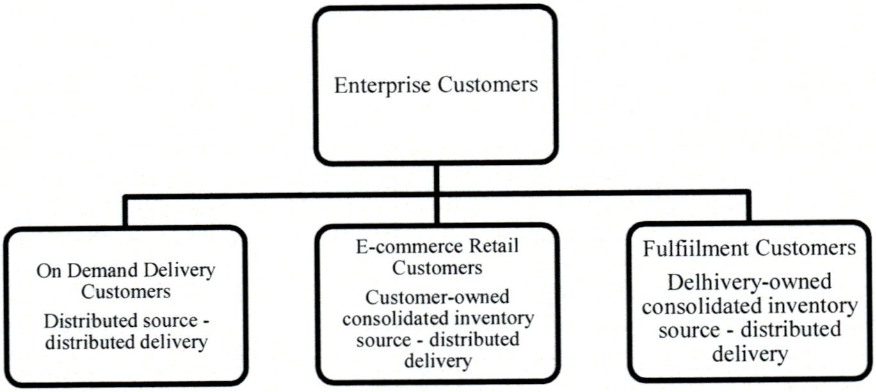

Fig. 14.2 Three kinds of enterprise customers. *Source* Authors' representation

Delhivery's Services

Delhivery provided a variety of services for its enterprise customers. They were organized into three distinct segments—customers for hyperlocal food delivery, where the sourcing address and the delivery address were uniquely provided for every order/transaction; customers for e-commerce retail, where the source was pre-defined as a specific customer warehouse/depot and the delivery address was provided uniquely for each transaction; and Delhivery's fulfillment customers, where the sourcing was from one of Delhivery's own or contracted warehouses to be delivered to an address provided for every transaction (see Fig. 14.2). For the enterprise customers, Delhivery provided significant value addition by enabling all three modes of logistics—distributed sourcing to distributed delivery; consolidated (customer-managed inventory) sourcing to distributed delivery; and consolidated (Delhivery-managed inventory) to distributed delivery. This enabled Delhivery to balance hyperlocal deliveries, e-commerce express deliveries, as well as express deliveries enabled by their fulfillment services. Mohit explained it thus:

> What we have built is a fulfilment platform where basically, the partners digitally interact with each other. After that, the physical service is connecting the goods or the services and payments is what we do; and that is what we call as our platform. So warehouse being one part of it, we need our enterprise customers to use it. That is where our network effects come in, with the size and spread of our warehouses. Now the objective is not to just scale up with the enterprise partners; it is to activate more and more buyers and sellers in the network., Basically what we do, for example, is that, we'll go to a market, let's say like Lucknow or Guwahati where not many people actually sell, they don't even know what e-commerce is all about. We'll go and enlist one of the sellers. There is no investment required for this from the sellers. We will train them, coach them; and then they start getting additional business volumes. Now, typically all these traders/suppliers are located in a cluster. And when they see what one of their own has gone on to e-commerce, they all get

> curious on the same, and they approach us. One of the qualities of any platform should be that it should be plug and play for anybody to connect with. So that's what we have created; sellers don't have to spend money to actually become a part of the e-commerce revolution.

On the warehousing side, Delhivery had signed up with 10 warehouse owners to stock products, either for fulfillment services or in transit. These warehouses were owned by independent entrepreneurs but would have been constructed to Delhivery's specifications. The warehouse owner would typically own the land, equipment, and property in the warehouse, and lease the same to Delhivery for a fixed time and commission. Delhivery added value to the warehouse owner by including him/her as part of the national network of warehouses. Being part of the warehouse network enabled visibility of his/her stock to the entire network, thereby optimizing inventory across the entire network, as well as increasing inventory turnarounds and capacity utilization of the individual warehouses.

Delhivery's fulfillment customers (sellers on e-commerce platforms/marketplaces) did not always use Delhivery as their last mile delivery partner. For instance, an e-commerce retailer could contract with its own subsidiary firm for last mile delivery. While sellers on that marketplace might use Delhivery's fulfillment services, they could be contractually required to use the captive logistics arm as their delivery partner while selling through the marketplace. On the other hand, if the same seller sold his/her products through another marketplace, he/she could choose Delhivery as the delivery partner. This flexibility of choosing the last mile delivery partner provided to the seller or the marketplace ensured that the inventory was optimized. Coupled with the retail point-of-sale (PoS) devices, real-time inventory data could be captured across the seller's physical offline store, as well as his/her affiliation with every other e-commerce marketplace.

Pricing

Delhivery has been an integrated platform which offers a range of services, with each service remaining modular. It followed a module-based pricing model for each of its services. A customer could choose to avail only fulfillment services or only transportation support of a specific kind from Delhivery and pay for that individual service module. If a customer wanted to utilize the entire platform on a single pricing basis, Delhivery could do that as well.

Transportation Services

Delhivery's transportation services consisted of two kinds of pricing models—one for standard express delivery and the other for on-demand delivery. Under the standard delivery model, it followed the industry structure and charge per delivery based on which of the four categories the delivery belonged to. The first category was the same city delivery or what they call as Zone A. The second was regional, which was any shipment to be delivered within 500 km from where it has been picked up. The third category was metro-to-metro deliveries, and the fourth was rest of India. In most instances, there was an additional charge for areas such as the Northeast, Jammu & Kashmir, and Kerala, because of specific costs of reaching there. There was an additional pricing for COD and for any other special services such as card on delivery and open delivery. Delhivery was in the middle of the bucket compared to its competitors in price. It was their clear strategic goal to be the most efficient player in the industry, and the intention of the team was to continue to find ways to reduce the cost of their services. Within its express model, it offered something called an all-India surface product, which had much commonality with the express pricing. The price was same for intra-city and regional, but it varied for national and anything that was sent far away. Typically, these were offered on a slab basis. A slab could be 500 g or 1 kg or 3 kg, with additional slabs being charged extra.

Another pricing model Delhivery followed under transportation was for on-demand deliveries where it charged on a per order basis in order to cover the delivery cost. In 2016, it offered this to restaurants in hyperlocal food delivery and was looking to offer the same model for all kinds of hyperlocal demand deliveries in the future. It operated on a per transaction basis for C2C deliveries as well, where it charged for transportation and packaging.

Fulfillment Services

Under its fulfillment services, it primarily charged for three parts—storage, processing, and packaging. Unlike general warehousing where a product was charged on basis of area, Delhivery charged per cubic feet on a per piece basis for storage of inventory, so that customers were not charged for the empty space on the racks. It charged for processing which included picking and packing the products, labeling them, and handing them over to the transportation partner. Since Delhivery handled the outer packaging of products, it charged for that as well.

Technology Services

There were various pricing models for the technology services Delhivery provided to its customers, most of which were either on a per month basis for usage of the software or on a per order processed basis. Its focus on pricing has been on the fulfillment and express side and not on the technology side. In fact, it viewed its technology services as a hook to bring in clients, whether they may be sellers, marketplaces, or enterprises, so that it could induce them to start using its physical services. This pricing structure for express delivery and fulfillment was common across all segments of Delhivery's customers. There were however a few nuances in pricing structures and additional sources of revenue from some segments of the customers.

Pricing of Bundles

Most of Delhivery's marketplace customers would opt for a pricing which was separate for the transportation and the fulfillment services. Some of them may also ask Delhivery for additional services on the platform such as sourcing sellers for them in particular areas. Delhivery charged for these services separately. However, Delhivery would source sellers in order to augment its own fulfillment business anyway. The first thing it seeded into this segment of small and medium business owners who were looking to start selling online was the marketplace panel. These marketplace panels are simple technology products which enable sellers to manage their inventory and allocate it across different marketplaces. Delhivery did not charge anything for this product at that time. When the sellers used this product, it became easier to manage their inventory across multiple marketplaces, which led to higher volumes. Then, Delhivery intended to cross-sell its fulfillment services to these sellers. In the future, it may choose to charge Rs. 0.5 or Rs. 1 per order since there might be sellers who do not need fulfillment services (such as a boutique owner). Other factors such as its offline–online mix and limited operational capacity could also prevent sellers from using Delhivery's fulfillment services due to which Delhivery could monetize from this product by charging for just the technology.

The sellers and the marketplaces would usually buy a service within the Delhivery platform. However, there were enterprise customers who required pure logistics services between their manufacturing/warehousing locations and their distributors/retailers located across the country. These customers bought the entire platform and offered a percentage of their sales as the price based on their current distribution cost to reach the end consumer with their existing distributor. Depending on the services they needed, Delhivery negotiated a price based on a percentage of the enterprise's sale value, MRP, etc., and the agreed-upon time for storage and delivery of products across India.

Delhivery was also trying to crack the problem of making the hyperlocal shopkeepers' inventory visible online. Delhivery was doing this by encouraging the store owners to use a PoS in order to manage their inventory better. This was Delhivery's entry point. Then, it educated these hyperlocal shopkeepers to liquidate their excess inventory by pushing it into the online marketplaces. This inventory visibility at the hyperlocal level was a huge value addition for e-commerce retail and hence could be leveraged by Delhivery in the future. Delhivery typically sold the PoS on a standard per month rental basis. Delhivery could provide this inventory information to someone who wanted it, say Grofers, for free. Still, Delhivery only charged the provider of information, the hyperlocal shopkeeper, in order to ensure that he/she provided only credible information. If he/she were not paying for the PoS, he/she would not have a dis-incentive to provide false information about his/her inventory.

Table 14.3 Pricing structure for different services offered by Delhivery

Service	Customer group	Pricing scheme
Transportation—express delivery	E-commerce marketplaces Sellers Enterprises	Charge per delivery based on type of zone to cover physical delivery cost
Transportation—on-demand delivery	C2C Hyperlocal food delivery	Charge per order to cover delivery cost
Fulfillment	E-commerce marketplaces Sellers Enterprises	Charge per cubic feet per piece and packing material for storage, processing, and packaging
Technology (IMS and WMS)	E-commerce marketplaces Sellers Enterprises Warehouse owners	Charged on a monthly basis or per order processed; hook into its physical services
Technology (marketplace panels and PoS)	Sellers Hyperlocal shopkeepers	Free of charge, to lock in and increase multi-homing and cross-sell express and fulfillment
Distribution	Enterprises	Negotiated percentage of customer's sales value/MRP, etc., for fulfillment and express delivery pan-India
Sourcing clients	E-commerce marketplaces	Charged separately for additional services

Source Company documents

Delhivery was looking to co-develop warehouses with entrepreneurs who had available rental space. In this model, it would provide the warehouse owners with the warehouse management system (the IT), train them and their employees on it, and enable the owners to start managing their own warehouse. Delhivery would even help with business development by getting them clients besides their existing clients. In turn, it would charge a technology fee and possibly take a small share of the owner's revenue since the warehouse would be a revenue generating entity then. However, it did not come across many entrepreneurs who are co-risk-sharing and revenue-sharing. All the warehouses Delhivery operated as of December 2016 were on lease. It paid a rent to the warehouse owners. Table 14.3 summarizes the pricing schemes for the different services offered by Delhivery.

Opportunities and Challenges

As the Delhivery leadership team sat down to review their performance, three themes continued to dominate their discussion. They continued to believe that their technology was the source of competitive advantage—it was through their technology that they could build switching costs for their partners, be it the warehouse management systems for their warehousing partners, be it the PoS solutions for their retail seller partners, or the technology that powered the fulfillment and last mile delivery services for their enterprise partners. Sandeep elaborated on their sources of competitive advantage with an instance.

> How we run a trucking operation is very different from everybody else. When I get to the required scale, I have a full truck load. So I'm not reliant on a bunch of transporters asking them 'Hey can I get one ton of yours and half a ton of theirs?'. I will put it into a 10, 15, or 20 ton truck. So as I consolidate across clients, the whole bunch of clients are getting a benefit of that. So one, I get better control on pricing because I'm actually getting value out of a full truck load rather than buying bits and pieces from different people. Second, I can say what kind of truck I want, how many drivers I want, how often the driver should change. Third, I can build predictability in the system. I can move my goods at whatever time I want. Say, all through the night, when I won't be able to fly anything by plane, I could use the truck, which would have helped me move my stuff towards the destination. Our data analytics optimizes the route that is the best for us. Plus, I have multiple redundancies built into the whole thing. At my scale and by using my technology and the experience curve that I'm building in allows me to overcome the infrastructure constraints faster and better than other people can.

Given this deep investment in technology, they began wondering about how much of this technology investments could be used for building predictive analytics? Could Delhivery transform from being a service delivery partner to a consulting/partnering role in their ecosystem?

The second theme they were discussing was about leveraging this advantage over larger markets. Should they go international at all? What specific resources would they leverage when they engage with cross-border enterprise customers? Would they be able to deliver packages to international last mile customers? What resources would they need to add to be able to leverage their existing competencies in international markets? Mohit commented:

> We've already started one as an experiment, in DAFZA,[5] Dubai. The idea is that people who want to import stuff into India, how do they do it more efficiently and faster? We can make the DAFZA facility as a transit hub. Customers can consolidate their load from Europe, USA, and everywhere in the Western hemisphere into DAFZA. Dubai has brilliant connectivity into India – air and sea both. So you can procure just in time. It allows for the importer to buy it in bulk, and stock it in DAFZA; and ship whatever your orders are into India just in time. Being a free trade zone, you don't pay any taxes; you save on your working capital. And you can return whatever is unsold directly back to the source from there or ship it to other parts of the world if required.

[5]Dubai Airport Free Zone Area.

This experiment at DAFZA had to be leveraged into a full-fledged fulfillment business. Not just for a small set of importers, but can this lead to significant learning and subsequent replications in other parts of the world, say in markets such as Hong Kong (for imports from China and Japan) or in Kuala Lumpur (for imports from the Far East)?

The third recurring theme was if their technology and processes were indeed resilient to changes in the regulation. For instance, when the GST bill would be passed by the Indian Parliament, the entire taxation regime would change. All those complications about having to return the goods to the seller's warehouse in the seller's state would become redundant.

They needed a clear roadmap for the next few years. Though as a platform they could say that technology was their core competence, it was becoming increasingly critical for them to leverage their investments in technology to do more and more things and more efficiently for more and more partners. How do they choose which direction to grow—introduce new products/services, improve their efficiencies, or serve newer clients? Or do they need to choose—can they do all of them simultaneously?

15 Winner-Takes-All Dynamics

Some markets are inherently dominated by one or few platforms. These markets are characterized by what is popularly known as, "winner-takes-all" (WTA) dynamics. It may not always be due to conventional first mover advantages or classic economies of scale—these traditional sources of advantages may result in oligopolies or monopolistic competition. In network markets, WTA dynamics manifest itself through the power of network effects, and the switching/multi-homing costs associated with the same. In this chapter, we will discuss the conditions for evolution of WTA markets, and persistence of WTA dynamics; its implications for platform firms; and the policy challenges of regulating these markets.

What Are WTA Markets?

Winner-takes-all markets are characterized by three conditions (Eisenmann, Parker, and Van Alstyne, 2006): The network effects are strong and positive, users experience multi-homing costs, and users have no special preferences for specific features. These markets, when the three conditions are met, may be dominated by one or very few platform competitors.

Strong and Positive Network Effects

These network effects ensure that more and more users join a specific platform and derive value from their affiliation and continued engagement. As these network effects are positive, the value derived exponentially increases, with the number of users engaged. And in some markets, platform competitors that manage to acquire more than the threshold of users (critical mass), not only continues to attract more and more users, but also manages to retain them on the platform.

R. Srinivasan, *Platform Business Models*, Management for Professionals,
https://doi.org/10.1007/978-981-16-2838-2_15

Take for example, a peer-to-peer social networking platform like Facebook. As users affiliate with these platforms, they seek and connect with their friends and family, and share content with each other. In some cases, these platforms provide an opportunity to track and reconnect with friends with whom they may have lost personal connects, long ago. The positive network effects greatly aid this discovery of friends and connections, and their continued engagement. The breadth of people to connect and the effort expended in the discovery and subsequent engagement enables high willingness to join (WTJ) and platform loyalty (willingness to stay or WTS).

High Multi-homing Costs

In certain product markets, users experience high multi-homing costs. Multi-homing is distinct from switching costs: While switching costs are costs incurred by users in leaving on platform and joining another, multi-homing costs are costs incurred by users in joining and staying engaged with multiple platforms at the same time, simultaneously. These multi-homing costs are typically variable costs that are incurred continuously through the period of engagement. And these variable costs across multiple platforms might outweigh the benefits derived from such multi-homing.

Take for example, drivers on ride-hailing platforms like OLA and Uber. In markets like India, where multiple such platforms compete, it is important for the drivers to choose a specific platform. These platforms incentivize drivers based on the number of rides they undertake on that platform, per day/week depending on the specific city. For instance, in larger and high-density cities like Mumbai, these incentives may be provided on a weekly basis, whereas in smaller cities like Trichy, where the market may not have matured (and the total number of rides may not be very high), these incentives may be calculated on the basis of number of daily trips. The multi-homing costs of affiliating across platforms manifest in the form of having to undertake a minimum number of rides per day or week in each of the platforms to keep their affiliation alive and maximise incentive-earning potential. Platforms may also penalize drivers with long periods of inactivity on the platform to dissuade multi-homing and attract serious committed driver partners. Apart from this, these platforms may require that only their App is installed in a specific device, requiring multi-homing drivers to invest in multiple phones and connections as well. Plus, the drivers need to ensure that when they are riding on one of the platforms, they do not attract rides on the other platform. Such issues lead to complex scheduling problems, like predicting which platform will provide more rides during the specific time of the day on weekdays/weekends; and making commitments to that platform for that time window. In markets with intense competition, competing platforms continue to increase driver multi-homing costs through a combination of strategies—penalties for periods of inactivity, device exclusivity, incentive structures, and other pricing schemes.

For the riders though, there may not be any multi-homing costs, as they can install multiple Apps on their phones and use those specific platforms when they need. Rider pricing is based on their variable use of these platforms, and there are no fixed costs; nor are there any opportunities lost through multi-homing.

User Preference for Special Features

The third condition for the existence and prevalence of winner-takes-all markets is the lack of user preference for special features on the platforms. If users preferred a special feature, there may be an opportunity for a platform that provides just that value. In such cases where the users prefer a special feature, the network effects may not be broad, and users might want to engage with only a subset of the platform features/users. And that allows for the market to be split across multiple platforms providing specific services to their specific user segments.

Take for example, user preferences in social networking. There may be users who would value sharing (and consuming) pictures and videos only, and therefore there is a niche for services like Instagram and Pinterest to sustain their network effects along with the generic Facebook. Similarly, the same user might want to share different content with their family and friends, and with their professional colleagues, and therefore create a market for a professional networking platform, like LinkedIn. For instance, if I went to Hawaii to receive a professional award, my award ceremony pictures would go to the professional networking platform, whereas my visits to the beaches and resorts would be shared in the social network platform.

Economics of WTA Markets

Even though WTA markets are dominated by one or few competing platforms, it cannot be safely assumed that the platforms that operate in these markets will be highly profitable. The users may have high multi-homing costs that prohibit users being affiliated with multiple platforms simultaneously; but it may be possible for users to switch platforms. That is, they could leave one and join another. These markets may also not guarantee first mover advantages. It is possible that a new platform could enter the market, rapidly acquire users on both (or all) sides of the platform, and challenge the incumbent platforms.

It is imperative for incumbent platforms, even in WTA markets, to stay update with both technological and consumer changes in order to remain competitive. Disruptive innovators[1] could enter WTA markets through targeting a small niche, an ignored consumer segment that valued specific features. Through market entry as a niche player, disruptors could then move up-market and start providing a wide range of services targeting the entire market. And such disruptors have displaced incumbents in a variety of industries, including in WTA markets.

For example, when Facebook entered the social networking market, it did not enjoy first mover advantage. There were many competitors like Orkut, MySpace and Friendster already in the market. Nor was Facebook the latest to enter the market; even Google entered the market with Google+ subsequently. Users switched from one platform to another, based on a variety of considerations, including but not limited to, specific features and brand name. Apart from these entry strategies, Facebook opened its social graph to third party complements, enabling them to produce a variety of complementary products like games and events, attracting more and more users.

Impact of WTA Markets on Complementors

The presence and evolution of WTA markets has multiple implications for users (demand side) and complementors (supply-side).[2]

Coordination Problems

Coordination problems arise when demand-side users cannot signal their intent of joining the platform unless the supply side has made specific investments in platform affiliation. The supply-side complementors need specific assurances of the demand-side users and the kicking-in of network effects to make specific investments. Even though this is a common problem across all multi-sided platforms with network effects, this gets accentuated in a WTA market. As the multi-homing costs are high, there is no opportunity to evaluate multiple platforms prior to the decision to affiliate.

Platforms operating in WTA markets need to signal their commitment to solving these problems in order to attract users and complementors, especially those who are expected to make significant asset-specific investments in platform affiliation.

[1] Christensen, CM., Reynor, ME., and McDonald, R., 2015. What is disruptive innovation, Harvard Business Review, December 2015.

[2] Church and Gandall (2004) citation here. Church, J., & Gandal, N. (2004). Platform Competition in Telecommunications (CEPR Discussion Paper No. 4659). C.E.P.R. Discussion Papers. Retrieved from http://ideas.repec.org/p/cpr/ceprdp/4659.html.

Tipping/Standardization

In WTA markets, there is an apprehension that once the complementors have made their asset-specific investments in joining the platform, there is a risk of hold up by the platform. That is, the platform can leverage its power over the complements and extract disproportionate rent from them, in terms of higher prices or even changing the terms of doing business. Due to this apprehension, some complements postpone adoption till such time the markets tip, and/or technical standards evolve. On the other hand, joining the platform early allows these complements to partake in the tipping process and gain significant advantage by shaping the market/technical standards, rather than only adopting the standards if they joined late.

Another related issue is the adoption of inferior standards by the market. Buoyed by the power of network effects, these inferior standards might become dominant designs and might not serve the needs of the complements. When products with inferior technologies become standards in WTA markets, both users and complements are forced to adopt those, and this widespread adoption could hinder innovation and new market development.

Multiple Equilibria

On the contrary, some markets may take a long time to tip and for standards to evolve and be widely adopted. While competing platforms might be fighting to set standards, it would be a significant dilemma for users and complementors to either wait for standards to evolve or to commit to one standard or the other. Till such time, there might be multiple standards operating in the market, and some complements might choose to incur multi-homing costs to have a head-start in every standard, for the fear of losing out when one of them becomes widely adopted as an industry standard.

Lock-In Costs

Lock-in costs represent the risk of hold-up by the platform once the standards war has been won. The winning platform typically intends to recoup the costs of the standards battle from its users, through either of the three means—increased prices, higher switching costs, and lack of investment in upgradation/improvement of technical standards. This lack of competition might restrict improvements in technology development, market orientation, as well as general deterioration in product and service quality.

Thus, there are three dilemmas for users complementors in WTA markets:

1. To join or not to join (will the network effects kick-in)?
2. When to join (will the market tip, and to which standard)?
3. To focus affiliation with one platform (hold up risks) or multiple platforms (incur multi-homing costs)?

Evolution of WTA Markets

Given the prevalence of penguin problems (experienced by the platform) and the consequent dilemmas for users and complements in WTA markets, there are six issues to consider in the evolution of WTA markets.

Pioneer's Dilemma and Penguin Problems

Platform businesses do suffer from pioneer's dilemma like most other businesses do. Pioneer's dilemma refers to the timing of launch of a technologically superior product/service by a start-up. If the start-up launches too early, it should invest in development of network effects, solving the penguin problems, and achieving critical mass of users and complements. If it launches too late, it should invest resources in differentiating its products/services from the incumbents (who had entered the market earlier) and acquiring users and complementors. In markets with high switching costs, this may be very expensive and may work only when the start-up adopts a significant superior technology and/or provides an improved product/service offering. In WTA markets, with the need for an undifferentiated product/service offering for the entire market (users do not value any special features) and the existence of multi-homing costs (platform users incur additional costs affiliation across multiple platforms), these costs may be very high and significant.

Take the example of cloud-based consumer email services. The market was dominated by Hotmail (the pioneer) and Yahoo Mail (a service provided by a diversified internet company). These two competitors had significantly grown the market and resolved all the issues faced by the pioneers—solving the penguin problem (by subsidising the users), generated critical mass required to monetize the other side (advertisers), and had erected significant switching and multi-homing costs (by making it a habit for users to share their email addresses as part of their visiting cards, as an electronic way of reaching them). In this market, the new entrant had to enter with a disruption, which is what Google did with its Gmail service. Gmail provided users with significantly large storage space, and effectively captured market share from the incumbents. The switching costs were worth incurring considering the benefits of the storage that Gmail offered. Plus, Gmail had successfully incorporated all the technological features of any cloud-based email service. Users switched *en masse*; some did multi-home for some time, but eventually Hotmail was acquired by Microsoft, and Yahoo Mail stopped growing. Gmail integrated tightly with the search engine Google.com and other products (to provide contextual advertising within Gmail) and monetized its mail service. Gmail disrupted the market and changed the dynamics of a WTA market. While Hotmail and Yahoo Mail (as well as numerous other similar email service providers) did their best to provide best quality cloud-based consumer email services, Gmail erected switching and multi-homing costs through its tight integration with other complementary products and services, including Google Drive (and other cloud storage driven products like Photos), Google Duo and Meet (peer-to-peer video calling and meetings), as well as with the Google Play Store (an applications market place on its shared mobile operating system—Android).

In summary, the way the pioneers solve the penguin problems does pave the way for evolution of the WTA markets. Additionally, strategies adopted by disruptive innovators may significantly shift the dynamics of WTA markets, in shaping switching and multi-homing costs, building preference for specific attributes, and the strength of network effects.

Subsidization and Monetization

One of the common strategies adopted by platforms for network mobilisation is to subsidize one set of users. The choice of subsidizing a set of users has implications for three outcomes—network growth (on all the sides of the platform), platform viability and its ability to invest in continued development/quality improvements, and the economics of complementors. The choices and implications of which side to subsidize and which side to monetize on network growth have been elaborated in detail in Chap. 5 on pricing.

While subsidies help the platform attract users, it may pose significant stress on the economic viability of the platform. Till such time the cross-side network effects kick-in and the platform on-boards adequate numbers of users on the money-side (who are willing to pay), the platform may have to keep investing money. Not every platform start up might be able to afford such upfront investments unless they are adequately funded. Such need for upfront investments restricts entrepreneurship to either large corporations or diversifying entrepreneurship (leveraging cash flows from another business to grow the platform). And therefore, we may not have very innovative start ups entering the ecosystem, as these large (multi-business) organizations might have already invested in certain technologies and standards. In WTA markets, such differences between well-funded platforms and others might result in an increased influence of incumbents and large corporations setting the standards/boundaries of growth.

Take for example, the evolution of ecommerce marketplaces across the globe. Given that these are typically winner-takes-all markets for the sellers on the platform (strong and positive cross-side network effects: Sellers value the large numbers of buyers on the marketplace; high multi-homing costs: Sellers invest in specific capabilities and processes for affiliating with each platform; and no special preferences: Most sellers value large number of buyers in the market more than specialised and curated segments offered by specialized ecommerce sites as a means of growth and diversification), they have evolved to attract only large competitors like Amazon and Walmart. In setting up such marketplaces, the costs of attracting, curating (the seller/product quality and process compliance) and retaining sellers mandate that there needs to be sufficient investments in building the supply-side before attracting the demand side (buyers). Given the low switching and multi-homing costs for buyers, one should subsidize buyers to attract them in large numbers. Given that buyers also value variety in such marketplaces, it becomes extremely difficult for focused ecommerce firms to compete in these markets. Hence, one can observe that in most markets, ecommerce marketplaces are dominated by large/diversified global firms like Amazon and/or well-funded ecommerce operations of large retail corporations (like Flipkart by Walmart).

Pivot Dilemma

As we saw in the previous section, in WTA markets, large and diversified platforms sustain their advantage over smaller focused start-ups. This presents a critical dilemma for platform start-ups on the timing of diversification and the extent of product breadth. It might be beneficial for the start-up to diversify early in terms of their ability to subsidize some users through revenue earned from other businesses. Such revenue streams could be accrued through other business models as well, say traditional pipeline businesses, like selling a product or providing something-as-a-service. Such revenue streams might provide the start-up enough headway to invest in subsidies for attracting new users. However, if the start-up diversified too early, it might lose focus and expend its energies on serving those markets. In WTA markets, such loss of focus might encourage entry of other platform competitors, who may be able to scale faster and therefore capture significant market share/value.

Remora Strategy

Some platforms with an intent to speed up its network mobilization follow a Remora strategy.[3] The Remora is a fish that attaches itself to a larger fish, like a shark, or a boat. While it is carried around the waters by the host (larger fish/shark/boat), it feeds on whatever it can get. It can swim on its own, but they prefer to attach themselves to the larger fish to hitch a ride to the deeper reaches of

[3]Don Dodge first used this phrase "Remora Business Model" to highlight this strategy: https://dondodge.typepad.com/the_next_big_thing/2007/05/widgets_the_rem.html. For a more detailed analysis of Remora strategies and their implications for platform start-ups, read: https://r-srini.in/2020/03/18/remora-strategies/.

the ocean, saving precious energy. Their relationship with the Shark is unique—they do not draw blood or nutrients from the Shark like a Leech. They feed on the food scraps of the larger fish by keeping their mouths open. While the Remora benefits from its attaching to the Shark, it does not significantly benefit or harm the Shark.

Let us fist understand the Remora strategy. A platform startup could piggyback on a larger platform to access its initial set of users, with no costs to the larger platform. Let us consider an example. A dating start-up struggles to get its first set of users. While it needs rapid growth of numbers, it should ensure that the profiles on the platform are of good quality (like avoiding bots and fake profiles). It has two options: developing its own validation algorithm or integrating with larger platforms like Twitter or Facebook for profile validation. It could create its own algorithms if it needs to validate specific criteria, though. It could use a Remora strategy, by attaching itself to a larger Shark in the form of Twitter or Facebook. This has no costs to Twitter or Facebook, and if at all, contributes to marginal addition of traffic to Facebook/Twitter. However, for the start-up, this saves significant costs of developing and testing its own user validation algorithms (swimming down the depths of the ocean).

By leveraging the users on a larger established platform, the first set of users could be sourced easily *en masse*. However, just having users is not sufficient—there is an issue of coordination: getting not just sign-ups but driving engagement. It is important that registered users begin engaging with the platform. Some platforms need more than just engagement, they are stuck with a real-time problem: Like in a multi-player gaming or a food-delivery platform, we need gamers to be engaged with each other real time. Some other platforms need users in specific segments, or the transferability problem: That users are looking for others within a specific segment, like in a hyperlocal delivery platform, a matrimony platform, or a doctor-finding platform. Such platforms need to have sufficient users in each of these micro-segments.

A Remora strategy could potentially help a platform start-up overcome these issues. By porting users from the larger platform, one could acquire sufficient users, and through tight integration with the content/algorithms of the Shark platform, the Remora (start-up) could get the engagement going. The decision to adopt a Remora strategy presents five trade-offs: (a) holdup risk; (b) ceding monetization control; (c) access to user data; (d) risk of brand commoditization; and (e) exit costs.

Hold-up risk: There is a significant risk of the established platform (host) holding the start-up adopting the Remora strategy (or just Remora) to a ransom, partly arising out of the start-up making significant asset-specific investments to integrate. For instance, the dating start-up would need to tightly integrate its user validation processes with that of Facebook or Twitter, as the need may be. It may have to live with the kind of data Facebook provides it through its APIs. It may be prone to opportunistic behaviour when Facebook decides to change certain parameters. For example, Facebook may stop collecting marital status on its platform, which may be a key data point for the dating start-up. Not making asset-specific investments to integrate with the host platforms might not provide the start up with the full benefits of its Remora strategy.

Monetization control: A significant risk faced by Remora start-ups is that of conceding the power to monetize to the Shark. For example, when a hyperlocal restaurant discovery start-up follows a Remora strategy on Google, it is possible that Google gets all the high-value advertisements, leaving the discovery start-up with only low-value local advertisements. There is also a risk of the larger platform defining what could be monetised on the start-up platform as well. For example, given that users have gotten used to search for free, even specialized search like locations (on maps) or specialized services like emergency veterinary care during off-working hours, may not be easy to monetise. Such platforms may have to cede control on which side to monetize and subsidize, and how much to price to the larger platform. To avoid conceding monetization control to larger platforms, Remora start-ups need to provide additional value over and above the larger platform. For instance, in the local search business, a platform start-up would possibly need to not just provide discovery value (which may not be monetizable) but include matching value as well.

Access to user data: This is the biggest possible risk of following a Remora strategy. Given that user data is the primary lever around which digital businesses customize and personalize their services and products, it is imperative that the start-up has access to its user data. It is likely that the larger platform may restrict access to specific user data, which may be very valuable to the start-up. For instance, restaurant chains who could have run their own loyalty programmes for its clients, may adopt a Remora on top of food delivery platforms like Swiggy or Zomato. When they do that, the larger platform may run a loyalty programme to its clients, based on the data it has about the specific user, which is qualitatively superior to the one that local restaurants may have. In fact, in the context of India, these delivery platforms do not even pass on basic user profiles like demographics or addresses to the restaurants. The restaurants are left with their limited understanding of their walk-in customers and a set of nameless/faceless customers in the form of a platform user, for whom they can generate no meaningful insights or even consumption patterns. It is imperative that platform start-ups define what data they require to run their business model meaningfully, including user data or even operations. It could be in the form of specific contracts for accessing data and insights, and/or co-creating analytical models.

Risk of brand commoditization: A direct corollary of the user data ownership risk is that the Remora start-up could be commoditized, and their brand value might be subservient to the larger platform's brand. It could end up being a sub-brand of the larger start-up. For user generation and network mobilization, the Remora start-up would possibly need to get all its potential users to affiliate with the larger platform, even if may not be most desirable one. On a delivery start-up, hungry patrons may be loyal to the aggregator and the specific cuisine, rather than to a restaurant. Given that patrons could split their orders across multiple restaurants, it could be the quality and speed of delivery that matters more than other parameters. Restaurants might then degenerate into mere "kitchens" that have excess capacity, and when there is no such excess capacity, these aggregators have known to set up "while label" or "cloud kitchens". It is important that Remora start-ups step up their branding efforts and ensure that the larger brand does not overshadow their brand. The standard arguments or relative brand strengths of complements in user affiliation decisions need to be taken into consideration while protecting the Remora's brands.

Exit costs: The last of the Remora's costs is that of exit costs. Pretty much similar to the exit costs from an industry, platform start-ups need to be clear if their Remora strategy is something temporary for building up their user base and mobilizing their networks in the early stages, or it would be relatively permanent. In some cases, the platform's core processes might be integrated with the larger platform, like the API integration for user validation, and therefore may provide significant exit costs. In some other cases, the platform may have focused on their core aspects of their business during the initial years and would have relegated their non-core but critical activities to the larger platform. At a time when the start-up is ready to exit the larger platform, it may require large investments in non-core activities, which may lead to disruptions and costs. Add to this, the costs of repurposing/rebuilding asset-specific investments made when joining the platform. Remora start-ups, therefore, need to have a clear strategy on what is the tenure of these Remora strategies, and at what point of time they would exit the association with the larger platform, including being prepared for the costs of exit.

Remora strategies allow for platform start-ups an alternative to scale their businesses very fast. However, it is imperative to understand the benefits and costs of such strategies and make conscious choices. These choices are at three levels—timing of Remora, what processes to Remora, and building the flexibility to exit. Some platforms may need to attach themselves right at the beginning of their inception to larger platforms to even get started; but some others can afford to wait for the first users to start engaging with the platform before integrating. What processes to integrate with the larger platform is another critical choice—much like an outsourcing decision, core and critical processes need to be owned by the start-up, while non-core non-critical processes may surely be kept out of the platform. While making these decisions, platform start-ups need to consciously decide the tenure and extent of integration with the larger platform, and therefore make appropriate asset-specific investments.

Integration Dilemma

Integration dilemma refers to the decision by platforms to integrate certain product features from outside their core into their core offering. The platform sponsor might vertically integrate (either backward in the providing of complements or forward in taking on certain intermediating roles) that may either be hard to develop by independent complementors. This difficulty could arise due to the need for its tight integration with the platform core, or high investments required by the complementor to create and capture value. Such features may have been hitherto provided by complementors, albeit with loose integration or with lower quality standards; and when these features become highly valued by the users, it presents a dilemma for the platform. Integrating these complements into the core allows for more value creation and capture by the platform by broadening its offering; but it risks spoiling the relationship it has with its complementors. If these complements were really valued by the users, the potential for value capture is higher with those complementors that produced and offered them to the users through the platform. And this may result in increasing complementors' bargaining power with reference to the platform. In this game for brand value between the platform and its complementors, it is tempting for the platform to integrate such complements. Such integration hurts the complementors significantly in WTA markets, where they may have limited choice if the users (on the other side) also have high multi-homing costs. In this competition between the platform and its own competitors, the platforms may also have the power to restrict the product features offered by the complements (by closing access to their core), set prices, and impose norms of engagement with end users (like payment processes and customer service norms).

For instance, when Apple launched iPhone, it had a lot of Google products as part of its ecosystems, including Google search, YouTube, and Google Maps. As the Apple ecosystem matured, it launched its own versions of search, videos, and maps.[4] In this market, users of iPhone could easily multi-home (as Google used Open API, allowing for even third parties to make Apps for these products) and download these Apps on their phones. However, when ecommerce platforms like Amazon launch their own white label products (like Amazon Basics) and house brands (like Solimo), it can hurt the sellers on the platform who compete in these categories.[5] For small sellers, who experience significant switching and multi-homing costs on the ecommerce marketplace, it can reduce greater value if Amazon's algorithm prioritized its own brands/private labels against that of independent sellers (as some claims have been made[6]).

Relationship Dilemma

Relationship dilemma refers to the abuse of bargaining power by the platform over its complementors. In WTA markets with low multi-homing costs for complementors, the terms of the agreement between the platform and the complementors may be highly skewed in favour of the platform. For instance, the question of who

[4]https://www.businessinsider.com/youtube-iphone-2012-8.

[5]For more details, see https://the-ken.com/story/amazon-private-labels/ (inside a paywall).

[6]See https://www.europeanceo.com/industry-outlook/regulators-push-back-as-amazon-expands-private-label-offering/.

owns the consumer data is a debate between the platform and complementors. In a typical marketplace platform, the sellers might have access to only transaction data that is relevant to their products and services, whereas the platforms may have full access to the buyers' search history and selection preferences. In performing their role as a sponsor, the platform might own the discovery/matching/transaction/evaluation algorithms. The dilemma in front of the platform in a WTA market is whether to use the data and build robust algorithms (based on descriptive, predictive, and prescriptive analytics of user data) to exponentially grow the market; or to share this data with the complements and allow them to monetize the same.

The additional risk for the complementors is that of the platform to monetize the data to cross-sell other products and services. Such monetization opportunities are disproportionately available with the platform, in comparison to the complementors. For instance, a platform with access to aggregate data on, say sales of a particular category of products, can intensify its marketing efforts and on-board more and more sellers on the platform. Such increase in sellers might also lead to congestion, and when these products are undifferentiated, cause negative same-side network effects. And motivate a few competitors (most likely those that are differentiated) to leave the market.

Take for example, the Indian doctor-finding platform, Practo. Practo entered the market with a clinic management solution, called Practo Ray. Practo Ray was sold as a Software-as-a-service (SaaS) to clinics to manage their end-to-end operations. One of the modules in Practo Ray was appointment management, and that was extended out as Practo.com, with patients seeking to discover doctors/clinics could use. Practo has the potential to use the data on clinics' performance to shape their ranking algorithm that prioritizes search results for users. This algorithm may be opaque to the users, and this could result in discontent and attrition of doctors from the platform. However, it is imperative for the platform to use "some" ranking algorithm to rank these results, else the search users may not find the platform easy to use. Given that the multi-homing and switching costs for the search users is lower, it is likely that they would leave the platform if they were confronted with congestion (too many options with too few parameters to discriminate amongst them).

Regulating WTA Markets

Traditional economic analyses of competitive markets provide us with a continuum between monopolies on one end and perfect competition on the other end. Democratic countries with capitalistic policies and open markets have almost always preferred perfect competition over other forms of competition. And have had significant regulatory control and oversight on markets that could even become monopolistic. Given the economics of platform competition favours one or a few competitors in winner-takes-all markets, governments and regulators are exploring ways to regulate these markets as well. However, before we proceed further, we need to distinguish between traditional monopolies and WTA markets.

A traditional monopoly is formed on the basis of either of three conditions—a natural monopoly (like roads or electricity distribution where infrastructure duplication is meaningless), advantages derived out of scale economies, and control over key resources (including government regulation). In other words, the barriers to competitive entry in monopolistic markets are high due to either of these conditions —control over infrastructure, key resources (including licenses), or high minimum economies of scale. However, in the context of winner-takes-all (WTA) markets, the source of advantage is through network effects; and consumer stickiness is due to their multi-homing costs.

In pipeline businesses, monopolies result in increased prices for the consumers, as the monopolist extracts rent based on the firm's dominant bargaining power over customers. There are WTA markets that are categorized by positive same-side network effects (also known as scale effects)—the more the number of users, the more valuable it is for other users on the same side. For instance, in a search engine like Google, more the number of users search on the platform, the more the machine learning algorithm running behind Google search learns about user search and preferences, and therefore returns much better search results to everyone else as well. In other words, more the users search on Google, more everyone else also benefits. In such WTA markets, users are provided the services for free (or at very low prices), and even if they are one of the few competitors in the market, scale economies are beneficial to the consumers as well.

It is not just that platforms competing in WTA markets provide their services for free. In the context of some WTA markets that charge prices based on variable costs, any increase in prices (beyond a threshold) might upset the network effects. Take for example, a WTA ride-hailing platform market. If the platform continued increasing the prices for riders, it would not only decrease the number of riders on the platform, but it may also attract more and more cab drivers as they would benefit more due to high prices. And such changes in the network structure with more drivers chasing less riders will lead to negative same-side network effects amongst the drivers (competing directly with each other), and eventually the weaker drivers (those that could not afford to compete) will exit the market. The market will correct itself to another equilibrium at lower volumes. This effectively provides an insurance for the riders against sustained price increases by the platform.

Predatory Pricing

Economists and policy makers concerned about market efficiencies and fair competition have been obsessed with the concept of predatory pricing for a long time. The most common definition of predatory pricing is through the application of the conventional Areeda-Turner test.[7] The Areeda–Turner test is based on two basic premises. The **recoupment premise** states that the firm indulging in predatory

[7]For more details, see: https://heinonline.org/HOL/Page?handle=hein.journals/jrepale10&div=4&collection=journals.

pricing should be able to predict and be confident of its ability to recoup the losses through higher profits as competition exits the market. The assumption is that the firm could reasonably anticipate the (opportunity) costs of predatory pricing, as well as have an estimate of the future value of monopoly profits; and the net present value of such predatory pricing to push competition out of the market should be positive and attractive. In other words, the firm should be able to project the effect of lower prices in terms of lower competition and higher profits in the future.

How low can this predatory price be? That is the subject of the second premise—the **AVC premise**. The firm's prices (at business-as-usual volumes) should be below its average variable costs (AVC), or marginal costs in the short run. If the prices were indeed above the AVC, the firm would argue that they are indeed more efficient than competition, due to any of their resources, processes, or organisational arrangements. It is when the price falls below the AVC that the question of unfair competition arises—the firm might be subsidising its losses. Take for instance, a start-up that is piloting an innovative technology. It may price its products/services at a price below the AVC to gain valuable feedback from its lead users, but in the absence of a recoupment premise such pricing might not qualify as predatory pricing. On the other hand, imagine a new entrant with superior technology who can bring costs down to a level where the prices fall below the marginal costs of the competitors but stay well above the firm's AVC, it is just disrupting the market. Only when both the conditions are met, i.e., when the predator's prices are below the AVC and the firm could project the extent of recoupment due to monopoly profits as competition exits the market, that we call it predatory pricing.

As we have seen before, subsidies are common in multi-sided platforms, and their prices may seem to reflect predatory pricing.

- Platforms may resort to subsidies to solve the penguin problems in the early days of their growth, and sometimes may offer their services for free as well.
- The platform might subsidize one side of users and make money from the other side, while incurring costs of providing services to both sides, depending on the relative price elasticities and willingness to affiliate with the other side of the platform. And the prices for the subsidy side would surely below costs for that side. It is imperative that the overall costs and prices are considered while analysing these pricing strategies.
- These cross-side network effects will force the platforms to price their services most efficiently across both the sides. Even for the money side, the platform might not be able to charge extraordinary prices as such prices would themselves act against the sustenance of these cross-side network effects. It is likely that these extra-normal profits would evaporate through subsidies on the other side to keep the network effects active. Imagine a situation where a B2B marketplace charged the sellers higher than normal prices. Only large (and possibly desperate) sellers would affiliate with the marketplace, leading to buyers (the subsidy side) leaving the platform. To keep the buyers interested, the marketplace might either have to broaden the base of sellers by optimising the prices or

provide extraordinary subsidies to the buyers to keep them interested. So, to maintain the equilibrium, the platform would have to price both the sides efficiently.
- Finally, in a competitive situation, not all competitors might follow the same price structure. So, a reduction of prices by one competitor for one side of the market may not force all other competitors to reduce prices; they may just encourage multi-homing (allowing users to use competitive products simultaneously) or manipulate the price on the other side of users.

Therefore, a direct application of the Areeda–Turner test might not be appropriate while studying predatory pricing in the context of MSPs. Let us imagine a market for home tutors supporting school students. The market is inherently geographically constrained; it is very unlikely that either the teacher or the student would travel across cities for this purpose. For the time being, let us assume that there is no technology (like video conferencing) being used. This market is apt for the entry of a multi-sided platform. Let us assume that the platform monetizes the students by charging a commission apart from the fee payable to the tutors (irrespective of which side the platform monetizes the analysis would be the same). Supposing it is faced with a competitive entry at lower prices. The new entrant sustains the same fees for the tutors (else they would not switch), while lowering the student prices. This could lead to temporary losses that the new entrant may be willing to cope with. Anticipating a larger surge in student numbers (at the same tutor fees), more tutors switch/multi-home to the new entrant; and seeing the number and quality of tutors on the new entrant's platform, students first start multi-homing, and some of them begin switching. The incumbent has four possible responses to this threat.

1. The incumbent can reduce the prices for the student-side as well as tweak the incentives for the tutor's side to match that of the new entrant. This is surely cost-enhancing and profit-squeezing strategy, and the battle becomes one of who has bigger pockets to sustain this price war.
2. Increase multi-homing costs for either or both sides, like providing either a multi-product bundle for students; and volume/exclusivity-based incentives for tutors. That is, tutors may earn exclusivity bonuses if they did not multi-home and engaged in a specified number of activities on the platform (designed in a manner to ensure that they have no time left for multi-home). Another means of increasing multi-homing costs are through increasing contract tenures—switch from monthly billings to annual billings, and therefore lock-in users for the whole year.
3. Increasing penetration: The incumbent can increase the overall size of the market by increasing the penetration of its services and target hitherto unaddressed niche markets. In the process, allow for a variety of niches to emerge and break the WTA dynamics in the market.

4. Perpetual matching: The incumbent platform can transform itself into a pure discovery and matching platform providing perpetual matches between tutors and students and highlight the value of such contracts to charge high upfront discovery charges.

Given the differences in the economics, tests like Areeda–Turner test would not be directly applicable in the context of platforms as they do in pipeline business models. Regulators should, therefore, ensure that they treat WTA markets and regulating platforms operating in WTA markets different from monopolies.

16 Tally Solutions Pvt. Ltd.: Orchestrating the Ecosystem

Introduction

In 2020, it had been over a decade since Tally Solutions had released its Tally.ERP 9 for micro, small and medium enterprises (MSME). It had also developed a platform, called Tally.Developer 9, in which the partner ecosystem helped develop customized solutions (Tally Add-On) and sold through the Tally Shop (a virtual online shop).

Tally's initial product contained a stand-alone accounting software. Tally provided after-sales services with an annual subscription model, where customers received free upgrades and access to online services (e.g., online bank reconciliation, online payment services through bank, and so on). It had developed from a boxed product to a platform and then subsequently to an ecosystem (as of 2020), enabling it to reach a new segment of customers, with infinite business opportunities.

Tally had faced several challenges through its journey. As it transitioned from an accounting-only software, it had transformed into an architect of the ecosystem model, the challenges mainly revolved around how Tally had evolved as an orchestrator of the ecosystem. In the ecosystem that it orchestrated, there were

---

R Srinivasan, Professor of Strategy, Sundararajan B (IIMB MBA Class of 2021), Sunil Ganesan (IIMB MBA Class of 2021) and Menaka Rao, prepared this case for classroom discussion. Tally Solutions Pvt. Ltd cooperated and provided information to the Indian Institute of Management Bangalore in connection with the preparation of this case and it was reviewed and approved before publication by a company designate. No funding was sought or received from Tally Solutions Pvt. ltd. for the development of this case. This case was also developed from available and permitted sources of information. This case is not intended to serve as an endorsement, source of primary data, or to show effective or inefficient handling of decision or business processes.

R. Srinivasan, *Platform Business Models*, Management for Professionals,
https://doi.org/10.1007/978-981-16-2838-2_16

significant decisions to be made around Tally's relationship with its complementors, including customization in the Tally Shop and its pricing strategy.

Evolution of Tally Solutions

Tally was founded by Shyam Sundar Goenka (SS Goenka or Goenka Senior), who was operating factories that supplied raw material and machine parts to chemical plants and textile mills in eastern and southern India. He realized that the manual processes that involved reading, consolidating, and cross-validating handwritten ledgers were time-consuming and tedious. The software that was available to perform these accounting tasks was really complicated and difficult to use. To simplify his accounting operations, SS Goenka tasked his son, Bharat Goenka (Bharat), with the responsibility of developing an accounting software product.

Tally the Boxed Product (1988–2012)

Bharat was challenged by this task and set out to create simple and easy to use accounting software, which could mimic the pencil noting of the Munshis.[1] The software was always tested by the senior Goenka; when he could not understand the software, he rejected it. Two years later, around 1988, Bharat developed a robust product called "the Accountant," which could perform accounting up to a simple trial balance.

The first sale was made by SS Goenka himself, to a computer accounting center that handled accounting services for 36 companies in the area. He convinced the firm to buy his software for US$500 with the guarantee that he would take it back and return the money if it did not help their business. Within 3 months, the firm was able to handle 400 companies with the same staff strength working in one shift, using the software. Slowly, Bharat added other features to the software and renamed it **Tally**.[2]

S S Goenka, with a very small team of 2–3 people, would roam the streets and towns of the country, essentially selling the product door to door. Soon, they also started appointing some of their customers as their "partners or sellers." This was the beginning of their most important business strategy of creating a network of partners.

Positioning Tally in the Financial Accounting Market

The financial accounting (FA) software revolution started in the late 80 s when the Indian software market was in its infancy. With the demand for PCs being low, FA

[1]Traditional Indian accountants in trading firms.
[2]Source: https://www.business-standard.com/article/companies/tally-tries-to-reach-for-the-stars-112010500087_1.html.

software packages were initially not popular. However, as basic accounting principles and rules were similar in user companies, software companies realized the huge potential that this segment offered and flooded the market with a host of products. Although the product revenues in the domestic software market were skewed toward imported products, the accounting software space was completely Indian. International brands such as Microsoft Money and Quicken had not made a dent in the Indian market owing to non-customization of the software to Indian conditions.

Tally was introduced in the market as a shrink-wrapped software product with a natural language interface having concurrent multilingual capabilities and remote functionality. It had reached customers through a dedicated partner network, and its focus on technology resulted in a robust product and partner system. Tally primarily sold its products under two brand names: **Tally and Shoper** (a product acquired from Vedha Automation). Tally was sold as silver and gold versions, where the silver version catered to a single user and the gold version catered to multiple users.[3] Shoper, a retail point-of-sale (PoS) management software product, was also sold in silver and gold versions. The Tally Partners used the development environment kit to customize and extend Tally. Customers could opt for two forms of usage—through a direct buyout of the software license and in the form of annual or monthly rentals. Beginning with Tally 4.5 through its timely upgrades to Tally 6.3 and subsequently Tally 7.2 in 2005, the brand was positioned as efficient "accounting software."

Tally also provided an exclusive tool—the auditors' edition, designed specifically for chartered accountants (CAs) keeping in mind the crucial role they played in a growing economy, where they had to deal with the widening of the tax net and increased compliance requirements. The Institute of Chartered Accountants (ICAI) had engaged with Tally as their technology service provider to facilitate the CAs in offering IT-assisted services to their clients. The Business Advisory Practitioners (BAP) Program run by the ICAI jointly with Tally helped accelerated development opportunities for CAs by facilitating and speeding up the audit process, which could be leveraged through the auditor's edition. There were several unique features in the auditor's edition; for instance, it enabled the auditor to access client's data and reports remotely, assist in regular statutory compliances, and create an audit dashboard (with the capability of generating annexure and reports for tax audits).

Bouncing Back from the VAT Debacle

In 2004, when value-added tax (VAT) was introduced in India, Tally already had a good standing in the market. Tally spent over US$8 million in promoting the adoption of VAT, stating that Tally had the best software solution to calculate tax across industries.[4] Tally planned to increase its user base by over half a million new users but achieved only 50,000 new customers. To promote VAT adoption and

[3]Source: https://www.business-standard.com/article/companies/tally-tries-to-reach-for-the-stars-112010500087_1.html.
[4]Source: Ibid.

Tally 7.2, the firm further commoditized the product by reducing its price from about US$450 to US$100. Even with the addition of new customers, which were a tenth of their planned target, the revenues of the firm shrunk to US$20 million (as against the targeted US$200 million).

The company right-sized itself to 550 people in the next 2 years (2007–2009), apart from increasing the price of the product to about US$270. Even through this tumultuous phase, the firm did not lose clarity on its intent and did not adopt the path of growing revenues from services.

The product's positioning as an easy, user-friendly tool that could be either bought or downloaded from the internet was reinforced with the growth in its customer base, especially the small and medium enterprise (SME) segment. Tally was being used by as many as 8 million SME customers, vindicating the various awards it had won.

Distribution and After-Sales Service/Support for the Product

Tally's distribution was an indirect partner-centric business. Tally operated a three-tier distribution system. Tally's first tier consisted of Master Tally Partners (MTPs); the second comprised local distributors (phased out in 2011); the third tier comprised the resellers, called the Tally Partners (TPs). The second and third tiers received the pricing structure through back-end commissions. This approach offered Tally better market coverage, as the partners' knowledge of the market was extensive. Partners had the ability to maneuver in local markets and possessed credit allocation capabilities. The software was sold only through the partner network. There was 25% margin on all sales to the end-seller and 15% margin on the sales to indirect sales partners. Tally employed 160 MTPs and approximately 16,700 TPs.

Since Tally was sold largely to SMEs in India who were not totally computer savvy, frequently, the Tally team of after-sales service partners had to customize the software for the end user. Another partner type, the Tally Service Partners (TSPs, about 1100 in number), would cater to after-sales service requirements such as implementation, data migration, and training requirements for customers. Technical partners, called Tally Integrators (TIs, about 150 in number), were partners who offered end-to-end technical solutions in and around the product. Tally also started approximately 800 Tally Academies (TA) to provide training on Tally.

Tally: The ERP Platform (2012–2020)

The financial accounting market grew at a compounded annual growth rate (CAGR) of 19.2% from 2010 to 2016.[5] Gradually, the industry consolidated, leaving behind a handful of national competitors, leveraging significant economies of scale. The

[5]Source: http://www.researchandmarkets.com/reports/1854812/india_accounting_software_market_outlook_2016.pdf.

users' expectations on the quality of software and support had also risen, which forced vendors to offer more robust features and functionality or shut down their companies.

The demands of the industry had grown beyond basic accounting, and small businesses would like to integrate accounting, inventory, and payroll management in the same database. Some customers sought integrated packages that included total financial management, supply chain management, and customized management information system (MIS). This led to many firms expanding their product features to include enterprise solutions (ERP) in the packages. ERP helped companies streamline different parts of their business, and its scope covered inventory, operations, budgeting, and human resources. A primary benefit of ERP was easier access to reliable, integrated information, the elimination of redundant data, and the rationalization of processes, which resulted in cost savings.[6]

In addition, there were five compelling reasons to implement an ERP system: (1) integrated financials with all other functions; (2) integrated customer order fulfillment information; (3) standardized and speeded-up core business processes such as manufacturing and financial services; (4) reduced inventory, nonperforming assets, etc.; and (5) standardized information available to the top management for decision-making. Although ERP was apt for business growth, the cost and cycle time in implementing and deploying the available ERP products was still significant; there were several hurdles in their implementation, especially in the SME segment.

Tally's Offerings

Tally's transition from a product to a platform began with Tally.ERP 9 A Series (Exhibit 16.1), which was launched in 2009 to help meet three objectives: (1) provide remote access capabilities and release valuable executive time that could be invested elsewhere; (2) provide affordable access to experienced professionals such as CAs, who with the support of an integrated support center could reduce the cost and time taken to resolve business problems; and (3) provide professional support to comply with various taxation requirements.

Tally realized that as business information spread across networks, access to data was exacerbated by problems of internet connectivity. When there was inadequate visibility, performance suffered, as the issues did not reflect on their radar. Hence, Tally supported supply chain visibility, an end-to-end line of sight across networks. Tally's supply chain visibility harnessed a wide reach to provide the last mile connectivity. Through the supply chain visibility feature of Tally, stakeholders in their business chain, including suppliers, customers, banks, and the government, could access timely reports.[7]

[6]Source: https://blog.e-zest.com/creating-business-value-with-erp/.

[7]Source: https://www.business-standard.com/article/companies/tally-tries-to-reach-for-the-stars-112010500087_1.html.

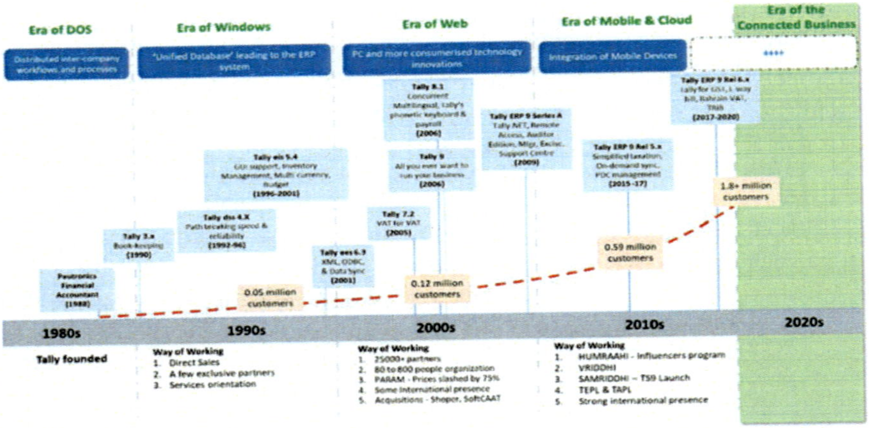

Exhibit 16.1 Tally Solutions Journey through the years. *Source* Company documents

Supply networks had footprints in various locations, sometimes even different countries, where factors such as distance, time zones, and even language posed challenges. Wide and diverse supply chains also meant disparate distribution systems, where data got isolated, leading to issues of comprehension and access. Human interventions to collect data from internal systems and external partners increased the likelihood of risk and simultaneously eroded efficiency. To address these problems, Tally's supply chain visibility was built on the customer's existing infrastructure without the need for integration or duplication. With Tally's software, customers saw great benefits, as the time to market reduced to 1 day from 3 days, and efficiency improved by 67%.

Tally.ERP 9 A had increased the turnover of the company from US$20 million to only US$44 million in 3 years, which was lower than their anticipated growth. With aspirations to reach a USD 1 billion turnover by 2015, they planned to launch Tally.ERP Series B in April 2013, followed by Tally.ERP Series C in April 2014 with additional functionalities and capabilities.[8] Tally used its existing channel of distributors to market its ERP. The most critical aspects of Tally.ERP Series B were related to delivering solutions for a "connected world," leveraging the advances in cloud computing and storage. Two key technology elements—labeled TallySpace and TallyScope—were the key enablers for the release of this transformational product. TallySpace—was coined to reflect the sentiment of being "beyond the cloud"—intended to completely remove the physical boundaries of operations for an enterprise, including the way they think about software deployment, data management, data access, workflows, security, integration, and operations. TallyScope—was a play on the word "telescope"—intended to take an enterprise

[8]However, both the products Tally.ERP Series B and Tally.ERP Series C had not been launched as of 2020.

beyond traditional boundaries, work with data, systems, and processes that transcend their organizations, and work with their partners (for instance, with banks including enabling cashless payments, with public data, with their suppliers and customers, and so on). To leverage this opportunity, Tally tied up with Standard Chartered Bank to facilitate transfer of funds from within the Tally software. Tally was also creating and operating a payment gateway within their solutions. There were plans to partner with more banks, and when that occurred in the Tally.ERP B series, it would help businesses move toward more optimized business processes.

In 2012, Tally launched several initiatives to be relevant to the times, for instance, Humraahi—an influencer connect program (for CAs, tax practitioners, etc.), Vriddhi—new partner structure, and Samriddhi, the launch of the server product TallyServer9. In addition, Tally created two subsidiaries—Tally Education Pvt. Ltd. and Tally Analytics Pvt. Ltd.

Tally eventually had six different types of releases. The first was a major release which entailed a new version of Tally with enhanced exhaustive and outstanding features. A minor release on the other hand was the theme or feature-specific enhancements, which were included with internal or external market fixes. The maintenance release was meant to fix defects and provide statutory updates. The hotfix release covered critical customer issues, which were generic in nature. The issues were solved via hotfixes made available on their website (download center), where customers were advised to use it for specific issues only. The issues solved by the hotfix release were eventually merged into the subsequent Gold Release. The Customer Release was made for a specific set of customers. The changes in this release were experimental. On completion of the experiment, they incorporated the changes in the subsequent Gold Releases. The emergency release was meant for statutory updates or showstopper issues caused by regression or fixes made in previous releases. This release was available to all stakeholders.

Release 5.X

In July 2015, Tally.ERP 9 Release 5.0 was launched. It offered new improved taxation and compliance experience. Release 5.0 was simple, fast, and a reliable solution to manage taxation. With the reconciled and triangulated tax returns, for excise, service tax, VAT, and TDS/TCS, Release 5.0 was designed to help businesses, accountants, and tax authorities to swiftly match returns with actual data. It provided the hand-prepared tax generation experience to ensure that customers enjoyed full visibility of the transactions used to compile the returns, thus helping them file their returns with complete accuracy.[9] Few states were covered in the first release, and subsequent releases provided simplified taxation experience to customers in all the states. This version of the release also made managing postdated cheques simple and efficient. The on-demand synchronization feature took business connectivity to the next level and provided scalability and convenience to customers.

[9]Source: https://www.dqindia.com/tally-set-to-transform-business-taxation/.

Release 5.0 occupied less memory space and enhanced performance; existing users could easily upgrade from previous versions. It also offered seamless migration, one-click installation, personalized product updates, and flexible licensing.

In June 2017, Tally launched Tally Release 6.x, GST Ready–GST Compliance software. According to a company spokesperson:

> Simply download and install Tally.ERP 9 Release 6 which takes a few minutes. Then set up your GST in five simple steps for GST-ready Tally.ERP 9 and its simplicity!

Release 6.0 was designed keeping in mind the need to break down the complexities of GST compliance and at the same time provide speed without faulting on accuracy.[10] GST-Ready Tally provided unique error prevention, detection, and correction capabilities at both the invoice and the tax return level with the combination of GSTN offline tool and GSTN Portal for GST compliance.[11] It helped manage tax rate setup and maintain GSTN details of suppliers and customers; it also created vouchers, which were GST compliant, including GST invoice printing. The release verified the correctness of transactions using GST rules in triangulation. Export data was formatted into Excel sheets that could be imported in GSTN. It made tax payment and adjustment entries in the books.

Tally for GST (Rel 6.x) in 2017–18 was a breakthrough release. It was the first release to have successful downloads of more than 100,000 in a single day, with 75% success rate, and breakthrough activations of 400,000 in one year. The customer base increased by 25% in 9 months from 950,000 to 1.3 million. The customer base was doubled during the VAT era and the same repeated with GST, and over 85% of their customers were on the latest major release.

Tally worked with both the government and several million businesses to transition into the GST era through various educational schemes. They were able to physically train almost one million businesses through on-ground efforts and more through digital efforts. The three challenges they faced while incorporating GST were educating the customers about the concepts and philosophy of GST, helping customers migrate to GST, and ramping up the customer care to support GST queries by customers. This was mainly done through GST events, blogs, and digital marketing efforts.

Tally's evolution as a brand was intricately woven with the senior Goenka's vision,

> there were only two types of businesses in India – one that used Tally and those that one day would.

This again was knit into the fabric of the growth of the product with Bharat's belief,

> If you want to build a successful product story, you have to make it the best and not the cheapest.

[10] Source: https://tallysolutions.com/blogs/.

[11] Source: https://m.timesofindia.com/business/india-business/tally-solutions-to-unveil-new-software-ahead-of-gst-rollout/amp_articleshow/59271410.cms.

The company positioned the product as a horizontal product as it was meant to cater to all segments of a pyramid, which consisted of small, medium, and large businesses, spread among various verticals. The conscious decision to remain a horizontal product and move from bottom-up was unique to Tally. Also, in contrast to other software products, Tally was against the notion of segmenting the market.

The only strategy for the growth of the product was by word of mouth with the underlying principle that if the company acquired 100 customers, they would be led to another 100 users, each who in turn would give the company access to 10,000 users. In addition to genuine users, there were a huge number of pirated copies of Tally being used in India, which also helped the organization to grow indirectly.

Tally also had three subsidiaries. The first was Tally (India), a distribution company that sold Tally software online, helped customers find right partners, and provided after-sales product. The second was Tally Analytics which collected and provided analytical services to the main Tally product (Tally.ERP 9). This mainly dealt with public data required for the functioning of the Tally product in a connected world, e.g., banking data such as bank/ branch lists and various codes, various interest rates, and various banking formats (cheque and payment files). The third was Tally Education, which collaborated with various universities and colleges to provide Tally product training to degree students. Tally Education had tied up with colleges to provide training and certification.

Tally's primary market was the MSMEs in India (Exhibit 16.2), but it also sold its product in over 100 countries including the Middle East and Africa. Tally had offices in 19 locations in India, one office in Dubai and one in Kenya.

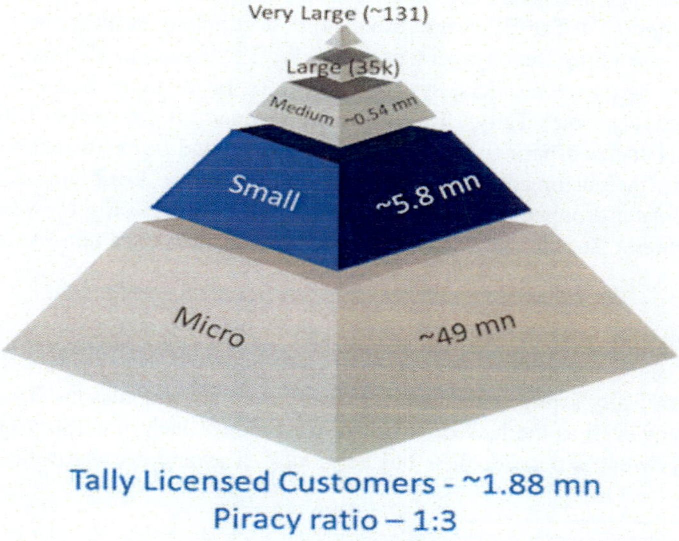

Exhibit 16.2 Business segments in India. *Source* Company documents

Tally's geographical spread had users in over 100 countries, and the company began tapping overseas markets in other developing countries stating that: "For us, manual bookkeeping is the only competition.[12]" In an ad hoc manner with virtually no planning or strategy, it journeyed smoothly among other players in the accounting software space. Tally took advantage of the changing landscape and the customer acquisition curve, and extrapolated it on technology and market space to evolve.

Tally Pricing

In 2012, the product pricing was changed from US$255 to US$340, including taxes.[13] Further, in 2017, the product pricing was again changed from US$340 all-inclusive to US$340 + taxes.

Distribution

Tally was distributed through two models: the MTP-TP model and distributor-AP-CP model. In the first model, Master Tally Partners (MTPs) and Tally Partners (TPs) were distributed to the customers, where the MTPs could do either direct sales or through TPs (indirect sales). TPs could only sell directly to the customers. As of 2020, Tally engaged with 160 MTPs who earned 15% on indirect sales and 25% on direct sales, and 28,000 TPs who sold directly and earned 25% on direct sales.

In 2015, Tally introduced the distributor model to replace the MTP-TP model. This model included Distribution Partner (DP), Associate Partner (AP), and Certified Partner (CP). The DPs were responsible for supply of software to both CPs and APs and sustaining the engagement with APs. The Associate Partners (APs) were typically hardware resellers, system integrators, or members in the IT ecosystem that reactively sold Tally. The Certified Partners (CPs) were Tally-invested and Tally-focused partners that committed a team and infrastructure to the business to serve the customers with high-quality experiences. Distributors earned 5% (which was later dropped to 4.5%), APs earned 12% (or 15% if they were Star Associate Partners), and the CPs earned 40% (or 25% if they were non-member CPs).

Dealing with Piracy

With Tally's piracy ratio at 1:3, there were several reasons for the existence of piracy such as the lack of access to the product, lack of ability to discover what to buy, what is best for their business, lack of awareness about the benefits that the

[12]Source: https://www.business-standard.com/article/companies/tally-tries-to-reach-for-the-stars-112010500087_1.html.

[13]1 US$ = INR 53.00 in 2012.

product offered, lack of information about the difference between pirated and the licensed product, and a perception regarding the product affordability and cost.

The company did not differentiate between licensed and pirated users and called them unpaid users. These users had the highest potential of becoming the company's licensed customers. The company did not attempt to strictly curb piracy; instead, it kept focusing on increasing the value and availability of their product and services.

There were four key factors which contributed to increasing their licensed customer base.

- External Triggers—Implementation of GST regime was a big shift, which changed the compliance game. GST required businesses to go digital and opt for business solutions to automatically synchronize invoice data, convert into GST-supported format, upload invoice details, rectify mismatches, and even file returns automatically. Thus, the need for licensed software got a huge push. Tally played a critical and crucial role in revolutionizing and ensuring tax compliance in the GST era.
- Internal Technology and Licensing Changes—Tally was in the process of creating more value to its customers through connected service offerings like synchronization, remote access, bank reconciliation, etc. Customers with a licensed copy and a valid TSS subscription (Tally Software Services) were able to access these features. Fear of missing out (FOMO) on key technology/feature updates, being connected with CA, and hassle-free GST compliance were some of the key factors changing customer perceptions. They also kept changing the licensing model, which made it difficult to crack the newer versions of Tally.
- In 2014–15, Tally revamped their partner structure and launched a new channel partner programs, including the launch of distribution network, which enabled their partner ecosystem to maximize reach and deliver higher-quality experience to customers. The new partner structure had a process of certifying partners based on their involvement, capability, and size, and was called Tally Certified Partners (CPs). These were further classified into 5 star partners and 3 star partners.
- Tally focused on customer engagements heavily, for instance, on personalized customer engagements to educate customers on software as a subject and improve awareness about their product/services and its benefits. Not only partners, but as a company, they regularly met customers through various customer connect programs like customer centricity, voice of customer (VoC), MSME day, etc.

Competitors

Tally was up against severe competition in both the accounting and ERP software space. India enterprise software market was a fragmented market and had several leading players across the value chain. Operating in a fragmented market, Tally software retained their loyal customers despite increasing competitive pressure from new players like Zoho, QuickBooks, etc.

The major competitors of Tally were Marg, Busy and SAP, who focused on the same customer segment as Tally solutions and offered a similar product.

Zoho was a software company that developed a range of business, collaboration, and productivity applications. Its products included CRM, mail, project management, invoicing, email marketing, and social media management apps. The company also provided network performance management, IT service desk and desktop management, data center and server management, log analysis, and security management. The accounting cloud product of Zoho was equipped to manage customer's finances. Zoho covered billing to purchasing, and from inventory management to tax readiness, making it one of the top accounting software in India. Zoho was a direct competitor to Tally[14] (refer to Exhibit 16.3).

SAP (Systems, Applications, and Products in data processing) was the name of the ERP software as well as the name of the company. They developed software solutions for managing business operations and customer relationships. The SAP system consisted of several fully integrated modules, which covered virtually every aspect of business management. SAP was #1 in the ERP market. As of 2010, SAP had more than 140,000 installations worldwide, over 25 industry-specific business solutions and more than 75,000 customers in 120 countries. SAP ventured into the SME space by offering customized products that were tailored for the small business enterprises. Their product offerings targeted toward SME had brought Tally in direct competition with SAP.[15]

Tally: Evolution of the Ecosystem (2020 Onward)

Tally believed that it could grow only if the ecosystem allowed the principal company to grow. To further its role in the ecosystem, Tally enabled partners to collaborate among themselves with a fixed rate card. For example, when a CP was required to deploy solutions across multiple locations (where it did not have scale to address these requirements), it was possible to leverage the extensive partner network in those locations, using the transparent fixed rate card. Over time, the partner network scaled up to cater to large accounts themselves now classified as Government and Very Large Account (GVLA) partners. The collaboration ensured timeliness and smoothness in the operational rollout. There were numerous such collaborative deployments in the partner network. With Tally's collaborative partner network, the company could bid, design, deliver, and deploy solutions quickly, which helped to cut across the partner's size and enabled geographical

[14]Source: https://tallysolutions.com/tally-software-service/ and https://www.zoho.com/.

[15]Source: https://www.guru99.com/what-is-sap-definition-of-sap-erp-software.html#2.

Comparison	ZOHO	TALLY
Customization	Yes	Yes
Multilingual support	All International Language	All Regional Language
Deployment	Web based & cloud	Mostly on Premise and cloud
Payment Term	Subscription	One-time payment
Technical support	Support on premise and phone	Support on premise and phone
Target Users	SMEs	SME's and Medium Enterprise
Platforms	Desktop and Mobile	Desktop
Pricing	Rs 2499 + GST per license (10 users)	Tally Silver 18000 + GST Tally Gold 54000 + GST

Comparison	SAP Business One	Tally ERP 9
Time involved in ownership, Implementation and Maintenance.	SAP implementation and integration involves long process, time, planning, cost etc. It cannot be implemented in short period of time.	It can be Implemented very or extremely fast quickly. It is as easy as thinking of a product, buying it either online or from supermarket, read instructions and start using it.
User friendly	Software is not much user friendly.	Software is absolutely user friendly.
Third party software support	Very High and reliable.	Not very good as Tally is developed with a core proprietary engine.
Technology	Three tier (R3) architecture technology. Completely based on coding.	Two tier (R2) architecture technology. It is code-less ERP System developed with a core proprietary engine and a Software Development Kit namely Tally Definition Language (TDL)
Data Handling Capacity	Large / Huge data sustains, there is no hurdle or limitation in processing large database. Data can also be processed in background	Software is not good in handling huge data, system stop responding in case of processing large database. Data cannot be processed in background.
Suitable for	Good and advisable only for large scale business heaving multinational, cross border, multi location operation with multi point control.	Good and advisable only for small and medium scale business where data volume is not very high and entire operation and management is very closely controlled.

Exhibit 16.3 Comparisons between major players in the ERP market. *Source* https://blogs.sap.com/2013/04/09/sap-erp-vs-tally-erp-comparative-analysis/

reach. Tally's intent was to build a solution exchange, which partners across the country could leverage for their own sales and support.

Apart from collaboration within Tally's partner network, external collaboration was also encouraged. For instance, Tally frequently collaborated as the transaction backbone for clients using other ERP solutions such as SAP or Oracle. In such collaborations, Tally provided the operational perspective, whereas other software solutions were focused on planning and optimization; hence, Tally complemented other packages. However, most of such external collaborations were informal, as neither Tally nor other competitors actively sold such collaborations.

TallyPrime

Tally endeavored to cater to the growing needs of the small and medium businesses, and in that spirit, on November 9, 2020, TallyPrime replaced Tally.ERP 9 as the flagship product of Tally Solutions, and the journey of Tally. ERP 9 finally ended after more than a decade. TallyPrime was designed keeping in mind the aspirations of new India and positioned as a worthy successor to one of India's most successful accounting software.[16]

Tally believed that the next significant shift would be toward connected business, as against the widespread belief that the next era in technology would be of big data, AI/ML, IoT, etc. According to Tejas Goenka:

> Networked Business is the future. We are building our new architecture of Series B/TallyWorld to enable creation of business networks powered by Tally Technology. Currently we are running the product architecture of "Series A

TallyPrime ensured that the famed simplicity of Tally.ERP 9 was retained so that users who were used to the Tally.ERP interface had a smooth user experience after transitioning to TallyPrime. Also, the TallyPrime took the UX to an altogether new level and Tally to a connected world, assisting companies with hassle-free accounting.

Using TallyPrime, users could manage invoicing, accounting, inventories, banking, taxation, payroll, and much more. The robust features understood user's business needs and simplified the lives of business owners through easy to use the software, insightful reports, multitasking capability, and much more.

The following features of TallyPrime transformed Tally from a simple ERP platform software to an ecosystem by connecting various stakeholders.

1. Simplified Interface and Insightful Business Reports

As the users of the prevailing business software were more concerned about the user experience, TallyPrime had simplified the screens while ensuring that the present Tally.ERP 9 users did not have to compromise with their experience after upgrading. The TallyPrime had a complete menu-driven interface that blended with the traditional commands to support Tally's current users. Most of the old shortcut commands worked seamlessly with the new TallyPrime along with the latest enhancement.

TallyPrime had a new and powerful search bar called "Go To." Using Go To, users could search and find things that Tally could do and simultaneously discover new insights to run businesses better.

TallyPrime came with more than 400 business reports as templates to assist business users. These reports were readily available to provide powerful insights to the users to help them make informed business growth decisions. TallyPrime also offered included features that assisted users in customizing their reports to their

[16]Source: https://tallysolutions.com/tally-prime/.

business needs. It also provided a user-friendly interface so that at the click of a menu, the user could change the view, modify the parameters of the reports, and enhance their report as per the changing business priorities.

2. **Invoicing and Accounting**

Since there were a lot of responsibilities (like invoicing) that come along with running a business, TallyPrime's all new business management software made it simpler to create and record invoices. Optimized invoice components, host of configurations, multiple billing modes, and so on, TallyPrime molded to the various businesses. Users could multitask and handle day-to-day interruptions with ease. Also, the personalization of the invoice option gave the user the flexibility to customize their invoice and save more details without disrupting the fixed invoice pattern of the company.

Electronic invoicing (e-invoicing) was the process of uploading all B2B transactions (sales invoices, credit and debit notes made to companies, including exports) in the invoice registration portal (IRP) for authentication. For every invoice uploaded and after authentication, IRP issued a unique invoice reference number (IRN). This IRN had to be converted into a QR code and other invoice information and printed on the face of the invoice for it to be considered valid. An e-invoice was a digital document exchanged between a supplier and a buyer and was validated by the government's fiscal portal. TallyPrime Release 1.1 provided an end-to-end connected e-invoicing capability in a very simplified and easy to use manner.

Tally was an official GST Suvidha Provider (GSP) due to which it could communicate directly with the IRP to upload invoices in real time. Once authenticated, Tally received the unique invoice reference number (IRN) as well as QR code information from IRP. This information was to be updated in the invoice seamlessly. The authenticated user could then print the required QR code and IRN on the invoice as part of their standard invoice printing procedure. In addition to the e-invoice, TallyPrime could also generate e-waybills, if applicable. TallyPrime users got a holistic view of the status of transactions and managed exceptions with the help of an exclusive e-invoice report and IRN register. Tally India Pvt. Ltd. (GSP) had followed all the information security policies as per international standards and was awarded the coveted ISO27001:2013 certification (Exhibit 16.4: steps to do e-invoicing and registering Tally as GSP IRP).

3. **Tally Business Report on Browser**

TallyPrime brought to customers the ability to access important business reports such as bills receivables and payables, stock summary, sales/purchase register, profit and loss A/C, balance sheet, and many such reports securely from one's Web browser. In addition, invoices could be downloaded and shared with customers on the go. All this could be done with the utmost security, where the data could be accessed only by the user.

Configuring e-Invoicing in Tally Prime is a very easy onetime process that can be done in under a minute.

1. Press F11 from any screen in Tally Prime and go to Step 1 or Select Alter under Masters in Gateway of Tally and select GST Details and go to Step 3.
2. On the screen which opens up, on the right side, under Taxation, you will see 'Enable Goods and Services Tax (GST)'. Since you have already configured GST, it will be showing 'Yes'. Double click on the same 'Yes' twice or click once and press Enter.
3. The GST configuration screen will now open. On the right-hand side, you will see two options; e-Way Bill applicable and below that e-Invoicing applicable. You can set both to Yes or only e-Invoicing depending upon the applicability to your company. Once you set it to Yes, you have to fill in the required information such as Bill from place etc. Press Ctrl+A to save and exit. The screenshot below shows the relevant details.

Your Tally Prime is now e-invoicing ready

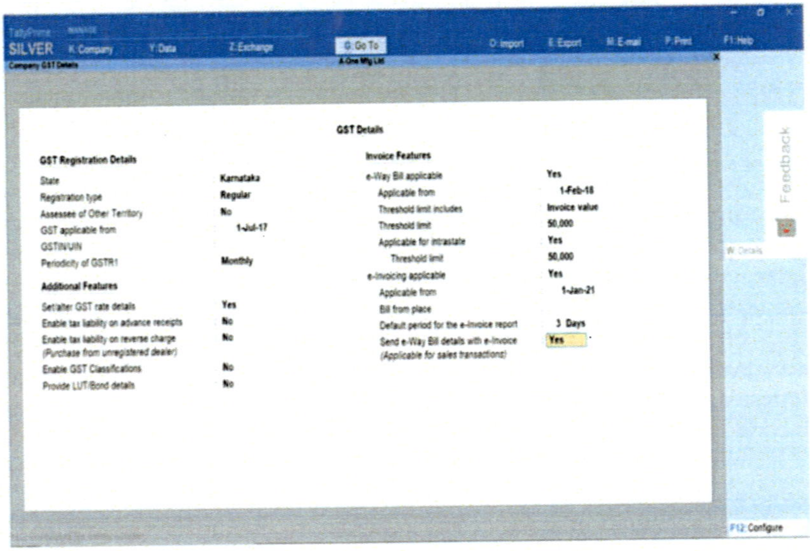

Exhibit 16.4 Steps to do e-invoicing and registering Tally as GSP IRP. *Source* Company documents

The user needed to connect the company to TallyPrime and log in to www.tallysolutions.com using the Tally.NET ID to access the browser reports. All it took was three simple steps to configure! Connect, login, and access the reports (refer to Exhibit 16.5 for the browser interface).

4. GST/Taxation Enhancement

With TallyPrime, users could generate a GST compliant invoice in seconds. Different types of GST invoices could automatically be downloaded such as tax invoice and bill of supply. The "prevention–detection–correction" technology of

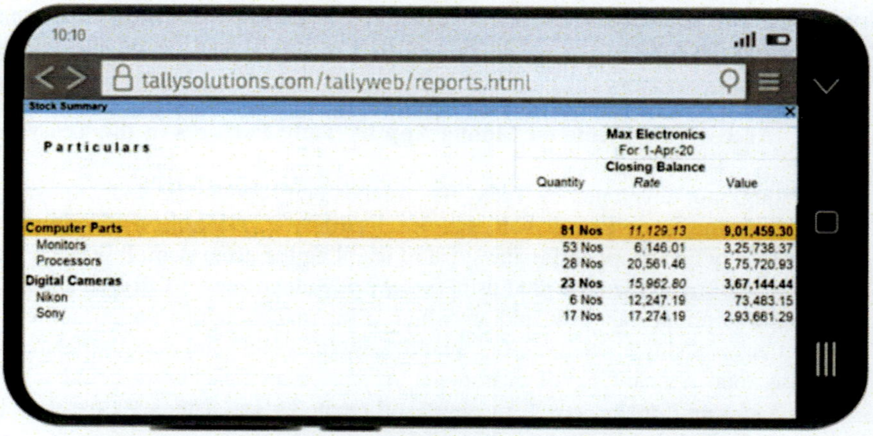

Exhibit 16.5 Tally's browser interface. *Source* https://tallysolutions.com/tally/faqs-tally-business-reports-on-browser/

TallyPrime helped users generate and file accurate returns.[17] Using TallyPrime's features, users could also manage TDS, TCS, and payroll, and other statutory items such as PF, ESI, and employee income tax.

5. **Inventory Management Enhancement and Multitask Capability**

The features of TallyPrime made it one of the most flexible systems for optimal inventory management. The wide variety of features in TallyPrime included godown management, stock valuation, manufacturing, batch and expiry date, job costing, etc. The powerful inventory reports made inventory management a cakewalk.

TallyPrime supported multitasking and helped the user handle day-to-day interruptions. If the TallyPrime user was in the middle of the sales invoice, he/she could record another new sale, could refer to a special report while in the middle of making a payment entry, or could print another report while in the middle of a voucher entry. Using TallyPrime, users were able to handle many such situations without the hassle of switching between multiple instances of Tally or the worry of losing progress.

6. **Cash Flow Management Enhancement**

By increasing the efficiencies in accounts' receivables and payables, inventories, and several other areas of business, TallyPrime helped users optimize cash flows. Using TallyPrime's features, users could automate and keep a complete track of the cycle of accounts' receivables and payables. With powerful inventory features such

[17]Source: https://tallysolutions.com/features/invoicing-and-accounting/.

as reorder level and actionable insights such as fast-/slow-moving goods, item-wise profitability, etc., users could plan their investment and be on the top of their business cash flow.

7. Access TallyPrime on Mobile App by Tally Partners in the Ecosystem

Though not developed by Tally, Biz Analyst had become the de facto synonym of TallyPrime on cell phones. It was developed by a partner in the Tally ecosystem that Tally had supported in the spirit of enabling the ecosystem. It was the preferred choice of more than 50,000 businesses worldwide to access TallyPrime on Android and iOS phones anytime and anywhere. Biz Analyst helped understand customers better on a single screen. Users could view their sales, receipts, performance, and also total outstanding of customers. At the same time, users could take punch invoices and orders, create receipts, and create ledger statements (refer to Exhibit 16.6 for Tally on cell phones).

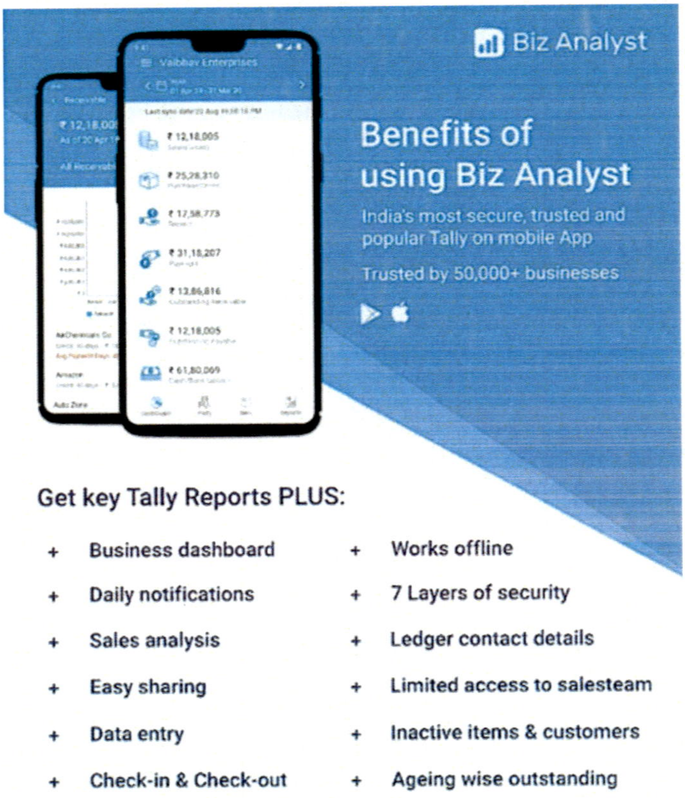

Exhibit 16.6 Biz Analyst TallyPrime on mobile. *Source* https://bizanalyst.in/

TallyPrime Versus Tally.ERP 9

To enhance the usability of Tally.ERP 9, TallyPrime introduced specific prominent changes that could improve the efficiency of the business as compared to Tally.ERP 9. The changes included some UI-based visible changes such as e-invoicing along with e-waybill. Some changes were not prominent. They would not catch the attention initially but were very helpful. The key differences between TallyPrime and Tally.ERP 9 along with the UX changes are listed in Exhibit 16.7.

Upcoming TallyPrime Features

The upcoming features of TallyPrime aimed to bolster the business of the users and build an ecosystem in which each component of the ecosystem could complement the other and bring in a synergy for the ecosystem as a whole.

8. **Multi-GST in a Company**

Multiple GST registrations were required for SMEs that functioned in more than one state. This was a challenge to the SMEs. From their customers' market study, Tally understood the needs and came up with a unique TallyPrime feature. TallyPrime users could create single company data for multiple GST registrations and file their returns easily.

9. **Connected GST Environment**

TallyPrime introduced a feature that would benefit all companies with GST registration. Users could compare the data in their books with that available on the GST portal. This gave them the confidence that the information in both systems matched. If there was any discrepancy, Tally users could take immediate corrective actions (refer to Exhibit 16.8).

10. **TCS Handling**

In the forthcoming releases of TallyPrime, users would experience a simplified item master setup and the introduction of new tax calculation methods based on "realization" and an amount exceeding threshold limit. Changes concerning 27EQ were also expected, which would further enhance the user experience. This TallyPrime feature would help in the day-to-day working of customers where TCS was applicable.

11. **Quick GST Report**

A frequent and long-standing complaint of most Tally users was that GST-related reports took a long time to open. In the upcoming releases, GST returns' related

#	Tally ERP 9	Tally Prime
1. Tally EXE/Application Logo	Tally ERP9	TallyPrime
2. Access Tally Data	Access company data by specifying a data path 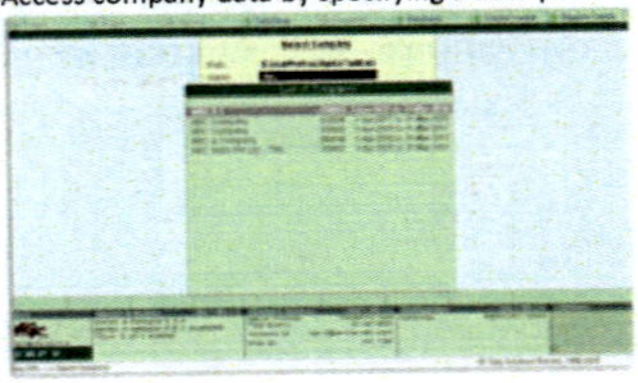	Access company data from any path or Drive or remote company and view the data status like Migration Required or Data Corrupted 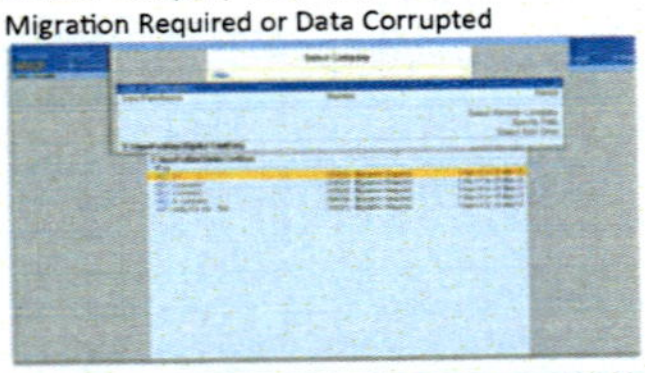
3. The Look and Color of Tally	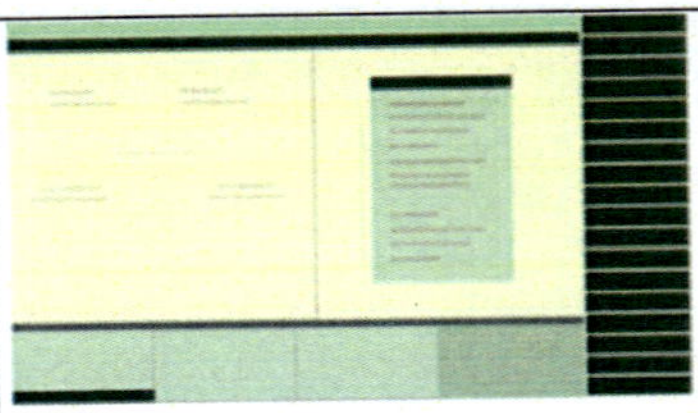	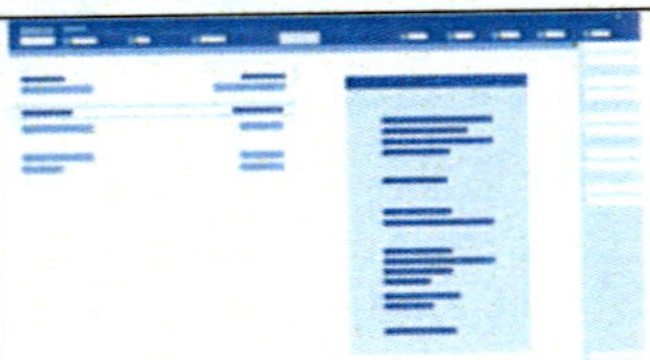
4. Multi-Tasking in Tally	Multi Tasking can be done by opening multiple Tally.ERP 9 Instances 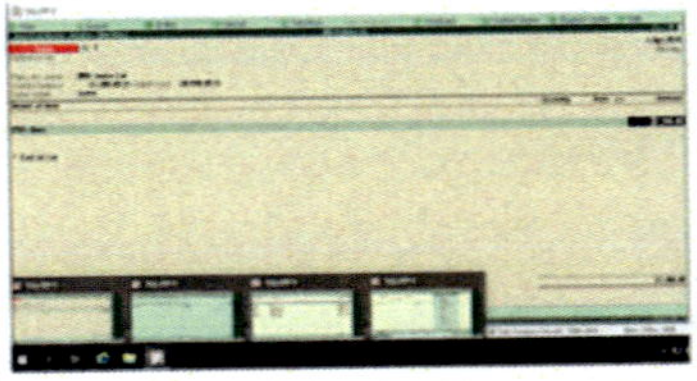	Multi Tasking can be done by in one Tally Prime Instance. Just check the Opened Reports in Go To Feature 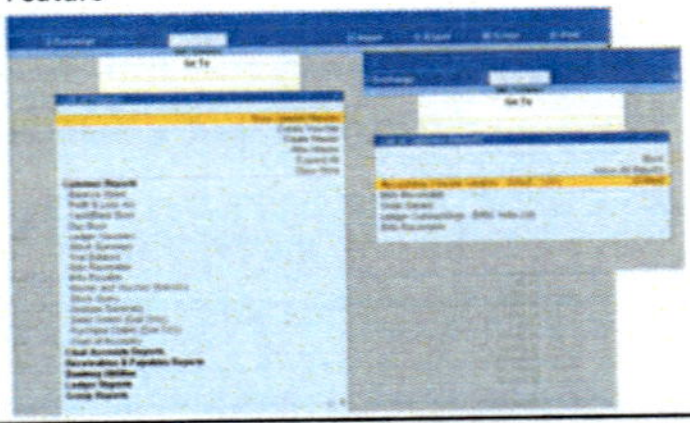
5. Chart of Accounts	In Tally.ERP 9 user had to make minimum 3 clicks to open each of these. In Gateway of Tally > Display > List of Accounts. 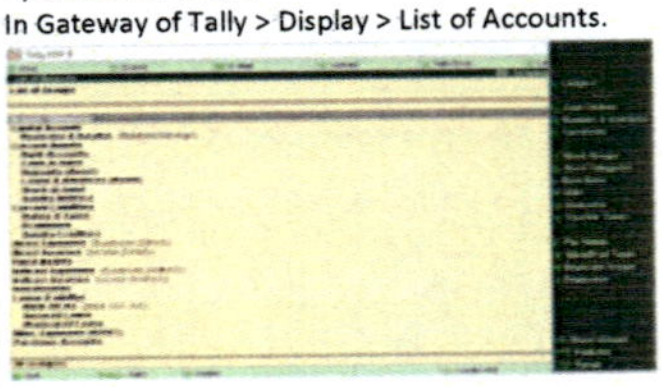	Option of 'Chart of Accounts' this allows you to access all your masters including groups, ledgers, voucher types, cost centre etc. can be accessed from one screen. 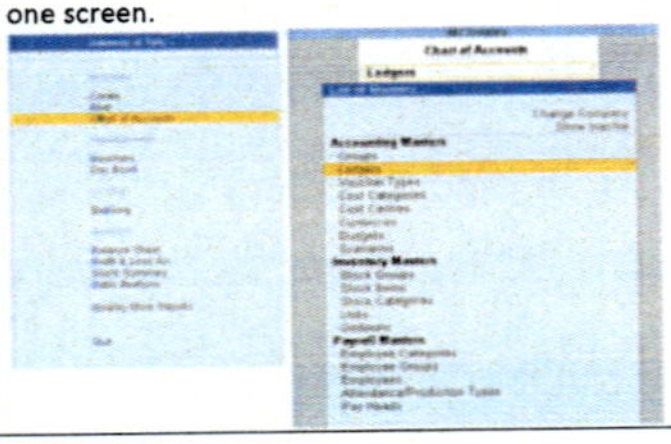

Exhibit 16.7 TallyPrime versus Tally.ERP 9 feature comparison. *Source* Company documents

6. **Supplementary Details**	In Tally.ERP 9, fill the required details and pass through complete Supplementary details 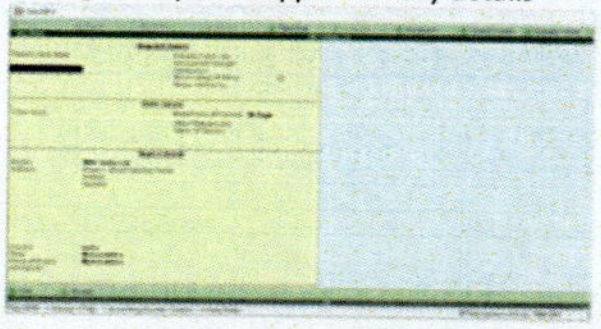	Add few details needed most of the time as 'Permanent details' in 'configuration' and get only those details in Supplementary details. 
7. **Copy/Paste in Tally**	Shortcut Keys Used to Copy and Paste in Tally.ERP 9 ctrl + alt + C ctrl + alt + V	Global Keys used to Copy and Paste in Tally Prime Ctrl + C Ctrl + V
8. **Change Voucher Mode**	In Tally.ERP 9 these options were available in 3 different places and hence navigation is now easier. 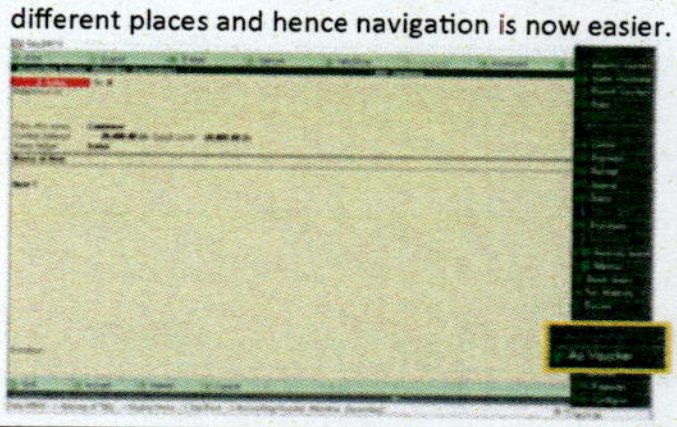	In sales voucher or any other voucher, the Change Mode gives you 3 options namely - Item Invoice, Accounting invoice and As invoice. 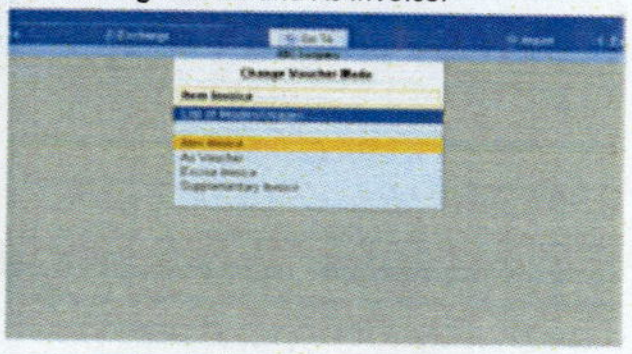
9. **Printing Invoice in Tally**	In Tally.ERP 9, when a user prints invoices with multiple items, the invoices are printed in multiple pages as unused blank space occupies the page that is not needed. 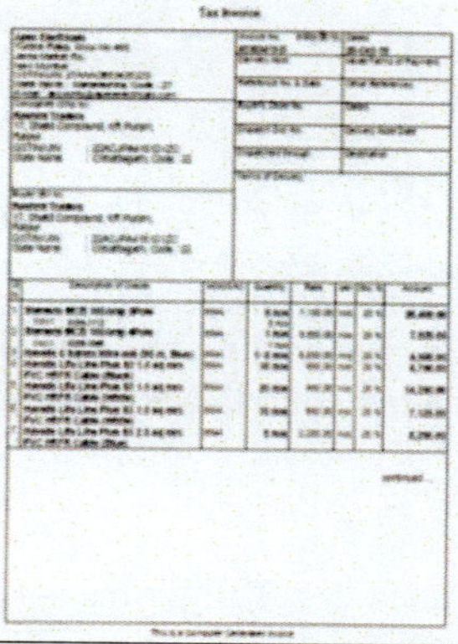	In Tally Prime, you can 'optimise printing to save paper'. This feature will reduce your 6-page invoice to a 2-page invoice, thus saving your printing costs, paper costs and other costs. 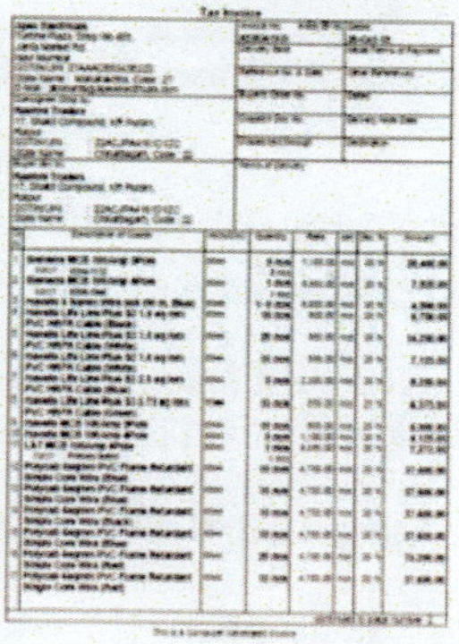

10. **Update details in Transaction**	In Tally.ERP 9, You need to pass through all items to update the details in specific item. 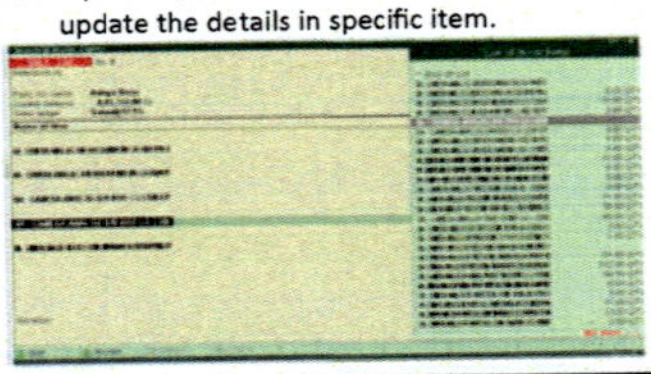	Use 'More Details' in Transaction and update details of specific item seamlessly 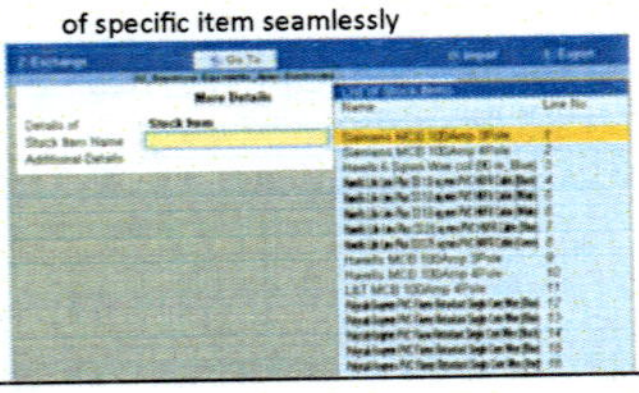

Exhibit 16.7 (continued)

Exhibit 16.8 GST reconciliation. *Source* Company documents

reports would open very fast like other accounting reports. This would save a lot of time spent on GST filing and associated compliance activities.

12. **Enhanced Report Filters**

New report filters were being planned for TallyPrime so that a user could get required information quickly, without wasting any time. With the option to apply single or multiple filters on a single screen, TallyPrime users could extract the most relevant information that they were looking for in the report effortlessly. This upcoming TallyPrime feature would significantly enhance the MIS reporting.

TallyPrime Pricing

The TallyPrime was available in two options: the Tally Silver, which was a single user edition for the stand-alone PC, and the other option was the Tally Gold, which was an unlimited multi-user edition for multiple PCs on LAN environments.[18]

Tally combined both the one-time pricing and subscription-based pricing models for its application. One-time pricing model was used for TallyPrime, and yearly subscription was used for Tally Software Services (TSS) subscription. The Tally Silver package was sold at USD 180 million, and Tally Gold was sold at USD 540 million. However, the TSS subscription costed approximately USD 40 a year and the TSS Gold costed approximately USD 146 annually.

Tally Software Services—The Ecosystem Enabler

Tally Software Services (TSS) was a software subscription for a collection of services that added tremendous value to TallyPrime by giving users the latest developments in technology and statutory laws.[19] It provided continuous product upgrades and updates, enhanced connectivity-driven functionalities such as online data exchange between multiple branches, remote access, and seamless banking and payment services contributing to users' business performance. The key benefits of TSS ecosystem are summarized in Exhibit 16.9.[20]

Bharat Goenka felt a sense of fulfillment looking at Tally as an ecosystem orchestrator. He had developed Tally as an alternative that mimics the manual ledgers that now defined how accounting and business processes were carried out in a large number of small and medium businesses in the country. Tally had added significant value to its users and other complementors in the ecosystem, including auditors, trainers, software developers, Tally Partners, and Tally Service Partners. At the same time, this came with a sense of accountability to steer the ecosystem to its most efficient path, lest they be enveloped by larger enterprise resource planning software and solution providers. At the heart of this dilemma lay another important question of how Tally would monetize this vantage position—higher prices would come at the cost of network growth, and too much subsidy might attract poor quality complementors into the ecosystem. It required a fine balance. Bharat wondered if the entire suite of TallyPrime (including the forthcoming releases) would allow them to keep the existing users locked in and attract new users, or would some users be wary of making such commitments to an ecosystem, and postpone adoption?

[18]Source: http://www.priztinesolutions.com/products.html.
[19]Source: https://www.visiontechtally.com/services.php.
[20]Source: https://tallysolutions.com/tally-software-service/.

Connected Service to Generate e-Invoice

Generating and printing e-invoice is amazingly simpler with TallyPrime's connected services. Tally being a recognized and ISO certified GSP (GST Suvidha Provider), TallyPrime directly integrates with IRP portal to seamlessly generate e-invoices.

- Auto-generate e-invoice instantly
- Print IRN and QR code automatically with no changes to the invoicing process that you follow.
- Flexibility to send individual/selective/ bulk invoices to IRP
- Generate e-invoice along with the e-way bill, wherever applicable
- e-Invoice report to get a bird's-eye view on the status (generated / pending / cancelled)

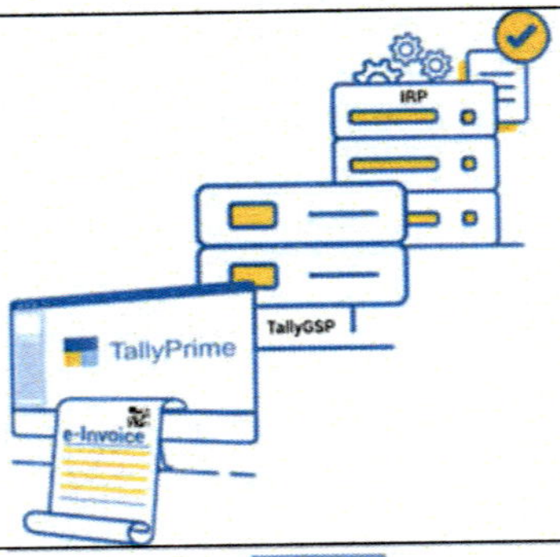

Business Reports on Any Device, Anywhere

Real-time and secure access to important business report from a web browser, on any device, anywhere.

- View your important business reports anywhere on a web browser
- Convenience of accessing your data anywhere while your data stays only with you
- Access important business reports such as Bills Receivable & Payable, Stock Summary, Sales/Purchase Register, Profit & Loss A/C, Balance Sheet etc on the go
- Helping you make the business decisions faster than before
- You can download an invoice or any report and share it on the go

Product updates

Regular product updates ensure that your TallyPrime caters to your ever-changing business requirements.

- Avail new product enhancements & major releases at frequent intervals
- Ensure compatibility with the latest technological and statutory changes

Banking & Payment

Experience smooth and ease of banking using Banking and Payment Services provided through TSS.

- Receive updates for all the latest cheque formats of banks available in your TallyPrime
- Automatically reconcile your books of accounts with your bank statements. It's quick, simple, accurate and stress-free. It saves your time, manpower and money

Exhibit 16.9 Tally Software Services (TSS)—ecosystem—benefits. *Source* https://tallysolutions.com/mena/tally-software-service/

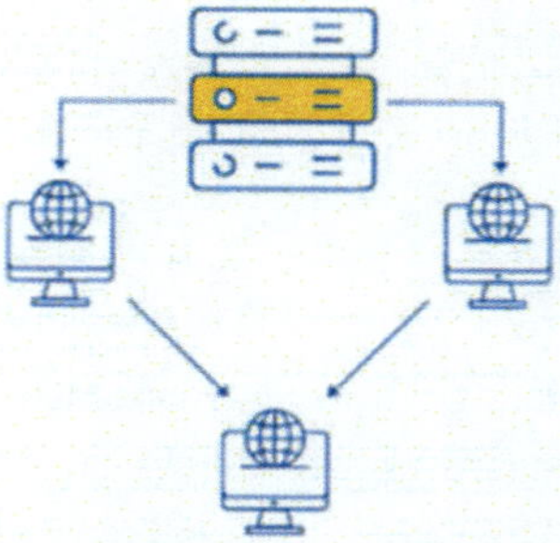

Online Data Synchronisation

Decentralisation of your books of accounts across branches is no more difficult. With TallyPrime's data synchronisation, you can synchronise data across your head office and branches, factories or warehouses.

- Exchange and consolidate Data across branches at click of a button
- Greater control on the direction of data synchronises and data to be synchronised
- Synchronise the data without needing to be 'connected to each other live' using on-demand synchronisation
- Complete visibility of business through consolidated reports of Head office and Branch office (Balance Sheet, P&L, Stock report, etc.)

Remote Access

24X7 business connectivity using our Remote Access Services and manage your business from anywhere in the world.

- Get round the clock access to crucial information about your business performance irrespective of the time or location
- Manage cash flows, bank accounts, stock positions or manufacturing time-lines even when you are not in your office
- Create and modify the business transactions and other details on the go
- Provide access to Chartered Accountants and their audit clerks to audit data

Exhibit 16.9 (continued)

17 Platform Envelopment

After having studied how platforms shape up to compete in winner-takes-all markets, we do appreciate that all markets do not exhibit WTA characteristics. In this chapter, we will talk about how platforms compete against each other and the idea of platform envelopment.

Platform Competition

Very similar to how we study competitive strategy in traditional pipeline firms, one should also study platform competition. Platforms can compete against other platform or pipeline firms on four strategies—platform scope; breadth and stickiness of the complementor network; switching and multi-homing costs for the users; and efficiencies in intermediation. Firms may adopt these strategies independently or in combination with each other.

Platform Scope

An important decision in platform design is that of scope. What activities will the platform sponsor internalize as part of the platform's core offering, and what activities will be provided by independent complementors. In the context of digital platforms, that are characterized by high modularity (a variety of complements can affiliate with the platform using standardised interfaces), this decision can affect platform competitive advantage. In an ecosystem with very strong and mature complementors, a lean platform core will allow for faster scaling and focus on user acquisition. On the other hand, in an ecosystem where the standards are yet to be set, and the complementor network is yet to mature, the platform sponsor may need to internalize a lot of operations themselves. Take the example of mobile operating system ecosystems. The platform sponsor (operating system producer) has to

R. Srinivasan, *Platform Business Models*, Management for Professionals,
https://doi.org/10.1007/978-981-16-2838-2_17

choose which applications need to be provided as part of the core offering; which applications could be exclusively developed by third party developers and offered through the applications marketplace; and which applications would be developed by both the platform sponsor as well as third-party developers and offered to the users as a choice in the application marketplace. This choice has implications for complementor variety and scale as well as users (demand side) switching and multi-homing costs. As we have discussed before, each platform sponsor should make these choices depending on their intent around scaling, capabilities, and their value architectures.

Breadth and Stickiness of the Complementor Network

Between competing platforms, platform scale has always been a critical metric for securing and sustaining competitive advantage. Scale in terms of number and diversity of complementors (independent providers of products and services) is important in platforms where cross-side network effects kick-in after the platforms attain critical mass. We have already seen that in order to attain this critical mass, platforms have been known to adopt a variety of measures, including subsidies and other incentives that attract complements to affiliate with the platform. Once the platform attains a critical mass, and the network effects kick-in, it would continue to scale without significant marketing investments or inducements. There are three competitive benefits that arise out of complementor scale and variety for platforms with strong cross-side network effects.

1. Complementor scale and diversity provide the users on the other side (that are looking to interact with these complementors through the platform) with increased choice. As the users evaluate competing platforms to affiliate, the extent of choice opportunities might tilt the scales in favour of the larger platform. Take the example of an ecommerce marketplace, where buyers would greatly value the variety of products (and brands/models amongst them) as well as the number of suppliers selling through the platform. Such variety might entice users to switch from other competing firms (platforms or otherwise) to this platform that offers most choice.
2. Complementor scale and variety also helps the users on the other side reduce their search costs—costs of searching for specific goods and splitting their transactions across multiple firms. This reduction in transaction costs may result in both users reduction in multi-homing costs, as well as increase loyalty to the platform. Take the example of enterprise software, where firms may prefer those platforms that provide an integrated solution spanning across all business functions, like accounting & finance, inventory management, warehouse management, retail operations, etc., rather than investing in stand-alone software for each of these functions. Even if the integrated software were to be inefficient in each of these specific functions, the value of integration might be highly

attractive to the firms, as it reduces their transaction costs of dealing with multiple software products (and vendors).

3. Complementor scale and variety would contribute to the platforms' maturity and learning. As more and diverse complementors affiliate with the platform, their varied expectations, transactions, and strategies will help the platform mature its own value creation and capture algorithms. Take for instance an event booking platform like bookmyshow.com. As the platform integrates movie halls in multiplexes, standalone theaters (for live performances), music concerts, contests (like quiz programmes), reality shows, and college festivals, the platform learns about the unique expectations of each of these complementors. And such learning may be transferable to their offerings to other complementors as well. In terms of discovery and transaction algorithms around marketing and filling the seats in an auditorium, the skills that the platform has acquired from multiplexes may be easily transferable to a live theater. However, a live theater might add additional constraints around, say restrictions around seating of infants in specific seats. Responding to this requirement may help the platform create differentiated seats in the audience, which it can leverage in seating VIP guests or judges in a reality show or a contest. The possibilities for learning from a complementor's context and integrating that learning into the platform core, so that it could be applied to other complementors' contexts creates significant value to the platform. A larger platform with learning and reapplication opportunities can sustain its competitive advantage over others with limited scale and diversity.

It is important to understand that in some contexts, just scale might not be valuable (it might lead to problems like choice overload). Similarly variety in itself might not be valued in the absence of critical scale, as the choice opportunities might be limited within each complement. Therefore, it is imperative that both scale and variety of complements is considered together.

Apart from focusing on the number and variety of complements, it is also critical to increase the stickiness of the complementors. By increasing the switching and multi-homing costs of the complementors, the platform can also sustain the competitive advantage. Platforms like bookmyshow.com, practo.com, and redbus.com increase their respective complementors' switching and multi-homing costs by tightly integrating their platform value-creating operations with the complementors' core operations. Each of these platforms also automates their complementors (movie halls, clinics, and bus operators, respectively) core operations (ticket sales, doctors' schedule management, and inventory of seats in every bus route, respectively) so that the platforms discovery and matching algorithms have access to high-quality and real-time data. If the complementors had low switching or multi-homing costs, it would be easy for competing platforms to imitate each other and shape the market dynamics into a situations like a free-for-all price competition.

Switching and Multi-homing Costs for Users

On the other side of the platform, the users' switching and multi-homing costs also have to be managed. In platforms where the demand-side users' switching and multi-homing costs are high, there is likely to be less churn of users, even when there is competitive entry of other platforms. Platforms adopt multiple strategies to increase switching and multi-homing costs for users.[1]

1. Tight integration with the platform's core products and services and that of the complementors' can help platforms increase user switching costs. For instance, when a user buys a device manufactured by Apple, the choice of operating system and other applications that will run on the device is pre-defined by Apple. If you would wanted to use an App, it better be available through the AppStore!
2. Adopting platform-specific nomenclature and processes can aid platforms increase the costs of users switching to other platforms. The costs of disruptions in unlearning the existing processes and learning something new might be very high and can significantly disincentivize switching and multi-homing. Imagine how enterprise software provide platform-specific training to their users' employees, so that they learn how to perform their tasks on that specific platform!
3. By adopting specific standards (including technology standards, data structures, definitions, and formats), platforms might restrict their users' switching to other platforms. Even when upgrading or updating the platforms to new standards, the platforms have the opportunity to enable backward compatibilities within their own platform ecosystem, thereby increasing switching and multi-homing.
4. Diversifying (breadth of complements) and providing the entire suite of products and solutions sought by their users can also aid the platforms disincentivize users' search in other platforms. Think how ecommerce firms have expanded to provide almost everything that the shoppers need, thereby reducing the need to shop in specialized stores.
5. Rewarding users for continuous association and repeated transactions can help the platform provide unique value to their users. This value could be distributed in multiple forms, including incentives/offers (like frequent flyer benefits from airlines), or customizations (like how search engines provide specific results based on one's search history and online activity).

Intermediation Efficiency

As with any other competition, efficiency of intermediation would contribute to the creating and sustenance of competitive advantage. How efficient is the platform in creating, delivering, and capturing value differentiates a platform from its

[1]See Shy, O., 2004. The Economics of network industries, Cambridge, UK: Cambridge University Press; and Shapiro, C., and H. Varian. 1999. Information Rules: A Strategic Guide to the Network Economy. Boston: Harvard Business School Press.

competitors. The maturity and accuracy of the platform's internal algorithms would help the platform increase user loyalty and help them scale. This is a virtuous cycle, as in most cases, platform scale helps platforms learn more and more, and mature their algorithms.

Thus, putting all of these together, in order to secure and sustain competitive advantage, platforms need to focus on complementors' scale and variety, user scale and switching costs, platform scope and efficiency. And each of these strategies reinforce each other—more the complementor scale and variety, more the users are likely to stay loyal to the platform; more the users interact with the complementors, more the platform learns and provides them with custom solutions/reduces costs that can be passed on to the users; which can help attracting new users/increase loyalty of existing users; and the like.

Platform Envelopment

In the context of platform firms, envelopment refers to the entry of a platform firm (enveloper) into another platform's (incumbent) market, combining its own functionality with the incumbent platforms' functionalities into a multi-platform bundle that leverages common components and/or shared user relationships. The enveloping platforms typically leverage the existing standards and product architectures; attract the same complementors (or those possessing similar capabilities); and address the same user segments. In doing so, they combine the value hitherto provided by the incumbents with theirs and provide an integrated bundle. In doing so, the complementors and users value the integrated bundle more than value provided by the independent platforms.

Take for example, a classified advertising platform. As the platform grows and builds networks on both sides of the platform—advertisers and readers, the platform becomes attractive for other multi-platform bundles like newspapers. When a local newspaper introduces classifieds column in its newspaper, it leverages its larger advertising base from its newspaper business to expand its advertiser-base for the classifieds; and expands the reader base at the same time. When such envelopment happens, independent classifieds platforms do not survive, as the advertisers and readers value the breadth of content and visibility provided by the newspaper, rather than the focused classifieds platform.

Imagine an App, where you would find a partner to date using your favourite dating app, plan your evening to a game/movie using an event ticketing app, find a restaurant & book your table using a hyper-local restaurant finder app, and hitch a ride using a car-hailing app whenever you are ready to move on, or better still, have an rented car waiting for you through the evening. All in one app. Wouldn't you love it, if all of it were integrated in one App? Just imagine the convenience if your restaurant-finder knew that you are in a particular concert at a specific place and you are likely to head out for dinner at a particular time. This specific knowledge could immensely help your restaurant-finder app to customize the experience for you—for instance, it could not only provide you those restaurant options that are open late in the evening after the concert was over, in a location that is close to the venue; it could possibly alert the restaurant that you were arriving in 15 min, based on your cab location. And through the evening, post your pictures on social media, check-in to all those locations in Facebook, and tweet your experience as well.

Yes, you would leave a perfect trail for the entire evening in a single place, and if you were to be involved in an investigation, it would be so easy for the officer to trace you! No need for any detectives here—the integrator app would take care of all the snooping for you!

Such envelopment is very commonly observed in converging markets, especially in the context of technology ecosystems. When technology standards have evolved and the interactions in the market stabilized, platforms from adjacent markets sense the opportunity and envelop these markets. Smart phones have historically enveloped a variety of functionalities, including photography, music, internet, and even payments. Each of these were independent platforms a few years ago, incorporating device manufacturers as one of the complements. However, as the relative power in these markets shifted from device manufacturing to software and application networks, the firms that dominate the mobile phone operating systems have systematically enveloped all these platforms into their larger platform offering. Independent platform providers like Spotify end up competing with Apple's own music streaming service, while accessing users as an App on the Apple ecosystem.

Follower Advantage

In these enveloping markets, fast followers enjoy a few advantages. The pioneering innovators have worked hard to establish the products and ignite the network effects. All that the fast follower has to do is then to differentiate their products and services from that of the incumbents to attract users. The business models are well set, and the firms have begun to understand what the users need (beyond the first few or lead users), as the market expands beyond the trial phase. These fast followers typically employ smart imitation (imitate the core value proposition and expand on the other features-based on user feedback on their existing products/services) and enter the market at a time before the market enters the exponential growth phase. And when these fast followers integrate the value proposition with their other value offerings, users begin switching.

Take the example of Google's consumer email service, Gmail. Google was not the first entrant in the cloud-based provisioning of consumer email services. There were competitors like Hotmail that had a significant market share. However, as the internet penetration showed signs of exponential growth, Google launched Gmail with the promise of a large storage. At a time when competitors were offering very little storage space (2 MB) on the cloud and users had to either delete their old emails or download those into their local computers, Gmail provided such a large storage (1 GB) that users overcame their switching costs and adopted Gmail. Gmail was able to provide such storage on the basis of their control over shared storage that they had built for their other products and services, including Google search. Falling storage costs and complementarity with Google products enabled Google to provide Gmail with differentiated features to users. These features were so valuable to the users that users switched their email addresses—the switching costs were non-trivial: Users had to communicate their new email address to everyone in their network; as well as keep their old email active for some duration, for a possibility that some business associate who had not been in touch with you for some time still remembers one's old email ID or uses an old business card to communicate.

Staircase Strategies

Some envelopment may happen through a carefully crafted set of product introductions that leverage on their existing products. Such stepwise diversification to envelop the market is known as staircase strategies. These new products increasingly reinforce each other and cumulatively enhance consumer value.

Take the example of Amazon, Inc. Amazon started as an ecommerce platform that brought together sellers and buyers. Gradually it expanded its merchandise mix to include its own private labels on the ecommerce platform. Leveraging on the technology evolution from compact disks as a medium for consuming music and video to streaming, Amazon adapted the change and introduced its own subscription-based streaming service. Similar is the case with its books—from physical printed books to electronic versions—and Amazon introduced its own ebook reader, Kindle (with proprietary format—epub). Leveraging its large servers and cloud storage, Amazon Web Services was introduced to provide cloud computing as a service. One by one, each product built on each other, and when one looks at the Amazon organization of today, it has enveloped many diverse platforms. It has backward integrated in its retail supplies (Cloudtail), diversified its products/services and therefore user segments (consumers, enterprises, families, as well as B2B customers), enabled payments through its own payment ecosystem, as well as expanded into a global corporation.

Competing Against Envelopment

When an envelopment threat is imminent, platform competitors have three strategies to compete. They could either focus on a specific niche, leverage its platform core, or enable complementors' growth.

Incumbent platforms could concede the larger market to the imminent enveloping platform but stay on to focus on a specific niche of customers that value the narrow, stand-alone platform. In doing so, it is possible for the incumbent to provide differentiated services to that specific segment and generate significantly stronger network effects. This could provide them with the required scale and resources required to attract more and more complementors and users and help them "tip" the market beyond the critical mass required. For instance, in the early days of smartphones, the Canadian firm Research in Motion (RIM) built a robust smartphone, Blackberry, and focused all its attention on positioning Blackberry as a business device. As against its rivals that were focused on the mass market, Blackberry's business focus helped it learn product design, features required, and the usage data of its primary users—the businessman. It enjoyed significant brand loyalty and market leadership in its segment till Apple and other Android-based competitors overtook the Blackberry powered by the breadth of Apps available in their application marketplaces.

Another strategy available for incumbents to defend against the onslaught of envelopers is to leverage the core across multiple products/platforms. By focusing on the core, it could be possible that the platform shrinks its scope, while expanding its complementors and user bases. Take the example of Apple's iTunes that was built for the iPod ecosystem, but was extended to serve the iPhone and the iPad ecosystems. While it could be easy for the envelopers to imitate and envelop the products and services, the core could be extremely difficult to replicate, given the strength of network effects.

The third strategy to compete against envelopment is to work with the complementors and ensure that they stay economically viable and sustain the innovation at appropriate pace. By enabling the complementors' business models and helping them achieve their economic goals will go a long way in competing against envelopers. Tight integration with the platform providers' roles will help the complementors leverage common resources thanks to modularity and compatibility. Platforms like Apple continue to engage with its App and content providers on its AppStore and iTunes store and help them market their products and services to the mass base of users. As early as 2007, Facebook opened its social network to third-party application developers. These developers could therefore utilize the data collected from the actual users and co-create better products and services.

Mitigating Envelopment

Apart from responding to envelopment, platforms could also adopt proactive strategies to mitigate envelopment. Platforms could either engage in racing strategies to acquire users faster than their potential new entrants (racing), protect their products and services from imitation and exploitation through legal means (IP protection), and by locking-in their users to their platform/ecosystem (caging of customers).

Racing (to Acquire Customers)

Companies have been known to race against competitors for a variety of reasons—to pre-empt access to critical resources (technology, patents, etc.), to set standards, or even set up capacity to limit competitor capacity addition. However, in the context of platform competition, we would exclusively focus on racing strategies platforms adopt to acquire customers (users and complementors). Before we elaborate on the specific racing strategies, let us first understand when to race, and when not to race. Platforms should engage in racing to acquire customers under the following conditions.

1. The market should reward scale with increasing returns. In other words, there should be increasing returns to scale, either through the presence of strong network effects resulting in higher willingness to pay by the users, or increase in platform efficiency, or both.
2. Proprietary nature of these network effects would provide platforms with the ability to lock-in customers (with high switching and multi-homing costs) and attract a variety of high quality complementors who are willing to make specific investments. When complementors invest in specific assets (assets that are almost exclusively useful in interacting with one platform ecosystem), they make a commitment to the ecosystem. This long-term commitment invites more and more users (on the other side) to join the platform, as they are assured of continued affiliation of the complementors.
3. The market does not possess late-mover advantages. Late-mover advantages typically include (a) opportunities to reverse engineer products to reduce costs; (b) leapfrogging opportunities through adoption of newer technology standards in a market where technology standards are rapidly evolving; (c) piggybacking on pioneers' (first movers) efforts in customer education and market creation; and (d) opportunity to create niche user segments that has been overlooked by the pioneers. If the market possessed any or a combination of these late-mover advantages, it is not advisable for the pioneers to race.

Thus, platform pioneers (first entrants in a market) should race when the market provides increasing returns to scale, it is possible to lock-in users, and there are no late-mover advantages. On the other hand, if the market provided late-mover advantages, it would make sense for the pioneers to wait for the market to mature—standards to be set and user segments to stabilize, before making investments in racing.

When the market is conducive for racing, platform competitors adopt four strategies to rapidly acquire customers (faster than competition).

1. *Focus on acquiring and locking-in marquee complementors*: One of the most common strategies in a market where standards are yet to evolve, this strategy is likely to yield immediate results. An affiliation by a marquee complementor, someone who is highly valued by the users on the other side, is an affirmation of

credibility of the platform. If the complementor further signals commitment to the platform, it provides further assurance for the users to affiliate and engage.

2. *Subsidize to acquire users*: Platforms have also known to subsidize users at the early stages of evolution. There is a significant trade-off in adopting this strategy —the subsidized prices should be justifiable with the unit economics of the platform in steady state. The platform should be able to raise the prices subsequent to the market stabilizing. If that would not be possible, then the subsidized price should be surely higher than the platform variable costs at the minimum, and in a reasonable time frame should also be sufficient to cover the fixed costs. If the subsidized prices are not economically justifiable at the targeted volumes, this strategy could seriously hurt the platform, as well as ecosystem development. In such contexts, there is also an issue of the economic viability of the complementors. The pricing and economics should not only ensure sufficient user growth, but also keep the complementors economically interested to keep investing and staying on the platform.
3. *Adopt pricing models that encourage frequent and/or exclusive transactions*: Following on the complementors' economic viability, it is imperative that the pricing models should encourage, if not incentivize exclusivity. If the platform could incentivize the complementors to transact exclusively on the platform, it would encourage the complement in its own marketing efforts, in addition to that of the platform's, to acquire users. As the frequency of transactions in the platform increases, it encourages users and complementors to invest in specific assets related to the platform.
4. *Adopt user acquisition strategies like referral programmes*: Such programmes like referral programmes on both sides of the platform, complementors bringing in "their own users" on to the platform, as well as "users get more users" can help in increasing scale substantially. In the absence of same-side network effects (if it did exist, more users would get more users), such referral programmes will assist platform marketing. These programmes will make users into promoters of the platform and contribute to increased net promoter scores (NPS).

In sum, racing is a viable competitive strategy under specific conditions; and platforms have a portfolio of choices to race.

IP Protection

Another classic means of mitigating envelopment is to protect one's business activities and products through protecting intellectual property. Platform owners regularly protect their core to deter any new competitive entry, let alone entry by an enveloping platform. Broadly, there are four forms of protection. Trademarks are typically used to claim names, phrases, logos, colours, and symbols exclusively, as a brand. Such trademarks help firms promote their brands and ensure that new entrants do not imitate the brands and imagery easily. Copyrights help protect firm's creations, including designs, books, processes, and even software. Patents on the other hand provide firms with rights over their novel inventions. Patents typically provide marketing rights to innovators for a specific tenure. Trade secrets are things that could not be registered but are kept confidential. Typically, formulas, algorithms, techniques, and routines are protected as trade secrets.

For instance, Amazon has patented processes like 1-click ordering, products like drones, and some computing protocols, all of which are core to their business of electronic commerce and cloud storage solutions.[2]

Caging of Customers

Caging as a concept is different from lock-in. Lock-in strategies are typically achieved through erecting high switching and multi-homing costs. It is an economic cost that could be overcome through investments and expending financial resources. Caging, on the other hand refers to contractual lock-in, wherein the costs of exit from the contract are typically far higher than what may be worth.

Caging could be observed when platforms lock complements and users into contracts to use specific technological elements and such use might require asset-specific investments that might become redundant without these technological elements. For example, in the Apple ecosystem, users have very little choice to use any other operating system, once they have made their choice of Apple hardware.

Platforms can cage users through a variety of contracts and commitments, including transaction costs of joining/exiting the platform, redundancy of asset-specific investments, and disruption in operations due to switching (as the platform processes are tightly integrated with the complementors' core processes).

Adopting caging as a defence against imminent envelopment is fraught with two downsides. Firstly, having understood the costs of caging, the platform might only attract limited complementors and users, denying the platform with scale. Second, the costs of caging might reflect in the complementors and users not willing to pay the fair price for the platform. On the other hand, in the absence of any contracts, whenever an enveloping platform enters the market, it is attractive for the new entrant to reduce prices and encourage complementors to break the contracts and adopt the new platform.

Therefore, it is important for platforms considering caging as a strategy to balance the needs of scale and willingness to pay on the one side and preventing customers from "escaping" to enveloping platforms on the other side. There could be possibilities for a middle path, that provide for sufficient contractual lock-ins, while enabling growth and profitability.

[2]For a more detailed list of Amazon's patents and copyrights, see: https://companyprofiles.justia.com/company/amazon.

Managing Multi-platform Bundles

Let us now turn our attention to the enveloping platforms. Envelopment as a strategy provides a few sources of advantage over stand-alone platforms. As a multi-platform bundle, there are opportunities to build their different platforms around a common core. This core could include common matching algorithms, shared user networks, common complementors, and even shared overheads. For instance, ecommerce platforms have been able to integrate multiple business models—marketplace models (where the platform only connects buyers and sellers) and inventory-led models (where the platform also carries inventory and performs the fulfilment role as well) under the same firm. At the outset, these two business models might look very similar—in fact, for the retail buyer, it does not matter what model the firm uses; but they are quite different when seen from the sellers' point of view. An efficient ecommerce platform might be able to make intelligent choices around specific contexts where to use marketplace models, or inventory-led business models. And these could provide significant learning to each other.

As we have seen earlier, multi-platform bundles could share valuable data collected from the users across platforms. For instance, a user's internet search history might be very highly valuable to customize offerings and recommendations when the same user looks for flight tickets. Having understood from the search history about her intent to travel to a specific location, the firm can provide specific recommendations around travel to, stay in, and tours around that destination. Such data sharing though has to comply with the legal framework of the specific countries.

Multi-platform bundles can easily resolve penguin problems faced by platform firms, by porting relevant users from related platforms to the new platform under development. In addition to all these, multi-platform bundles can easily tip across markets—leverage the technological core from one market context to adjacent markets as well.

On the other hand, multi-platform bundles also have to incur some additional costs as compared to focused platforms. Pretty much similar to the arguments against diversification, multi-platform bundles need to manage their overhead costs efficiently. The costs of coordination across different platforms with different complementors and users might be non-trivial and may require considerable managerial and executive attention. Synergies are typically difficult to achieve when the businesses are very different from each other. Resource sharing and integration of activities across different platforms may cost significant amounts and dent the benefits accrued from synergies.

There is also a risk of such multi-platform bundles moving too far away from their core. Sometimes, sequential diversification and expansion might require additional resources and competencies, which may be specialised to specific platforms. For instance, when a peer-to-peer messaging platform seeks to integrate a variety of applications on the platform, it might leverage its existing competencies in certain markets like social commerce. However, the diversification from social commerce to managing payments might look synergistic, but managing payment platforms may require different regulatory interfaces, and may attract different segments of users to the platform. The social commerce and payments ecosystems may have overlaps, but there may be very little overlap between the platform's core —peer-to-peer messaging and payment platforms.

Apart from all of these, multi-platform bundles run the risk of reputational spill overs from one platform to another. For example, a scam attack on the payment platform might enrage the users of the messaging platform and might lead to significant customer attrition.

In summary, the decision to operate a multi-platform bundle has to be thought through as a diversification decision, where the synergies and benefits have to weighed against the costs of such diversification and bundling. Like most corporate strategy decisions, there may be opportunities for firms to operate different levels of diversification and integration across different platform combinations (tapered diversification strategies).

Tarnea Technology Solutions: Competing in a Winner-Takes-All Market

18

Introduction

It was a rainy evening in the city of Bangalore. Suresh Satyamurthy, CEO and Founder of Tarnea Technology Solutions, sat in his makeshift office in the comfort of his home and pondered where his company, a platform business in the pharmaceutical retail industry, was heading. On the other side, over a video call, was his Co-founder and CTO of the company, Madhav.

The COVID-19-induced pandemic had derailed all the carefully laid plans for the year 2020. Supply chains over the world had been thrown into disarray. The pharmaceutical supply chains on which Tarnea had built its platform had also seen disruption. The industry was seeing supply-side challenges as well. Raw materials from China were not flowing into the country anymore; and in India, interstate transport movements were restricted owing to the countrywide lockdown. Distributors were facing shortages, which were driving them to overstock

This case is an extension of Chapter 16 Platform Envelopment.

This chapter does not have the copyright statement as in other case studies. Please check and confirm if this is fine.

R Srinivasan, Professor of Strategy, Chandrasekar Venkatesan (IIMB MBA Class of 2021), Ishan Verghese (IIMB MBA Class of 2021) Manish Kumar (IIMB MBA Class of 2021) and Menaka Rao, prepared this case for classroom discussion. Tarnea Technology Solutions cooperated and provided information to the Indian Institute of Management Bangalore in connection with the preparation of this case and it was reviewed and approved before publication by a company designate. No funding was sought or received from Tarnea Technology Solutions for the development of this case. This case was also developed from available and permitted sources of information. This case is not intended to serve as an endorsement, source of primary data, or to show effective or inefficient handling of decision or business processes.

R. Srinivasan, *Platform Business Models*, Management for Professionals,
https://doi.org/10.1007/978-981-16-2838-2_18

inventory. They were hesitant to give credit to the retailers, who were getting squeezed. This lack of capital caused some retailers to shut shop.

Amidst this chaos, however, there was an opportunity for Tarnea. The COVID-19 pandemic would undoubtedly accelerate the digitization of retail. However, beyond this, there were several paths available to Tarnea to grow its business. Suresh and Madhav weighed the options available to them. Should the company pursue geographical expansion, horizontal expansion, or continue to refine its product to meet evolving customer needs?

Birth of Tarnea

Tarnea Technology Solutions was born out of a need to provide digitalization of the pharma value chain, especially the hundreds of thousands of small pharmacies. After earning a Master's in Electronics Engineering and a PostGraduation Diploma in Rural Management, Suresh worked for a European multi-national company. His close friend Senthil Rajagopalan, with whom he co-founded Tarnea, had completed his post-graduation in management and worked in the USA as a consultant. Suresh and Senthil were intrigued by the role that information technology played in the transformation of supply chains. They both shared a vision of starting a venture together in this domain.

However, it was not until 2011, when Suresh embarked on a "Bharath Darshan"—a cross-country road tour that the vision started to take shape. During this tour, Suresh spent a large amount of time trying to understand how supply chains were managed at the micro-level, the issues that plagued retailers and distributors, and how technology could be leveraged to offer solutions to these problems. There were three major problems that he wanted to address.

- How to bring about digitalization to the numerous small pharmacies, whereby data would play a huge role in bringing about better efficiencies to these retailers?
- The role of data in improving supply chain efficiency: Distributors faced a high cost for the acquisition of orders. As distributors did not have inventory stock visibility at the retail pharmacy, they had to employ sales personnel to visit retail pharmacies physically. Prioritizing the customers was critical in this model, as the cost of not being the first to respond to orders meant that a competitor would grab it.
- Inventory management: There was a high cost associated with the expiry of medicines due to the lack of turnover and stockouts. Suresh sought to address these issues.

Armed with these insights, Suresh set about developing a business plan that would provide supply chain solutions to the Indian retail pharmaceutical industry. Drawing inspiration from Walmart's proprietary RetailLink®, Suresh decided to use the software as a service (SaaS) model as the business plan's centerpiece.[1] He could

[1]RetailLink® is a registered trademark of Walmart, Inc.

utilize the cloud's centralized storage capabilities to enable real-time data access for retailers and distributors.

Pharmaceutical Retail in India

The total turnover of the Indian pharmaceutical market was US$20.03 billion in 2019[2] and was expected to grow at rates between 10 and 12% till 2022.[3] The Indian pharmaceutical firms were also exporting drugs to over 200 countries in the world, and in 2020, Indian exports were valued at US$16.28 billion.[4] Together, it was estimated that the total market was expected to grow to US$59 billion by the year 2023,[5] largely driven by increasing incidences of chronic diseases and lifestyle changes.

Pharmaceutical retailing in India was fundamentally different and unparalleled in the world. The industry was dominated by approximately 850,000 small unorganized pharmacies run by independent owners, accounting for about US$ 33 billion in annual sales.[6] By comparison, a country like USA had only 88,000 pharmacies[7] accounting for approx. US$ 300 billion.[8] According to a report by Deloitte, China which had a population similar to India had only 388,000 pharmacies[9] catering to retail sales of about US$ 270 billion.[10] The small size of the pharmacies and the immense geographic spread across India had made previous attempts in organizing or consolidating them to fail. As a result, 1% of the pharmacies today could be considered as organized doing a daily sales turnover of a mere US$ 129 a day![11]

Pharmacy retail in India was dominated by brick-and-mortar retailers. Based on the format, the market was segmented into the organized sector, unorganized sector, and online retail. The unorganized sector was the largest with a 93% market share. The

[2]https://www.ibef.org/industry/pharmaceutical-india.aspx.

[3]India's Pharma Supply Chain: Does the Industry Have What It Takes to Win? OPPI, ATKearney, https://www.indiaoppi.com/wp-content/uploads/2019/12/Indias-Pharma-Supply-Chain-Does-the-Industry-Have-What-It-Takes-to-Win.pdf.

[4]https://www.ibef.org/industry/pharmaceutical-india.aspx.

[5]https://www.statista.com/statistics/1027563/india-retail-pharma-market-size/ last accessed on 08-11-2020.

[6]https://www.statista.com/statistics/1027563/india-retail-pharma-market-size/.

[7]https://en.wikipedia.org/wiki/Pharmacies_in_the_United_States.

[8]https://www.statista.com/statistics/197635/annual-pharmacies-and-drug-store-sales-in-the-us-since-1992/.

[9]https://www.researchgate.net/publication/236675299_Community_pharmacy_practice_in_China_Past_present_and_future.

[10]How pharma companies can address the retail market transformations in China, https://www2.deloitte.com/cn/en/pages/life-sciences-and-healthcare/articles/industry-transformation-new-opportunities-pharmaceutical-companies.html#.

[11]https://www2.deloitte.com/content/dam/Deloitte/cn/Documents/life-sciences-health-care/deloitte-cn-lshc-four-transformation-pharmaceutical-retail-market-en-200609.pdf.

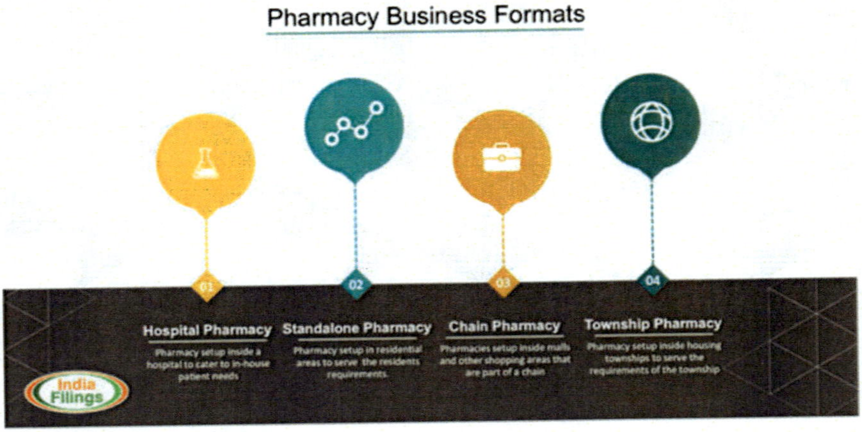

Exhibit 18.1 Indian retail pharmacy business formats. *Source* https://www.indiafilings.com/learn/how-to-start-a-pharmacy-business/

organized sector was estimated to increase steadily.[12] The online retail segment was projected to expand at a CAGR of approximately 34%. According to a FICCI report, pre-COVID, 3.5 million households were using a pharmacy online (e-pharmacy) in 2020. During COVID-19, the number of households increased to 9 million.[13]

Retail pharmaceuticals in India could be broadly divided into three categories: 1. hospital pharmacy, 2. independent pharmacy, and 3. chain pharmacy (see Exhibit 18.1). The business of the independent pharmacies was very dependent on its location—the "high-street" pharmacies typically did brisk business, where the "side-street" pharmacies had only a modest value of business.

Retail Pharmaceutical Value Chain

Exhibit 18.2 shows a simplified diagram of the Indian pharmaceutical value chain.

Principal

India ranked third worldwide for pharmaceutical production by volume and 14th by value. The country's domestic pharmaceutical industry had a network of 3000 drug companies and 10,500 manufacturing units. The principal or manufacturers were the

[12]Analysis on India's Pharmacy Retail Market, 2016–2024—Shares by Retail Channel, Drug Type and Therapeutic Area, March 13, 2020, https://www.globenewswire.com/news-release/2020/03/13/2000142/0/en/Analysis-on-India-s-Pharmacy-Retail-Market-2016-2024-Shares-by-Retail-Channel-Drug-Type-and-Therapeutic-Area.html.

[13]Maji Navneel, "E-Pharmacy: The Growth Story Of 2020", Business World, December 12,2020, http://www.businessworld.in/article/E-pharmacy-The-Growth-Story-of-2020/12-12-2020-352919/

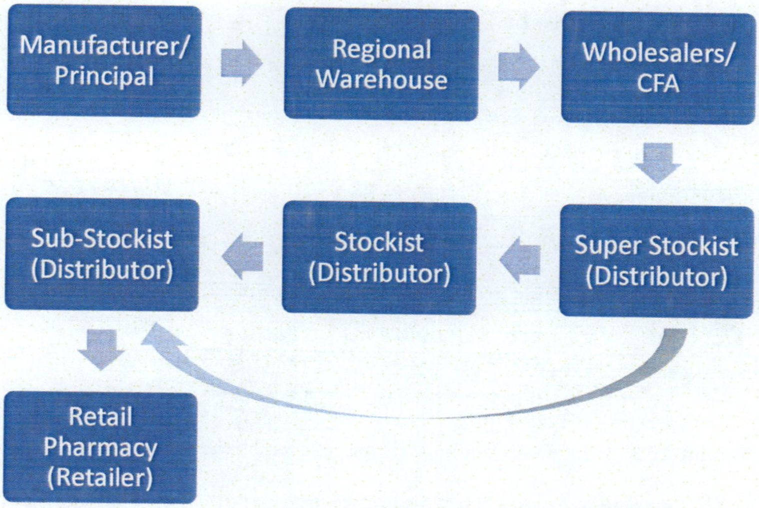

Exhibit 18.2 Simplified value chain. *Source* Authors' representation

large and small pharmaceutical companies that formed the $33 billion pharmaceutical industry in India.[14] The industry was going through an exciting phase. Companies endeavored to become a hub for low-cost manufacturing and R&D. They faced a unique set of local and global pressures to regulate the end-to-end operations. A key challenge was that the business differentiator was shifting from reverse engineering capabilities to operational parameters such as service level and delivery costs.

Companies were pursuing the next phase of growth, but there was a large gap between their strategic vision and the existing operational situation. Products had increased exponentially, and their formulations had become a lot more complicated, driven by the evolving therapeutic and medical needs of patients. Fragmentation across the value chain eroded the supply chain efficiency—widespread quality issues and pressure on prices across the value chain had triggered regulatory scrutiny. Infrastructure, although much improved, was still a concern. Despite these challenges, the pharma companies were expected to increase revenues and grow profits while also improving shareholder value.

Distributors

With 850,000 pharmacies and 85,000 distributors,[15] catering to various retail pharmacies across the country, the distribution network was highly fragmented in India.[16] The distribution system was multi-tiered. Clearing and forwarding agents

[14]https://www.ibef.org/industry/pharmaceutical-india.aspx last accessed on 13-11-2020.
[15]Pharmacy consolidation may disrupt domestic drug market …www.business-standard.com.
[16]https://www.biopharminternational.com/view/pharmaceutical-distribution-india last accessed on 17-11-2020.

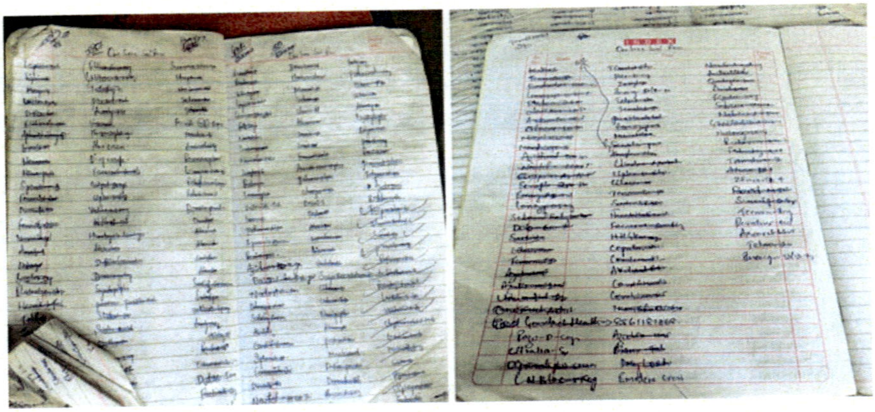

Exhibit 18.3 Want book. *Source* A sample sourced by the authors from a retailer

(CFA) established and own warehouses and depots. These agents were responsible for maintaining the principal's product stock and forwarding the SKUs to the distributor. On average, a principal worked with 25 CFAs and paid the CFA based on the total turnover of products.[17] The CFA, in turn, worked with anywhere between 300 and 500 distributors. Distributors catered to 2000–3000 retailers. A distributor handled stock from anywhere between 100 and 200 principals, and they usually received a 30–45-day credit period from the principal. Distributors received approximately 8–10% margin on the SKUs that they provided to the retailer.[18]

The distributor typically received orders through two modes. The distributor's salesmen visited the retail shops to deliver orders, and at the same time, took orders from the retailer's "want book" (see Exhibit 18.3). The second mode was carried out over the telephone. The distributor's "feet on the street" was a significant operational expense.

The distributor's importance to the retailers cannot be ignored as the distributors were the retailer's financiers. Most retailers were small stores with insufficient capital to finance their inventories. Thus, the distributor was the critical element of the value chain that provided the retailers with capital and credit terms that allowed the retailer to do business profitably.

The distributors were aware of the important retailer touch points in a market. Thus, the distributor acted as a center of data aggregation. The distributor could identify sales trends, market coverage, and the popularity of different products. The distribution system of the pharmaceutical industry in India was dynamic and challenging. In such an environment, managing relationships with stakeholders was complicated owing to the lack of coordination. Therefore, the use of sophisticated communication and information tools was necessary and would be inevitable.

[17]http://dolcera.com/wiki/index.php/Indian_Pharma_Industry_-_Distribution_&_Sales_Force_Structure last accessed on 17-11-2020.

[18]http://dolcera.com/wiki/index.php/Indian_Pharma_Industry_-_Distribution_&_Sales_Force_Structure last accessed on 17-11-2020.

Retailer

Indian retail pharma industry was widely fragmented throughout the country, with over 850,000 retailers in India.[19] However, the organized pharma industry was estimated to penetrate 13% of the retail market in 2021.[20]

New products, new forms of dosage, improved formulations, and packaging and labeling changes to cater to emerging markets widened the product portfolio. Leading Indian manufacturers launched about 15–30 products a year. This posed several implications for the retailer, including higher inventory costs and a more extensive distributor base.

The prices and margins of the drugs for the stockists and retailers were set by the National Pharmaceutical Pricing Authority (NPPA) under the drug price control order (DPCO). Prices were determined by whether the active constituent in the product was a scheduled or a non-scheduled drug. Scheduled drugs were price-controlled, while non-scheduled drugs were not. To keep prices accessible to the underprivileged population, the government had included 860 of them by 2019, impacting a significant part of the market (estimated to be around 30–35% of the total market).[21]

Online Pharmacy

With increased internet penetration and smartphone ownership, there had been significant growth in online e-pharmacy. According to Frost and Sullivan, India's e-pharmacy market was estimated to reach $3 billion by 2022.[22] There were around 60 online pharmacy delivery start-ups in India. The Tracxn reports on e-pharmacies in India stated that there were 282 start-ups in India.[23]

Cash burn in the e-pharma industry was a problem as the discounts (up to 35% for some) exceeded the margins in the chain (about 30–32%). While the race to scale up required greater adoption and discounts which was an integral part of growth, profitability could not be achieved only by operational efficiency and lowering of delivery costs; discounts had to come down to reasonable levels to

[19] https://www.biopharminternational.com/view/pharmaceutical-distribution-india last accessed on 18–11-2020.

[20] Sandhya Keelery, Organized pharmacy and wellness retail penetration India 2012–2021, Oct 23, 2020.

https://www.statista.com/statistics/1044055/india-organized-pharmacy-and-wellness-retail-market-penetration-rate/ last accessed on 18-11-2020.

[21] https://www.emerald.com/insight/content/doi/10.1108/EEMCS-06-2015-0137/full/html last accessed on 19–11-2020 Khan **Amir Ullah, India's drug price fix is hurting healthcare,** ***The mint***, 29 Oct 2019, https://www.livemint.com/politics/policy/india-s-drug-price-fix-is-hurting-healthcare-11572334594083.html.

[22] https://ww2.frost.com/frost-perspectives/spotlight-e-pharmacy-india-exponential-growth-opportunity/ last accessed on 20-11-2020.

[23] https://economictimes.indiatimes.com/small-biz/startups/have-e-pharmacies-found-the-growth-pill/articleshow/61515197.cms?utm_source=contentofinterest&utm_medium=text&utm_campaign=cppst.

achieve breakeven and any meaningful profitability.[24] A substantial amount in the online pharmacy route went toward raising "awareness" about their platforms and goading people to make the switch from round-the-corner chemists to apps or websites.

They operated with a significantly negative margins, while they had to maintain huge inventories. They offered low prices and steep discounts. However, e-pharmacies were steadily gaining market share. Though consumers were initially reluctant to avail e-delivery of medicines, there was a significant change in the trend. Nevertheless, there was still a long way to go, as the primary revenue was derived from selling of "over the counter" (OTC) drugs which offered meager margins.

The COVID-19 outbreak led to rapid growth in e-pharmacies. Frost and Sullivan reported that e-pharmacies penetrated about 9 million households in India due to the COVID-induced lockdown, and the sector was expected to reach 70 million households by 2025.[25] The major players in this sector were 1 mg, PharmEasy, Netmeds, and Medlife. With the big corporations like Reliance, Amazon, and the Tata Group showing interest in online pharmacy, it was expected that the fledgling e-pharmacy sector would see a phase of consolidation and growth. The increased acceptance of online pharmacy was also exerting pressure on traditional chemist shops to embrace digitization.

One of the e-pharmacies PharmEasy connected patients to local pharmacies and diagnostic centers across India through a mobile app. PharmEasy catered to the chronic-care segment through services such as doorstep medicine delivery, at-home sample collection for diagnostic tests, teleconsultation, as well as a subscription-based healthcare service. The start-up catered to over 20 lakh families annually and had added more than 20,000 new postal codes to its service network over 2017–19. PharmEasy entered into a partnership with Brand Capital, the strategic arm of Times of India Group, was present in over 1000 cities in India, and delivered within 24 h of ordering.[26]

Retail Pharmacy Chains

Organized retail in pharmacies was carried out by licensed retailers, who were registered for sales tax. The retail chains and privately owned large retail stores were included in this division. Organized retails were also growing at a considerable rate at an average of 25%.[27]

---

[24]https://www.franchiseindia.com/wellness/e-pharma-vs-offline-pharmacy-which-segment-to-invest-in.13400.

[25]https://ww2.frost.com/frost-perspectives/epharmacy-expected-to-penetrate-70-million-households-in-india-by-2025/ last accessed on 6-12-2020.

[26]https://economictimes.indiatimes.com/industry/healthcare/biotech/healthcare/pharmeasy-and-brand-capital-create-indias-no-1-health-tech-platform/articleshow/65994581.cms?utm_source=contentofinterest&utm_medium=text&utm_campaign=cpps.

[27]Ravichandran v, retail pharmacy market scenario in India, *journal of composition theory*, issn: 0731–6755, nov 2019, http://www.jctjournal.com/gallery/106-nov2019.pdf, last accessed on 12-12-2020.

With the increased need for people to make an informed decision, organized retailers enabled the consumers by having more educated support staff and giving them more options. The margins these stores obtained were around 16–22%.[28] The retail chains also introduced promotions and loyalty programs to retain consumers.

The following players dominated the organized retail chain:

1. **Apollo Pharmacy**: Apollo Pharmacy was India's largest retail chain, with over 3766 stores across India. It was part of the Apollo Hospital—Asia's largest health group. Operating 24 h a day, Apollo pharmacy was well stocked with medicines, OTC, and FMCG products and had a computerized system taking care of the backend operations. It also expanded its online pharmacy and omni-channel strategy and considered it as new growth prospects.[29]
2. **MedPlus**: MedPlus was the second-largest pharmacy retail chain in the country, with over 1650 pharmacies throughout India. Its online pharmacy and general store, MedPlusMart.com, was launched in 2015 and was one of India's largest e-pharmacy. It served over 350,000 customers daily and employed over 10,000 people. Its goal was to create a world-class IT system.
3. **Wellness Forever**: Scattered around Maharashtra, Goa, and Karnataka, Wellness Forever had 161 stores. The largest organized retail chain in Mumbai was backed by a consortium of HNIs and had plans to open 450–500 stores in the next three years. The stores were open 24 × 7 and used technology extensively to improve supply chain management and network the stores and warehouses. The annual revenue was close to US$ 140 million in 2020 with significant growth from US$ 80 million in 2008, when it was founded.[30]
4. **Fortis Healthworld**: With an over 110 store pan-India footprint, Fortis Healthworld was one of the significant pharma-organized retail chains. It operated retail, worksite, and hospital pharmacies across ten cities—Delhi, Mumbai, Bangalore, Pune, Gurgaon, Noida, Faridabad, Jaipur, Kangra, and Amritsar. It had online presence in the retail healthcare market space with its e-store fortishealthworld.com.[31]
5. **98.4 Pharmacy**: 98.4 chain of retail chemist stores was a global health line brand that operated in Delhi and NCR. Established in 2002, it had 23 stores with a total carpet area of over 10,000 square feet. They were poised to open 200–300 stores by 2022.[32]

[28]https://pharmafranchisehelp.com/profit-margin-pharmaceutical-sector-manufacturing-marketing-distribution-pharmacy-chemist/ last accessed on 17-12-2020.
[29]https://economictimes.indiatimes.com/markets/stocks/news/for-apollo-hospitals-online-pharmacy-is-the-new-growth-frontier/articleshow/76690534.cms last accessed on 17-12-2020.
[30]https://www.businessinsider.in/business/news/how-a-drug-retail-chain-grew-from-8-crore-a-year-to-1000-crore-without-the-msme-tag/articleshow/76869600.cms last accessed on 17-12-2020.
[31]http://rhcholding.com/group_HealthWorld.html last accessed on 17-12-2020.
[32]https://www.globalhealthline.com/about-us.html last accessed on 19-12-2020.

Independent Retail Pharmacy

Independent retail pharmacy referred to the local, low-cost retailing, owned and managed privately or by a partnership with 1–2 membered supporting staff. Primary research and interviews revealed that a typical pharmacy would be 10–15 m^2 in size and could be developed by investing US$ 7000–8000. The rental or land cost, and labor cost depended on the location of the shop. The margins were around 16–20% for regular medicines and 20–25% for rare drugs and special medicines. The average estimated profit of a pharmacy located in a semi-urban area, with moderate demand would be approximately US$ 250-$350 per month.

Despite the odd challenges that this type of pharmacy faced, they were the undisputed winner in India. With 93% of total medicine sales happening through such stores, they offered employment to millions of people and were still growing due to their high sales base.[33] Though the major players in the organized retail had good back end, supported by enterprise resource planning (ERP) system for maintaining the inventory, most of the unorganized traditional/local pharmacy operated on registers (*Bahi Khaata*).

Traditional pharmacies were fraught with the following issues that hampered their day-to-day operations:

1. Real-time visibility of inventory at the retailer: The salesperson did not have any inventory visibility at the stores. This led to one of the significant issues of the expiry of medicines in brick-and-mortar pharma stores. Since the record maintenance was done manually in a notebook/diary, the first in first out (FIFO) method of inventory management was not followed due to the lack of inventory visibility.
2. Order fulfillment issues: As they were not linked to the retailer–distributor supply chain, retailers had no idea when they would receive the required stock from the distributors and about the quantity. This information asymmetry led to overstocking (leading to the expiry of drugs on the retail shelf in the future) and loss of sales due to the non-availability of medicines on time.
3. Discrepancy in pricing and invoicing—Due to the unavailability of accurate sales data at the retailer, distributors did not pass on the principals' offers. Due to the lack of records, distributors preferred their relationship, not the sales performance of the shops, while fulfilling their orders.
4. The retailer had to perform physical verification of inventories. One of the retailers remarked that "*We close down our shutter for 2–3 h on Saturday afternoon to count and match the inventory available at the shop. It is a very tedious job and results in loss of sales in those hours.*"
5. Other issues included tax evasion as consumers did not insist on taking bills, medicine sales without prescription, less insurance penetration, etc.

[33]https://www.globenewswire.com/news-release/2020/03/13/2000142/0/en/Analysis-on-India-s-Pharmacy-Retail-Market-2016-2024-Shares-by-Retail-Channel-Drug-Type-and-Therapeutic-Area.html last accessed on19-12-2020.

Evolution of Tarnea

Creating the Product

With their focus set on the retail pharmaceutical industry, Suresh met a major pharmaceutical manufacturer in India and pitched their product idea. The firm's CEO was impressed by the concept and believed that such a product could provide the much-needed visibility of stocks and sales at the retail level throughout the supply chain and thus increase supply chain efficiencies. This confirmation gave Suresh the impetus to take his idea forward.

Product development posed the first challenge for Tarnea. As Suresh was the only employee of the company, he decided to outsource its development. He drafted the scoping document and the product's architecture and then outsourced the rest, hoping to reduce the development cost. This decision, however, did not produce the required results. After going through several developers and still not achieving the desired results, Suresh was forced to design and develop the product himself. Though Suresh was not inherently a designer, the repercussions of failure drove him to develop the skills required to build the minimum viable product.

The Pilot

Suresh decided to run their test pilot in Erode. There were several reasons for selecting Erode as the location for their pilot. (a) Erode had one of the country's highest per capita hospital beds and catered to a progressively affluent municipality; (b) Erode consistently produced the best salespeople in the industry in terms of performance; (c) Erode was sufficiently isolated, easily accessible, and adequately dynamic; and (d) Tamil Nadu had a far more organized distribution network than some of India's eastern and northern states.

The pilot was a resounding success, but during their pilot phase, Suresh met a professor from a leading business school in Bangalore, where they were headquartered. Initially approached to provide advice on the product, the professor quickly pointed out that their solution was not a product but had the potential to be a "platform" that mediated between two networks—the distributors and the retailers, with significant cross-side network effects. Exhibit 18.4 shows the product evolution tree.

Product Development at Tarnea

Requirements Phase

Product ideas emerged from four different sources: (1) The product team generated a new idea that was not a specific industry requirement and had no market reference. These ideas were intended to create the next big thing in the system or change

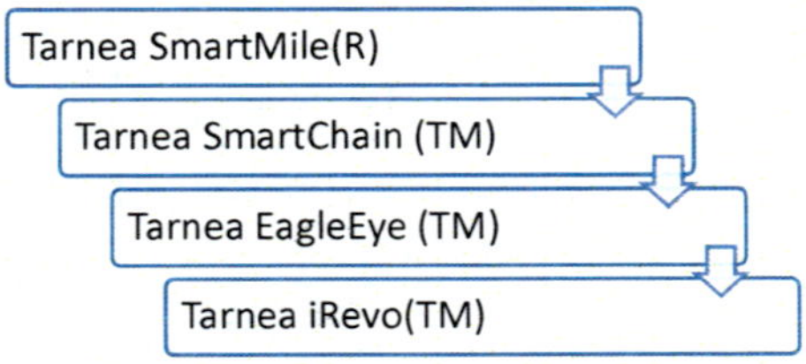

Exhibit 18.4 Product evolution tree. *Source* Authors' representation

how the work was done. (2) The sales team recommendations on a new feature would help them sell the product. (3) The requirements of customers would remove their day-to-day issues and pain points. (4) The new regulatory and compliance requirements such as Goods and Services Tax (GST) were driven by the industry.

Prototyping

Product teams examined the requirements, analyzed them, and noted the specifications. If it was an established requirement with a known specification such as Goods and Services Tax (GST), it went directly into the development phase. However, if it was a new product, they would build a hypothesis and test it. Then, customer mock-ups were created to obtain feedback and assess the feasibility of the solution.

Development

In the development cycle, projects were prioritized to meet the business and market needs. The product team created details needed to develop the product. Quality assurance (QA) started building test cases, and the design team was involved in designing the user interface and the user experience. QA and design teams worked in sprints to create the product.

Testing

Much testing was done before releasing the product, such as unit tests and $(n - 2)$ version compatibility tests to ensure that lagging customers were on board, performance testing, and a sanity check for security loopholes. Finally, the product was released with a publication describing the software version, significant feature changes, and training material.

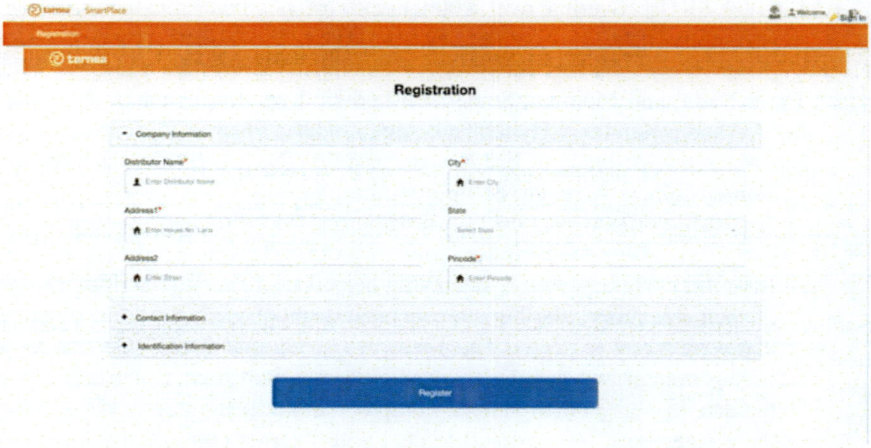

Fig. 18.5 Retailer–distributor registration page. *Source* Company Sources

Tarnea—the Platform

Suresh had initially envisioned their solution as a SaaS primarily targeted at retailers. Retailers would not have to install any software on their computers or face restrictions in terms of minimum system requirement configurations. Instead, retailers would simply register themselves on the Tarnea website (see Exhibit 18.5), by providing essential identification information and then use the solution for a small annual subscription fee.

However, having considered the professor's insights during the pilot phase, Suresh decided to pivot their business model to cater to both the distributor and the retailer. There were, however, several issues to be considered. How does Tarnea scale up to become a platform? At what point does a product become a platform? How do you develop an organization for a platform business model? How do you fund a platform business model?

Over several consultative meetings, the professor helped the Tarnea team build a platform business model around their solution. The result was the **SmartMile** platform. Tarnea's vision was, "*Every retailer will sell like an Amazon and buy like a Walmart.*" Through digitization and information flow, Tarnea tried to bring value to all stakeholders at all levels.

Tarnea launched the SmartMile platform as the first cloud-based platform for pharma retailers. The platform was available in over 100 locations serving over 32 million transactions. It offered automatic data management to retailers of over

120,000 SKUs covering over 2000 brands of pharmaceutical, fast-moving consumer goods (FMCG), over the counter (OTC), and clinical supply products.[34]

SmartMile catered to hundreds of customers in Andhra Pradesh, Telangana, Tamil Nadu, and Mumbai. Some well-known drug stores such as Pradhan Mantri Jan Aushadhi Kendra in Hyderabad, Arogyaraksha Pharmacy group in Vijayawada, and Maaruthi Medicals in Erode were users of the SmartMile platform. Over 1.2 million customers were served through the platform.[35]

SmartMile offered retailers and distributors the following features.

- **Inventory Management**: SmartMile helped retailers and distributors keep track of their inventory, alerting store managers about medicines and other products that were likely to expire. The platform also equipped each salesperson with the billing system and thereby reduced customer wait time. SmartMile could store the data locally on the retailer's computer and later transmit it to the cloud when the connectivity was restored to deal with internet connectivity loss.
- Tarnea's system enabled tracking of the batch number of every product that sat on the retailer's shelf. It could generate prompts to the retailer well before the expiry date to return a product to the distributor and claim full reimbursement. On sending back the medicine to the pharma company, the distributor also received reimbursement. Though the pharma company incurred substantial loss from the unsold medicine, the potential liability of the expired medicine was huge and critical. On comparison, it was better to have monetary losses.
- **Purchase Optimization**: By onboarding distributors on the platform, SmartMile provided retailers with price transparency, empowering retailers to get the best price and quickest deliveries.
- **Loyalty Service**: One of the biggest attractions of SmartMile was the integrated loyalty program feature. This feature allowed retailers and stores to provide customers with special offers or issue loyalty cards.

SmartMile had created an enviable solution for independent pharmacies. However, Tarnea did not have a solution that addressed the specialized needs of pharmaceutical retail chains in a hub–and-spoke model. In 2018, Tarnea launched a new product for pharmacy chains called SmartChains. The solution provided five key benefits to retail chains. It allowed digital engagement with customers, including the possibility of online and offline sales. It improved operating efficiency and, thus, maximized profitability. It enabled rapid growth and scalability; it centralized all functions, and finally, it helped guide stock transfers between outlets for inventory optimization.[36]

[34]https://www.financialexpress.com/industry/tarnea-technology-solutions-new-startup-digitises-medical-stores/1372473/?cv=1 last accessed on 23-12-2020.

[35]https://www.financialexpress.com/industry/tarnea-technology-solutions-new-startup-digitises-medical-stores/1372473/?cv=1 last accessed on 23-12-2020.

[36]https://www.expresshealthcare.in/news/tarnea-technologies-launches-smartchains-a-cloud-based-software-platform-for-pharmacy-chains/400515/ last accessed on 23-12-2020.

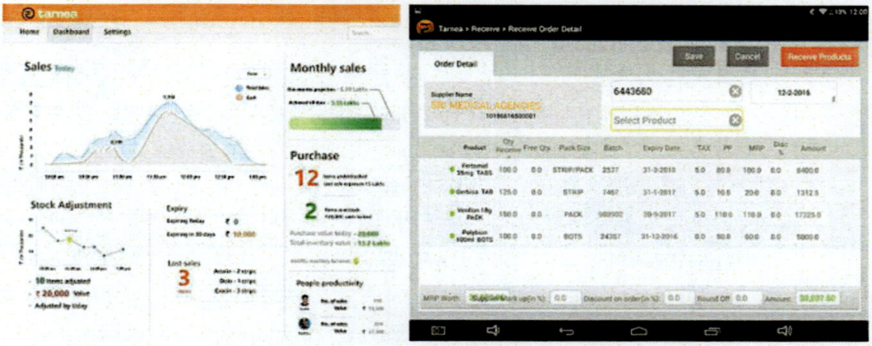

Exhibit 18.6 Analytics and billing. *Source* Company Sources

In addition to these, SmartChains continued to offer loyalty service as in SmartMile. Perhaps the most attractive feature of SmartChains was its ability to bring data analytics and business intelligence to retail pharmacy chains through the Eagle Eye app (Exhibit 18.6). Tarnea's SmartChains, thus, recreated a hub-and-spoke model for the retail pharmacy chain management. The central hub for operations gained full visibility and control over all branch business functions, including product and stock management, discount management, customer management, business reports, etc.

In 2020, Tarnea launched the iRevo application for Android devices. This application allowed retailers to gain visibility of the best supplier offers and deals running in the market from their smartphones. It also offered the capability of an all-in-one payments medium, which essentially integrated swiping machines, UPI, digital wallets, order books, and bill books into a single device. Bills could be sent directly to the customer via SMS and Email. Further, retailers could offer discounts on the next purchase, thus providing customers with a holistic digital experience. Retailers could also send regular customers reminders to refill a medication before the stock got exhausted.

Tarnea's Ecosystem

Usually, a market is segmented geographically or demographically, but Tarnea segmented its platform business in terms of interactions (Exhibit 18.7). These interactions are as follows:

1. Consumer to retailer
2. Retailer to distributor
3. Distributor to principal
4. Retailer to principal
5. Retailers to others (credit companies, payments, last mile logistics companies, etc.).

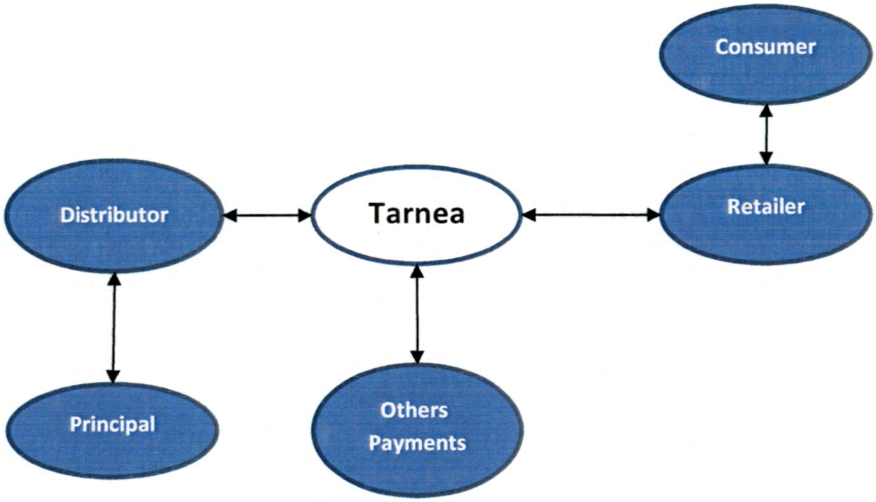

Exhibit 18.7 Tarnea's segmentation based on interaction. *Source* Authors' representation

Tarnea initially focused on retailer–distributor interaction and aimed to solve supply chain inefficiencies and order acquisition. They identified medicine expiry at retailers' shops and sales loss due to drug non-availability as the main challenges. One major issue that they stumbled upon while solving these supply chain issues was the owner's control over the business. With the existing software, owners were not aware of what was going on in the pharmacy in their absence. Tarnea, with its cloud-based solution running on the Android platform, provided the owner's visibility and control on the stocks, expiry, payments, stock adjustments, etc., from anywhere. They introduced a well-established product Tarnea SmartMile in this domain.

Tarnea enabled interaction of retailers with credit companies by closing a few deals with banks and non-banking financial companies (NBFCs) in the early part of the lockdown (April–May 2020). They integrated online payments in their existing products with tie-ups with payments and FinTech companies such as First Data Corporation, Worldline, Pine Labs, and HDFC Bank.

Retailer to consumer interaction products were also at the threshold of a launch. COVID-19 breakout presented an enormous opportunity to link the customer with retailers as customers were wary of visiting crowded places such as pharmacies, which had the potential of spreading the disease. This new product would enable online ordering of medicines and offer the functionality of loyalty points.

Retailers to principal interactions were also established through pilots. They planned to scale it up in the next quarter (January–March 2021). The principal could bypass traditional distributors and directly connect with retailers using this product, which provided a curated list of retailers with all the details, analytics of sales/volumes, and an online lending facility.

Ecosystem View

Tarnea identified four ecosystems in the retail chain with the retailer as the fulcrum.

1. **Inventory Ecosystem**: The inventory at the retailers was prone to two issues; the first was expiry, and the second was overstocking and understocking due to lack of visibility in the supply chain. Tarnea, with its range of products, provided real-time visibility of inventory and analysis of quantity to be stocked.
2. **Payment Ecosystem**: It consisted of billing and invoices from retailers to consumers and purchases orders and invoices from distributors to retailers. SmartMile and iRevo had built-in features to carry out these transactions. After revolutionizing the inventory management system, the payment ecosystem was a big focus area for Tarnea as it enabled both consumer–retailer and distributor–retailer interactions. While enabling online ordering, invoicing, and payment for retailers and consumers, banks and financiers could also use Tarnea's billing data to provide credit to the retailers, which was one of the distributor's significant activities.
3. **Physical Delivery Ecosystem**: It consisted of the physical movement of goods from the distributor to the retailer and from the retailer to the consumer. The distributors owned the goods, and their employees distributed them to the retailer. In retailer to consumer transactions, either the retailer's employees performed last mile delivery, or some third-party agents took over delivery responsibilities from the retailer.
4. **Financing Ecosystem**: Traditionally, distributors were financiers of this trade, and they bought the goods with cash or on credit from the big pharma manufacturers and sold it to retailers on credit. Now, with Tarnea in the picture, the financier could be a third party. Banks and credit card companies could finance the retailers based on their credit transactions and credit history, available on the Tarnea platform.

As of December 2020, Tarnea focused solely on the inventory ecosystem. In the inventory ecosystem, the company focused on developing its capabilities in the replenishment model. The forecasting model of inventory management required large volumes of historical data to gather seasonality and cyclicality information. Tarnea had and continued to build its capabilities in this ecosystem. The payments ecosystem was a highly attractive ecosystem that was also increasing importance to Tarnea's customers. It thus represented a growing opportunity. However, in terms of the capabilities required to deliver these features, Tarnea would have to develop new capabilities. This would undoubtedly require a significant investment.

Similarly, in the financing ecosystem, Tarnea would have to establish partnerships with banks and other non-banking financial institutions to make capital available to distributors and retailers. These were capabilities that Tarnea would need to build from scratch, and the company would have to develop credibility with these financial institutions. In the delivery ecosystem, Tarnea would have to develop an interface for the end consumer where it would be possible for them to order the medicines online and track their orders as they were delivered to their homes. Tarnea certainly had the capabilities to develop such a product. However, there was uncertainty about the value addition that it would bring to customers over the existing arrangement of telephone ordering and delivery management.

Pharmaceutical Retail—A Winner–Takes-All Market

Multi-homing Costs

Multi-homing costs are the costs associated with the distributors and retailers being on more than one platform. In the pharmaceutical retail market, there were high costs associated with multi-homing. For distributors and retailers, switching to a new platform involved onboarding costs as these platforms managed inventory for both sides. There were also the costs involved with leaving the existing platform as the subscription charges were levied annually. It was difficult to manage inventories and reputation scores on more than one platform. Retailers would lose out on the volume discounts that were offered by the platform. Therefore, we can conclude that there was little incentive in multi-homing for distributors and retailers.

Network Effects

Platforms benefited from positive cross-side network effects in the retail pharmaceutical industry. The platform's value to the distributor increased with the increase in the number of retailers on the platform and vice versa. The platform was capable of connecting the distributors to the retailers and extending its reach to customers and principals. Also, by bringing banks and credit card company services to the platform, a multi-dimensional network was created.

Opportunities for Differentiation

There were limited opportunities in differentiation for platforms catering to the pharmaceutical retail market. Platforms had sales in multiple product categories, and there was a little scope for vertical differentiation.

Therefore, we can conclude that the pharmaceutical retail market displayed a decisive winner-takes-all dynamics.

Pharmaceutical Retail—A Density Business

It is important to note that the pharmaceutical retail market was a density business. A density business is a market in which a platform needs to obtain critical density to take advantage of scale economies. This is important so that the platform can have a cost advantage over its competitors. In order to drive adoption, platforms must focus on distributors and incentivize them. In turn, distributors connected to numerous retailers in an identified market would be able to incentivize adoption by retailers. Through these interactions, a platform could gain market share and achieve critical density. It is at this point that a platform should look to expand its markets geographically.

COVID-19 Acceleration and Challenges

The COVID-19 lockdown came up with different kinds of challenges and opportunities. On the one hand, retailers were suffering from supply-side challenges as the supply lines were broken. On the other hand, online pharmacies were threatening to take away the business from offline merchants. Poor visibility across the supply chain was causing stockouts or retailers to overstock. As the financial pressure was mounting, distributors were also not willing to give credit to retailers. In this uncertain environment, to allay the fears of offline merchants and to win in a post-COVID-19 scenario, Tarnea proposed three mantras.

1. Transformation of offline pharmacy into digital pharmacy: Employ a set of digital technologies such as Tarnea SmartMile, which would enable these brick-and-mortar pharmacies to stay connected with their customer and suppliers 24 × 7, to their offers, promos, schemes, and loyalty programs, to offer electronic bills and receive digital payments, to place orders electronically, and to track their delivery.
2. Last mile delivery: As the consumer preference changed due to the epidemic, there would be an increasing home delivery trend. Therefore, retailers would have to tie up with logistics companies to ensure last mile delivery. Tarnea as a platform allowed retailers to control their last mile operations by connecting the end consumer to the retailer and allowing the consumers to track the status of their order.
3. Personalization: This would involve driving the business and serving the customer better by using the power of data. As the customers were not going to come to the shops, the retailers had to find ways to reach them. Using data analytics, they could send targeted offers and promotions to their customers.

The belief that the retail pharmacies had the unparalleled advantage of local presence, fastest fulfillment, and human touch, Tarnea continued its digitization efforts even during the lockdown. As the spread of the virus increased and the lockdown extended, Tarnea faced the challenge of onboarding new retailers on its platform. They started the virtual and digital onboarding to meet the retailer's requirements.

Digital Onboarding

Digital onboarding of retailers was viewed as a necessary measure to improve customer experience and operational efficiency. Initially, when a retailer signed up for a subscription with Tarnea, the company would first provide an account to the retailer. Tarnea worked hard to automate this process and design it such that the retailer himself could set up the operation. The retailer had to answer a sequence of questions on the app and fill in a few details and could get operationally ready. The provisioning of the account and setting up of billing systems would take place automatically in the back end. Tarnea continued to support the retailer remotely, assist him through his first few transactions, and take him through the process of updating his inventory in the software.

In the words of Tarnea Chief Technical Officer Madhav,

> Digital on-boarding has removed the requirement for a support person to be physically present and has eliminated the worries of travelling to the retailer's location. Instead, the retailer is now supported by a helpdesk that can guide him through installation and setup remotely. This is extremely important in order for us to scale our operations. It would be impossible to have a person physically visiting a retailer's location multiple times to have him set up as the scale of our operations increase. Furthermore, COVID has only accelerated the rate of adoption as retailers do not want people visiting them unnecessarily.

Way Forward

While thinking of the road ahead, Suresh and Madhav carefully weighed their options. COVID has surely changed pharma retailing forever. How will it shape the market for medicines now? How should Tarnea's business model adapt to these changes?

1. Race ahead? Tarnea could expand geographically at a breakneck pace before the competitors set their foot into the market. In 2020, Tarnea was present in three states, i.e., Andhra Pradesh, Tamil Nadu, Telangana, with 150+ locations. They also had a small presence in Madhya Pradesh and Maharashtra and were planning to scale up across India.
2. Expand to more verticals? Tarnea could expand the product in another industry that had inventory-driven retail business such as Kirana stores.
3. Exploit adjacencies in healthcare space? Tarnea could expand deeper into healthcare services such as linking doctors to consumers and laboratories to consumers.

On hearing the news of the successful trials of the COVID-19 vaccine, Suresh felt slightly more hopeful, got up from his chair, and moved toward the dining hall.

Complementary Business Models 19

The technology business world of today is characterized by a range of business models. Even though this book is focused on platform business models, it is imperative to understand how different and alternate business models complement each other. In this chapter, we explore different business models and highlight complementarity across different business models.

Leveraging on three levers of business change—unbundling driven mass customization, re-intermediation of value exchanges between user groups driven by extensive preference and transaction data, and the prevalence of winner-takes-all markets dominated by global technology giants—five dominant business models have emerged.

(a) Unbundling driven mass customization: Digital technologies has greatly aided in unbundling of products and service bundles across industries and geographies. Take the example of music industry—no one buys full albums anymore, but only single songs (or singles). This has had significant impact on the economics of music publishers, who relied on a few hit songs driving up sales of entire albums that contained them. These industries, popularly known as "blockbuster economies," where a few unpredictable "hits" subsidized the costs of producing, marketing, and distributing the entire portfolio, including "flops" and "also-rans." As digital music proliferated market, consumers only bought hits, and it was impossible to charge different prices for hits, as it could not be predicted *apriori*. This unbundling of products and services into singles enabled collection of user-specific data and helped create custom portfolios/ bundles for specific users.

(b) The extensive and detailed data collection was also powered by new forms of intermediation between producers and consumers of products/ services. While users sign up for a platform like a music streaming service, their preferences are captured—both during sign-in as well as when they sign up to specific channels, representing genres or a mix of artists. In addition, there is also an opportunity to collect data on their actual listening and downloading habits,

R. Srinivasan, *Platform Business Models*, Management for Professionals,
https://doi.org/10.1007/978-981-16-2838-2_19

which represents their revealed preferences. Such combination of expressed and revealed preferences can greatly aid in customization of the product/ service offering to a user segment of one. This personalization would be largely driven by the evolution of new intermediaries than the traditional. These intermediaries design their products and services around organizing the supply side depending on the specific preferences of the demand side dynamically.

(c) Such mass customization (unbundling) and personalization (extensive profile and preference data) have enabled the erection of multi-homing costs for most platform users. These multi-homing costs and extensive diversification by global technology corporations (like Facebook acquiring Instagram and WhatsApp, and Microsoft acquiring Skype) have helped these corporations to integrate their services across domains and create strong ecosystems. It has created globally dominant technology firms that operate in winner-takes-all markets.

These trends—mass customization, data-driven personalization, and globally dominant firms in winner-takes-all markets—provide firms with a variety of business model choices. We will elucidate five dominant business models, with an understanding that each firm can configure their business model design adopting one or combining a few of these business models.

Dominant Business Models

Multi-sided Platforms

As we have seen before, platforms intermediate between multiple sets of users, and create value through network effects. By enabling exchange of information/ products/services/content between networks of users, platforms help reduce transaction costs, including costs of search, matching specific preferences across user groups, fixed and variable costs of transaction, and collecting/collating user reviews and feedback. The key resource that platform firms leverage to secure and sustain their competitive advantage is their network effects.

Servitization and SaaS

Servitization is a significant business model that dominates the technology businesses in the post-internet era. Driven by the power of fractionalization of usage, it might be economically viable for users to lease/ rent products for specific periods rather than exclusively own the assets. Such renting of assets for specific usage was not restricted to technology businesses and had been even popular in holiday assets like time-share rentals or short-term car-rentals.

With the ubiquitous availability of the internet for business usage, firms have adopted a variety of service models driven by the internet. By using cloud services for storage and computing, firms can optimize on their capital investments in servers and software that they would have had to purchase outright otherwise. One of the most popular business models that have proliferated in the recent years is providing software as a service (or SaaS). Typically organized as a pipeline (or a linear) business, software vendors host the software on the cloud for their clients to use, rather than an outright sale. Cloud hosting helps clients try these products without making long-term commitments, thereby helping the vendors with rapid adoption and user feedback as well. It also helps in vendors installing updates to the software products, by updating it on the cloud and pushing the updates to the clients over the air (OTA, or through the internet), with no manual intervention. These SaaS models have helped rapid scaling up of software firms across geographies and domains at very low marginal costs of marketing, distribution, and rolling up of upgrades.

Clusters

Clusters are typically referred to as a geographical agglomeration of businesses, interconnected with each other as customers-suppliers-technology providers or other such transactions. One of the primary motivations for businesses operating in clusters is to develop competitive advantage at the level of the collective, with respect to other competitors. Clusters help firms develop standards, leverage economies of scale and scope among complementary products and infrastructure providers, and rapidly enable adoption of innovations emerging from the cluster.

Cluster management organizations (CMO) typically act as intermediaries and evangelists. These CMOs perform one or many of the following roles: (a) identification of best-in-class technologies and benchmarks among the cluster firms; (b) enabling knowledge and technology transfer within and from outside the cluster firms; (c) help in securing and distributing institutional funding for research and development, product development, and setting standards; (d) project management for the execution of infrastructure and other projects; and (e) evangelizing the cluster technologies and marketing the brand(s) to stakeholders outside the cluster. These cluster organizations derive their competitive advantage over other clusters through accumulation of right kinds of cluster firms, enabling effective cooperation among these firms, and a strong brand of the cluster in the industry.

Communities and Networks

While clusters attract organizations that operate in the same industry (including offering products and services across the value chain), communities bring together a motely set of players, typically non-competing in their core businesses. Most communities share assets (like infrastructure) and resources (like access to talent) that are critical to their businesses but not their core. For example, an association of automobile manufacturers may jointly support an innovative industry-oriented diploma course in a high-quality engineering institution. The firms may be competing in their core business of automotive products but collaborate in the creation and sustenance of high-quality engineering talent (critical, but not core). Another typical form of communities is that of identity-driven associations, like a community of animators. In such identity-driven communities, the membership is typically closed to include only those that possess specific professional certifications and skillsets. Communities are typically organized by industry- or identity-level associations with monetary and moral support from its member firms.

Networks as a business model is a subset of communities, where the express purpose is to enable interactions among members. The belief is that such interactions would promote communication and cooperation among them and help them achieve synergies arising out of cooperation. Members of a network expect firms to support each other with their own resources, access to resources, or even connections with those that have the desired resources. Examples of network organizations include the Indian IT-industry lobbying group, NASSCOM and the network of global business schools, the GNAM.[1]

Ecosystems

The word ecosystems is borrowed from a biological (ecology) discipline that refers to a self-contained system of flora (plants), fauna (animals), natural resources like water bodies, soil, and other micro-climatic conditions. When we use that metaphor in the context of technology or business ecosystems, we refer to a collection of firms (competitors, complementors, suppliers and other value chain contributors), customers and users, technology providers, regulators, and even expertise providers (experts and consulting firms). Such ecosystems have their own technology standards and business practices; consist of interconnected firms; and demonstrate resilience. In the business context, resilience refers to the ability to maintain its inertia, yet absorb exogenous shocks from the environment.[2] The ecosystem needs to arrive at a fine balance between the abilities to maintain inertia within and evolve in response to shocks from outside. This equilibrium between stability and evolvability is the hallmark of ecosystems. There are five critical competencies that help ecosystems maintain this equilibrium.

---

[1]See https://nasscom.in/ and https://globalnetwork.io/ for the respective websites.

[2]Read: Baldwin, CY., and Woodard, CJ (2009) The architecture of platforms: A unified view, Platforms, Markets, and Innovation, 32. and Boudreau, KJ., and Hagiu, A 2009. "Platform Rules: Multi-Sided Platforms As Regulators." In Platforms, Markets and Innovation, edited by Annabelle Gawer. Cheltenham, UK: Edward Elgar Publishing, 2009.

(a) A relatively stable core that allows for standardized processes and help provide economies of scale and scope, so that the infrastructure investments could be amortized.
(b) A robust platform architecture that enables complementors and other users to affiliate with this core for their primary functions but have the ability to adapt to changes in the environment.
(c) An optimal sharing of economic benefits between the core (platform provider and sponsor) and the complementors. Depending on whether the core is for-profit or not, the way the ecosystem core (development, maintenance, and overhead) costs are compensated define the sustenance and growth of the ecosystem.
(d) A strong mechanism for governance that facilitates complementary innovation —helping the complementors' development and offering of outputs to serve their customer needs, without compromising on the core.
(e) A system/process of managing the economics of complementors, including gatekeeping (defining who can participate and who cannot), regulating (what can the complementors do and what they cannot), and managing their identities (balancing the ecosystem core brand vs. individual complementors' brands).

In sum, technology ecosystems need to balance three paradoxes—standards and variety (variance in outputs); control and autonomy (complementary innovation); and individual and collective identity (investments in core and complements).[3] Depending on how the ecosystems resolve these paradoxes, they could evolve in different ways. For instance, an ecosystem that is highly standardized, controlled, and focused on collective identity might not foster much complementary innovation and enterprise; whereas at the other extreme, if the ecosystem were to value variety, high autonomy, and individual identities might not make sufficient investments in those core, reusable knowledge/processes of the platform.

An example of a tightly governed ecosystems would be Apple iOS with the strong core processes owned and governed by the platform sponsor (Apple). At the other extreme may be the Android ecosystem, where there is minimal governance and too much variety.

It is likely that some ecosystems have more than a few platforms operating, with more than one of them performing the facilitation and orchestration roles. Irrespective of whether the ecosystem is orchestrated by single or multiple focal firms, these platforms should define their scope—what activities and businesses will be internalized by the focal firm, and what will be owned by the independent complementors. This decision is contingent upon four parameters—the interdependencies between the (focal) firm and the complementors; the levels of differentiation and competition among the complementors; the architecture of the ecosystem (open or closed, and shared or proprietary), including modularity (ease

[3]Warenham, Fox, and Giner (2014). Technology ecosystem governance, Organization Science, 25, 4.

of complementor affiliation with the ecosystem); and the levels of competitiveness of the ecosystem against other ecosystems.

- *Interdependencies*: If the firm has the resources and capabilities to perform certain activities but has chosen to divest it to independent complementors, the firm holds much more bargaining power than when the firm reasonably cannot integrate into those activities.
- *Competition among complementors*: The more the complements (products and services produced by the complementors) are undifferentiated, the more there would be direct competition among complementors, and that would cede a lot of power to the orchestrator firm to set standards and boundaries for exchange. The more differentiated they are, the more opportunities for the complementors to create unique value to the ecosystem users and other complementors.
- *Ecosystem architecture*: The more open, shared, and modular the ecosystem architecture, the easier it is for the complementors to affiliate with the ecosystem and create/ capture value. On the other hand, a closed, proprietary, and specific (less modular), the ecosystem may enable the focal firm to disproportionately capture more value.
- *Ecosystem competition*: The more the competition between the ecosystem and other ecosystems, the more motivated the focal firm to take more control over the ecosystem emergence and differentiation. In order to compete efficiently against other competing ecosystems, the focal firm might invest in developing "ecosystem-level competencies" that are difficult to imitate and substitute by other ecosystems/ platforms.

Combined Business Models

The five dominant business models—multi-sided platforms (MSP), SaaS, clusters, communities and networks, and ecosystems—are pure types. It is very likely that any firm would use not just one of these pure types but may adopt a combination of these. It is also possible that a firm evolves from one business model to another as part of their strategy and resultant growth plans. For instance, in their strategies to solve the penguin problem, platforms might adopt another business model till such time the platform is established and scaled. Let us explore why some of these combinations are necessary and how they create value. We will specifically focus on how platforms leverage these combinations.

MSPs and SaaS

This the most found combination in the world of platforms. Platforms with strong cross-side network effects have to solve their penguin problem (no one joins unless everyone joins) that manifest in many ways, including cold-start problems. The cold-start problem refers to the platform not having sufficient user base or transactions to be of value to its users. Imagine an intercity bus ticketing service being introduced. Unless there are sufficient bus owners on the network offering rides to a large number of cities, the platform will not be useful to the user (commuter) looking to join the platform. To resolve this, the firm has to get the bus owners on board before they attract riders to join the platform. For attracting the bus owners to join the platform, it may be possible for the platform to provide them with some value that is independent of the number of riders on the platform. Here is where the SaaS business model can help. By providing them with a standalone service, the platform attracts the supply side first and then scales it up to introduce the demand side (riders) later.

Take the example of the bus ticketing platform, RedBus. RedBus began their growth story by aggregating inventory of bus operators (buses and seats availability) through a SaaS solution, then called Bus Operating System Software (or BOSS), which is now called RedBus Plus.[4] Once the inventory of seats available across different operators–routes combination was available, it was easy for RedBus to launch the platform and bring in the other side—bus riders looking to book tickets. The availability and visibility of the bus/seat/route inventory on the cloud through the SaaS offering enabled RedBus to provide high-quality services to the riders.

Practo leveraged its SaaS-based clinic management system, Practo Ray, to not just onboard clinics on to the platform, but have access to valuable data, that would form the basis of their proprietary Practo Ranking Algorithm, when the launched the patient-facing appointment booking platform Practo.com. These SaaS offerings helped them mature their artificial intelligence (AI)/machine learning (ML) applications that formed the foundation of their doctor–patient discovery and matching algorithms.[5]

As we can see, a combination of SaaS and MSP business models is useful for (a) resolving the penguin problem faced by MSPs by on-boarding one side of the platform first; (b) where the platform can solve a standalone problem for the supply side of the platform through a SaaS model; and (c) the SaaS model thus executed provides valuable data for maturing their algorithms. This data-driven approach to scale the platform also helps platform firms to solve the lonely user problems.

[4]Thomas, Sujo & Pathak, Bharthi & Vyas, Pavak. (2014). The Growth of Online Bus Ticketing Industry: RedBus Route to Success in the Indian Market. International Journal of Business and Management. 9.; and https://www.verzeo.in/startup-redbus.

[5]See: https://cio.economictimes.indiatimes.com/news/next-gen-technologies/how-practo-uses-artificial-intelligence/77902912.

MSPs and Communities

While the cold-start problem manifests in platforms with cross-side network effects, the lonely user problem is more visible in platforms with same-side network effects. In platforms with same-side network effects, the value of new users is dependent on the number of users (from the same side) already using the platform. Take the example of a platform that uses crowdsourcing of content to provide recommendations to users on certain issues. A good dating platform needs to continuously learn from the users' activity on the platform—their expressed preferences at sign-up, specific choices made during sign-in, and the observed behavior during the engagement (like click-throughs of specific links or time spent on specific pages). This learning should help the platform evolve its recommendation engine, so that the users get better and better matches as they engage more with the platform.

Take the example of platforms like Big Biking Commune[6] and Cycling Cities[7] that built communities of bikers and cyclists. These passionate members of the communities are leveraged for various events and activities. These events and activities that bring together communities of users attract brands and other sponsors who are willing to pay to reach these communities. For example, Big Biking Commune integrates motorcycle brands, riding clubs, accessories, bike rental firms, tour operators, and even government-owned tourism departments under one roof. All these partners are attracted primarily due to the size, quality, and engagement of the community of riders on the other side of the platform. Given that these community members are likely to be lead users of these brands, it is highly likely that the firms will engage with the community for sourcing product feedback, design ideas, and participating in their product development and innovation journeys as well.

In summary, investing in building communities as a business model helps building platforms in three ways: (a) aggregate users with similar interests and passion into a mutually reinforcing community; (b) attract a large number of diverse partners that are willing to pay to access the large and passionate community on the other side; and (c) extend the community value proposition to provide innovation opportunities.

MSPs and Clusters

While SaaS and communities as business models help platforms solve the penguin problems by addressing the cold-start and lonely user problems, clusters help platforms in addressing issues of monetization by establishing industry standards that members of a cluster value and therefore may be willing to pay. Typically monetization dilemmas occur when users are price sensitive and have very low switching costs. In such a context, providing free access to services might

[6]See: https://bigbikingcommune.com.

[7]See: https://cyclingcities.in.

contribute to a large user base but not result in revenues for the platform. If the platform begins to charge for their products and services, then the users would switch to other platforms that provide the same/similar services. It can be argued that in the context of information goods that are provided digitally, the marginal cost per user might be negligible. It might not be zero, but even if we assume that it is close to zero, there are other costs. The fixed costs of building the platform, the marketing costs incurred for user acquisition, the costs of providing them with service, the bandwidth and energy costs associated with providing quality services and access, and the like might be significant. And these need to be monetized from the other side.

However, there is another trade off in providing platform services to one side completely free. A platform that is free to access might attract a large number of poor quality and less engaged users, who might not be valued by users on the other side, who are paying for the access/ transaction. In other words, indiscriminate growth of users due to the free nature of the platform might create negative network effects (either cross-side or same-side or both) and will degenerate the platform into a "market for lemons." Therefore, for platform to avoid these negative network effects, it is imperative that irrespective of the prices charged, the platform needs to ensure adequate quality checks on user quality.

One of the best means to manage this issue is for platforms to coexist with clusters as a business model. By investing in a cluster (or a network business), where firms are looking to cooperate in sharing non-core critical assets, and seeking synergies in their operations, a platform firm might be able to increase their switching costs.

Take the example of business clusters like the Medical Valley E.M.N.[8] Situated in the Nuremberg region of Germany, the Medical Valley cluster brings together large firms, start-ups, researchers, healthcare providers, policy makers, investors, and citizens interested in a variety of healthcare products and services. It provided a myriad range of services to their members, including innovation support, visibility to public funding opportunities, a platform for engaging in cooperative projects among members, organizing events, and even in internationalization efforts. The Medical Valley cluster integrated these members on one side and therefore enabled access to the other side of the platform—access to firms in the cluster to others, including multi-lateral funding agencies, manufacturing companies (say in Asia), product developers looking for talent, and governments interested in accelerating their own capabilities around health care. The Medical Valley as a platform leverages the cluster in the Nuremberg region on one side (supply of products, services, and capabilities) to access the demand side. Given that the switching costs for the supply side is high due to their cluster membership, it is easy for the Medical Valley to monetize the supply side and subsidize the demand side. It may not be completely free for the demand side, but surely the Medical Valley platform can afford to just recover the marginal costs of adding the demand-side user from them and monetize the fixed costs from the supply side. For the supply side, Medical

[8]Visit: https://www.medical-valley-emn.de/en/.

Valley may also adopt a freemium model, including some free users and some paid users, who value differentiated and premium services.

MSPs and Ecosystems

A critical element of ecosystems, especially in the context of digital technologies, is how they are facilitated and orchestrated. And these roles are often performed by a platform firm. The facilitation roles include providing for the infrastructure and other enabling mechanisms for the interactions to happen between the focal firm and the complementors, as well as among complementors. On the other hand, orchestration roles include defining the norms of interaction/ exchange, articulating (and ensuring) the boundaries of the ecosystem as well as the focal firm and the complements, governing the synergies and complementarities among the various actors (including dispute resolutions), and managing the three paradoxes—of standards and variety; control and autonomy; and individual and collective identities. These roles are similar to the roles performed by platforms—platform providers and platform sponsors, respectively.

Therefore, in every ecosystem, one would find one or few platform firms performing these roles to ensure sustainability and effectiveness of the ecosystem. In effect, there cannot be an ecosystem without a platform firm facilitating and/ or orchestrating the exchange.

A good example of an ecosystem facilitated and orchestrated by multiple platforms is the EkStep Foundation.[9] The EkStep organization brings together diverse communities related to primary and secondary education, including learners, teachers, parents, content creators, technology developers, artists and illustrators, simulation designers, assessment creators, and school administrators. This ecosystem is orchestrated by the EkStep Foundation (ekstep.org) and facilitated by the Sunbird community.[10] The high modularity and the open architecture of the Sunbird community enables scaling up the digital infrastructure to a variety of applications apart from education (like healthcare provision or even micro-credit) and therefore spawn across multiple ecosystems.

[9]Visit: https://ekstep.in/.

[10]Visit: https://www.sunbird.org/.

QWIKCILVER™ and WOOHOO™: Developing a Complementary Platform

20

Introduction

On a late Wednesday afternoon in September 2017, Kumar Sudarshan (Kumar) and Pratap T P (Pratap), co-founders of Qwikcilver, awaited the arrival of the rest of the core leadership team. They were to discuss the operational details that would lay the foundation for gift card sales during the upcoming festive season. With key Indian festivals such as Diwali, Navratri, and a host of other national holidays and long weekends around the corner, this period of the year was a great gifting season. The festive season became even more interesting with the announcements of mega sales events by major e-commerce portals in the country. Year after year, the festive seasons were getting bigger and better for the entire Qwikcilver team. They always looked forward to the onslaught of seasonal promotional programs launched by retail chains across the nation.[1] They were wondering how the Woohoo.in platform would complement their traditional Qwikcilver gift card business. They listed three points on the whiteboard:

[1]Firms such as Qwikcilver and Itz Cash Card look to tap growing Rs. 9,000-crore gift cards business. *Source: The Economic Times* https://goo.gl/fsXC9R *Accessed on:* 10 October 2017.

This case is an extension of Chapter 18 Complimentary Business Models.

R Srinivasan (Professor of Strategy), Sandeep Lakshmipathy (Research Scholar) and Padmavathi Koride (Post-Doctoral Research Scholar), prepared this case for class discussion. This case is not intended to serve as an endorsement, source of primary data, or to show effective or inefficient handling of decision or business processes.

R. Srinivasan, *Platform Business Models*, Management for Professionals,
https://doi.org/10.1007/978-981-16-2838-2_20

1. Penetration of gift cards from the urban to tier-2 and tier-3 towns required significant behavior change in their customers
2. Such increase in penetration and growth required partnering with a larger and more diverse set of partners and complementors
3. Balance between corporate gifting (institutional sales) and individual gifting (consumer sales) businesses is key to the direction and sustainability of growth.

As the team members began walking into the meeting room, Kumar and Pratap began organizing their notes.

The Qwickcilver Enterprise Journey

Qwikcilver was a venture born out of the passion of two BITS Pilani alumni—Kumar and Bhaskar Vasudevan (Bhaskar) who were soon joined by a third BITS Pilani alumnus Pratap. As an end-to-end solution provider for gift card management in India, Qwikcilver, headquartered in Bengaluru, revolutionized the gift card market through its innovative platform. While Bhaskar was associated with the firm actively until 2011, Kumar and Pratap carried forward the dream of building the country's first comprehensive prepaid card management solution.

An initial attempt was made in 2004 to start off a product development firm. However, for over 2 years, until 2006, both Kumar and Bhaskar were contemplating different ideas for the start-up venture. The idea of starting a venture took off only by November 2006 when Kumar decided to quit his full-time job at an MNC to dive head-first into the entrepreneurial journey. The fundamental premise for the founders was an urge to build a product company out of India. Services powered venture was not an option, although India was then known more for the outsourced IT services than for product development. Kumar registered a firm that would look into building a technology-based product out of India. With a focus on zeroing in on a niche area to build a new product offering, the founders explored various product development opportunities. With the bare-bones necessities of a start-up taken care of by the end of November 2006, Kumar was now a full-time entrepreneur ready for the uncertain ride ahead.

Brainstorming over countless coffee sessions, the founders rejected many ideas early on, as they were not appealing enough as problems worth solving. Few other areas were crowded with multiple players trying to grab a piece of the same pie. The founders were looking at identifying a market segment that held great growth potential over the next 5–10 years, and something that could be first done for India, and then taken to the overseas markets. While exploring multiple avenues, one that struck a common chord with the founders was the opportunity to revolutionize the gift card segment which had remained mostly paper-based. By early 2007, based on conversations with various retail business outfits, it was clear to Kumar that they should be looking at disrupting the gifting market in India. It was also clear that they wanted to be a gift card processing technology provider more from the merchant side, rather than working for the bankers. Other players in the industry were already trying to serve the banking side, to handle prepaid and loyalty services. Banks also did not show any special interest in the gift cards, but it was a key differentiator to a merchant who was issuing the gift cards. Gift cards for the merchants represented an opportunity to acquire a new customer who may not have yet experienced the brand and thus have a captive new customer. Convinced by their initial research findings and to give the venture its best chance to flourish, Bhaskar also joined Kumar in the venture full time in June 2007.

The founders had zeroed in on the product they were building out and started to work closely with a few retailers. This was a new experience for the founders as they had to take people in the retail space into confidence, for getting a feedback. One of the acquaintances referred the founders to investors at Helion Ventures Partners who, in turn, helped connect with the COO of Landmark. The Landmark store in Chennai was the first to show keen interest in the solution that Qwikcilver was building. Its COO offered to work closely with the founders to influence the way the gift card platform would evolve. Several nuances such as integrating to the point-of-sale (PoS) system at Landmark stores, handling gift card inventory, making the accounting sections take cognizance of the gift card sales for revenue recognition were the challenges that the team had to deal with. Toward the end of 2008, as the integration work with Landmark progressed, another start-up, Printo in Bengaluru worked closely with Qwikcilver toward deploying the early version of the gift card management solution at its stores. Printo became the first customer to deploy the end-to-end gift management solution from Qwikcilver and operationalize across its chain of over ten stores. Similarly, Rex Fashions in Mylapore area in Chennai city was yet another early adopter of the solution across its three-store chain.

Around late 2007, the founders also started talking to friendly investors to understand how to go about raising some venture fund to keep the firm afloat. A serial entrepreneur advised Kumar to first raise money from family and friends, before approaching the venture capital firms. Based on this sound advice and having decided to only raise funds from investment savvy friends, the founders raised some initial amount by January 2008 which kept them afloat for a few more months. Around this time, Pratap joined the Qwikcilver founding team and brought in the marketing know-how which was critical to the growth of the early stage start-up that was fast taking shape. The solution had also evolved to be more of a generic stored value platform which could handle gift cards, loyalty points, prepaid cards, conditional promotions, cash backs, food-court management, and refund management amongst other uses. By late 2008, the founders could articulate with great clarity the value addition that their gift card solution brought to the retail store chain.

The team accessed samples of gift cards from the USA and Europe to understand the workflow better and in turn, fine-tune Qwikcilver's gift card offerings. The founders worked with the retailers to understand the reasons that held back these stores from launching gift card solutions and the inherent complexities. These in turn helped Qwikcilver build the required competitive differentiation versus an in-house gift card management solution that any of the major retailers could have launched. By 2009, the Qwikcilver team had increased to five members, and with an external development team in Bengaluru, the team continued to expand its customer base.

Around May 2011, impressed by the disruption that Qwikcilver was creating in the gift card segment and wanting to be part of the team that was reinventing the gift card space, Shankar Balan joined as the head of sales in India for Qwikcilver. Shankar's experiences with the hospitality, services, fashion, and lifestyle sectors made him a retail expert at Qwikcilver. Shankar also brought in the perspective that Qwikcilver should be an end-to-end gift card management provider without restricting itself to pure technology solution alone for the gift card processing business. From the point of designing a gift card program, to physical card design templates, to managing the logistics for gift card packaging, distribution and answering customer complaints, Qwikcilver could handle the end-to-end gift card management for the retailer (see Exhibit 20.1 for details). According to Kumar and Pratap, this comprehensive solution approach became attractive to the retail chains which began to perceive Qwikcilver as a valuable and trusted partner to work with (see Exhibit 20.2 for more details). Kumar recalled:

> From 2011 onwards, we were launching about 5 to 10 large gift card programs for major retail brands in India with end to end integration to the billing systems. These retailers were given complete access to our APIs to integrate into the gift management platform so that the PoS could be seamlessly tied into our gift processing network.

When the gifter purchased a gift card from a retail outlet, the outlet used the system provided by the gift card issuer to hand out a gift card of certain value and expiry date. Based on the type of gift card purchased, the person who received the gift card (redeemer) had the choice of either redeeming it in the same retail chain as the card was purchased (closed loop gift card) or within the partner network (semi-closed loop gift card) of the gift card issuer. When the gift card was redeemed to pay for some in-store or online purchases, the gift card processing system checked out the card details and the PIN to ascertain the remaining gift card value and authorized the PoS to account for the correct payment details. In this transaction model, there was no direct interaction of the gift card buyer or redeemer with the gift card processing entity such as Qwikcilver (see Exhibit 20.3). The retailers' system and the Qwikcilver backend processing interacted with each other as trusted entities to make the end-to-end transaction possible in real time.

The Gift Cards Industry

Gifting posed several questions to givers. What to buy? Where to buy? And how much to spend? If the intent was to make the recipient feel special, in many instances, the opposite was true. Inappropriate gifting created transactional

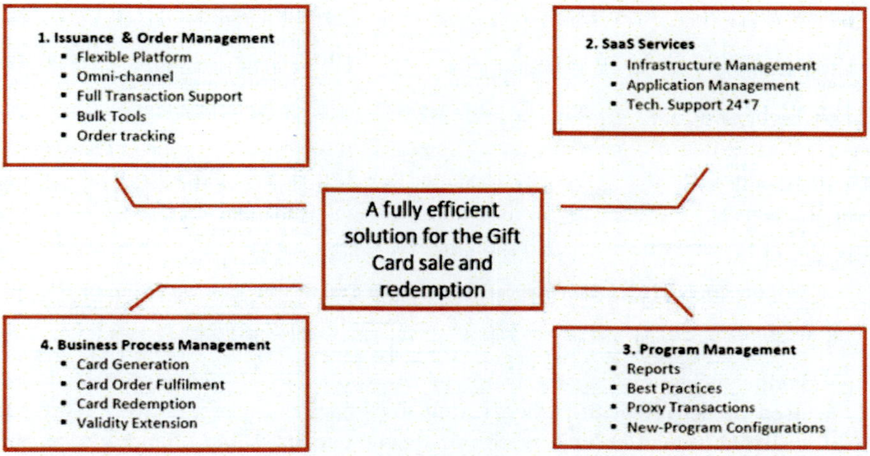

Exhibit 20.1 Complete solution for gift card management. *Source* Company documents

Exhibit 20.2 Versatile technology for end-to-end stored value management. *Source* Company documents

Exhibit 20.3 Traditional pipeline model of gift card transactions. *Source* Author's visualization

inefficiencies, making the recipient worse off. Social taboos prevented cash to be used in lieu of a gift, often taxing the imagination of the giver. Gift purchases centered around holiday season or special occasions and often happened just 48 h before the event. The countless choices offered by the market added to the stress of choosing a gift. To circumvent the problem of time scarcity, to understand the needs of the recipients and to choose the right gifts, gift card companies created platforms linking scores of retailers to millions of customers. By gifting a card, the giver essentially transferred the burden of choice to the recipient, saving himself the stress of choosing, and saved time in the process. The system further allowed the gift receiver to have the flexibility of buying based on his/her needs. Gift cards added the allure of flexibility and convenience to the giver and the recipient.

Traditionally, gifting has been a social activity across the country, and no family event in India missed the opportunity of being an occasion for gifts. Gifts have been largely in the form of cash or household items. Usage of gift cards for family gifting was a recent phenomenon, and as technology penetration increased in India, there was more openness to explore new forms of gifting. Aided by retail platforms such as Flipkart and Amazon, the gift cards expanded customer choices. Propelled by categories such as hospitality and fashion, gift cards were also designed for the well-travelled and market-savvy customers. Gift cards were handy when loyalty points from a retail store did not score. For a single retailer, the problem of storing a gift card in lieu of cash was a hassle, as cards were unaccounted for in the books and yet were as valuable as cash. For an ever-zealous customer, repeat visit to a single retailer or restaurant may not be appealing. This was where gift card platforms, with multiple retailers on board, came in handy. See Appendix 1 for a description of types of gift cards. Both Kumar and Pratap stated:

> Retailers were happy to join our gift card bandwagon because gift cards helped expand retailers' customer base, which added to the existing direct marketing effort.

Market Size—India and the USA

In the backdrop of digitally oriented customers with eclectic tastes, gifting was becoming a complex heuristic. The gift card industry was becoming increasingly popular the world-over. The United States, for instance, registered a growth of 6% in the gift card industry in 2015–16, taking the market size to a staggering USD 131 billion.[2] It was further predicted to reach USD 160 billion by 2018, out of which e-gifting would constitute USD 18 billion. In the UK, the gift card market was expected to reach USD 13.1 billion by 2020.

In India, where the minimum gift card value can be as low as ₹850 (around USD 8),[3] the growth of the market has been far higher than the western counterparts. Gift cards-based gifting in India was poised for major growth from the existing 1.5% of the gift market to over 20% as seen in mature markets such as USA and UK (see Exhibit 20.4 for details). In the four years from 2012 to 2016, the gift card sale increased by 20 times 2, with the average gift card value rising from ₹850 to ₹3400 (around USD 13 to USD 52). Offline gift cards increased to 25%, and the gift card market grew 40–45% in three years. The growth story in India was mainly propelled by e-gifting (see Exhibit 20.5 for details). As per Economic Times report, over 70% of the Indians surveyed prefer gift cards over cash.[4] Over 70% of corporate employees preferred gift cards over gifts. As a response, some corporates developed gift card-centric engagement programmes for their employees, customers, and partners. Sensing the opportunity, retailers jumped on to the bandwagon and launched novel innovations with gift card programmes. Nevertheless, the actual growth of this segment appeared to be propelled by e-gifting (see Exhibit 20.6 for details).

Competition and Envelopment Threats

As of 2017, even though Qwikcilver owned 90% market share in India, the company had to be wary of local competitors entering the Indian gift card market. Many international players could also foray into India to take a slice of the rapidly growing gift cards business.

Stellr

Stellr was a prepaid gift card mall headquartered in Singapore which was vending cards for global malls through a network of physical and electronic outlets. Stellr

[2]Indians taking to gift cards over cash, physical gifts. *LiveMint E-Paper*. *Source:* https://goo.gl/iHHnHm *Accessed on:* 20 October 2017.
[3]1 USD = INR 63.66 as on January 2, 2018.
[4]Blackhawk Network. *Source:* https://www.crunchbase.com/organization/blackhawk-network *Accessed on:* 20 October 2017.

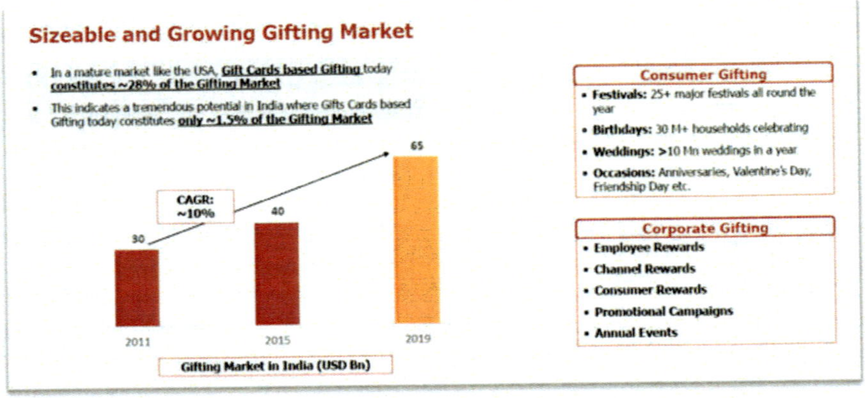

Exhibit 20.4 Gifting market in India. *Source* Company documents

distributed gift cards of BookMyShow, Hungama, and Cleartrip. The retail network of Stellar included over 15,000 stores, e-commerce companies and wallet players, some of which were Reliance Digital and Croma. It was active in international markets such as Russia, China, Turkey, Brazil, and other South East Asian countries.

Blackhawk Network Holdings

Blackhawk Network Holdings, a listed firm headquartered in California, had subsidiaries and partners across the world. With its network spread across 25 countries, it offered a large selection of branded value products such as gift cards, reloadable prepaid debit cards, rebate cards, prepaid telephone calling cards, ticket, and sports cards. The products from Blackhawk were marketed through different retail networks including grocery store chains, drug stores, and convenience stores.[5] Along with physical and gift card offerings, the firm also operated automated and kiosk-based services. Its solution portfolio covered B2C as well as B2B gift card offerings, and the firm introduced themed gifting to enhance customer flexibility, convenience, and choice.

Blackhawk Network made a series of acquisitions in the prepaid and gift cards segment over the years to boost its market presence and to improve its offering to the customers through mobile payment solutions and digital gifting innovation. The intent has been to capture customers dealing in cash, helping them digitize their transactions and allowing mobile bill payments. Blackhawk products included patented restricted authorization network (RAN), reloadable and non-reloadable

[5]Blackhawk Network Obtains New RAN Patent. *Source:* https://blackhawknetwork.com/blackhawk-network-obtains-new-ran-patent/ *Accessed on:* 10 October 2017.

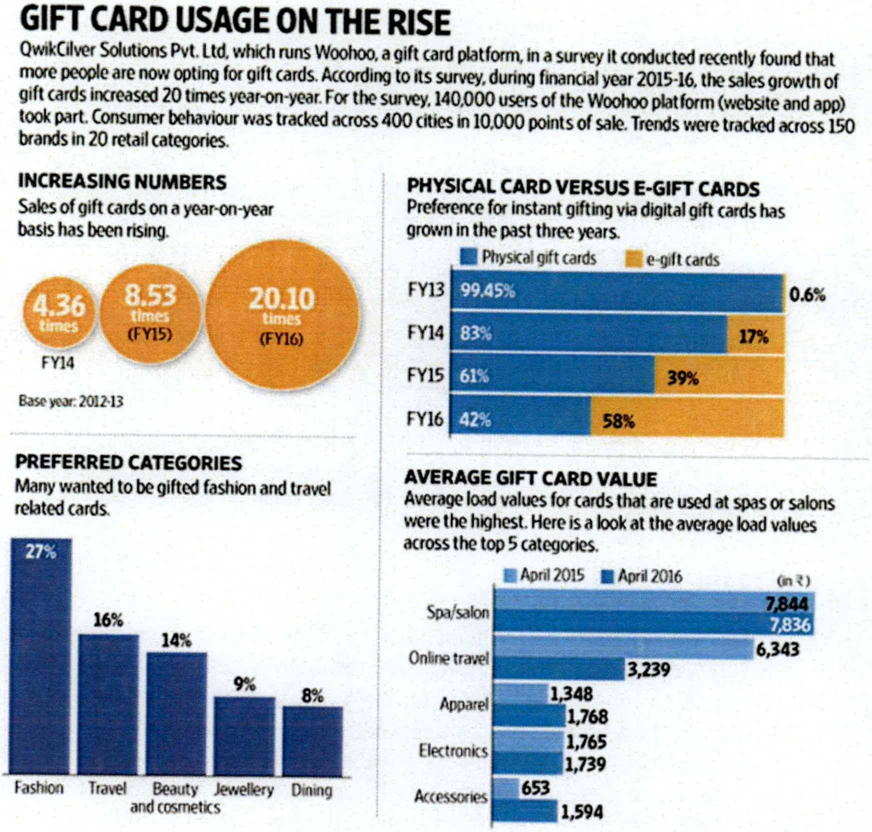

Exhibit 20.5 Overview of the gift card market in India. *Source* Live Mint, 10 October, 2017

network branded programs, and other retailer cards that attracted new customers.[6] For consumer incitement, Blackhawk offered rebates, managed promotions for retailers, processed rebates, and performed a rule-based validation. Blackhawk acquired CashStar for \$175 million.[7] CashStar developed a suite of digital prepaid card technologies with a special focus on the first-party market. The first-party segment of the gift card market was the fastest-growing segment, and the acquisition was expected to power Blackhawk's growth.

[6]Blackhawk Network Acquires CashStar For Digital Gift Cards. *Source:* https://seekingalpha.com/article/4103890-blackhawk-network-acquires-cashstar-digital-gift-cards *Accessed on:* 21 October 2017.

[7]InComm Claims Two Top Honors at 2017 Pay Awards. *Source:* https://www.prnewswire.com/news-releases/incomm-claims-two-top-honors-at-2017-pay-awards-300479339.html *Accessed on:* 8 October 2017.

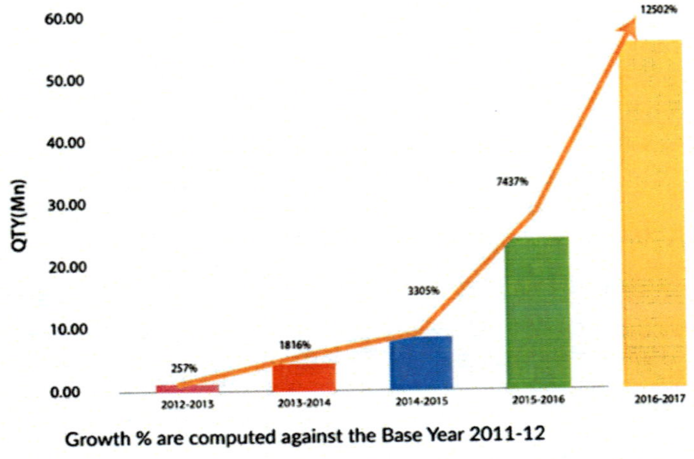

Exhibit 20.6 Y-o-Y gift card and e-gift card issuance trend. Source Company documents

InComm

InComm touted itself as a financial technology firm that was transforming the shopping experiences through payments technology in the gift card market space. Headquartered in Atlanta, GA, in the USA, InComm had a broad footprint in the US market. Leveraging deep integrations into retailers' point-of-sale systems, InComm provided connectivity to a variety of service providers allowing consumers to conduct everyday business at more than half a million retail distribution points.[8] Whether those consumers were activating prepaid products, paying bills, enjoying discounts through a membership card, purchasing digital goods in-store or adding funds to an online account, they benefitted from InComm's gifting opportunities, catering to on-the-go shoppers, as well as cash-based consumers. Launched in 2005 in partnership with Visa and MasterCard, the InComm Vanilla gift card allowed customers the benefits of a prepaid open loop card that was accepted at all locations that took a Visa or MasterCard debit card.[9] Customers had the flexibility of using these Vanilla cards for online or in-store redemptions, and as of 2017, InComm was expanding the footprint of these cards into other countries.

InComm had a presence in more than 30 countries in addition to owning 206 global patents. InComm's solutions were powered by Qualtrics, a data analytics system, which told the retailers more than the operational information—they would not only know which products were selling how much but why, which helped them understand consumers better. In 2017, InComm partnered with American Express

[8]Celebrating 10 Years of Vanilla Gift. *Source:* http://www.incomm.com/blog/Pages/Blogs/Celebrating-10-Years-of-Vanilla-Gift.aspx *Accessed on:* 10 October 2017.
[9]AmEx's $300 Million Prepaid Tech Experiment Ends in a Sale. *Source:* https://goo.gl/JFNQSj *Accessed on:* 3 October 2017.

to acquire the exclusive distribution rights of American Express's prepaid reloadable and gift card products in the US.[10]

Ceridian Stored Value Solutions

Ceridian Stored Value Solutions (SVS) was founded in 1996 and headquartered in Louisville, KY, in the USA. It offered gift card solutions to large retail brands in the USA by working with casinos, fashion, supermarkets, airlines, retailers, and enterprises to offer customized prepaid card solutions. Along with enabling retailers and enterprises to design their custom gift card solutions, Ceridian SVS also catered to production and packaging of cards along with fulfillment and card delivery. It partnered with top global retailers to offer stored value solutions, where the offerings included payroll, benefits, tax services, compliance, and human resources. In order to enhance its international footprint, SVS has partnered with retail chains in the UK, Australia, and New Zealand.[11]

Gyft

Started as a mobile-first gift card firm in San Francisco in 2010, Gyft aimed at disrupting the over $100 billion physical gift card market to completely take it to the mobile.[12] Being an early mover in the fully digital gift cards space in the USA, Gyft brought the plastic gift card industry to the mobile, as opposed to focusing on new “social gifting” experiences similar to some of the other gift card start-ups operating in this space. While the Gyft app supported storing a variety of gift cards, users could also check their balances on the cards. Gyft obtained the required retailer partnerships, owing to the app’s ability to interoperate with the retailer’s backend systems. In the updated app, passbook integration was offered on a per card basis, wherein instead of a generic “Gyft” card being stored in the passbook app, the customer appeared to have individual store gift cards. For the start-up retailers, the passbook app increased mobile downloads, potentially increasing their market share. In 2015, Gyft furthered its innovation by developing a trading platform for easing gift card exchange. Termed Gyft Block, it was part of Gyft's broader mission to digitize gift cards so that they could be securely traded using bitcoin's public ledger, the block chain.[13]

---

[10]InComm to Become Exclusive Distributor of American Express U.S. Prepaid Cards. *Source:* https://goo.gl/EkcyP2 *Accessed on:* 21 October 2017.

[11]Ceridian Stored Value Solutions (SVS) Launches B2B Gift Card Portal. *Source:* https://goo.gl/xzuZFH
Accessed on: 8 October 2017.

[12]Gyft Unveils New Tech for Blockchain-Powered Gift Cards. *Source:* https://www.coindesk.com/gyft-chain-blockchain-gift-cards/ *Accessed on:* 20 October 2017.

[13]This is the most requested gift for 8 years in a row. *Source:* https://goo.gl/jB6fyf *Accessed on:* 10 October 2017.

Qwikcilver Business Model

The year 2008–09 was a period of growth for the organized retail industry in India as the e-commerce portals such as Flipkart and Amazon had not yet overtaken the brick & mortar stores. Big retail brands such as Shoppers Stop, Croma, Westside, and others were looking at scaling up their retail operations. It was not easy to convince the retailers to allow Qwikcilver to handle gift cards for them. These stores did not have the technology to issue gift cards, despite having the best technology for managing stores. They had to be convinced of the safety and revenue potential of gift cards. Most stores were new to any form of ERP solutions other than what was needed for bare bones accounting and inventory management. Cloud-based solutions were even more alien. Some of the stores were perturbed to learn that all the gift card-related data would be stored on the cloud servers along with data from other competitors.

Foray into Distribution Business—GiftBig Portal

When Qwikcilver contracted with Flipkart to launch gift cards in India, the first set of e-gift cards or digital gift cards were introduced. Consumers visiting Flipkart could buy e-gift cards which could be delivered over email or buy physical gift cards which could be shipped to them. Similar efforts with MakeMyTrip portal also resulted in the adoption of Qwikcilver's solution by the online travel portal to reward returning customers as part of brand loyalty promotion. Rewards through gift cards instead of cash paybacks were seen to retain positive association with the customers, and this motivated retailers to switch to increased usage of gift card-based rewarding. All this convinced Qwikcilver to consider entry into the distribution business as they started to see the potential of going directly to the enterprises to promote gifting experiences for their employees, channel partners, or customers (see Exhibit 20.7 for details). Around 2011, the founders realized that their solution was ready to take on a bigger mantle in the B2B space with a foray into the distribution business. As it was an established opportunity in the USA where several portals offered digital gift cards to enterprises, Qwikcilver wanted to cash in on this opportunity by becoming an end-to-end player. This seemed to serve two main purposes—getting closer to the enterprise market that was growing at a very rapid pace in India and offering online presence for brick-and-mortar retail partners and resellers.

With an intention to focus on both the enterprise and consumer sections of the gift card buyers in 2011, Qwikcilver launched GiftBig.com portal to directly sell gift cards. Leveraging the tie-ups with the retail brands that already existed, Qwikcilver offered a variety of gift cards on the GiftBig portal. If someone wanted to buy a Domino's Pizza gift card for ₹500 (around USD 8) for their employees, they could just go to the GiftBig portal to purchase physical gift card that would get shipped or an e-gift card that arrived over email. This solved the gifters and

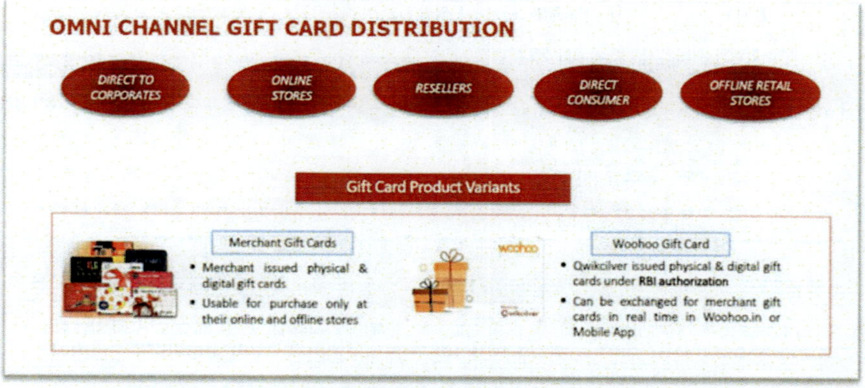

Exhibit 20.7 Channel Reach. *Source* Company documents

redeemers the trouble of visiting the physical store and improved the online presence of physical retail stores, who otherwise had almost no internet presence.

By 2014–15, based on customer and enterprise demands, the gift card resellers started to include gift cards in their portfolio. This was a big shift for many of the gift card resellers who were holding large inventories of gift cards. It slowly began to dawn on these resellers the advantages of moving to an electronic model as they could shrink their inventories by adopting the digital gift card model. They could further offer flexibility of variable card value where they were no longer restricted to providing just fixed denominations. While coupons from retailers have a mere 10% redemption rate, gift cards enjoyed redemption rates of 50–80%, causing retailers to value gift cards more for brand promotions.[14]

In order to turbocharge the B2B side, Qwikcilver started forming small teams by 2012 to convince corporates to adopt Qwikcilver solutions for meeting all their gifting needs. Although corporates used gift cards, they had to offer a single type of gift card to all the employees, and that provided little flexibility in choice. For the ease of processing, Qwikcilver issued GiftBig cards which the recipients could exchange for any retailer's card on the GiftBig portal. These GiftBig cards were more like catalogue cards wherein, instead of the employer choosing the gifts for all the employees, the latter could exchange them for any other card of their choice. If an employee had a GiftBig card, then she could exchange it partially for a Domino's Pizza gift card while the rest could be converted to a Levi Strauss gift card. Toward late 2017, Qwikcilver had over 400 large corporate tie-ups to provide them with gift card solutions, constituting nearly 85% of the spend.

[14]Qwikcilver has a lion's share of the Indian gift card market. Now, it plans to go global. *Forbes India*. *Source:* https://goo.gl/cNZKU2 *Accessed on:* 12th Oct 2017.

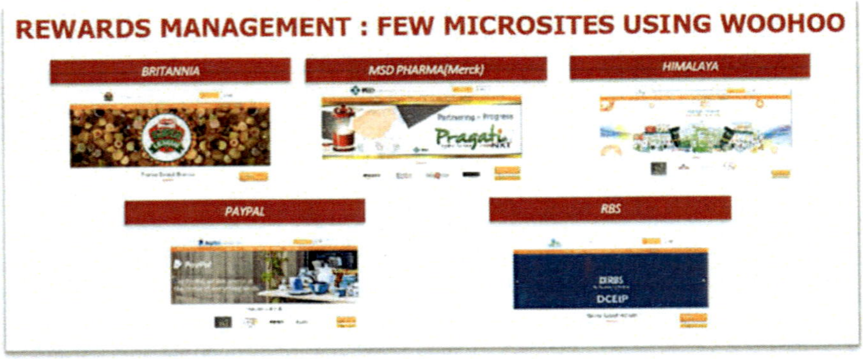

Exhibit 20.8 Powering enterprise portals through micro-sites. *Source* Company documents

Qwikcilver also provided micro-sites for the existing retailers to allow customers to purchase and redeem gift cards. To address corporate demands, Qwikcilver started to introduce customized corporate cards through existing partnerships with retail brands. Qwikcilver could setup a www.Britannia.GiftBig.com portal if Britannia wanted to leverage the enterprise connect that GiftBig brought to the table (see Exhibit 20.8 for details). The GiftBig mobile interface could also be embedded within the mobile app of partners similar to a micro-site. Foray into the distribution space helped Qwikcilver improve the valuation of the firm as much venture money in 2011–15 was chasing B2B and B2C start-ups. Enterprises or individuals had the ability to buy physical or e-gift cards by visiting GiftBig.com portal without having to go through a third party.

From when a retail brand decides to launch a new gift card program to when the customer redeems such a card gifted to her, Qwikcilver helped the retailers and customers handle the entire sequence of events end to end. QwikCilver's end-to-end gifting solution addressed the different inefficiencies for the retailer and the customer. See Appendix 2 for a detailed description of a gift card life cycle and the critical success factors for the industry. The gift card life cycle involved multiple stages, and the card changed hands multiple times before it finally got redeemed. All through the life cycle, the gift card issuers such as Qwikcilver could make the process seamless for the retail brands, store keepers, gifters, and redeemers.

Evolution of Pricing Model

From the Landmark store experience during the initial years, the founders understood that the retail stores would be willing to pay a percentage share of the card value from the sales of gift cards. Over the decade, the revenue model for Qwikcilver has remained mostly unchanged. Alternative models such as software-based licensing approach or a fixed charge or charge per transaction have not appealed either to retail store chains or to the Qwikcilver team. With the transactions-based charging, the retail stores would not be sure what value each transaction brought them, as the value of each gift card could vary. With a slab-based pricing model where the gift management solution got a percentage of the card value, the Qwikcilver team was taking over the overhead of managing the life cycle of the gift card from the store. The cost for the retail store was directly linked to the return on investment they earned. According to Kumar and Pratap, shopping using gift cards also exhibited a *going-premium effect* wherein a consumer, who would normally not shop at the store, would visit the retail outlet to redeem the gift card and would end up exploring the store for other purchases too. The retail stores began to see these multiple benefits, and how these operational charges for gift cards could lead to better customer experiences. Different percentages prevailed for different slabs: 0–20 million Indian rupees had one fixed rate, while 20–50 million had another, and so on.

QwikCilver's pricing model was also attractive as it was independent of the number of stores the retail brand had, or the number of cards sold per brand, or the number of gift card programs running for a given retail brand. By tightly linking the growth of their business with the growth of the gift card category, the founders were pegging the future of the firm to the growth their retail partners witnessed. The retailers in turn were confident as they saw a firm that was not looking at a one-time transaction but someone who would be incentivized to see the retailers benefit from the year-on-year growth.

Woohoo—Qwikcilver's Multi-Sided Platform

With the GiftBig portal focusing more on the corporate gifting aspects, the founders were looking to foray into building direct connect with the consumers. In early 2015, Qwikcilver decided to directly enter the B2C segment with an entirely new brand called Woohoo. The consumer-to-consumer (C2C) side of gifting was still a nascent market with immense potential for growth as gifting was only getting bigger in the Indian context. The GiftBig portal had become more synonymous with corporate gifting and micro-site usage, and the team felt the need to create a new consumer brand. The idea then was to create a wallet of wallets such that the new brand could be more than just a digital gift card. All this resulted in Qwikcilver using the investments from venture funds for various strategic initiatives, including building a consumer brand, which was a pilot move. By this time, the digital gift cards in India were picking pace, and most of the retailers working with Qwikcilver had added e-gift and mobile-based gift cards to their portfolio which already included physical gift cards. These trends were aided by the increasing mobile phone and internet penetration in India. The existing GiftBig physical cards were also easily rebranded as Woohoo cards, and the Woohoo mobile application was launched on the iOS and Android marketplaces.

The idea with Woohoo was to finally realize the vision of the founders to allow a customer to have seamless gifting experience. What if one could walk into a Shopper's Stop store and redeem her bank credit card points to pay for the purchases? With the introduction of the Woohoo card, the founders were finally close to the possibility of allowing anyone a complete flexibility in expending their gift card points. With the ability to generate digital gift cards on the fly, Qwikcilver soon realized the potential a consumer-based service such as Woohoo. The consumer card allowed Qwikcilver to create a digital spending network for the end user who could convert the Woohoo card to that of any other retailer to suit the shopping needs. Card personalization features of Woohoo have been migrated on to the B2B offerings from Qwikcilver. Ability to customize the look and feel, add audio and video messages, scheduling delivery of a card for a future date are the popular features of Woohoo. With backend integrations to a variety of e-wallets such as Mobikwik, Paytm, Oxicash, and others, the Woohoo mobile app had become the most personalized omni-potent mobile gifting solution. Similar to a mobile wallet usage, the consumer with a prepaid Woohoo app could generate a gift card coupon code of a retail chain, to be redeemed at its counter.

Woohoo mobile app enabled C2C transactions by allowing consumers to trade in gift cards through a fully digital experience (see Exhibit 20.9 for more details). Consumers had the opportunity to buy discounted gift cards or partially used cards that other consumers were selling on the Woohoo secondary marketplace or exchange unused cards. Users could also convert their partially used gift cards to cash or trade their unused ones for other cards that are of interest to them. When converted to cash, Qwikcilver took a commission to exchange the unused portion of the gift card to money in the customer's bank account. Gift card trade on the Woohoo marketplace proved a win–win for the consumers and retailers. The secondary market place helped reduce the spillage rates, while expanding the customer base for the retailers. This marketplace allowed the consumer to acquire only the required card that suited her tastes with higher likelihood of not going unused, while allowing retailers access to those customers who were fans of the retail brand. This helped spread the positive shopping experience while generating additional incremental revenues for the retailer when such customers upspend beyond the value of the card. Gift cards do not accurately capture the value the recipient desires, leading to *uplift or upspending*, a phenomenon where the receiver spends more than the card value. According to a report by GC Incentives, it was found that 51% of those who had received a gift card in a rebate offer went on to spend more than the card's face value with that merchant.

As more consumers became comfortable using digital gift cards in the form of Woohoo mobile app, user participation and exchange of gifts increased. The Woohoo app offered the customer a choice of over 150 brands. It offered group gifting option, where customers pooled in money for gifting the recipient. The Woohoo secondary marketplace for digital gift cards also offered safety to the buyers in terms of remaining gift card value while trading with semi-used cards. It saved the trouble of physically picking up the discounted cards from the seller. With support for extensive customization of gift cards sent to family and friends,

Exhibit 20.9 Wooing B2C with Woohoo. *Source* Company documents

the Woohoo app made it convenient for people to change their gifting habits and embrace the new dynamics of gifting. While the Indian gift card market grew at 300% annually, QwikCilver's additional gift card transactions popularized the usage of digital gift cards for all occasions.

Referred to as a super store by Kumar, the Woohoo app gave the receiver of gifts the choice to choose from over 150 brands that had partnered with Qwikcilver. Based on the level of integration with the retailer, Qwikcilver had the visibility into the specific buying habits of the customers and what they spent the gift cards on. These could in turn be leveraged by Qwikcilver to run specific promotional campaigns for the retailers based on the needs. Although Woohoo sales accounted for less than 20% of the gross merchandise value (GMV) for Qwikcilver in 2017, with additional features such as group gifting and secondary marketplace, the app was growing. For instance, when a gift card buyer wishes to buy a Croma gift card through an e-commerce portal, then the entire processing was done through the Woohoo system through its integration with the portal so that a digitally activated Croma gift card was delivered to the buyer. According to Kumar, the Woohoo platform had created the C2C ecosystem for gift cards that did not exist in India. For the first time, customers could sell their unused gift cards directly to other customers and instead pick up what they were interested in. Thinking about how the Woohoo and Qwikcilver business models related to each other, Pratap recalled an analogy:

> Woohoo business model and the traditional Qwikcilver model could be better understood by considering the analogy of innovations introduced in Forumula-1 cars by car manufacturers. If an innovation succeeded on the Formula-1 track, then that same innovation could be transferred and adapted to the passenger car market over time. But when it failed, such failures were insulated from the outside market and did not have any bearing on the broader business.

A successful innovation on the Woohoo platform was soon made available to the retail stores on their micro-sites which made it even more valuable for the retailers. With these innovations, selling the solution to retailers coming onboard became easier. Woohoo remained an experimental ground for Qwikcilver to continuously learn from the consumer market, even though no additional marketing expenditure was made for B2C and C2C push. By continuing to maintain presence in the direct to consumer space, the Qwikcilver team was confident of stepping up its activities at any moment on the consumer front as the inflection point emerged.

The traditional Qwikcilver model of powering the prepaid cards for the retailer was a pipeline business, wherein the Qwikcilver technology and logistics powers the gift card solutions for the brands. But with the Woohoo model, Qwikcilver opened itself up as a true multi-sided business model powered by a proprietary platform[15] with the retailers and customers playing a critical role on the platform driving transactions (see Exhibit 20.10). With consumers on one side and retail brands on the other side of the two-sided gift card platform, there were same side network effect on the retail side, wherein no retail brand wanted to lose out on the opportunity to get access to consumers who would be transacting using gift cards. With more brands available, the cross-side network effects would entice even more consumers onboard the Woohoo platform.

Sustaining Growth

At the time Qwikcilver started operations, the gift card market was an opportunity that was ripe for disruption and transformation. It had remained mostly paper based with very low penetration even in the Indian metropolitan areas. The founders were contemplating the situation of a newly married couple in the Indian context—inundated with gifts from relatives and friends, most of which consisted of traditional bed-linen and crockery. While the gift givers were well-meaning, they could little understand the needs of the newlyweds. A perfectly rational gift giver would offer cash, and a perfectly rational recipient would accept it, where the satisfaction was 100%. But the world was not perfectly rational, but boundedly rational. Consequently, Kumar reminisced:

> Billions of dollars were spent on gifts with uncertain impact on the recipient, creating huge market inefficiencies. Gift cards had the opportunity to address this gap.

From the outset, gift card management seemed to be an adjacency which any of the major players in the financial products space or a retail software space could get into and disrupt. Kumar quickly acknowledged that nimble competition, more than established players, could challenge Qwikcilver's dominant market position. But the real entry barrier for most newcomers would be the myriad integrations that they

[15]Reserve Bank of India. (2009). Draft Guidelines for issuance and operation of Prepaid Payment Instruments in India. *Source:* https://rbi.org.in/scripts/bs_viewcontent.aspx?Id=1902 *Accessed on:* 10th Oct 2017.

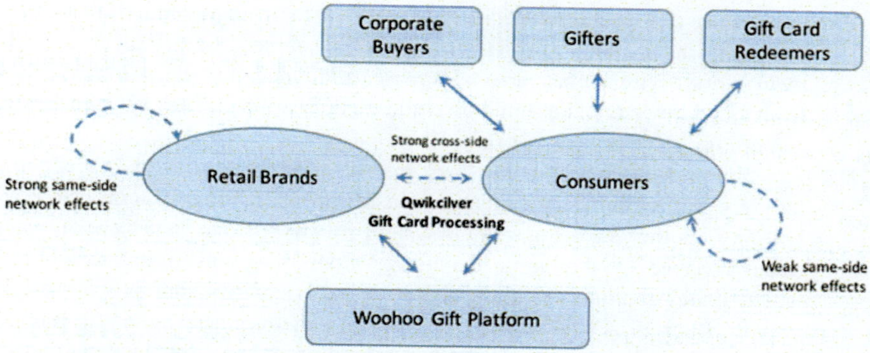

Exhibit 20.10 Woohoo—A Multi-Sided Platform business. *Source* Author's visualization

need to comprehend with, while rolling out the technology to work with every possible PoS out there. Over the years, according to Kumar, Qwikcilver had integrated with nearly 30 odd PoS systems in India and abroad.Apart from regulatory licenses and technology challenges, these relationships with the retailers across the country and abroad were significant entry barriers that were helping Qwikcilver cement its leadership position. At this point, Pratap reiterated:

> Retailers' trust was something competition would have to work very hard to achieve.

Qwikcilver, according to its founders, had painstakingly put together an entire ecosystem to handle the gift card programs for a retail store chain including design of cards, deliver to all the outlets in the country, seamless redemption of gift cards by customers or even exchange of unused card value. Along with the tools needed for operationalizing the gift card programs, the entire order fulfillment process had to be replicated by competition if they have to grab a share of the lucrative gift cards market. Retailers also had access to rich reporting through real-time dashboards and detailed reports with analytics that helped visualize the progress of the gift card programs. Qwikcilver managed the entire workflow for the retailer without stopping at providing a technology solution alone. Yet the founders remained vigilant about competition from adjacent solution providers, since the gift card market was sustainably profit making. The founders stressed on the fact that only constant innovation would help the Qwikcilver platform stay ahead of the pack.

Technology Choices

With an experience in handling large transaction processing systems, the founders were initially tempted to fully build the product in-house end to end. However, as early as in 2007, when they realized the need to continuously engage with the retail stores to understand the evolving solution and integrate the critical needs of the merchants, the founders decided to restrict their involvement to defining and designing the technology platform. They outsourced the actual product development work. With some personal savings ploughed into the venture and support from angel investors, the founders could identify a local IT firm as partner for all the technology development work.

Coming from a payments background, Kumar leveraged his experience in building high-volume multi-tenant transaction processing systems. He envisioned building another such transaction system for the gift card market. Kumar's experiences shaped Qwikcilver's technology strategy—build highly scalable software which could provide seamless customer experience, which propelled the firm's growth. Back in 2007–08, with the internet penetration in India still picking pace, and when mobile-based transactions were still in infancy, the decision to build out a multi-tenant fully hosted solution was not only uncommon, but was also frowned upon. Even in the USA, the enterprise acceptance of cloud computing was still evolving, and the viability of infrastructure-as-a-service (IaaS) providers such as Amazon Web Services (AWS) was still being proved in real business terms. However, the call to build the technology platform in the form of a hosted software offering or software as a service (SaaS) was a key decision as even a decade later, it continued to enable the firm to roll out increasingly robust offerings. With the concept of a multi-tenant SaaS offering still new to the Indian IT providers, there was considerable effort involved in determining the right deployment that could scale horizontally as the needs evolved.

Integrating with PoS

While working with the Chennai-based Landmark store's IT team to integrate with the book chain's backend systems, the founders realized the major challenges that they would face. Every single retail store chain had a different proprietary home grown or customized off-the-shelf IT system that needed special integration to reconcile with the gift card transaction system. The gift cards were a sensitive inventory as it was just another form of cash that anyone could walk away with—inventory management was critical for accounting purposes. Most systems in those days were decentralized, and inventory reconciliation took place at the end of the day from each store to the central IT system. There was no centralized authentication system where all stores could closely monitor who issued gift cards and when. From the beginning, these aspects could be easily tracked on the Qwikcilver network. The Landmark systems were the training ground for these first-time entrepreneurs. With a clear understanding that the store cashier should be able to handle gift card issuances with ease, the Qwikcilver team had its task cut out. The solution needed to ensure that there was no scope for fraud where one could just walk away with a set of activated cards. While working with the Landmark team, Qwikcilver plugged in as many loopholes of the new system as possible. The initial deployment of the gift card management solution had to seamlessly work across the

18 different Landmark stores across the country as part of the full-fledged solution deployment, after the pilot at the T-Nagar store.

Even after a decade of Qwikcilver's operations, its integrations with the PoS variants in the retail stores had remained a key differentiator and an entry barrier for competition. Although the PoS variants reduced over the years, integration remained more of a logistical challenge than a technological one. Qwikcilver brought down the time needed to integrate with a new variety of PoS through their ever-improving ability to define better interfaces. Although these APIs were designed to handle complex integration scenarios, the challenges remained. The window of time to integrate with the PoS due to down time needs was a challenge. The IT teams managing the PoS units for the retailer were mostly small-time vendors different from the principal of the retail chain. Often these could be resellers or a just-in-time technical team put together for implementing the solution for the retailer. Working with several such teams for rolling out the gift card processing solution was a time-consuming process. The Qwikcilver team had rolled out many such integrations with thousands of retail stores across the country and abroad over the last decade.

Working with Card Manufacturers

One of the challenges for Qwikcilver in 2009 was to identify a card manufacturer who could consistently supply high-quality cards. The cost per card was still high in India, and none of the existing players could supply a high volume at an affordable price. The vendors who supplied cards to the credit and debit card industry were expensive and did not fit the economics involved in gift cards. Spending ₹20–25 (around USD 0.3–USD 0.4) for a magnetic strip-based card with just ₹500 (around USD 8) loaded on a gift card was not appealing. With the e-gift cards having few takers due to fears on data security and lower internet and mobile penetration at that point, Qwikcilver had to explore various options including paper-based gift cards, magnetic strips on paper, and so on. Some of the low-cost vendors had high error rate even in correctly encoding the gift card information onto the magnetic strips.

Much of the ecosystem needed for closed-loop gift card market did not practically exist in 2007–08 in India, impeding the growth opportunities. For a brief period in 2008, the team also explored Chinese card manufacturers who could supply printed magnetic strip-based cards to India for about ₹4 (around USD 0.06) as the landed cost. However, as the Indian Rupee began to weaken considerably against the USD, this price arbitrage soon disappeared. From 2008 to late 2017, the cost of printing a gift card in India has come down significantly over time. Owing to the advancement in mobile and internet penetration, the e-gift cards in 2017 appeared to have taken over from the need to handle logistics of physical cards. Pratap commented:

> Every year we had new set of retailers show interest in gift cards and come on-board to try out a new gift card promotional program for their customers. In 2016, we had the travel portals try our gift cards and such organic growth was good to see. We have persuaded them for years to try out our offerings and those efforts seem to be paying off now. When the customers visit the retailer outlet to redeem a gift card, she gets exposed to the full range of products on offer and retailers see an upspend happen when customers come to redeem their gift cards.

Influencing the Regulatory Framework

In late 2009, Reserve Bank of India (RBI) issued guidelines for businesses dealing with prepaid instruments (PPI), and the gift cards issued by Qwikcilver under its own brand (GiftBig) would be categorized as a semi-closed loop gift card needing a license from RBI. As per RBI guidelines, banks and non-banking financial companies (NBFCs) would be permitted to issue all categories of prepaid instruments as long as they complied with the eligibility criteria. Only those banks allowed by RBI to provide mobile banking were permitted to launch mobile-based prepaid instruments. Non-banking enterprises would be allowed by RBI to issue only closed loop and semi-closed loop prepaid instruments. The rule clearly mandated that mobile service providers would be permitted to issue mobile prepaid cards, but it stated that "*in addition to talk-value, the use of such pre-paid value as a payment instrument shall be restricted to the purchase of only such value added digital contents or services for use on the mobile phones*[16]". Use of mobile prepaid value for purchase of any other consumer goods or services was prohibited by RBI. There was also another subtle but important differentiation between gift cards and prepaid cards: While gift cards issued by retail stores were designed for use until the original balance existed, the prepaid cards which were issued by banking entities were reloadable and were designed to be similar to debit cards. Kumar said:

> We were one of the early movers with respect to regulatory compliance, and by 2012, we had started working towards procuring a license from RBI so that we could soon issue gift cards under our own brand. Even the RBI was handling for the first time a request by a venture funded start-up that was looking to obtain a PPI license. There was ambiguity around what guidelines of Foreign Investment Promotion Board (FIPB) were applicable to the gift cards segment. It took them over a year, something like six quarters almost, to close out the regulatory formalities wherein the gift card segment was identified as similar to other stored value cards.

By August 2013, after further clarifications from Department of Industrial Policy and Promotion (DIPP) and completion of all required security and regulatory audits, and introducing a mandatory Disaster Recovery (DR) solution, Qwikcilver obtained the coveted semi-closed loop license from RBI which allowed them to issue prepaid gift cards. Later, when the Indian government issued marketplace guidelines which

[16]The Gift-Card Economy. *Source:* http://www.nytimes.com/2007/01/07/magazine/07wwln_freak.t.html *Accessed on:* 13 October 2017.

prohibited online retailers such as Amazon and Flipkart from issuing their own closed loop cards usable on their marketplaces, the RBI license held by Qwikcilver allowed it to be the preferred gift card management solution provider on these e-commerce portals. So around 2014, the Qwikcilver powered gift cards, issued, and fulfilled by Qwikcilver backend processing, began selling on Amazon and Flipkart. This development triggered a fresh growth stage not only for the firm but also for the gift card market segment as a whole. This was soon followed by a set of online retailers such as Myntra, ShopClues, SnapDeal, and others. Along with Qwikcilver, Mobikwik and Paytm also received the RBI license to issue semi-closed loop cards. Although Flipkart and MakeMyTrip were using Qwikcilver powered gift cards earlier, they were only closed loop cards. Of these, MakeMyTrip continues to issue closed loop cards, powered by Qwikcilver. Struck by the Indian government's regulation around marketplaces, the seamless transition to semi-closed loop offered by Qwikcilver was most welcome for these online retailers as they migrated to the full-fledged card issuance and fulfillment solution on offer.

Issues with Traditional Gift Cards

For most part, gift cards posed a win–win for all parties involved—retailers, card buyers and recipients, corporates, and the platform itself. Yet, there were a few issues in the gift card value chain. Gift cards were not always fully utilized on time as every card came with an expiry date. Spillage as it was called amounted to a staggering USD 8 billion of the USD 80 billion gift card market in America, as on 2006.[17] This spillage essentially meant the gift giver paid the retailer for a mere plastic card, without any tangible benefits to the recipient. The taboo on exchange of cash led one to present gift cards, which could be of little or no value to the recipient with 10% to 33% of value lost in holiday gifting alone. Yet, levying junk fee or the fees for idle cards decreased the instance of spillage in America which stood at 1% of the total gift card spend.[18] Interestingly, the practice of exchanging cash for gift cards, albeit at a fee, was introduced to control spillage.

In 2007–08 when Qwikcilver ventured into the gift card space, gift cards across the world were mostly physical in nature. Some of these were paper or plastic cards with a magnetic strip that contained the encoded information related to the gift card amount, issue and expiry date. As these physical cards were predominantly a bearer instrument, without including much of the information of the owner or recipient of the card, it carried the risk of getting lost. Risk of losing a paper voucher or ensuring multiple redemptions does not happen through photocopies of paper vouchers, forgetting to redeem a card, needing to visit a physical store to both buy a gift card for an occasion and to redeem a card gifted by family or friends, inability

[17]Retailer gone bankrupt? What cardholders should do. *Source:* https://goo.gl/n13EYH *Accessed on:* 8 October 2017.

[18]Qwikcilver aims to capture global markets. *Business Line*. *Source:* https://goo.gl/MAZRvo *Accessed on:* 8 October 2017.

to customize the gift cards for the occasion, lack of flexibility to buy gift cards of any desired denominations, and inability to understand the buying behavior of customers who redeem these gift cards were just some of the pitfalls of the physical cards. Pratap pondered over the challenges of a typical retailer:

> With the risk of fraudulent use of gift cards and duplicate card redemptions always present, the retailer had to safe-guard the gift cards against theft, losses during transportation, manage its inventory and misuse by his own staff.

Opportunities in International Markets in 2017

After dominating the Indian gift card market, Qwikcilver forayed into the Middle Eastern market through tie-ups with major brands in the region. The Al-Futtaim Group in UAE used the full suite from Qwikcilver to manage loyalty and promotion programs for over 40 brands that it held licenses for, in the Middle East markets. The Lulu chain of malls and others across the GCC countries started using the Qwikcilver platform for managing a variety of stored value cards for their customers. From selling gift cards at the gold souks in Dubai to running promotional programs in the various super markets during the Dubai Shopping Festival, the platform was able to handle the needs of new markets in the Middle East. After piloting the platform for a year in the GCC countries, the Qwikcilver team set up offices to build its partnerships in the region and enhance presence in West Asian countries. Qwikcilver powered the luxury retailer Al Tayer group in the region by offering prepaid cards covering fashion, jewelry, home, and department store categories. Kumar was quick to state:

> Although our platform is not restricted to pre-paid card issuance and processing side of the business, in future we do have plans to enter the distribution side in the GCC region.

By late 2017, Qwikcilver aimed to have presence in the USA, Australia, and Singapore markets. In Singapore, Qwikcilver partnered with the retail giant Lazada Group to offer prepaid gift cards for in-store and online usage. With the Lazada Group being the largest e-commerce marketplace in Singapore, Malaysia, Thailand, Philippines, and Vietnam, the Qwikcilver platform was aiming for presence in these countries through this partnership. In Australia, the company entered into retail markets through a retail chain that picked up Qwikcilver's gift card processing system over an incumbent solution it had in place for several years. With such inroads into new markets, the company strived to maintain its leadership position in the gift cards category. The lack of innovation, hassle of having to deal with multiple vendors, lack of digital gifting solutions, and quality of service of the incumbents in these markets have been key issues. With gift cards accounting for nearly 30% of the US gifting spend, it was imperative for Qwikcilver to enter the US market to capture a portion of the pie.

Road Ahead

As of 2017, the size of the gifting industry in India was over $40 billion (see Exhibit 20.4), and gift cards were predicted to take in a majority share in the coming years. There was competition in the mobile wallet space amongst mobile-operated, bank-operated, and independent wallets, where each operator tried to provide an increasing range of services in a likely winner-takes-all market. With RBI guidelines specifying exemption from Foreign Exchange Management Act (FEMA) to gift card transactions, flexibility was no longer an issue. The government's focus on cashless transactions, coupled with the increasing popularity of independent e-wallets such as Paytm, held a promise for the gift card markets as well. The consumer's shift of focus from physical gifts to gift cards to e-gifts indicated that the market was set to grow further. From getting discouraged by the retailer storekeeper while attempting to buy a gift card, to buying gift cards on the Woohoo app, the gifting experience in India seemed to have come a long way.

Kumar and Pratap believe that a nimble competition can throw up a challenge to Qwikcilver's market dominance, and they remain ever watchful for the upcoming disruption. Over the last decade, the founding team was constantly innovated to stay ahead. The Woohoo B2C model was a platform business wherein the firm encouraged customers to connect with enterprises and retail brands with a belief that the gift cards could become the largest selling SKU for a retailer and could contribute 12–15% of a retailer's top line. As the consumer side of the business improved, with more digitally distracted and instant gratification seeking younger generations opting for e-gifts, Qwikcilver could become a market leader. Having built a business with significant entry barriers, along with continued presence as a market leader in a potential winner-takes-all market, the Qwikcilver story was also one of massive envelopment wherein it has leveraged inherent competitive strengths to enter all possible adjacencies without losing sight of resource relevance and profitable growth. With an aim to maintain its status as the "visa of the (semi-) closed loop", Kumar and Pratap foresee an exciting time ahead for their venture.

As Kumar and Pratap contemplate the road ahead, some key questions lingered in their minds:

- With vast sections of Indian population yet to buy their first gift card, how should Qwikcilver go about encouraging the shift toward gifting to go digital? What other platforms or brands or resellers should they collaborate with so as to influence the gifting behaviors?
- What are the envelopment threats they need to watch out for as they expand footprint into other countries, as gift card processing and distribution becomes a lucrative business that attracts competition?
- When and how to re-invigorate the B2C push so that they can realize the yet-to-be-fulfilled portion of their original vision? How could Woohoo unravel the immense potential it offered to disrupt consumer gifting?

- What changes were needed in their distribution strategy to take digital gift cards to the tier-II and tier-III cities which hold the next big growth opportunity?

Appendix 1: Types of Gift Cards

Gift cards are preceded by prepaid cards, used for a variety of purposes. In the USA, general purpose reloadable (GPR) cards offer popular prepayment options for a variety of purposes, including food, apparel, holidays, and gifting. GPR cards are typically used by those with lower education and incomes, with an eye on the budget. Gift cards in contrast are popular with the younger and the better-educated. In India, mobile wallets are closest to GPRs, where competition existed for moving up the value chain to prepay for movies, cabs, restaurants, and even homes. Broadly speaking, prepaid instruments are of two types—the closed loop and the open loop.

Closed Loop Payment Instruments
These instruments are issued by retailers to facilitate purchases from stores owned by the retailer. Consumers need to use the payment cards exclusively within the retail store, and customers prefer this when these prepaid cards are available at a good discount (e.g., Macy's or BigBazaar shopping card).

Semi-Closed Loop Payment Instruments
Compared to the closed loop instrument, the semi-closed loop cards are redeemable at a group of retailers who have specifically contracted with the issuer to accept these cards. These instruments do not permit cash withdrawal or redemption by the holder (e.g., Qwikcilver's Woohoo card or the Mobikwik e-wallet).

Semi-open Loop Payment Instruments
More permissible than the semi-closed loop cards are the ones that can be used to purchase at any card-accepting retail store. However, these instruments are specifically designed to not allow cash withdrawal by the card holder (e.g., InComm's Vanilla gift card).

Open Loop Payment Instruments
The most common form of card was the credit or debit card that can be used for any transaction and also permits cash withdrawal at ATMs and other locations (e.g., RuPay, Visa, or Mastercard).

Appendix 2: Gift Card Life Cycle and Critical Success Factors (*Source* Author's Visualization)

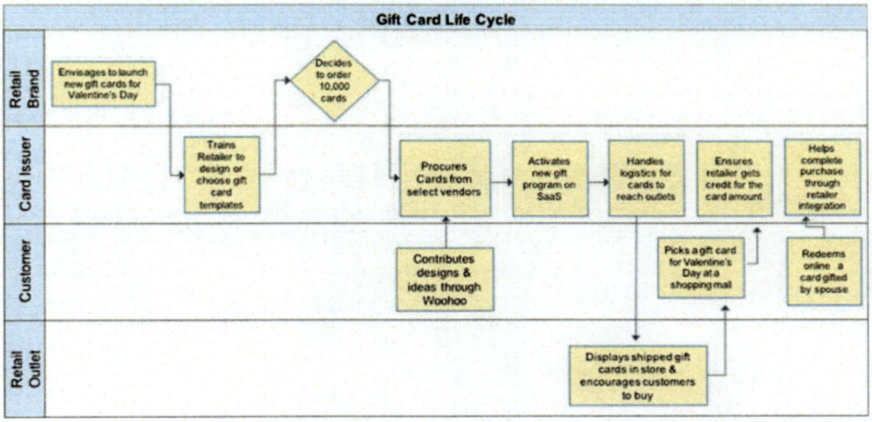

Critical success factors in the gift card industry included setting targets and incentivizing the retail store managers for selling gift cards. As part of launching a gift card program and rolling it out to the retail outlets across the regions, it was important to also handle the following:

- Retailer needed to be clear about the objectives of the new gift card program being launched.
- Important to set well-known targets and incentives so that retailer's employees participate in making the gift card program a success
- Further breaking down targets into measurable goals at the store level
- Closely tracking the performance of the newly launched gift card program through analytics and reporting
- Investing in educating and training of store staff
- Periodic strategic review and program improvement strategies.

21 Contemporary Issues in Platforms

We live in a world where platforms are ubiquitous everywhere—right from the sources of news and entertainment, doing business, dealing with the government, and engaging with the larger society. It is therefore important to understand the impact of these platforms on society and how governments and regulators view platforms and their strategies. Given the way these large technology platforms have diversified and globalized, their power to shape our lives is unfettered. In this chapter, we discuss the societal impact of platforms, governance and regulation, and their impact on industry structures and economics.

Social Impact of Platforms

We live in a world that is dominated by a variety of platforms, right from the sources of information, news, commerce, social networks, and entertainment. And quite a few of these markets are winner-takes-all (WTA) markets, dominated by one or a few global firms. These global corporations are typically privately owned (for-profit) public spaces that dominate the societal narrative and discourses across various countries and over time. For instance, social media and the internet have been an effective tool for amplifying electoral messages in democracies. We will discuss the specific impact of platform firms on the society on three axes: content, data, and competition.

Content

Typically, platforms that work around news and information manage user-generated content (UGC) or third-party content (TPC) on their platforms. Take the example of Google or Facebook—neither of them generates their own content, as they intermediate in the information markets. Google collates and organizes

R. Srinivasan, *Platform Business Models*, Management for Professionals,
https://doi.org/10.1007/978-981-16-2838-2_21

websites and news available, either as search results or through its own products like Google Maps, for use by search users. In some products like Google Maps, Google collects basic data around topology and maps the cities and countries, and crowd sources-specific details about businesses and landmarks on the same. The quality and accuracy of such third-party data could be highly variable and subject to a variety of questions. Similarly, Facebook does not publish any data on its own—all its content is user-generated (UGC), both in the form of posts, events, or even links to news articles.

A key issue in such managing UGC and/or TPC is that of content moderation. What are the boundaries of the platforms? How do we ensure reliability of content provided by platforms that provide UGC and/or TPC? As these platforms replace our traditional means of information filtering (editorial processes, research protocols, and trusted institutional frameworks) with algorithms, there is a trade-off between content moderation and control on one side, and monetization on the other. These algorithms are typically designed to highlight and prioritize content that are most valued by the users on the other side, based on their analytics of the profile and preferences of the users. It is such customized content that sustains engagement with the users, which is highly valued by the other side of these platforms—the advertisers. In such a marketplace, a profit-maximizing platform is more likely to depend on algorithms that amplify specific information, rather than moderate the same.

Though platforms in the recent years have made investments in content moderation, there are serious questions about the transparency around these algorithms and moderation tools. Add to this, the vast differences that exist in many countries in digital literacy. With low to moderate levels of digital literacy, some of these markets are more prone to amplification of misinformation and disinformation, rather than fact checking and establishing provenance of information. This creates a world that is dominated by fake news and targeted information campaigns that push people into echo chambers—a context where people are pushed only that information that conforms to their own belief systems, and pretty much nothing that contradicts. Such echo chambers are highly useful in mobilizing public opinion around social issues, political movements, or even targeted campaigns by government and semi-government organizations. It can have major impact on what the entire segment of population believes in and can have major impact on even public health programs.

A more worrying issue in the management of these UGC and TPC is that of liability. The platforms have continued to deny any liability arising out of the quality and reliability of the content distributed/hosted on their platforms, as they were generated outside the platform and that platforms only role is to make things available and accessible. Across countries, various governments have tried placing liabilities on these intermediaries with limited success. These are more designed as information marketplaces, where the demand and supply conditions determine inventory and transaction of specific information, rather than as publishers, where the liability rests with the editorial function of the publishing house on the basic quality and veracity of content hosted/ published/ transacted on the platform.

Data

Possibly, the most contentious issue in the impact of platforms on society is that of data. Platforms collect a variety of data from the users to provide them with customized and personalized content, products, and services. These data could be collected at sign-up (as profile information), at sign-in (as context information) and during the engagement process (as preferences and priorities). These data that are collected are critical in most cases for the platforms in order to provide appropriate services to the users. For instance, profile information like age and gender act as important filters in choosing to provide adult/ sensitive content; location (of sign-in) and language preferences enable targeting the users with appropriate local advertisements; and the specific search terms and navigation behavior within the platform provides valuable "expressed preference" of the users to dynamically provide engaging content. Platform sponsors argue (and rightly so) that these profile, context, and preference information are critical in providing a satisfying user experience.

What matters therefore, is who owns this data? What are the accountabilities of the platform in using this data? Questions around how platforms can monetize this data are tricky. Given that a lot of these patterns are discerned through algorithms, it is likely to have significant social consequences. Well before the emergence of platforms, there have been instances of such patterns uncovering certain information about users, including drug abuse, suicidal tendencies, or even teenage pregnancies.[1] Dilemmas exist about whether the platforms are accountable to share with relevant stakeholders, including law-enforcement authorities, when these patterns are illegal. Should Facebook and Twitter alert a users' suicidal tendencies to his friends and family at all? What about his privacy? Should drug abuse information about specific individual users be reported to the law-enforcement and/ or healthcare systems?

Algorithmic accountability is not an easy problem to solve. On the one hand, we can claim that it was a person that designed the algorithm in the first place and therefore, the platform that got the algorithm made should be accountability. However, the fact that the algorithms learn and make predictions about user behavior makes it nearly impossible for human agents to define the specific outcomes (apart from broad boundaries).

Managing (user) data privacy is a significant issue for such platforms. There are three layers of rights—right to use the data within the platform to customize and personalize their products and services; right to monetize the data within the platform by targeting third-party advertisements and content to users, and the right to share the data to third parties (both commercial entities or governments/ regulatory bodies). The European Commission had taken giant steps in this direction by

[1]See https://www.forbes.com/sites/kashmirhill/2012/02/16/how-target-figured-out-a-teen-girl-was-pregnant-before-her-father-did/ for an interesting news story about how a retailer figured out a girl was pregnant well before her parents.

enacting the General Data Privacy and Regulation (GDPR) Act in 2018.[2] Other countries are catching up, including India with its proposed regulation (still under discussion in the Indian Parliament), Personal Data Protection (PDP) Bill, 2019.[3] Germany has passed the Network Enforcement Law (NetzDG), 2017 that made the companies liable for illegal speech propagated through their platforms.[4] This NetzDG Act is hailed as one of the first attempts (not without significant controversies) that balances the demands of freedom of speech and privacy on one side and online hate on the other.

Competition

One of the major issues in competitiveness of platforms is that these firms operate largely in winner-takes-all markets, with little or no effective competition. The dominance and hegemony of these platforms is difficult to control through traditional anti-trust and monopoly regulations. As we have seen before, traditional tools are ineffective in regulating the market power and dominance of these platform firms. Given that these firms are also multi-national corporations, international regulations around information exchange and commerce are tricky as well. What may be acceptable in some markets may not be legal in some others.

Some countries like China have very strong regulatory frameworks in allowing multi-national technology firms operating in their countries. Country-specific requirements like data localization might impose significant costs on the platforms. However, specific regulatory frameworks like blasphemy, sedition, and national security laws in various countries pose different risks for the platforms. For instance, a platform like Twitter might not be held accountable to something a Canadian resident writes about an anti-government protest in India. While the content may attract legal action for Indian citizens/Indian residents, it may require very different action on the part of law enforcing agencies to act against such content. Twitter may be forced to remove the said content, block the user for a specific period, or even permanently disable that user from using the platform, by the government. But, as we can see, these are reactions rather than proactive regulation and moderation.

Taxation has also been a very thorny issue in the context of global platforms. These firms have known to avoid taxation by setting up their office and global headquarters in low-tax regime economies, bypassing a variety of international regulations. Apart from moving their administrative headquarters, some of these platforms also shift significant value creating activities to global locations. Like moving their research and development centers to cities like Bangalore, they save

[2]See https://gdpr.eu/what-is-gdpr/ for more details.

[3]For details about India's PDP Bill, see http://164.100.47.4/BillsTexts/LSBillTexts/Asintroduced/373_2019_LS_Eng.pdf.

[4]For a good commentary on the NetzDG Act, see: https://www.politico.eu/article/germany-hate-speech-internet-netzdg-controversial-legislation/.

on significant employee costs (as compared to locating the same in a city like San Francisco or Seattle).

Patents and copyrights on these algorithms and designs are another issue in platform competition. Given the geographic nature of some of these patent laws, it has become very difficult and costly to enforce global patents and copyrights on product design, trademarks, and copyrights.

There are no easy answers to these questions of moderation, transparency, and liability of content; ensuring data rights and algorithmic accountability; and competitive behavior of these platforms, and various governments are trying different measures to govern platforms. At stake are major issues around liberal values of free speech and privacy, access to public data, easy political participation, and the very pillars of democratic governance.

Platform Governance

As we had discussed before, platform firms are private entities that work for private gains, even though they provide public goods. Most of them remain privately owned public spaces, driven by commercial interests. The impact that platforms have on widening information asymmetry, amplification of misinformation and disinformation, inability to curb hate speech and fake news, overall decline in the reliability of information, creation and propagation of information echo chambers resulting in heightened polarization of public opinion, and questions around psychological health of users (due to addiction and screen time) has been the concern of many public policy professionals. Add to these, the issue of winner-takes-all markets, where these markets are captured by a single or at best a handful of firms, who shape public discourse and opinion. These near monopolies have also known to collude with other firms within and outside their network to maximize their returns. For instance, the role of Cambridge Analytica (CA) in sharing raw data about millions of Facebook users through exploiting a loophole in Facebook APIs, for targeted political advertising shook the world.[5] CA ran a quiz on Facebook that collected not just data about the quiz takers but also friends of quiz takers without their knowledge and sold the data. It has been argued that it was not so much about a scam by CA, but Facebook's inadequate protection of its users from a third-party application designed with the specific purpose of collecting user data without their knowledge. This is complicated by the fact that these are multi-national corporations with their algorithms operating in black boxes, and an architecture that makes it difficult to separate the liabilities of the platforms and their users.

The power of platforms to intervene and interfere in our daily lives has been documented by many scholars and policy practitioners, especially by the "Amsterdam school of critical platform studies" (Hargittai, 2007; Introna & Nissenbaum,

[5]Read https://www.vox.com/policy-and-politics/2018/3/23/17151916/facebook-cambridge-analytica-trump-diagram for an executive summary of the scandal.

2000; Nieborg & Poell, 2018; and Van Dijck, Poell, and de Waal, 2018[6]). These scholars argue that with their epistemic power of filtering information that is accessible to different actors in the ecosystem, digital platforms engage in some form of regulation themselves. With their choices of platform architectures and algorithms, these platforms are more likely to perpetuate biases prevalent in the society, rather than addressing them.

Therefore, it is imperative that platforms need to be governed by the very stakeholders that they seek to serve[7]—the complementors, users, governments and other state actors, and the civil society. How they are governed has implications for scale, social impact, and upholding modern values (including transparency and non-discriminatory service delivery, civility of discourse, and content promoting diversity of perspectives). Platforms could be governed internally, like any other corporation, accountable to its stakeholders, and within the law of the land, they operate in. Such governance has been known to be problematic, as these for-profit corporations should prioritize the demands of the principal stakeholders, their shareholders as their fiduciary duty. They may be compliant with the regulations, but technology change has often outpaced regulation. These platforms may be complying with the letter of the law, without actually following the spirit of the same.

Platforms as Marketplaces, Gatekeepers, and Editors

There are three ways at looking at these platforms—as marketplaces, as gatekeepers, and as editors. When we consider these platforms as marketplaces, they take no responsibility to the products, services, content, and behaviors by their users or complementors that use their platform. As in a typical marketplaces, platforms own the discovery and matching algorithms, and are not accountable for the specific behaviors of the complements and users, beyond basic quality verification. Such models may work with platforms around ecommerce, where the markets are efficient, and buyers can efficiently evaluate the quality of products/ buyers. However, when markets are lesser efficient, the platforms need to take more accountability in assuring quality of the complementors, the products and services offered, as well as the quality of transactions. Take for instance, a financial intermediary. As compared to a traditional ecommerce firm, a financial intermediary needs to ensure that the complementors on their platform are regulatorily compliant, the products are

[6]Hargittai, E. 2007. The social, political, economic, and cultural dimensions of search engines: An introduction. Journal of Computer-Mediated Communication, 12 (3), 769–777; Introna, LD., Nissenbaum, H. 2000. Shaping the Web: Why the politics of search engines matters. The Information Society, 16 (3), 169–185; Nieborg, DB., and Poell, T. 2018. The platformization of cultural production: Theorizing the contingent cultural commodity. New Media & Society; Van Dijck, J. Poell, T., and de Waal, M. 2018. The platform society: Public values in a connective world, NY: Oxford University Press.

[7]For a more detailed argument on governance principles, read: Gorwa, R. 2019. What is platform governance? Information, Communication & Society, 22 (6), 854–871.

approved by the appropriate authorities, and the processes are secure. A simple marketplace model that ensures compatibilities and a robust matching algorithm may not be sufficient in this case. In such cases, we need to conceive of the intermediating platform as a gatekeeper. The platform must not only earn the trust of the users and complementors on their products and services but should also ensure that only quality users and complementors are affiliated with the platform. In a sense, it should play the gatekeeping role.

In between the two extremes of completely *laissez faire* marketplaces and tightly controlled gatekeepers, we could also conceptualize platform intermediaries as editors. As editors, the platforms might be required to allow for user-generated content and third-party content to be available for dissemination, with certain controls. The accountability here is shared between the content creator and the platform. Traditional media organizations have been operating in this model, with their content being generated from a combination of their own employees, through tie-ups with syndicates and agencies, as well as from independent columnists. The split of accountabilities might be different across the three sources of content, but the platform surely takes some responsibility even in the case of columns by famous writers—after all, the writer was chosen by the editor.

The Problem of Many Hands

However, technology-driven platforms of today have achieved such scale and enjoy network effects that make it difficult to effectively perform these editorial roles efficiently. Most often, the business model involves motivating users to engage more and more and in the process enhance volume and diversity of interactions. Gatekeeping and editorial roles are extremely difficult to perform, and if at all, done post-hoc., i.e., when a specific content is flagged as inappropriate, action is taken. *Apriori* evaluation of content and controlling the flow might actually be counter-productive to the scale and scope that lies at the heart of the business. Pragmatically, regulators would prefer to have a central actor with full accountability to create and/ or cause harm and therefore own legal responsibilities. Such a centralization of responsibility is easier to administer by the law enforcement authorities.

This is a manifestation of what is referred to as the *problem of many hands*.[8] The problem of many hands occurs when multiple uncoordinated entities contribute in different ways to a problem (or in solving the problem) in a manner where it might be difficult to accurately place accountabilities and responsibilities to actions and consequences. Issues like climate change and air pollution are examples of the problem of many hands, where multiple actors contribute to the exacerbation and escalation of the problem, as well as in their own ways, mitigate the same problems.

[8]For an introduction to the problem of many hands, please read: Thompson, DF (1980). Moral responsibility of public officials: The problem of many hands. The American Review of Public Administration, 44 (3). 259–273.

It would be practically impossible to assign values to activities like deforestation, fossil fuel usage, mining and civil construction, altering the course of rivers through dams and canals, as well as increased economic activity for climate change. Even when one could scientifically separate out part values of the various causes, it would be very difficult to legally hold specific actors responsible for each of these actions.

Modern platforms clearly suffer from the problem of many hands. For instance, to hold Twitter or Facebook accountable for hate speech posted by one its users is preposterous so is placing accountability on a few group administrators in WhatsApp groups, where members generate ideas bordering illegality (like say sedition, national security, or harassment/bullying). By the same token, absolving these platforms of any accountability for the existence and promotion of hate speech or illegal content. Clearly, it is the responsibility of these platforms to ensure that such content do not enter, remain, or get disseminated through their platforms. They have a variety of means to ensure that, ranging from carefully selecting and ratifying content, educating its users, using technologies like AI to discover offensive content, crowdsourcing the flagging of content, and removal of such content/ offenders when there is a breach in accepted norms. In order to solve this problem of many hands, Helberger, Pierson & Poell (2018) suggest a system of cooperative responsibility.[9] They suggest that these platforms should (a) collective define the essential public values that they intend to uphold; (b) acknowledge that they have a role to play in realization of these values through their activities and decisions; (c) develop a multi-stakeholder process of public deliberation and exchange; and (d) translate the outcomes of these deliberations into shared codes of conduct, rules, and design principles for their platform architecture.

Platforms in Contestable Markets

The theory of contestable markets was defined as an extension of perfect competition and has the following characteristics.[10]

(a) The market is accessible to potential entrants, where the same customer needs can be served using the same technologies (that are easily available) as the incumbents.
(b) Therefore, the new entrants' evaluation of the market attractiveness is based on the incumbents' pre-entry prices.

[9]Helberger, N., Pierson, J., and Poell, T. 2018. Governing online platforms: From contested to cooperative responsibility, The Information Society, 34 (1), 1–14.
[10]For more details, read: Baumol, William J., Panzar, John C., and Willig, Robert D. 1982. Contestable Markets and the Theory of Industry Structure. New York: Harcourt Brace Jovanovich, Inc.

(c) Therefore, the entry into such markets is absolutely free, as the new entrants face no disadvantage in comparison to incumbents (easy technology access or no consumer lock-ins with the incumbents).
(d) This market is also characterized with costless exits. In other words, competitors face no exit barriers—no sunk costs to recover. Therefore, contestable markets are vulnerable to hit-and-run strategies.

In such a market, where the threat of new entrants is always imminent, the incumbents will keep their prices close to the competitive equilibrium with very low profitability. Given the low entry and exit barriers, when a new entrant enters the market, the only feasible response by the incumbents is to compete with them by lowering the prices. It may still be possible for the new entrant to match the lowered prices for some time, but when the incumbents have scale and learning advantages, for whatever they are worth in such markets (in perfectly contestable markets, such advantages do not exist at all), they may not be able to sustain. And a few firms may exit the market.

It may not be always the case that contestable markets will have hundreds of competitors, but even when there are a handful of firms, the threat of new entry will keep the firms behaving as if they were in perfect competition. Contestable markets are efficient and increase consumer wealth, as the prices are kept to the minimum possible. Given that there are no switching and multi-homing costs faced by the users, competitors also have to maintain acceptable quality standards.

Let us consider an example. The conventional banking industry had significant costs of entry, including fixed costs of setting up a network of branches; resources like branding and customer services were differentiators that provided incumbents with competitive advantage; and the costs incurred in branding, promotion, and customer acquisition/retention are sunk costs (cannot be recovered at exit). However, the class of digital banks has no costs of entry—all that they need is a set of servers that could be rented from a cloud computing service; online banking provides very little differentiation opportunities across different banks; and the user acquisition and retention costs are minimal with electronic and social commerce penetration. Therefore, if we can consider digital (online) banking as a contestable market. In order to facilitate the contestability of these markets, governments and regulators across countries have also framed policies to ease switching costs across banks (as well as integrate physical banking and online banking).

The increased internet penetration has helped a lot of industries become more and more contestable; by reducing entry barriers (easy user access), removing fixed costs (growth of the sharing economy), information proliferation (easier discovery and evaluation), and reduced sunk costs (opportunities for coring).

Platform firms play a key role in enhancing the contestability of markets. Platforms, with their network effects, help competitors access users easily. Some firms may enter adjacent markets through tipping strategies and port the entire user base to the market. The consumer cloud storage market is an excellent example of contestability created by coring platforms. For instance, firms like Google and Apple have entered consumer cloud storage markets (Google Drive and iCloud) by leveraging their user base from products and services in other markets. The barriers to entry is very low, given that these firms already have sunk costs around cloud storage; exit barriers are also low, due to the lack of any specific investments required to be made for offering these services; and there are no differentiated services in the core offering. As more and more firms enter the market, the specialized incumbents like Dropbox and Box are forced to compete on prices and/ or differentiated features, in a market characterized by no consumer lock-ins, low switching and multi-homing costs, and low loyalty. Prices fall as new entrants threaten to enter the market, and there is increased homogeneity in the range and quality of services offered by the competitors.

The Rise of Platform Conglomerates—FANGAM

Such opportunities for platform firms to enter new markets relatively at no entry costs have given rise to what practitioners label as platform conglomerates. Platform conglomerates refer to those large technology corporations that started their journey as a specialized platform, but slowly diversified into adjacent markets that are contestable, leveraging their user base and core technologies. Abbreviated in a variety of ways, the six large platform firms have become to control users and businesses across the globe—Facebook, Amazon, Netflix, Google, Apple, and Microsoft. Each of these businesses started in a different business but has increasingly converged and has made more and more markets contestable.

- Facebook began as a peer-to-peer social network but has entered into social commerce (small businesses setting up webpages and event pages on Facebook), peer-to-peer messaging (WhatsApp chat), payment solutions (WhatsApp Pay) and video (Instagram reels) as well.
- Amazon began as an ecommerce retailer but has diversified into payments (Amazon Pay), video streaming (Prime Video), and voice assistant consumer devices (Alexa) among others.
- Netflix began as a DVD rental firm embraced video streaming of third-party content (movies, TV shows, documentaries animations, and short films) and began producing its own content (Netflix originals).
- Google began as a search engine and has possibly the most diversified portfolio among tech platforms, with businesses ranging from video sharing (YouTube), mobile operating systems (Android), browsers for PC and mobile phones (Chrome), applications marketplace (Play Store) navigation products (Google Maps), and even self-driving cars (Waymo).
- Apple is an integrated competitor that produces hardware—computers, tablets, phones, televisions, and music players; operating systems and application software (iOS, iPadOS, and other applications), applications marketplace (AppStore), cloud storage (iCloud) and a voice assistant (Siri), among other products, software, and services.

- Microsoft, a market leader in PC operating systems (Windows) and business productivity software (MS Office Suite) has acquired the professional networking site, LinkedIn (that includes a jobs marketplace, blogging, and learning solutions), and peer-to-peer communication platform Skype to complement their own collaboration platforms like MS Teams.

One could see that each of these firms competes with each other in certain businesses, and despite these overlaps, they seem to be dominating their own markets. Do you realize how one could make simple Venn diagrams to represent where these firms compete with each other? Such competition where major competitors compete with each other in multiple markets have their distinct strategic characteristics, which is known as multi-market competition.

Platforms in Multi-market Competition

Competitive strategy scholars define multi-market competition as occurring when firms compete against their competitors across multiple markets/industries.[11] When competitors face each other in a variety of markets, it may induce mutual forbearance and reduce rivalry among them. The theory of multi-market competition highlights how strategic similarity among firms reduces competitive intensity; and mutual forbearance is greater in more concentrated markets.[12]

As we had discussed, enveloping platforms diversify and compete against each other, they engage in multi-market competition. Such platforms have the potential to demonstrate mutual forbearance—reduce competitive intensity in markets where they are weaker than competition, in lieu of receiving the same favor in another market where they are stronger than competition. In other words, across multiple markets, competitors just do not compete hard enough for fear of stronger retaliation in some other markets.

For instance, Amazon's Kindle did not expand its capabilities beyond book reading, even though it had the opportunity to expand into a fully functional tablet. Similarly, Apple has not (yet) launched a voice assistant hardware to complement Siri's capabilities. Therefore, in both markets (handheld devices and voice assistants), these competitors do not compete directly with each other—Kindle remains an ebook reader against the multi-functional iPad; whereas in Alexa is integrated into a standalone device Echo, whereas Apple's Siri remains an App on the iPhone/iPad.

[11]For a more detailed study of multi-market competition, see Edwards, CD (1955) Conglomerate bigness as a source of power, In: NBER Conference Report: Business Concentration and Price Policy. Princeton, NJ: Princeton University Press, pp. 331–352. Available at: http://www.nber.org/chapters/c0967.pdf.

[12]See: Fuentelsaz and Gomez (2006). Multipoint competition, strategic similarity, and entry into geographic markets, Strategic Management Journal, 27, 477–499.

Platforms and International Regulations

When these platforms compete in international markets, there are specific issues of regulatory compliances. The tussle between news organizations and content platforms has come to the fore in markets like Australia and Germany. As platforms like Twitter, Facebook, and Google become the primary sources of news to many users, news organizations have been severely hit, as they begin losing advertisement revenues. News organizations claim that they had invested heavily in hard and soft infrastructure to collect, validate, and edit news to provide it to the users in a credible form, both in digital and physical forms. These activities of news collection and distribution cost money and they recouped the same from advertisers. However, with the emergence of these big technology platforms, the users began sourcing their news through these platforms (which had linked the news content from the news websites), and consequently, advertisers moved over to the platforms. The platforms claim that these links allow for the news companies to market their content to a wider audience, as these links brought in many more click-throughs to their websites.

In July 2020, the Australian Competition and Consumer Commission (ACCC) recommended a code to compensate the news organizations with a fair compensation for their journalism. Calling on the tech platforms to pay for the content, the code allowed these firms to partner with consortia of news organizations for the content.

The two firms that were primarily affected by this code, Facebook and Google, have responded differently.[13] Google initially threatened to withdraw its search engine from Australia but subsequently announced that it had signed an agreement with the media firm, News Corp for sharing news content from its news websites in exchange for payments. Facebook announced that they would stop users posting news content on their pages. It also blocked Australian news companies from posting any of their stories or links on their Facebook pages.

Germany, on the other hand, was in the process of enacting a new framework, Bundeskartellamt, that would proactively frame a set of rules that technology giants would need to follow.[14] Especially in markets with winner-takes-all dynamics, the German regulator claims that these gatekeeper corporations need to ensure that they do not give preferential treatment to their own products and services and hindering interoperability with other services. This could become the framework for a broader European regulation in the near future.

[13]See: https://www.bbc.com/news/world-australia-56107028 for details about the proposed code and the platforms' response.

[14]See: https://www.politico.eu/article/germany-shows-eu-the-way-in-curbing-big-tech/ for more details.

India has also been working on regulating how data collected by digital technology platforms are stored and used. In the year 2020, Indian regulators banned a slew of mobile applications, including the popular short video-sharing platform, TikTok, on cross-border data sharing concerns.[15] The government is also close to enacting the Personal Data Protection (PDP) Bill into an Act that would specify how these platforms will treat user data. Discussions around India's ecommerce policy have also intensified—especially during the COVID-19 induced lockdown, while the local grocery shops gained significant ground in comparison to the national ecommerce firms. The concerns around ecommerce in India are centered around both ends of the business—how fairly are small and medium businesses are treated as suppliers on these platforms, and how much has this competition contributed to consumer welfare in terms of prices and convenience.

Conclusion

The emergence of platform business models has had a variety of consequences. The proliferation of digital technologies aided with network effects and the convergence of standards has significantly contributed to rapid growth of these platform firms. On the one hand, this growth had expanded the user base and broadened the range of services experienced by the users, including personal, social, and commercial benefits. However, on the other hand, these have come with their own costs—the emergence of winner-takes-all markets and the resulting dominance by global corporations.

Any discourse around emerging topics like platforms where technologies, business models, and regulation are constantly changing should co-evolve with the context. However, there are some foundational building blocks that need to be appreciated for sustaining the conversation. As in most other topics, there are many perspectives that one can take—one could discuss platforms from a policy and governance perspective, from the perspective of a marketer, from the users' perspective, from small businesses that complement these platforms, the gig workers that serve these platforms, as well as from the strategic perspective—that of the platform owner/ manager. Each of these perspectives will provide different nuances around understanding the import and dynamics of these business models.

In this book, we took the perspective of the entrepreneur-manager that is building/ operating a platform business firm. We focused on the economics and strategy of these firms. We introduced the basic concepts and differentiated platform firms from traditional pipeline firms and elaborated on the core properties of platforms—network effects, penguin problems, and winner-takes-all dynamics. We analyzed a variety of platforms, including their value architectures and network mobilization strategies. We elucidated the choices around platform architecture,

[15]See: https://www.businesstoday.in/technology/news/india-bans-tiktok-permanently-app-evaluates-notice/story/429086.html.

discussed platform competition and envelopment, and highlighted how multiple business models could come together to create synergies. We conclude the book with a discussion on contemporary issues facing platforms across different countries.

JOSEPHS®: the Service Manufactory

22

There was a sense of déjà vu among the team members of "JOSEPHS®—The Service Manufactory" (hereinafter referred to as JOSEPHS®) as its first birthday approached. They had the same feelings as they had a year before, when JOSEPHS® first opened its doors to customers in May 2014. Designed as a space for tenants (spots) to engage in open innovation with customers who would walk into the "store," it was to operate as an open innovation laboratory. It was May 2015, and preparations were on for the celebrations. As Dr. Frank Danzinger, Project Manager, JOSEPHS®, got his team together to review the arrangements, a few questions lingered on—could they say that JOSEPHS® had been successful? What parameters were appropriate to measure the success of JOSEPHS®? Also what was the future for JOSEPHS®; did it require any course corrections?

The Birth of the Idea

The Fraunhofer Institute for Integrated Circuits IIS (hereinafter referred to as Fraunhofer IIS) was an application-oriented research institution for microelectronic

---

Professor Srinivasan R, Professor of Strategy, prepared this case for class discussion. This case is not intended to serve as an endorsement, source of primary data, or to show effective or inefficient handling of decision or business processes. The author would like to gratefully acknowledge the financial support provided by the FAU Wi1 chair; and the Fraunhofer IIS and FAU Wi1 staff for support in documenting the case.

R. Srinivasan, *Platform Business Models*, Management for Professionals,
https://doi.org/10.1007/978-981-16-2838-2_22

and IT system solutions and services.[1] It offered commercial and industrial organizations a variety of collaborative options, ranging from R&D services, licensing of technologies and systems, technology integration and the development of components to project support and advice, and conducting market studies. The major research areas included the following.

- Audio and multimedia
- Communication systems
- Energy management
- IC design and design automation
- Imaging systems
- Medical technology
- Nondestructive testing
- Positioning and navigation
- Safety and security technology
- Sensor systems
- Supply chain management.

The Fraunhofer IIS was exploring the setting up of a laboratory on service innovation, and they approached Prof. Dr. Kathrin Möslein (Kathrin), Chair of Information Systems 1, Innovation and Value Creation (hereinafter referred to as FAU Wi1), Friedrich–Alexander University Erlangen–Nuremberg (FAU), to join their advisory board as they had heard of her work on open and user innovation. During one of their discussions, the former head of Fraunhofer IIS, Prof. Dr.-Ing. Heinz Gerhäuser, introduced Dr. Angela Roth (Angela), who was working on service innovation, to Kathrin. They were exploring the idea of setting up a service innovation laboratory; when Kathrin suggested to them that for such a laboratory to be open and leveraging consumer insights directly, it should be located closer to consumers, say at the city center, rather than other scientific laboratories. The dominant model of working at Fraunhofer IIS would have been to invite a market leader into the laboratories and design an innovative service or technology, leveraging each other's knowledge. Given that Fraunhofer IIS was interested in taking the innovation process closer to the users, they had invited Kathrin to the annual meeting of the advisory board to deliver a keynote address, where she talked about the power of open innovation. The Fraunhofer IIS management was excited about the opportunity to bring the business and consumer sides of the innovation together, and began exploring the physical idea of an open innovation laboratory. Kathrin and her team at FAU were looking at open innovation as a process that was conducted using virtual platforms over the internet, but when Fraunhofer IIS began talking about a physical laboratory, it was a big challenge to bring the two ideas together.

Prof. Dr. -Ing. Albert Heuberger, Director of Fraunhofer IIS remarked:

> The JOSEPHS® concept of an open lab environment challenges the traditional, rather technology-driven understanding of a research laboratory. In traditional labs, we rather

[1]For more information on Fraunhofer IIS, please visit: http://www.iis.fraunhofer.de/en.html.

exclude the public in order to keep intellectual property of developments. However, it is a great opportunity, as a lot of technologies interact directly with people – their reactions, acceptance, and feedbacks can hardly be designed in a closed lab environment. I think it is the interplay between open and closed labs that create synergetic effects.

Through the next few months, the idea evolved into a "boundary object" where potential users and innovators could come together with entrepreneurs and firms and develop something. Kathrin did not have an idea of how the actual laboratory would look, but rather had some ideas of the specific location and the architecture. From there, one decision led to another, and the service manufactory idea was born. The Fraunhofer IIS team was exploring various options such as hiring a high-rise department store or even one of the city towers along the city's historic wall. However, Angela and Kathrin held on to this idea of a compact facility, kept the owners engaged through the renovation, and leased it when the opportunity arose.

Another of the key design elements was a storefront to attract walk-in customers. The team had thought of a coffee shop such as Starbucks, where customers would sit and spend some time, and possibly become curious about what was happening at the back end. Given that Starbucks was an American brand, which may not be very appropriate for Nuremberg, they began exploring other options. Angela had a connection with the family that ran the Mr. Bleck coffee chain and they approached them.

Kathrin summarized the synergies between FAU and Fraunhofer IIS:

At the core, there was a joint interest in each other's topics. I was an open innovation researcher, and was talking a lot of how open innovation was different from closed innovation. But I was never really involved in a closed innovation system. Whereas the whole Fraunhofer IIS was a closed innovation laboratory and they wanted to hear a lot about open innovation. From products, they had already begun working on service innovation, but all this open and user innovation was very different for them. During the annual meeting, Albert introduced me to the audience as, "now Kathrin will talk about all the dangerous stuff", which was cool. That is how different our outlooks were, but we know from our research that we could do both of these things together, something like ambidexterity.

As Angela joined the FAU team, Frank left FAU and joined Fraunhofer IIS as the project manager for the service innovation project (that included JOSEPHS®). The entire JOSEPHS® project was then managed between Frank and Angela—they actually had no specific organization structure defined. However, the decisions were being taken and the idea was evolving into something tangible. When JOSEPHS® finally opened in May 2014, Heike and a team of guides joined the team at the operational level. Heike came from a retail background and brought in much professional retail discipline to the whole place. However, at the strategic level, it was purely between Angela and Frank who were listening to ideas from a variety of stakeholders and implementing them. As in a true service design project, the entire JOSEPHS® project was an outcome of a set of non-sequential, interdependent decisions generated out of a variety of stakeholders not formally connected through an organizational structure!

There were times when certain decisions would fall through the cracks—no one would have felt responsible for something, for instance, the decisions on who was responsible for securing the next set of companies for JOSEPHS®. FAU Wi1 had great interest in introducing a variety of firms, but they were not obliged to do so. However, the Fraunhofer IIS team (Frank) were required to, but still had to establish an effective dissemination and acquisition mechanism. In spring 2015, Kathrin and the entire team had a meeting at JOSEPHS® and brainstormed about where the next funding would come from. Then, someone suggested that they could offer the *Denkfabrik* to interested innovators and companies, and so on. People took on specific roles, and along the way, JOSEPHS®' organization developed.

The Concept and Architecture

JOSEPHS® was designed to operate as an open innovation laboratory, set up in the Nuremberg city center. The intent was to attract a wide range of walk-in customers, who would see it as an extension of a retail store. JOSEPHS® was built on the core belief that when customers engage with a product or service innovation at its earliest possible stages, true customization and value addition were possible. The later the customer interaction in a product development/innovation life cycle, as in pilot testing of prototypes, takes place, the lesser value addition was expected. This was especially true in the context of services, where customer engagement can shape the way businesses design their products, services, and business models by leveraging early interaction with real customers.

JOSEPHS® was designed to look and operate as a retail store and a workshop (*Werkstatt*) area at the same time (see Exhibit 22.1 for a drawing). The workshop design was achieved with a special focus on the ambience and interiors that signaled a certain degree of seriousness and formality. The customer interaction area (the manufactory) was therefore designed to look similar to a workshop with a high table and spaces for documentation of feedback and interactions. Handheld devices were preferred over fixed terminals for this purpose, as they could be moved around the entire area, as well as shared among JOSEPHS® employees, company representatives, and customers, as required (see Exhibit 22.2).

The retail store aspect of the design was set up in the front of the store in the form of a dining partner. In order to attract customers to walk in and participate in the innovation co-creation process, JOSEPHS® had a coffee shop, Mr. Bleck, at the front. The presence of the coffee shop was intended to attract footfalls into the JOSEPHS® as well as work toward helping customers overcome their hesitation in engaging with the various spots/workshop areas. The coffee shop was chosen over other retail formats, as it would attract customers who would have some time to spend, as well as small groups of people.

The third aspect of JOSEPHS®' design was the meeting area, also known as the *Denkfabrik* (or thought factory). This was a specialized conference/meeting room facility that supported special types of interactions (see Exhibit 22.3). Such interactions could include meetings and events by participating companies, by the sponsors, viz., FAU or Fraunhofer IIS, or even rented out by other firms for a special purpose. This conference/meeting area was one of the major pivots around

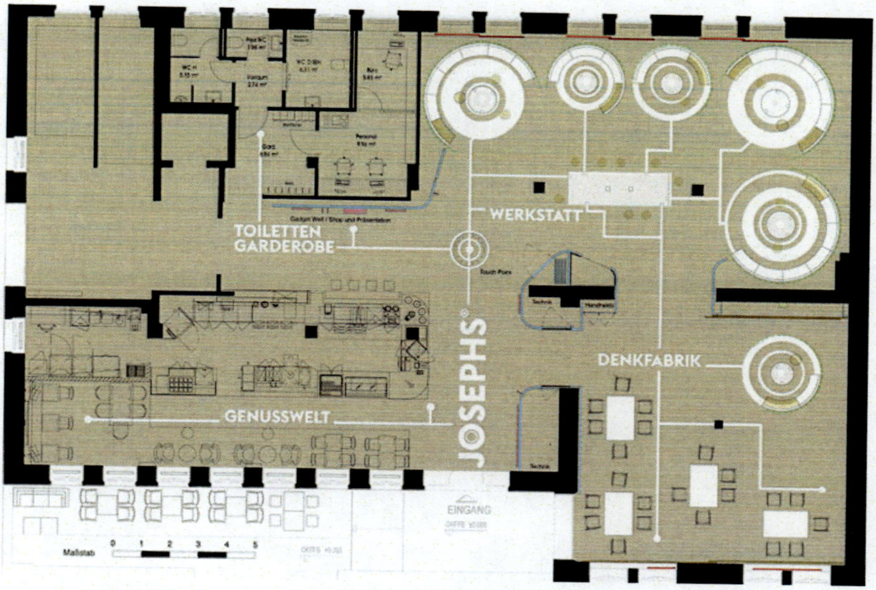

Exhibit 22.1 A drawing of JOSEPHS®. *Source* Website of JOSEPHS®: https://www.JOSEPHS-service-manufaktur.de/index.php?id=11&L=1, accessed on October 28, 2015

which JOSEPHS® operated. Although it was important to encourage people come in and interact with the companies at their respective spots, it was also critical for the companies to have a place to commune with their customers and other stakeholders as a group. It also provided for an interactive communication space with diverse stakeholders, who intended to participate in the value creation phase.

The fourth dimension of JOSEPHS®' design was the set of spots—the specific real estate where each of the participating companies was housed. These "spots" were a part of the *Werkstatt* and were crafted carefully to be generic enough for being used by different customers, but flexible and customizable as the tenants' requirements changed. For instance, a jeweler might have different consumer interaction points and needs than a technology-driven firm developing a "talking product" (see Exhibit 22.4). These spots were built on basis of an open design that provided for the company to place its specific infrastructure, have a person or two interacting with the customers, enough space for a group of three to four customers to interact with the infrastructure, as well as some space for interacting with/capturing the feedback from customers.

These four dimensions of JOSEPHS®' architecture—the ambience of a workshop and a retail store at the same time that ensured seriousness as well as innovative/creative behavior; the coffee shop; the *Denkfabrik* (thought factory); and the spots for housing the firms—ensured that it became a multi-sided platform with significant same-side and cross-side network effects.

Exhibit 22.2 The workshop area at JOSEPHS®. *Source* Author

Exhibit 22.3 Denkfabrik at JOSEPHS®. *Source* Author

JOSEPHS® as an Open Innovation Intermediating Platform

As an entity, JOSEPHS® added value to a range of stakeholders as a multi-sided platform. Various sides that experienced JOSEPHS® included (a) customers who walked into the store; (b) the firms using the open innovation infrastructure for own user-specific research questions and workshops; (c) Fraunhofer IIS that used JOSEPHS® to study consumer behavior and preferences; and (d) the FAU Wi1 team that performed research with JOSEPHS® as the site.

Exhibit 22.4 The spots (the service manufactory) at JOSEPHS®. *Source* Author

For the consumers walking into JOSEPHS®, it provided an opportunity to contribute early in the value creation process, a critical component of open innovation. The design self-selected customers interested in open innovation, as they demonstrated curiosity, experimentation, and willingness to share ideas/experiences. For the firms resident on JOSEPHS®, it presented a well-designed infrastructure for engaging with customers self-selected for open innovation and design. For the Fraunhofer team, JOSEPHS® provided an open innovation laboratory to provide their corporate customers with an open innovation value proposition. Also, the academic researchers at FAU gained access to real-life data on open innovation research.

Customers

In order to attract customers walking into the store, JOSEPHS® was located right in the city center, surrounded by many retail stores, restaurants, and public spaces (see Exhibit 22.5). In addition to its location, JOSEPHS®' design included a local brand of coffee shop: Mr. Bleck. The location and the coffee shop ensured that JOSEPHS® attracted the consumers that was appropriate for open innovation—random as well as self-selected. Random, as they were located in the city center and attracted retail customers who walked in to have coffee as well; and self-selected, as only those interested in what was happening around the coffee shop would walk in to explore. Further, when they did walk around, a JOSEPHS®' team member was always around to explain what was going on and introduce various spots.

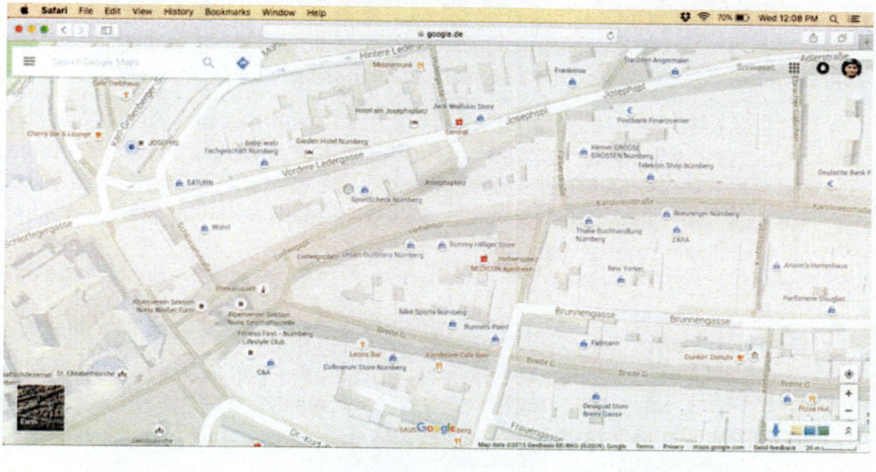

Exhibit 22.5 Map of the location (JOSEPHS®. *Source* Google maps (maps.google.de)

As Dr. Albrecht Fritzsche, FAU, commented:

> The coffee shop is one of the most important aspects of JOSEPHS®. It is definitely part of the innovation process. It reduces the threshold for people who are not used to doing this innovation to come in and join. This helps provide a smooth transition from people who just want to enjoy something (like coffee) to those who want to be active contributors. I think this is a key success factor for the whole thing, to make sure we get all kinds of people, including those who are committed to contribute to the innovation process.

As compared to other retail formats, a food and beverage format suited the innovation process best, as it provided a space for people to sit and interact, and help people overcome their barriers to experimentation. Most customers needed support in terms of explanation about what the JOSEPHS® was about, and had to be convinced to experiment.

A regular visitor to JOSEPHS® recalled:

> I come here for coffee at least 2-3 times a week (my work place is about 2 minutes away). This man (Stefan) once started talking to me and asked if I was curious to see what was inside, as I was actually staring at all the fancy iPads being used. He took me to a couple of shops (spots). I did come back after that one day and saw a music chair. I spent around two hours that day at the music chair shop (spot).

Frank Danzinger reminisced:

> We did talk about how to get people interested to enter JOSEPHS®, when we were making the initial decisions. We wanted to have something that would be more social in nature. Unlike a bookshop, where people would be individually searching for, engaging with a book, a coffee shop brings groups of people together. They (the coffee shop customers) are more likely to walk into JOSEPHS®. On the other hand, a toy store could be dangerous. It would encourage people to play. Unlike for younger kids where playing and experimentation could be the same, for adults they are different. We are looking for inspiration and creativity – a toy store rather kills creativity, as with most toys there is a certain way of doing things, there is a right solution to a problem in a toy or a game. In JOSEPHS®, we do not have a right solution, but are looking for creative ideas. A toy store may sure look very colorful and fancy, but might be detrimental to the seriousness of the research we do at JOSEPHS®.

The coffee shop thus provided JOSEPHS® with a communication and a meeting space that was informal without losing the seriousness of the communication; experimentation and feedback while capturing and documenting the ideas required for user innovation; and one that provided for one-on-one interaction without losing its social nature of groups.

Tenant Firms

The money side of the JOSEPHS® was the tenants who would use the spots and JOSEPHS®® team's support for a period of 3 months in order to answer their user-specific questions.

The JOSEPHS® team carefully chose the tenants for these spots. In order to ensure that these firms really understood the concept of JOSEPHS® and the service manufactory, the JOSEPHS® team would engage with the managers and founders of these firms for extended periods of time before the actual engagement. Some of these tenants discovered the JOSEPHS®' opportunity through either online or offline media coverage and contacted them. Some others were reached through direct calls from the JOSEPHS® team. Either way, it would be very rare for the firms to come up with the specific research questions at the first instance. There could be firms that were looking at JOSEPHS® as a product/prototype-testing place, where real customers would provide feedback to the firm around various product/service design options. These firms could look at JOSEPHS® as an infrastructure for collecting consumer data on pre-defined product/service options. On the other hand, there could be firms that were looking at JOSEPHS® as a trade fair booth, a place to showcase their innovative products/prototypes. The JOSEPHS® team therefore engaged with these firms, asking pointed questions on what contribution they expected during face-to-face customer involvement in the product development/prototyping process. During this phase, the emphasis was laid on sharpening the research question around user-driven open innovation and set the expectations right. This engagement could last for around 6 months to sometimes over a year.

Once the firm was convinced, it signed an R&D contract with JOSEPHS®. The contract explicitly stated the specific research questions to be answered during the tenure and the analysis commitment from JOSEPHS®. The teams would then agree upon the specific design of the spot, the infrastructure required, and other basics. It took utmost 2 days for the firm to move in and set up the spot. Once the spot was set up, the firm representatives would provide a detailed briefing on how the customer interaction was best managed to the JOSEPHS® team. This was an iterative process, as the JOSEPHS® team would also provide feedback to the firm representatives on what might succeed and what might not, based on their prior experience. The effort was to get the customer experience right, first time. Sometimes, the process of designing the customer interaction process could undergo revisions during the first few days.

Once the firms had set up their spots and were functional, they used several methods to attract customers to visit them. Through the first year of operation (May 2014–May 2015), there were three kinds of customers whom the firms engaged with. The first set consisted of those customers who walked into the coffee shop and intrigued about what was happening behind, and stepped in. On a typical weekday, about 30 customers would walk into the spot areas of JOSEPHS®. The numbers were significantly more during Saturdays. Among the coffee shop customers, roughly 10–15% of the customers would explore the spots. The second set of customers included those who had heard of JOSEPHS® in the media, and walked into the *Denkfabrik* or the spots directly. These customers were typically repeat customers, were aware of JOSEPHS® concept, and walked in whenever they found time or when they heard of a spot refresh through the media. The third set of customers included those that were customers of the specific firms in the spot. For instance, one of the tenants MyBoshi had a strong fan base, before they entered JOSEPHS®. The firm then sent out mailers and communication to their customers inviting them to visit their spot at JOSEPHS®. This set also included customers the firms invited to attend a special event or a meeting they organized at the *Denkfabrik*. The ratio of the second and third set of customers was about 60:40 in the first year. As more and more firms with established brand names entered JOSEPHS®, the proportion was likely to increase in favor of specific brands.

At the end of three months, the JOSEPHS® team summarized the results of the customer interactions, answered the specific research questions that was set out in the beginning (possibly modified a little during the first few days), and provided the firms with an analytical report. This report would be based on the specific customer journeys, including their emotional journeys captured through the emotion cameras, the comments they wrote, the words they spoke, and their specific interactions with the firms in the spots in specific.

The firm typically held the intellectual property that was generated during the tenure, and if Fraunhofer wished to use them, they would seek the firm's approval. However, given the nature of user-driven open innovation, most of the knowledge was in the public domain.

Each of the firms obtained different insights and returns, depending on what their research questions were when they entered JOSEPHS®. The returns varied from generic feedback on the business models to specific product design elements. Olga Dick, from Amoonic, an online provider of customized jewelry, one of the first tenants at JOSEPHS® reminisced:

> Our returns from tenure were very big. Since we were one of the first companies here, we got a lot of PR. We got a lot of opinions from a lot of customers, lots of big people, important people; and got a lot of feedback on what we should do.
>
> During our tenure at JOSEPHS®, we had actually learnt that the customers want to get inspired. If you just had a computer, it was not sufficient. They need the inspiration – the need to touch the gem stones, they want to see how it fits into the metal with their own eyes. We also learnt that they needed help in design. They would appreciate professional help in informing them about the fine stones and their quality. It is too expensive and complicated to make a decision with a few clicks.
>
> So, when I set up a retail (offline) store, I would display a set of mixes (of gems and metals); but not have large storage (inventory) like most jewelry stores have. As a fashion item, the millions of Euros of working capital lying in inventory is just waste.

Herbert Galster from BewegtbildPlus, a start-up that provided innovative video footage and online–offline interaction (e.g., with the help of beacons), had a different idea on the returns from their tenure at JOSEPHS®:

> We learnt from JOSEPHS® that, apart from targeting the city administrators and retailers, we need to focus our marketing on the customers, citizens. Now, we are expanding to all cities of Bavaria, getting all these three elements together.
>
> In Germany in the past, such beacons had failed because they were not installed properly. At JOSEPHS®, we learnt how many, and how to install these beacons that they do not disturb or annoy people.

Fraunhofer IIS

Fraunhofer IIS has been a significant enabler of the JOSEPHS® platform. As an entity, Fraunhofer had deep interests in various technologies and their application. For Fraunhofer, JOSEPHS® served as an open innovation laboratory, where they could test the application of their own technologies (such as the emotion cameras) and highlight them to business customers. It was also a great opportunity for Fraunhofer to help solve many research questions raised by their current and potential customers through the open innovation platform. Fraunhofer had a long tradition of building laboratories to research customer-relevant questions; for instance, firms could use one of Fraunhofer laboratories for testing their logistics processes. In their endeavor to support service innovation, they realized the need to include extensive customer and end-user involvements. JOSEPHS® provided Fraunhofer with a perfect platform to set up an end-user-driven open innovation laboratory which they use in customer projects (businesses looking for service innovation solutions) as a non-traditional laboratory infrastructure.

Albert Heuberger summed up the intent behind JOSEPHS®:

> Our goal was providing a platform for, both innovative companies and active prosumers. We wanted to establish a physical open innovation space where co-creators and companies can develop products and services together. We also wanted to build a living and innovative place that supports the region and provides a visible platform for new developments – no matter if they are developed by Fraunhofer or other companies.

FAU

The university partner in the JOSEPHS® platform was the Friedrich–Alexander University Erlangen–Nuremberg (FAU). The FAU Wi1 was specifically working toward open and user innovation as a research theme, and JOSEPHS® provided the researchers in the university a laboratory to explore various research questions that required end-user interface. Compared to a random survey experiment, JOSEPHS® provided them with a self-selected group of participants with an interest to contribute to the cause of open innovation.

As Albrecht Fritzsche remarked:

> JOSEPHS® provided us with an opportunity to create an environment where we can use the ideas of design and action research on a microscopic site. Normally, we do these studies at a macroscopic level. At JOSEPHS®, we have micro-design activities and we have the discourse that happens around it. This discourse is around the design activities. This is something that is not described in the scientific literature so far as a research method. This is something new that we have explored by now. I think we have (at the moment) five or six students there that do research on Masters' theses. So, there are quite a few things going on in terms of research.

JOSEPHS® provided the FAU researchers with an excellent micro-site to examine multiple case studies about user/open innovation and explore multiple research questions. The contract between the companies and Fraunhofer IIS ensured confidentiality of data collected through the tenure. However, the FAU team helped Fraunhofer IIS in publishing, based on the data.

Angela Roth elaborated:

> Given the confidentiality agreements between the firms and Fraunhofer IIS, what FAU cannot do is to publish the specific names of the companies. However, what we are writing is about the general nature of how co-creation takes place, what customers do here, and so on. There are also reactions of companies, but these data comes from what FAU has collected directly from the companies, based on interviews FAU conducted with the companies. So, this is our data.

There were three sets of research relationships that were working at JOSEPHS®—where the companies contracted with Fraunhofer IIS for their specific research questions; the studies FAU researchers conducted by studying companies and customers at JOSEPHS® through their own data collection; and the relationship between Fraunhofer IIS and FAU through which FAU helped Fraunhofer IIS publish papers based on JOSEPHS® data (including FAU students interning at Fraunhofer IIS). The FAU–Fraunhofer IIS relationship was governed by the master contract that allowed FAU to contact companies. It also provided an innovative and unique location for hosting special lectures and events at the *Denkfabrik* (see Exhibit 22.6 for a sample of events held at the *Denkfabrik*).

Network Effects in the JOSEPHS® Ecosystem

JOSEPHS®' success as a platform was dependent on a set of four network effects (see Fig. 22.1).

1. The firms/tenants sign up to engage with JOSEPHS® expecting a steady stream of visitors—consumers who walk into JOSEPHS® to explore and co-create. More the number of consumers visiting the spots, more value the firms generate during their stay at JOSEPHS®. The presence of a coffee shop is a significant attraction for retail customers to walk in. The various events and meetings that are hosted in the *Denkfabrik* (thought factory) also contribute to bringing people into JOSEPHS® and help them get interested in various tenants. The tenants were also encouraged to organize events and talks specific to their products and services, so that they attract the right number and kind of consumers to visit their spots.
2. On the other hand, the consumers who walk into JOSEPHS® would be willing to engage with a wide variety of spots. The short tenure (3 months before each refresh) of the set of spots retains the interest of the consumers to keep coming back to JOSEPHS® to check out the new firms/tenants. As discussed above, the coffee shop and the *Denkfabrik* also help increase the number and frequency of visitors.

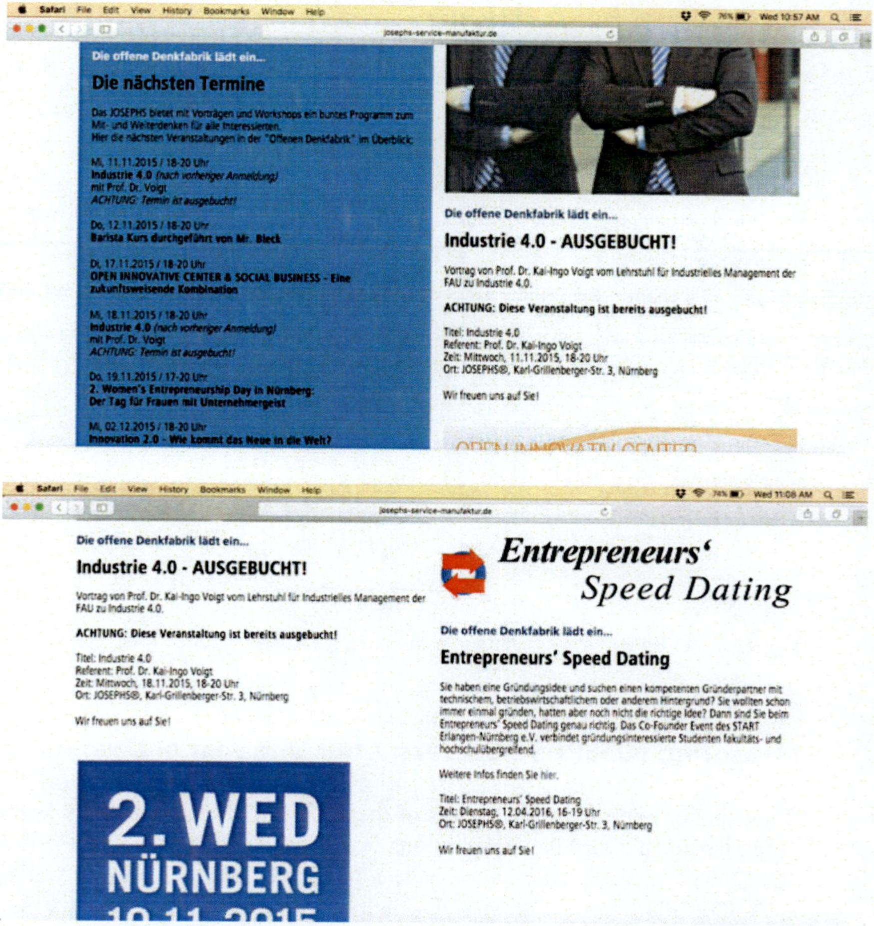

Exhibit 22.6 The event page at the JOSEPHS®' website. *Source* http://www.JOSEPHS-service-manufaktur.de/veranstaltungen/ accessed from the internet on November 4, 2015

3. With a focus on open innovation, FAU researchers would significantly benefit from a larger number of customer interactions at JOSEPHS®. The larger the number of customer–firm interactions, and the larger the variety of these interactions, data on user innovation becomes richer and richer.
4. As for Fraunhofer IIS, with a commercial focus of providing a platform for service innovation capabilities to its research partners/business customers, it is important for them to also have a range of firms that benefit from JOSEPHS®. For them, the success of the tenants in JOSEPHS® becomes an instance of significant use for highlighting to their business customers. As the variety of tenants increases, the richer is the experience that Fraunhofer as an institute gains for leveraging with their other clients.

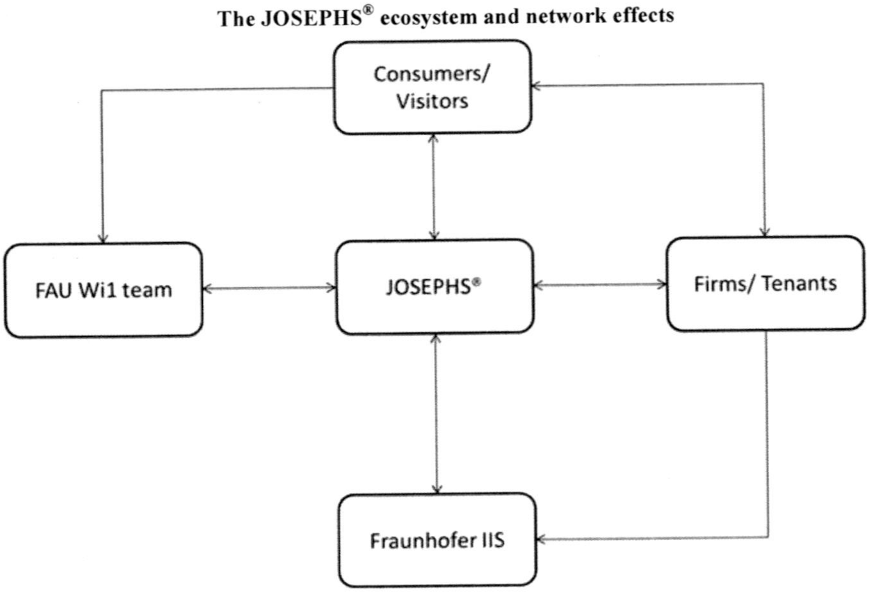

Fig. 22.1 JOSEPHS® ecosystem and network effects. *Source* Author's representation

Measuring JOSEPHS®' Success: After One year of Operations

The primary question in the minds of the JOSEPHS® team members as they were preparing for the birthday celebrations was the metrics they would use to measure JOSEPHS® success. There were quite a few ideas, but more clarity was required.

If JOSEPHS® was a service that helped companies innovate, then its success must be measured in terms of how much the company became innovative after the tenure. However, if JOSEPHS® was a specific infrastructure for the companies to use for innovation, then the metric should include the specific innovations that resulted as a consequence of their tenure at JOSEPHS®. However, given that different companies were in different stages of the innovation maturity, it would be difficult to generalize the metrics for all companies.

Another perspective was to look at whether and how the companies were able to answer the specific research questions they set out to answer when they entered JOSEPHS®. A good metric therefore would be to measure a "before–after" state of their clarity on the research questions. How satisfied were they with the progress toward answering the specific research questions. For instance, a company that signed up for a spot at JOSEPHS® wanted clarity on their business model. They had a technical idea—creating 3D-printed vases based on sound. When they came into JOSEPHS®, they did not know whether customers would like the idea, what kind of sounds would they like to be converted, and what prices would they be willing to pay. At the end of the tenure, they had a good business plan in hand, including some surprise learning. They learnt that customers would not just want to record any meaningful sounds, but things such as music, and that they wanted the vase to be aesthetically pleasing as well.

To enable JOSEPHS® to measure these metrics, it was important to document the progress of the specific firms after their tenure at JOSEPHS®. However, there was a tricky part of causality—did JOSEPHS® directly contribute to the firm's success? Or was JOSEPHS® just involved in the specific part of helping them think differently about their business? How much of the success story can be attributed to JOSEPHS® is a question no one has an answer yet.

From a Fraunhofer point of view, the metrics would include how much visibility Fraunhofer obtained through JOSEPHS®, how many of the spots in JOSEPHS® were booked, and possibly the spillovers from JOSEPHS® into Fraunhofer's business. From the FAU perspective, the metrics could be in terms of the richness of the research they were able to perform, compared to the study of the same phenomena in real settings of specific companies. Given that such comparative data would be difficult to procure, these metrics remained qualitative and output-focused and reveal the number of research papers published using JOSEPHS® as a context.

In terms of JOSEPHS®' design, there were certain things that were pre-defined. For instance, the tenure for all firms at the spots was defined as 3 months, and they were arranged into a theme. Even though there were specific research questions that required shorter or longer tenures, it was difficult to sign contracts with firms for varying tenures, as that would affect the way the themes were structured. Though there was sufficient flexibility to define themes, there could be instances of sub-optimal tenures being offered to the firms in the spots.

The nature of the contract with Fraunhofer IIS required that all firms using these spots had to share the data with Fraunhofer IIS, which would analyze the same and provide them with the results/reports. Given the nature of Fraunhofer IIS' mandate and JOSEPHS® design, it was not possible to "rent" the spots to companies to perform their own research, without Fraunhofer IIS' involvement. As far as the *Denkfabrik* was concerned, it was a space that could be used by firms independent of Fraunhofer IIS/FAU involvement. For instance, any firm in the area could make use of the *Denkfabrik* space for its event, bring its own facilitators and participants, and let the participants/facilitators contribute to various spots as visitors/consumers.

Also, significant design changes were to be considered if and when JOSEPHS® had to be replicated in places such as airports, shopping malls, or residential areas. Angela Roth commented:

> Maybe at airports, we will have two different kinds of customers – those who have a lot of time (bored due to a long layover between flights), and those who have very limited time. Between these two sets of customers, the customer journeys may be different. Also, repeat customers may be difficult – we may need to question our five-spot design and talk about two-spots; we may need to refresh it faster than every three months; the research questions may not change, but the way the customer relates can change. Airports also provide us with the opportunity to have a wide variety of customers with different nationalities. And we

would also have a different segment of customers – business people who would not have time to come to the city center may engage at the airport; maybe our sample is biased with only those who can afford to fly. Maybe, we can work on a research problem with the companies spending two months at the Nuremberg city center and one month at say, at an airport.

As the birthday celebrations came closer, it was important that these questions were answered with clarity to all stakeholders. Much media coverage was expected through the event—local radio and print media journalists were likely to raise questions. And the team at JOSEPHS® needed to be ready with coherent answers.